Automata and
Formal Languages

Automata and Formal Languages

An Introduction

Department of Mathematics and Computer Science
Gustavus Adolphus College

PRENTICE HALL, Englewood Cliffs, New Jersey 07632

Library of Congress Cataloging-in-Publication Data

Kelley, Dean.
    Automata and formal languages: an introduction / Dean Kelley.
        p.   cm.
    Includes bibliographical references and index.
    ISBN 0-13-497777-7
    1. Computer science—Mathematics.   2. Programming languages
(Electronic computers)   3. Automata.
QA76.9.M35K45 1995
511.3—dc20   94-22953
                                                      CIP

Acquisitions editor: *Marcia Horton*
Editorial/production supervision: *Raeia Maes*
Cover design: Sue Behnke
Manufacturing manager: *Lori Bulwin*

 ⓒ 1995 by Prentice-Hall, Inc.
A Simon & Schuster Company
Englewood Cliffs, New Jersey 07632

Printed in the United States of America

10   9   8   7   6   5   4   3   2   1

ISBN 0-13-497777-7

Prentice-Hall International (UK) Limited, *London*
Prentice-Hall of Australia Pty. Limited, *Sydney*
Prentice-Hall Canada Inc., *Toronto*
Prentice-Hall Hispanoamericana, S.A., *Mexico*
Prentice-Hall of India Private Limited, *New Delhi*
Prentice-Hall of Japan, Inc., *Tokyo*
Simon & Schuster Asia Pte. Ltd., *Singapore*
Editora Prentice-Hall do Brasil, Ltda., *Rio de Janeiro*

For Mom and Dad
... and Uncle Fudd

Contents

Preface

This book arose from my course notes for an introductory course in the theory of computation at Gustavus Adolphus College. At Gustavus, this course covers formal languages and their automata, Turing machines, and computability via decidability. The course is intended for students in their second year of the computer science curriculum and until recently had as its main prerequisite a course in reading and understanding mathematical proofs.

The book is intended to be read by students having minimal mathematical background. Chapter 0 covers the mathematical preliminaries necessary for a reading of the entire text. The level of mathematics in the subsequent chapters is initially quite low, but rises as the material demands it and the students' abilities (maturity?) increase. I have tried (occasionally with success) to avoid mathematically rigorous demonstrations where possible, certainly in the earlier chapters. Consequently, many tedious details of many proofs are missing. On the other hand, I have tried to state theorems and definitions precisely. Most of my arguments are intended to be motivational rather than mathematically complete or elegant.

I believe that homework exercises contribute heavily to the learning process. The exercises at the end of each section are intended to emphasize, illustrate, review, and extend the material of the sections. The exercises range from quite easy to very hard. Many of the easier exercises reinforce ideas from the section, whereas the harder ones illustrate and extend that material. Chapters 1 through 7 end with a collection of chapter problems. These problem sets are designed to encourage investigation on the part of the reader. Generally (although not always), the material dealt with in the problem sets represents what I consider to be interesting side excursions from the main train of development in the text.

The text consists of eight chapters. The following is a short description of the contents of each of them.

Chapter 0, the initial chapter, covers mathematical and logical preliminaries. It is intended as a quick review of logic and set theory, although the chapter is quite complete. All the mathematical background necessary for the rest of the text is covered in this chapter.

In Chapter 1 we present the basic definitions and notation of alphabets, strings, and languages. Elementary string and language operations are defined and investigated.

Chapter 2 covers regular languages and regular expressions. Finite automata are defined and their relationships to each other and to regular languages are established. Nondeterminism is introduced. The fundamental properties of regular languages are established (pumping lemma, decision algorithms, and the like).

Chapter 3 introduces the concept of grammars and then develops the properties of context-free grammars, languages, and pushdown automata. Various grammar simplifications and normal forms are presented.

Chapter 4 is the first of four chapters centered on Turing machines. This chapter covers the basic definitions and various alternative formulations of the Turing machine and introduces the idea of Turing computable functions and language acceptance via Turing machines.

Chapter 5 explores the connection between Turing machines and formal languages. The Chomsky hierarchy is established.

Chapter 6 covers decidability. It begins with the halting problem for Turing machines, covers the undecidability of the Post correspondence problem (via the modified Post correspondence problem) and looks at some undecidable problems for context-free languages and grammars. The chapter closes by investigating computable integer functions.

Chapter 7 is an introduction to the computational complexity of language recognition. We discuss complexity in terms of time and space resources (of Turing machines).

While almost all this material is consistent with the usual content of an introductory theory course, the novelty of this text is perhaps the level at which it is approached. I have tried to bring this material to mathematically unsophisticated students in a manner that they can grasp while simultaneously developing their mathematical ability.

I have found that this is more than enough material to cover in a one-semester course meeting four days a week. I usually cover Chapters 1 through 5 in their entirety at whatever speed the students can comfortably handle. This material is the absolute core of any course in formal language theory, and I am not unhappy to take whatever time is necessary to allow the students to digest it. Depending on the audience, I may spend several lectures in Chapter 0 or simply assign homework from it. Much of the material in Chapter 0 came from a short course (essentially 2 credits) on mathematical proofs that was at one time offered at this college. I always completely cover Chapter 6, as well, although the depth depends on the time remaining in the semester. I was initially surprised to find that, when pressed for time, decidability can be presented quite well in a short sequence of lectures.

I would like to thank my friend Ding-Zhu Du of the University of Minnesota, Minneapolis, for suggesting Problem 1.7, which deals with the McMillan inequality. The development that leads to Lemma 2.8.3, using Arden's lemma, was suggested by one of the original reviewers of the book. I would like to thank him or her for bringing this approach (due to Brzozowski) to my attention. I would also like to express my appreciation to my friends T. J. Morrison and D. J. Malmanger for their encouragement and moral support throughout this seemingly endless project. Finally, I would like to thank the following for their comments when reviewing the manuscript: Moon Jung Chung, Michigan State University; Ronald K. Friesen, Texas A&M University; Micha Hofri, University of Houston; Robert Kline, West Chester University; S. A. Kovatch, General Electric.

Dean Kelley

Automata and
Formal Languages

0

Mathematical
Preliminaries

0.1 ELEMENTARY LOGIC

Three basic mathematical tools are necessary for the study of the theory of computation. They are a facility with set theoretic notation, a concept of functions and relations, and an understanding of mathematical induction. The ability to use set theoretic notation depends, largely, on an understanding of certain basic definitions of symbols and their meanings. Acquiring the other two tools depends on the ability to understand logical arguments. We begin, therefore, with a presentation of fundamental ideas from logic and then proceed to establish the required mathematical devices.

In logic a *statement* or *proposition* is any sentence for which truth or falsity can be determined. Thus the sentences "$2 + 1$ is 5," "$3 > \sqrt{8}$," and "17 is a prime number" all are statements, whereas "come to our party," "what time is it?" and "this statement is false" are not. If P and Q are statements we say that P is *equivalent* to Q if they have the same truth value in all cases. Thus the statements "$3 < 5$" and "π is irrational" are equivalent, as are the statements "$\frac{1}{2}$ is an integer" and "$4 < 3$," since their truth values are the same.

If P is a statement, its *negation* or *denial* is denoted $\neg P$. If P is true, $\neg P$ is false, and if P is false, $\neg P$ is true. $\neg P$ is read as "not P." Thus, if P is the statement "$3 < 5$," we have that $\neg P$ corresponds to "$3 \geq 5$." Since the truth value of $\neg P$ depends on the truth value of P, we may use a table, called a *truth table*, to indicate the dependency:

P	$\neg P$
T	F
F	T

The truth table tabulates truth values of $\neg P$ for corresponding truth values of P.

The *conjunction* of propositions P and Q is denoted $P \wedge Q$ and is read "P and Q." The compound statement $P \wedge Q$ is true only when *both* P and Q are true simultaneously. Thus, in a truth table, we have the following:

P	Q	$P \wedge Q$
T	T	T
T	F	F
F	T	F
F	F	F

Note that the truth table for a compound statement must account for all possible combinations of the truth values of the constituent statements.

Consider the conjunctions

1. $3 < \sqrt{17}$ and $25 = 5^2$.
2. $3 < \sqrt{17}$ and $26 = 5^2$.
3. $3 \geq \sqrt{17}$ and $25 = 5^2$.
4. $3 \geq \sqrt{17}$ and $26 = 5^2$.

Of these four compound statements, only the first is true. In all the others at least one component statement is false, making the entire conjunction false.

The *disjunction* of the statements P and Q is denoted $P \vee Q$. It is true whenever *at least one* of P and Q is true. Another way of saying this is that $P \vee Q$ is false only when both P and Q are false. Since this closely resembles the English use of the word "or," $P \vee Q$ is read "P or Q."

The proposition $P \rightarrow Q$ is called the *conditional* and has the truth table

P	Q	$P \rightarrow Q$
T	T	T
T	F	F
F	T	T
F	F	T

The conditional is usually read "if P then Q." To understand the truth values of $P \rightarrow Q$, consider the statement "If the sun is shining, then Karl is playing baseball." To determine when this statement is true, let's ask ourselves when the person making it is telling the truth. We have four cases corresponding to the four lines in the preceding truth table.

In the first case (the sun is shining and Karl is playing baseball), the truth has been told. In the second case (the sun is shining, but Karl is not playing baseball), the truth has not been told. In the last two cases (the sun is not shining, and Karl is playing baseball; the sun is not shining, and Karl is not playing baseball), we would not want to call the person making the statement a liar because the sun is not shining and he or she only said that something would occur if the sun were shining.

In the conditional $P \rightarrow Q$, the statement P is called the *hypothesis*, *condition*, or *antecedent*, while Q is called the *conclusion* or *consequent*.

The *converse* of the conditional $P \rightarrow Q$ is the statement $Q \rightarrow P$.

The *contrapositive* of $P \rightarrow Q$ is $(\neg Q) \rightarrow (\neg P)$. Note that $P \rightarrow Q$ and its contrapositive are equivalent since they have the same truth value in all cases, as shown by the following truth table:

P	Q	$P \rightarrow Q$	$\neg Q$	$\neg P$	$\neg Q \rightarrow \neg P$
T	T	T	F	F	T
T	F	F	T	F	F
F	T	T	F	T	T
F	F	T	T	T	T

Consider the statement $(P \rightarrow Q) \wedge (Q \rightarrow P)$. It is easy to see that this statement is true only when P and Q have the same truth values. This statement is often abbreviated $P \leftrightarrow Q$, which is read "P if and only if Q." It is called the *biconditional*.

The statements $\neg (P \wedge Q)$ and $(\neg P) \vee (\neg Q)$ are equivalent (this is one of De Morgan's laws; see Exercise 0.1.2). Consider the statement

$$(P \wedge Q) \leftrightarrow (\neg P) \vee (\neg Q)$$

Because of the equivalency of the statements, we have that both sides of the biconditional have the same truth values in all cases. Thus this biconditional is true in all cases. This suggests the following theorem:

Theorem 0.1.1.   Let P and Q be statements for which $P \leftrightarrow Q$ is always true. Then P and Q are equivalent. On the other hand, if P and Q are equivalent, then the biconditional $P \leftrightarrow Q$ is always true.

A statement is a *tautology* if it is always true. Note that if P and Q are equivalent then $P \leftrightarrow Q$ is a tautology by the previous theorem. We may thus also define equivalence as: P and Q are equivalent if $P \leftrightarrow Q$ is a tautology.

When the conditional statement $P \rightarrow Q$ is a tautology, we write $P \Rightarrow Q$. Similarly, we write $P \Leftrightarrow Q$ if the biconditional $P \leftrightarrow Q$ is a tautology. Note that this means substantially more than that the conditional (or biconditional) is a true statement. The truth of $P \rightarrow Q$ depends on the truth values of P and Q. On the other hand, $\neg (A \wedge B) \rightarrow (\neg A) \vee (\neg B)$ is a true statement regardless of the truth values of its constituent statements A and B. Thus we may write $\neg (A \wedge B) \Rightarrow (\neg A) \vee (\neg B)$.

A *contradiction* is a statement that is always false. Thus the negation of any tautology is a contradiction.

An *open sentence* or *propositional function* is a statement involving a variable. For example, the sentence "$x^2 + 2x + 16 = 0$" involves the variable x, as does the sentence "x was the first president of the United States." The collection of objects that may be substituted for a variable in an open sentence is called the *set of meanings* of that variable. The set of objects in the set of meanings for which the open sentence becomes a true statement when substituted for the variable is called the *truth set* of the open sentence. If the set of meanings for the open sentence $x^2 + 2x + 16 = 0$ is taken as the real numbers, then the truth set has no objects in it. If the set of meanings includes either of $1 \pm i\sqrt{15}$, then the truth set has something in it.

If P is an open sentence involving the variable x, we write $P(x)$. Generally, when presented with an open sentence, the set of meanings for the variable(s) involved is either explicitly stated or is clear from the context. Certain operators indicate to us how we may select items from the set of meanings. These operators are the universal and existential *quantifiers*.

A sentence of the form "for all x in the set of meanings $P(x)$ is true" is said to be a *universally quantified* sentence. It indicates that the truth set of $P(x)$ consists of all objects in the set of meanings for x. We abbreviate this as $\forall x\, P(x)$, which is read "for all x, $P(x)$." Note that $\forall x\, P(x)$ is no longer an open sentence because its truth or falsity may be determined. For example, if $P(x)$ is the open sentence "$x + 1 > x$" and the set of meanings is the collection of all real numbers, then $\forall x\, P(x)$ is a true statement.

A sentence of the form "there exists an x in the set of meanings for which $P(x)$ is true" is said to be *existentially quantified*. It indicates that somewhere in the set of meanings is a value that, when substituted for x, makes $P(x)$ true. That is, some object in the set of meanings is also in the truth set of $P(x)$. This is abbreviated $\exists x\, P(x)$ and is read "there exists an x such that $P(x)$," or "for some x, $P(x)$." Note that $\exists x\, P(x)$ is no longer an open sentence.

Theorem 0.1.2. $\neg(\forall x\, P(x))$ is equivalent to $\exists x\, \neg P(x)$.

Proof.   Suppose that $\neg\forall x\, P(x)$ is true. Then $\forall x\, P(x)$ is false, and so the truth set of $P(x)$ is not the entire set of meanings of x. The truth set of $\neg P(x)$ then contains some object. Hence the statement $\exists x\,(\neg P(x))$ is true.

Now suppose that $\neg\forall x\, P(x)$ is false. Then $\forall x\, P(x)$ is true, and so the truth set of $P(x)$ is the entire set of meanings of x. Therefore, the truth set of $\neg P(x)$ contains no objects, so the statement $\exists x\, \neg P(x)$ is also false.

We have shown that the two statements have exactly the same truth values and so are equivalent. ■

If $P(x)$ is an open sentence in x, then a *counterexample* to $\forall x\, P(x)$ is an object, t, in the set of meanings such that $P(t)$ is false. Statements of the form "If for each $x\, P(x)$, then $Q(x)$" may be proved by proving that $\forall x(P(x) \rightarrow Q(x))$ is true. They may be disproved by providing a counterexample. For example, the statement "if n is prime then $2^n - 1$ is prime" would be disproved by providing a counterexample, such as $n = 11$.

Exercises for Section 0.1

0.1.1. Give a truth table for $P \vee Q$.

0.1.2. Show that $\neg(P \wedge Q)$ is equivalent to $(\neg P) \vee (\neg Q)$. Show that $\neg(P \vee Q)$ is equivalent to $(\neg P) \wedge (\neg Q)$. These two equivalencies are known as *De Morgan's laws*.

0.1.3. Show that $P \wedge (Q \vee R)$ is equivalent to $(P \wedge Q) \vee (P \wedge R)$ and that $P \vee (Q \wedge R)$ is equivalent to $(P \vee Q) \wedge (P \vee R)$.

0.1.4. Show that P and $\neg(\neg P)$ are equivalent.

0.1.5. Simplify $\neg((\neg P) \vee (\neg Q))$.

0.1.6. Simplify $\neg((\neg Q) \wedge (\neg P))$.

0.1.7. Are $P \to Q$ and $Q \to P$ equivalent?

0.1.8. Which of the following are tautologies?

(a) $P \leftrightarrow \neg(\neg P)$.

(b) $\neg(P \vee Q) \leftrightarrow \neg P \wedge \neg Q$.

(c) $P \vee \neg P$.

(d) $(P \vee \neg P) \wedge (Q \vee \neg Q)$.

(e) $P \wedge \neg P$.

(f) $(P \wedge \neg P) \to Q$.

(g) $(P \leftrightarrow Q) \to (P \to Q)$.

(h) $(P \to Q) \leftrightarrow \neg P \vee Q$.

0.1.9. Show that the following are contradictions:

(a) $(P \to Q) \wedge (P \wedge \neg Q)$.

(b) $((P \vee Q) \wedge \neg P) \wedge (\neg Q)$.

(c) $(P \wedge Q) \wedge (\neg P)$.

0.1.10. Show that $\neg \exists x P(x)$ is equivalent to $\forall x \neg P(x)$.

0.2   BASIC DEFINITIONS

We now begin with the basic notions of set theory.

A *set* is a collection of objects called *elements* of the set. If A is a set and a is an element of A, we use the notation $a \in A$ (read "a is an element of A") to denote this. We use the notation $b \notin A$ when it is necessary to indicate that b is *not* an element of A.

If we know that A contains exactly the elements $a_1, a_2, \ldots, a_n$, we can denote this fact by writing $A = \{a_1, a_2, \ldots, a_n\}$. For example, the set of all natural numbers less than 6 may be written $A = \{0, 1, 2, 3, 4, 5\}$. Also, we may extend this notation to sets for which it is inconvenient to list all the elements, such as $\mathbb{N} = \{0, 1, 2, \ldots\}$ or $\mathbb{N}^+ = \{1, 2, 3, \ldots\}$. A set is characterized only by its elements and not by the order in which they are listed. Thus $\{1, 2, 3\}$ and $\{2, 1, 3\}$ denote the same set.

Sets A and B are *equal* if they contain exactly the same elements. Thus, if $A = \{1, 2, 3\}$ and $B = \{2, 1, 3\}$, we may write $A = B$. Note that $\{a\}$ and a are not the same. We have $a \in \{a\}$, but $a \neq \{a\}$. Also, the set $\{\{a, b\}\}$ has a single element, which is the set $\{a, b\}$. On the other hand $\{a, b\}$ has two elements, a and b. Consequently, $\{\{a, b\}\} \neq \{a, b\}$.

If A and B are sets and all elements of A are also elements of B, we write $A \subseteq B$ and say that A is a *subset* of B. Thus, for $A = \{1, 2, 3\}$ and $B = \{0, 1, 2, 3, 4, 5\}$, we have $A \subseteq B$. On the other hand, B is not a subset of A, for the elements 0, 4, and 5 of B are not in A.

Note that if $A \subseteq B$ and $B \subseteq A$ at the same time then all elements of A are in B and all elements of B are in A. Thus, if $A \subseteq B$ and $B \subseteq A$, we must have that $A = B$.

Theorem 0.2.1.   If $A \subseteq B$ and $B \subseteq C$, then $A \subseteq C$.

Proof.   Let $x \in A$. Then, since $A \subseteq B$, we have that $x \in B$. Finally, since $B \subseteq C$ and $x \in B$, we have $x \in C$. Thus, since x was an arbitrary element of A, we have that $A \subseteq C$. ∎

For purposes of completeness it is convenient to define a special set $\emptyset$, called the *empty* or *null* set, that has *no* elements. The empty set is a subset of all sets; that is, for any set A, we may write $\emptyset \subseteq A$.

Sometimes it is convenient to describe the contents of a set in terms of a characteristic property of all the elements in the set. Let $P(x)$ be a statement about x's. The notation $\{x \mid P(x)\}$, which is read "the set of all x such that $P(x)$," denotes the set of all x's for which $P(x)$ is a true statement. For example, $\mathbb{Z}^+ = \{x \mid x \in \mathbb{N} \text{ and } x > 0\}$ describes the set of positive integers. Also, $A = \{x \mid x \in \mathbb{N} \text{ and } x < 5\}$ is the set $\{0, 1, 2, 3, 4\}$.

Let A be any set. We define the *power set* of A to be $2^A = \{B \mid B \subseteq A\}$. For example, let $A = \{a, b, c\}$. Then 2^A is the set

$$\{\emptyset, \{a\}, \{b\}, \{c\}, \{a, b\}, \{a, c\}, \{b, c\}, \{a, b, c\}\}$$

Note that $\emptyset \in 2^A$ and $A \in 2^A$.

Let I be some set. If for each $\alpha \in I$ we have that A_α is a set, then $\{A_\alpha \mid \alpha \in I\}$ is called an *indexed family of sets*. For example, if for each $n > 0$ we let $A_n = [-1/n, 1/n]$, then $\{A_n \mid n \in \mathbb{Z}^+\}$ is the family of closed intervals from $-1/n$ to $1/n$ for $n = 1, 2, 3 \ldots$.

0.3 SET OPERATIONS

In arithmetic we can add, subtract, or multiply two numbers. In set theory there are three operations that are analogous to these operations. The *union* of sets A and B is denoted $A \cup B$ and consists of those elements that occur in A or in B or in both A and B. Thus $A \cup B = \{x \mid x \in A \text{ or } x \in B\}$.

The *intersection* of A and B is the set $A \cap B = \{x \mid x \in A \text{ and } x \in B\}$. Note that if $x \in A \cap B$ then we must have that x occurs in both A and B simultaneously.

For example, if $A = \{0, 1, 2, 3, 4, 5\}$ and $B = \{2, 3, 5, 9\}$, then $A \cup B = \{0, 1, 2, 3, 4, 5, 9\}$ and $A \cap B = \{2, 3, 5\}$.

As another example, note that we have $\mathbb{Z}^+ \cup \{0\} = \mathbb{N}$, while $\mathbb{N} \cap \mathbb{Z}^+ = \mathbb{Z}^+$.

Sets A and B are said to be *disjoint* if $A \cap B = \emptyset$.

Theorem 0.3.1.   For sets A and B, we have the following:

1. $\emptyset \cup A = A$.

2. $\emptyset \cap A = \emptyset$.

3. If $A \subseteq B$, then $A \cap B = A$.

4. If $A \subseteq B$, then $A \cup B = B$.

5. $A \cap A = A = A \cup A$.

6. (a) $A \cup B = B \cup A$.

   (b) $A \cap B = B \cap A$.

7. (a) $A \cup (B \cup C) = (A \cup B) \cup C$.

(b) $A \cap (B \cap C) = (A \cap B) \cap C$.

8. (a) $A \cap (B \cup C) = (A \cap B) \cup (A \cap C)$.

(b) $A \cup (B \cap C) = (A \cup B) \cap (A \cup C)$.

Proof.   We leave the proofs of most of these statements to the reader.

7. (a) An element x satisfies

$$
\begin{aligned}
x \in A \cup (B \cup C) &\Leftrightarrow x \in A \text{ or } x \in (B \cup C) \\
&\Leftrightarrow x \in A \text{ or } (x \in B \text{ or } x \in C) \\
&\Leftrightarrow (x \in A \text{ or } x \in B) \text{ or } x \in C \\
&\Leftrightarrow x \in (A \cup B) \text{ or } x \in C \\
&\Leftrightarrow x \in (A \cup B) \cup C
\end{aligned}
$$

Thus we have that $A \cup (B \cup C) \subseteq (A \cup B) \cup C$ and also $(A \cup B) \cup C \subseteq A \cup (B \cup C)$ so the two are equal.

8. (b) An element x satisfies

$$
\begin{aligned}
x \in A \cup (B \cap C) &\Leftrightarrow x \in A \text{ or } x \in B \cap C \\
&\Leftrightarrow x \in A \text{ or } (x \in B \text{ and } x \in C) \\
&\Leftrightarrow (x \in A \text{ or } x \in B) \text{ and } (x \in A \text{ or } x \in C) \\
&\Leftrightarrow x \in (A \cup B) \text{ and } x \in (A \cup C) \\
&\Leftrightarrow x \in (A \cup B) \cap (A \cup C)
\end{aligned}
$$

so we have that each of the sets $A \cup (B \cap C)$ and $(A \cup B) \cap (A \cup B)$ is a subset of the other. Thus the two sets are equal. ■

If A and B are any two sets, the *complement* of B in A (also called the *relative complement*) is the set

$$A - B = \{x \mid x \in A \text{ and } x \notin B\}$$

That is, $A - B$ consists of all of A's elements that are not also in B. For example, if $A = \{0, 2, 4, 6, 8, 10\}$ and $B = \{0, 1, 2, 3, 4\}$, then $A - B = \{6, 8, 10\}$, while $B - A = \{1, 3\}$.

Frequently, it is convenient to think of all sets under discussion as being subsets of some *universal* set U. Complements can be formed relative to this universal set. If A is some set, then $U - A$ is the set of all elements not in A. It is often convenient to denote such complements by $\overline{A}$; thus $U - A = \overline{A}$. Note that $\overline{\emptyset} = U$ and $\overline{U} = \emptyset$.

Theorem 0.3.2.   For sets A and B:

1. $A - B = A \cap \overline{B}$.

2. $\overline{(A \cap B)} = \overline{A} \cup \overline{B}$.

3. $\overline{(A \cup B)} = \overline{A} \cap \overline{B}$.

4. $\overline{\overline{A}} = A$.

Proof. We prove parts 1 and 3 and leave the rest for the reader.

An element x satisfies

$$
\begin{aligned}
x \in A - B &\Leftrightarrow x \in A \text{ and } x \notin B \\
&\Leftrightarrow x \in A \text{ and } x \in \overline{B} \\
&\Leftrightarrow x \in A \cap \overline{B}
\end{aligned}
$$

Thus $A - B \subseteq A \cap \overline{B}$ and $A \cap \overline{B} \subseteq A - B$, so we have $A - B = A \cap \overline{B}$ and (1) is proved.

For part 3, an element x satisfies

$$
\begin{aligned}
x \in \overline{A \cup B} &\Leftrightarrow x \notin A \cup B \\
&\Leftrightarrow x \notin A \text{ and } x \notin B \\
&\Leftrightarrow x \in \overline{A} \text{ and } x \in \overline{B} \\
&\Leftrightarrow x \in \overline{A} \cap \overline{B}
\end{aligned}
$$

Thus we have $\overline{A \cup B} \subseteq \overline{A} \cap \overline{B}$ and $\overline{A} \cap \overline{B} \subseteq \overline{A \cup B}$, so the two sets are equal. ■

Note that parts (2) and (3) of Theorem 0.3.2. are known as De Morgan's laws for sets.

Given any two sets A and B, their *Cartesian product*, $A \times B$, is the set of all ordered pairs whose first element is from A and whose second element is from B. Thus

$$
A \times B = \{(a, b) \mid a \in A \text{ and } b \in B\}
$$

For example, if $A = \{1, 2, 3\}$ and $B = \{5, 6\}$, then

$$
A \times B = \{(1, 5), (2, 5), (3, 5), (1, 6), (2, 6), (3, 6)\}
$$

Note that ordered pairs are equal if and only if corresponding elements in them are equal. Thus $(a, b) = (c, d)$ only when $a = c$ and $b = d$. Consequently, an ordered pair is different from a set of two elements.

Exercises for Section 0.3

0.3.1. Prove the following:

(a) If $A \subseteq B$, then $2^A \subseteq 2^B$.

(b) If $A \cap B = A \cup B$, then $A = B$.

(c) If $A = B$, then $A \cap B = A \cup B$.

0.3.2. If $A \subseteq B$, then for any set C, we have $A \cup C \subseteq B \cup C$ and $A \cap C \subseteq B \cap C$. Prove this statement.

0.3.3. If $A \subseteq C$ and $B \subseteq D$, is it the case that $C \cup D \subseteq A \cup B$?

0.3.4. Prove or disprove the following:

(a) If $A \cup B = A \cup C$, then $B = C$.

(b) If $A \cap B = A \cap C$, then $B = C$.

0.3.5. Let $\{B_\alpha \mid \alpha \in I\}$ be an indexed family of sets. We use the notation $\bigcup_{\alpha \in I} B_\alpha$ to indicate the union of all the B_α and $\bigcap_{\alpha \in I} B_\alpha$ to indicate the intersection of all the B_α. Prove that for any set A we have the following:

(a) $A \cap (\bigcup_{\alpha \in I} B_\alpha) = \bigcup_{\alpha \in I} (A \cap B_\alpha)$.

(b) $A \cup (\bigcap_{\alpha \in I} B_\alpha) = \bigcap_{\alpha \in I} (A \cup B_\alpha)$.

0.3.6. Prove the following:

(a) $A - B = A - (B \cap A)$.

(b) $B \subseteq \overline{A}$ if and only if $A \cap B = \emptyset$.

(c) $(\bigcap_{\alpha \in I} B_\alpha) - A = \bigcap_{\alpha \in I} (B_\alpha - A)$.

(d) $(A - B) - C = (A - C) - (B - C) = A - (B \cup C)$.

(e) $A \cap \overline{B} = \emptyset$ and $\overline{A} \cap B = \emptyset$ if and only if $A = B$.

0.3.7. Is it the case that:

(a) $2^A \cap 2^B = 2^{A \cap B}$?

(b) $2^A \cup 2^B = 2^{A \cup B}$?

0.3.8. The ordered pair (x, y) is often formally defined by the statement $(x, y) = \{\{x\}, \{x, y\}\}$. Using this definition, show that $(a, b) = (c, d)$ if and only if $a = c$ and $b = d$.

0.3.9. Let A, B, and C be any sets. Show that:

(a) $A \times (B \cap C) = (A \times B) \cap (A \times C)$.

(b) $A \times (B \cup C) = (A \times B) \cup (A \times C)$.

(c) $A \times (B - C) = (A \times B) - (A \times C)$.

0.4 RELATIONS AND FUNCTIONS

A *relation* from the set A to the set B is any subset of $A \times B$. Thus, if $R \subseteq A \times B$ and $(a, b) \in R$, we say that *a is related to b* under the relation R. For example, if $A = \{2, 3, 4, 5\}$ and $B = \{1, 3, 5, 7, 9\}$, then $R = \{(2, 1), (2, 3), (5, 4), (5, 5)\}$ is a relation, and 2 is related to 1 under this relation.

Often A and B are the same set and, in that case, we speak of a relation as a *relation on A*. For example, let $R \subseteq \mathbb{N} \times \mathbb{N}$ be defined by $(x, y) \in R$ if and only if $x \leq y$. R, here, is the usual "less than or equal to" relation on $\mathbb{N}$.

The relation $R \subseteq A \times B$ defines two subsets, one a subset of A and one a subset of B. They are

$$\text{Dom}(R) = \{a \mid a \in A \text{ and } (a, x) \in R \text{ for some } x \in B\}$$

$$\text{Im}(R) = \{b \mid b \in B \text{ and } (y, b) \in R \text{ for some } y \in A\}$$

and are referred to as the *domain* and *image* of R, respectively.

For example, if $A = \{a, b, c, d, e\}$ and $B = \{1, 2, 3, 4, 5\}$ with $R = \{(a, 1), (a, 2), (b, 5), (c, 4)\}$, then we have

$$\text{Dom}(R) = \{a, b, c\} \quad \text{and} \quad \text{Im}(R) = \{1, 2, 4, 5\}$$

If $R \subseteq A \times B$ is a relation from A to B, then the set $R^{-1} = \{(b, a)|(a, b) \in R\}$ is a subset of $B \times A$. Consequently, it is, itself, a relation from B to A. R^{-1} is called the *inverse* of the relation R.

Let A be a nonempty set. A collection $\mathcal{A}$ of nonempty subsets of A is a *partition* of A if the following hold:

1. If B and C are sets in $\mathcal{A}$, then either $B = C$ or $B \cap C = \emptyset$.
2. $A = \bigcup_{B \in \mathcal{A}} B$.

Intuitively, a partition of A cuts A up into nonempty, disjoint pieces. For example, let $A = \{x|x \in \mathbb{N} \text{ and } x \leq 10\}$ and let

$$\mathcal{A} = \{\{0, 2, 4\}, \{1, 3, 5\}, \{6, 8, 10\}, \{7, 9\}\}$$

Then $\mathcal{A}$ partitions A. On the other hand,

$$\mathcal{B} = \{\{0, 2, 4, 6\}, \{1, 2, 3, 5, 7\}, \{9, 10\}, \emptyset\}$$

is not a partition.

As another slightly more interesting example, let $\mathbb{Q}$ be the rational numbers. For each $r \in \mathbb{Q}$, let

$$Q_r = \{(x, y) \in \mathbb{N} \times \mathbb{Z}^+ | \frac{x}{y} = r\}$$

Thus $Q_{3/8}$ contains $(3, 8)$, $(6, 10)$, $(9, 24)$, and so on. Note that the collection $F = \{Q_r | r \in \mathbb{Q}\}$ is a partition of $\mathbb{N} \times \mathbb{Z}^+$. To see this, first note that if Q_r and Q_s are elements of F and if $(x, y) \in Q_r \cap Q_s$, then $s = x/y = r$ so that $s = r$ and thus $Q_r = Q_s$. Since $Q_r \subseteq \mathbb{N} \times \mathbb{Z}^+$ for all r, we have that $\bigcup_{r \in \mathbb{Q}} Q_r \subseteq \mathbb{N} \times \mathbb{Z}^+$. Conversely, if $(x, y) \in \mathbb{N} \times \mathbb{Z}^+$, then $x/y \in \mathbb{Q}$, and so $(x, y) \in Q_r$ for the rational number $r = x/y$. Thus $(x, y) \in \bigcup_{r \in \mathbb{Q}} Q_r$. It follows that $\bigcup_{r \in \mathbb{Q}} Q_r = \mathbb{N} \times \mathbb{Z}^+$.

Yet another example of a partition of a set is the collection $\{\mathbb{Z}_0, \mathbb{Z}_1, \ldots, \mathbb{Z}_{m-1}\}$, where m is a fixed positive integer and $\mathbb{Z}_i$ is defined as

$$\mathbb{Z}_i = \{x|x \in \mathbb{Z} \text{ and } x - i = km \text{ for some integer } k\}$$

Note, for example, if $m = 3$, we have $\mathbb{Z}_0 = \{0, \pm 3, \pm 6, \pm 9, \ldots\}$, $\mathbb{Z}_1 = \{\ldots, -5, -2, 1, 4, 7, \ldots\}$, and $\mathbb{Z}_2 = \{\ldots, -4, -1, 2, 5, 8, \ldots\}$.

Suppose that $\mathcal{A}$ partitions the set X. Let us define a relation on X by

$$R = \{(x, y)| x \text{ and } y \text{ are in the same set in } \mathcal{A}\}$$

For example, if $X = \{0, 1, 2\}$ and $\mathcal{A} = \{\{0\}, \{1, 2\}\}$, then R would be the set $R = \{(0, 0), (1, 1), (2, 2), (1, 2), (2, 1)\}$.

A relation defined in this way has certain interesting properties. First, note that if $a \in X$ then, since $\mathcal{A}$ partitions X, there is some $A \in \mathcal{A}$ for which $a \in A$. Thus $(a, a) \in R$.

Second, note that if $(a, b) \in R$, then a and b are in the same set of $\mathcal{A}$, and so b and a are in the same set of $\mathcal{A}$. Thus $(b, a) \in R$.

Finally, note that if $(a, b) \in R$ and $(b, c) \in R$ then a, b, and c are all in the same set in $\mathcal{A}$. Consequently, we have that $(a, c) \in R$.

Summarizing, for the relation

$$R = \{(x, y) | x \text{ and } y \text{ are in the same set in } \mathcal{A}\}$$

we have the following:

1. $(a, a) \in R$ for all $a \in X$ (reflexive property).
2. If $(a, b) \in R$, then $(b, a) \in R$ (symmetric property).
3. If (a, b) and (b, c) are in R, then $(a, c) \in R$ (transitive property).

Any relation having these three properties is said to be an *equivalence relation*.

Suppose that R is an equivalence relation on the set X. For each $x \in X$, define the set $[x] = \{y \in X | (x, y) \in R\}$. The set $[x]$ is called the *equivalence class of x.*

Theorem 0.4.1.   The equivalence classes of an equivalence relation R on a set X form a partition of X.

Proof.   To prove this theorem, we must show that the equivalence classes are disjoint from each other and that their union is all of X. We first show that they are disjoint from each other.

Suppose that $z \in [x] \cap [y]$. Then $(x, z) \in R$ and $(z, y) \in R$. Since R is transitive, we then have that $(x, y) \in R$. Consequently, $x \in [y]$ and $y \in [x]$. Thus $(x, y) \in R$ and $(y, x) \in R$. Now, if $t \in [x]$, then we have $(t, x) \in R$ and so $(t, y) \in R$, by R's transitivity again. Thus $t \in [y]$, giving $[x] \subseteq [y]$. Conversely, if $t \in [y]$ then $(t, y) \in R$, and so $(t, x) \in R$, giving $t \in [x]$ so that $[y] \subseteq [x]$. Hence, if $[x] \cap [y] \neq \emptyset$, we must have that $[x] = [y]$.

Now, since R is an equivalence relation on X, any $x \in X$ must satisfy $(x, x) \in R$, so $x \in [x]$. That is, any element of X appears in some equivalence class, namely its own.   ∎

Our earlier discussion gives the following theorem:

Theorem 0.4.2.   Any partition $\mathcal{A}$ of a nonempty set X defines an equivalence relation on X.

Thus we have a very close connection between equivalence relations and partitions.

A *function* from A to B is a relation from A to B that meets additional criteria. The set $f \subseteq A \times B$ is a function if Dom $(f) = A$ and whenever (x, y) and (x, z) are in f then $y = z$. This means that every element x of A has a uniquely determined y such that $(x, y) \in f$. We generally write $f: A \rightarrow B$ and use the notation $f(x) = y$, where $(x, y) \in f$. This notation can, in fact, be extended to relations in general, as we have done with the R-image of Exercise 0.4.3.

Theorem 0.4.3.   Let $f: A \rightarrow B$ and $g: A \rightarrow B$ be functions. Then $f = g$ if and only if $f(x) = g(x)$ for all x in A.

Proof.   Suppose that $f = g$. Let x be any element of A. Then if $y = f(x)$ we have that $(x, y) \in f$, and so $(x, y) \in g$. Consequently, $y = g(x)$.

Conversely, suppose that $f(x) = g(x)$ for all x in A and suppose that (x, y) is an arbitrary element of f. Then $y = f(x) = g(x)$ so that $(x, y) \in g$, giving $f \subseteq g$. On the other hand, if (x, y) is an arbitrary element of g, we have that $y = g(x) = f(x)$, and so $(x, y) \in f$, giving $g \subseteq f$. Thus $f = g$. ■

For $f \subseteq A \times B$ to be a function, we have required that $\text{Dom}\,(f) = A$. This is actually somewhat more restrictive than necessary for our purposes in this text. Let us define *total function* to mean the kind of function that we have defined previously. We will define *partial function* to mean a relation f satisfying the conditions that $\text{Dom}\,(f) \subseteq A$, and if (x, y) and (x, z) are in f, then $y = z$. Note that the only difference is that in a partial function from A to B the domain of the function need not be the entire set A. We will use the term function, unmodified, to mean either partial or total function and will qualify only when necessary.

Let $f: A \to B$ be a function. If $X \subseteq A$, we define the *image of X under f* to be

$$f(X) = \{y \in B | y = f(x) \text{ for some } x \in X\}$$

If $Y \subseteq B$, the *inverse image of Y under f* is the set

$$f^{-1}(Y) = \{x \in A | f(x) = y \text{ for some } y \in Y\}$$

Theorem 0.4.4. Let $f: A \to B$ be a function.

1. $f(\emptyset) = \emptyset$.

2. $f(\{x\}) = \{f(x)\}$ for all $x \in A$.

3. If $X \subseteq Y \subseteq A$, then $f(X) \subseteq f(Y)$.

4. If $X \subseteq Y \subseteq B$, then $f^{-1}(X) \subseteq f^{-1}(Y)$.

5. If X and Y are subsets of B, then $f^{-1}(X - Y) = f^{-1}(X) - f^{-1}(Y)$.

Proof.   The proofs follow easily from the preceding definitions and are left to the reader. ■

A function $f: A \to B$ is said to be *one-to-one* or *injective* if, whenever $(x, y) \in f$ and $(z, y) \in f$, then we have that $x = z$. This says that if $f(x) = f(z)$ then $x = z$. A function f is said to be *onto* or *surjective* if, whenever $y \in B$, there is some $x \in A$ for which $f(x) = y$.

The function $f: \mathbb{N} \to \mathbb{N}$ defined by $f(n) = n$ is both one-to-one and onto. The function $g: \mathbb{N} \to \mathbb{N}$, where $g(n) = n + 1$, is one-to-one but *not* onto, for there is no $x \in \mathbb{N}$ for which $x + 1 = 0$. The function $h : \mathbb{R} \to \mathbb{R}$, where $h(x) = x^2$, is neither one-to-one nor onto.

If f is both one-to-one and onto, it is called a *bijection* or *one-to-one correspondence*. Note that if $f: A \to B$ is onto then $f^{-1}(\{b\}) \neq \emptyset$ for all $b \in B$. If f is one-to-one and onto, then $f^{-1}(\{b\})$ is a singleton set for all $b \in B$. Thus when f is a bijection, $f^{-1}: B \to A$ is a function.

Both functions and relations can be combined in a convenient manner. Let $R \subseteq A \times B$ and $S \subseteq B \times C$ be relations. We define the *composition* of R and S as

$$S \circ R = \{(a, c) \in A \times C | \text{ for some } b \in B, (a, b) \in R \text{ and } (b, c) \in S\}$$

Thus if $R = \{(0, 1), (0, 2), (1, 1)\}$ and $S = \{(1, a), (2, b)\}$, we would have $S \circ R = \{(0, a), (0, b), (1, a)\}$. Note that, on the other hand, $R \circ S = \emptyset$, since there are no symbols that appear simultaneously as a first component of an element of R and as a second component of an element of S. Thus, in general, $R \circ S$ and $S \circ R$ are not the same.

Composing functions is done in exactly the same manner:

$$g \circ f = \{(a, b) | \text{ for some } y, f(a) = y \text{ and } b = g(y)\}$$

For example, let $f : \mathbb{R} \to \mathbb{R}$ be defined as $f(x) = x + 1$ and $g : \mathbb{R} \to \mathbb{R}$ be defined as $g(x) = x^2$. Then we have

$$g \circ f(x) = g(f(x)) = g(x + 1) = (x + 1)^2$$

and

$$f \circ g(x) = f(g(x)) = f(x^2) = x^2 + 1$$

Exercises for Section 0.4

0.4.1. Let A and B be the sets $A = \{2, 3, 4, 5\}$ and $B = \{1, 3, 5, 7, 9\}$. Let R be the relation

$$R = \{(x, y) \in A \times B | x < y\}$$

List the ordered pairs in R.

0.4.2. Show the following:

(a) $\text{Dom}(R^{-1}) = \text{Im}(R)$.

(b) $\text{Im}(R^{-1}) = \text{Dom}(R)$.

0.4.3. Let $R \subseteq A \times B$ be a relation from A to B. Let $X \subseteq A$. We can define the *R-image* of X to be

$$R(X) = \{y \in B | (x, y) \in R \text{ for some } x \in X\}$$

Note that the R-image of X is just the image of the relation R when restricted to the subset $X \times B$ of $A \times B$. Let D and E be subsets of A. Prove the following:

(a) $R(D \cup E) = R(D) \cup R(E)$.

(b) $R(D \cap E) = R(D) \cap R(E)$.

(c) $\text{Dom}(R) = R^{-1}(B)$.

(d) $\text{Im}(R) = R(A)$.

0.4.4. Let $R \subseteq A \times B$ and $S \subseteq A \times B$ be relations. Then $R \cup S \subseteq A \times B$ is also a relation from A to B, as is $R \cap S$. Show the following:

(a) $\text{Dom}(R \cup S) = \text{Dom}(R) \cup \text{Dom}(S)$.

(b) $\text{Im}(R \cup S) = \text{Im}(R) \cup \text{Im}(S)$.

(c) $(R \cup S)(X) = R(X) \cup S(X)$ for any $X \subseteq A$.

(d) $(R \cup S)^{-1} = R^{-1} \cup S^{-1}$.

(e) $(R \cap S)^{-1} = R^{-1} \cap S^{-1}$.

0.4.5. Let $m = 5$. Find the sets $\mathbb{Z}_0, \mathbb{Z}_1, \mathbb{Z}_2, \mathbb{Z}_3, \mathbb{Z}_4$.

0.4.6. Show that $\{\mathbb{Z}_0, \mathbb{Z}_1, \ldots, \mathbb{Z}_{m-1}\}$ forms a partition of $\mathbb{Z}$ for any fixed $m > 0$.

0.4.7. Determine if each of the following relations is an equivalence relation on the set

$$A = \{0, 1, 2, 3, 4, 5\}$$

(a) $R_1 = \{(0, 0), (1, 1), (1, 2), (2, 2), (3, 3), (4, 4), (5, 5)\}$.

(b) $R_2 = R_1 \cup \{(2, 1)\}$.

(c) $R_3 = R_1 - \{(1, 2)\}$.

(d) $R_4 = R_2 \cup \{(2, 3), (1, 3), (3, 1), (3, 2)\}$.

0.4.8. Let $\{\mathbb{Z}_0, \mathbb{Z}_1, \mathbb{Z}_2, \mathbb{Z}_3, \mathbb{Z}_4\}$ be the partition of $\mathbb{Z}$ defined on page 10. What is the equivalence relation on $\mathbb{Z}$ that this partition gives rise to?

0.4.9. Let $\{A_1, A_2, \ldots, A_m\}$ be a partition of A and $\{B_1, B_2, \ldots, B_n\}$ be a partition of B. Show that the following set is a partition of $A \times B$:

$$\{A_i \times B_j \mid i = 1, 2, \ldots, m \text{ and } j = 1, 2, \ldots, n\}$$

0.4.10. Let A and B be sets defined by

$$A = \{0, 1, 2, 3\}$$

and

$$B = \{-1, 0, \frac{1}{2}, 1, \frac{3}{2}, 2, 3, 4\}$$

Which of the following relations are total functions, which are partial functions, and which are not functions at all?

(a) $f = \{(0, 1), (1, 2), (2, 3), (3, 4)\}$

(b) $f = \{(0, 0), (1, \frac{1}{2}), (2, 1), (3, \frac{3}{2})\}$

(c) $f = \{(0, 0), (1, 1), (1, -1), (2, 3)\}$

(d) $f = \{(0, 0), (1, 3), (2, 2)\}$

(e) $f = \{(0, 0)\}$

0.4.11. Let $f: A \to C$ and $g: B \to D$ be two functions with $f(x) = g(x)$ for all $x \in A \cap B$. Show that $f \cup g$ is a function from $A \cup B$ into $C \cup D$.

0.4.12. Let $f: A \to B$ be a bijection. Show that f^{-1} is also a bijection.

0.4.13. Show that if $f^{-1}(f(X)) = X$ for all $X \subseteq A$ then f is one-to-one. Show that if $f(f^{-1}(Y)) = Y$ for all $y \subseteq B$, then f is onto.

0.4.14. Let $f: A \to A$ be a function for which $f(f(x)) = x$ for all $x \in A$. Show that f is a symmetric relation on A.

0.4.15. Let $f: A \to B$ and $g: C \to D$ be functions and assume that $A \cap C = \emptyset$ and $B \cap D = \emptyset$. Show that $f \cup g$ is onto if both f and g are. Show that $f \cup g$ is one-to-one if both f and g are.

0.4.16. Let f and g be defined by

$$f = \{(x, y)|x \in \mathbb{N} \text{ and } y \in \mathbb{Z}^+ \text{ and } y = |x| + 1\}$$
$$g = \{(x, y)|x \in \mathbb{Z}^+ \text{ and } y \in \mathbb{N} \text{ and } y = -2|x|\}$$

Note that $f \subseteq \mathbb{N} \times \mathbb{Z}^+$ and $g \subseteq \mathbb{Z}^+ \times \mathbb{N}$ so that $f \circ g$ and $g \circ f$ are defined. Describe $f \circ g$ and $g \circ f$.

0.4.17. Let A be any set and define the relation

$$I_A = \{(a, a)|a \in A\}$$

(a) Prove that I_A is a function.

(b) Prove that I_A is a bijection.

(c) Let $f: X \to Y$ be a function. Show that $f \circ I_X = I_Y \circ f = f$.

(d) If $f: X \to Y$ is a bijection, show that $f \circ f^{-1} = I_Y$ and that $f^{-1} \circ f = I_X$.

0.4.18. Let $f: A \to B$ and $g: B \to C$ be functions. Show the following:

(a) If f and g are one-to-one, then so is $g \circ f$.

(b) If f and g are onto, then so is $g \circ f$.

0.5   INDUCTION

A subset A of $\mathbb{N}$ is said to be an *inductive set* if, whenever $a \in A$, then $a + 1$ is also in A. For example, the set $\{5, 6, 7, \ldots\}$ is inductive, but the set $\{0, 2, 4, 6, 8, 10, \ldots\}$ is not. Note that for a set to be inductive it cannot contain a finite number of elements. Many sets of natural numbers are inductive and do not contain 0. Many sets of natural numbers contain 0, but are not inductive. That there is only one collection of natural numbers that is both inductive and contains 0 is called the *principle of mathematical induction* (PMI). Stated succinctly the *principle of mathematical induction* is:

> Let $A \subseteq \mathbb{N}$ satisfy the following:
> 1. $0 \in A$,
> 2. if $n \in A$, then $n + 1 \in A$,
> then $A = \mathbb{N}$.

The principle of mathematical induction is useful for many things in mathematics. It provides a convenient mechanism for defining sets of objects in which there is a first object, a second object, and so on. In such definitions the first object is defined and the $n + 1^{st}$ object is defined in terms of the nth.

For example, the factorial of a natural number can be defined inductively as

$$0! = 1$$

and

$$(n + 1)! = (n + 1) \cdot n!, \quad \text{for } n > 0$$

The PMI is also useful for proving statements about things that at some level or another can be indexed by $\mathbb{N}$. In such a proof we show that the collection of indexes is inductive and contains 0 and, consequently, is $\mathbb{N}$.

For example, the statement "$n + 3 < 5(n + 1)$ for all natural numbers n" can be proved as follows:

Let $A = \{n \in \mathbb{N} \mid n + 3 < 5(n + 1)\}$. We must show that A is $\mathbb{N}$. Note that if n is 0 then we have $n + 3 = 3$ and $5(n + 1)$ is 5, so the statement holds. Thus we know that 0 is in A. Now suppose that $n \in A$. We wish to show that $n + 1$ is also in A. Note that $(n + 1) + 3 = n + 4 = (n + 3) + 1$. Then

$$
\begin{aligned}
5((n + 1) + 1) &= 5n + 10 \\
&= 5(n + 1) + 5 \\
&> (n + 3) + 5 \\
&> (n + 3) + 1 \\
&= (n + 1) + 3
\end{aligned}
$$

Thus the statement holds for $n + 1$ when it holds for n, and so we have $n + 1 \in A$ when $n \in A$. By the PMI, we have $A = \mathbb{N}$, and so the statement holds for all natural numbers. ∎

The steps of a proof using the PMI are quite easy to remember.

1. Show that the statement holds for 0.
2. Assume that the statement holds for n and show that this forces it to hold for $n + 1$.
3. Conclude that the statement holds for all of $\mathbb{N}$.

Step 1 is called the *basis step*. The assumption that the statement holds for n in step 2 is called the *induction hypothesis*. Step 2, itself, is called the *induction step*.

It is often convenient to use the PMI to prove statements about collections of natural numbers that do not contain 0. For example, the statement of the formula $1 + 2 + \cdots + (2n - 1) = n^2$ doesn't make sense (nor is it true) for $n = 0$. Nevertheless, this formula holds for all $n \geq 1$. In this case we choose a different inductive set S. Note that the formula holds for $n = 1$. Let

$$
S = \{n \in \mathbb{N} \mid \text{the formula holds for } 1 + n\}
$$

Note that $0 \in S$. Also if $n \in S$, then we know that

$$
1 + 2 + \cdots + (2(1 + n) - 1) = (1 + n)^2
$$

We then show that the formula holds for $n + 1$. That is, $n + 1 \in S$ whenever $n \in S$. For $n + 1$, we add the appropriate value to each side, getting

$$
\begin{aligned}
1 + 2 + \cdots + (2(1 + n) - 1) + (2(1 + (n + 1)) - 1) &= (1 + n)^2 + (2(1 + (n + 1)) - 1 \\
&= 1 + 2(n + 1) + (1 + n)^2 \\
&= (1 + (n + 1))^2
\end{aligned}
$$

It then follows from the PMI that $S = \mathbb{N}$, and so the formula holds for all $n \geq 1$. ∎

In actual practice we usually do not specify the set S. If a property is expressed as $P(n)$ for all $n \geq k$, the proof usually takes the following form:

1. (*basis step*) Show that $P(k)$ holds.
2. (*induction step*) Show that if $P(n)$ is true then $P(n+1)$ is true for any $n \geq k$.
3. (*conclusion*) By steps 1 and 2 and the PMI, $P(n)$ is true for all $n \geq k$.

Thus the proof in the preceding example could be redone as follows:

Let $n = 1$. Then we have $1 = 1^2$, so the formula holds. Now assume that for $n \geq 1$ the formula holds. That is,

$$1 + 2 + \cdots (2(1+n) - 1) = (1+n)^2$$

Then we have

$$\begin{aligned}
1 + 2 + \cdots + (2(1+n) - 1) &+ (2(1 + (n+1)) - 1 \\
&= (1+n)^2 + (2(1 + (n+1)) - 1 \\
&= 1 + 2(n+1) + (1+n)^2 \\
&= (1 + (n+1))^2
\end{aligned}$$

and so the formula holds for $n + 1$. Then, by the PMI, the formula holds for all $n \geq 1$. ∎

Exercises for Section 0.5

0.5.1. Show that, for all $n \in \mathbb{N}$,

$$2^0 + 2^1 + \cdots + 2^n = 2^{n+1} - 1$$

0.5.2. Show that, for all $n \geq 1$,

$$2^1 + 2^2 + \cdots + 2^n = 2^{n+1} - 2$$

0.6 CARDINALITY

Bijections, one-to-one onto functions, between sets are especially useful when comparing the relative sizes of sets. Two sets A and B are *equivalent* if there is a bijection between them. We employ the notation $A \cong B$ to denote this. Thus we have $\{x, y, z\} \cong \{1, 2, 3\}$, while $\{x, y, z\} \not\cong \{1, 2\}$.

Example 0.6.1

As a slightly less trivial example, let $\mathcal{F} = \{f \mid f\colon \mathbb{N} \to \{0, 1\}\}$ be the set of all functions from $\mathbb{N}$ to $\{0, 1\}$; then $\mathcal{F} \cong 2^{\mathbb{N}}$. To see this, we need a bijection $H\colon \mathcal{F} \to 2^{\mathbb{N}}$. That is, we need a rule that associates each function in $\mathcal{F}$ with some subset of $\mathbb{N}$. For $g \in \mathcal{F}$, let $H(g) = \{x \mid g(x) = 1\}$. Note that all functions in $\mathcal{F}$ have an image under H. We now show that H is one-to-one and onto.

To see that H is one-to-one, let g_1 and g_2 be functions in $\mathcal{F}$ and assume that $H(g_1) = H(g_2)$. Let $x \in \mathbb{N}$. We must have that either $x \in H(g_1)$ or $x \notin H(g_1)$. If $x \in H(g_1)$, then, since $H(g_1) = H(g_2)$, we must have that $g_1(x) = g_2(x) = 1$. On the other hand, if $x \notin H(g_1)$, then $g_1(x) = g_2(x) = 0$. Thus, in either case, we have $g_1(x) = g_2(x)$ for arbitrary $x \in \mathbb{N}$, and so $g_1 = g_2$.

To see that H is onto, let $A \in 2^{\mathbb{N}}$ be an arbitrary subset of $\mathbb{N}$. Define the function g: $\mathbb{N} \to \{0, 1\}$ by

$$g(x) = \begin{cases} 0, & \text{if } x \notin A \\ 1, & \text{if } x \in A \end{cases}$$

Note that $g \in \mathcal{F}$ and that $H(g) = A$. Thus, for an arbitrary element A of $2^{\mathbb{N}}$, we may find a function in $\mathcal{F}$ that maps to A. It follows that H is onto.

Theorem 0.6.1.   Suppose that $A \cong C$ and $B \cong D$ with $A \cap B = \emptyset$ and $C \cap D = \emptyset$. Then $A \cup B \cong C \cup D$.

Proof.   Since $A \cong C$ and $B \cong D$, there are bijections $g: A \to C$ and $h : B \to D$. Define f: $A \cup B \to C \cup D$ by

$$f(x) = \begin{cases} g(x), & \text{if } x \in A \\ h(x), & \text{if } x \in B \end{cases}$$

By Exercise 0.4.15, f is a bijection since both g and h are. Consequently, $A \cup B \cong C \cup D$. ∎

For each natural number $k \geq 1$, let us define $\mathbb{N}_k = \{1, 2, \ldots, k\}$. We will use the $\mathbb{N}_k$'s as "standard-sized" sets against which other sets will be compared.

A set A is *finite* if either:

1. $A = \emptyset$, in which case we say A has *cardinality* 0.
2. $A \cong \mathbb{N}_k$, in which case we say A has *cardinality* k.

A set is *infinite* if it is not finite.

Thus, for example, $A = \{a, b, c, d, e\}$ is finite with cardinality 5 while $\mathbb{N}$, itself, is infinite. For simplicity, if A is finite, we will write $|A| = k$ to represent its cardinality.

Suppose that A is finite and has cardinality k and that $x \notin A$. Note that $\{x\} \cong \{k+1\}$ so that $A \cup \{x\}$ is also finite with cardinality $k + 1$. This follows immediately from Theorem 0.6.1. This idea extends to the following:

Theorem 0.6.2.   If A and B are finite disjoint sets, then $A \cup B$ is also finite and $|A \cup B| = |A| + |B|$.

Proof.   If $A = \emptyset$, then $A \cup B = B$, so

$$|A \cup B| = 0 + |B| = |B|$$

If $A \neq \emptyset$ and $B \neq \emptyset$, then let $f: A \to \mathbb{N}_m$ and $g: B \to \mathbb{N}_n$ be the bijections that establish $|A| = m$ and $|B| = n$. Define $h: \mathbb{N}_n \to H = \{m + 1, m + 2, \ldots, m + n\}$ be defined as $h(x) = m + x$. It is easy to see that h is a bijection and so $\mathbb{N}_n \cong H$. Note that

$\mathbb{N}_m \cup H = \{1, 2, \ldots, m + n\} = \mathbb{N}_{m+n}$ and the function $\widehat{f}\colon A \cup B \to \mathbb{N}_{m+n}$ defined by

$$\widehat{f}(x) = \begin{cases} f(x), & \text{if } x \in A \\ h \circ g(x), & \text{if } x \in B \end{cases}$$

is one-to-one and onto. Consequently, $A \cup B$ is finite and $|A \cup B| = m + n = |A| + |B|$. ∎

There is a very useful property for finite sets called the *pigeon-hole principle*. It says, essentially, that if you have more pigeons than pigeon holes you must put more than one pigeon in some pigeon hole.

Theorem 0.6.3.   (*Pigeon-hole Principle*) Let A and B be finite sets with $|A| > |B| > 0$ and $f\colon A \to B$ be a function. Then f is not one-to-one.

Proof.   The proof proceeds by induction on $|B|$.

If $|B| = 1$ and $|A| > |B|$, then A contains distinct elements a_1 and a_2. But then $f(a_1) = f(a_2)$, and so f is not one-to-one. Thus the statement holds for $|B| = 1$.

Now suppose that the statement holds for any set B with $0 < |B| \leq n$. Let B be a set with $|B| = n + 1$. Fix some element $b \in B$. Note that $|B - \{b\}| = n$. Suppose that A is any set with $|A| > |B|$ and $f\colon A \to B$. We consider the set $f^{-1}(b)$ in two cases.

Case 1:   Suppose that $|f^{-1}(b)| \geq 2$. In this case there are distinct elements a_1 and a_2 of A, with a_1 and a_2 in $f^{-1}(b)$, or, equivalently, $f(a_1) = f(a_2) = b$. In this case, f is not one-to-one.

Case 2:   Suppose that $|f^{-1}(b)| \leq 1$. Note, here, that $|A - f^{-1}(b)| \geq |A| - 1 > n = |B - \{b\}|$. Define the function $g\colon A - f^{-1}(b) \to B - \{b\}$ by $g(x) = f(x)$. Note that since $|B - f^{-1}(b)| = n$ and $|A - f^{-1}(b)| > |B - \{b\}|$, the induction hypothesis is satisfied. Thus g is not one-to-one and so there are a_1 and a_2 in $A - f^{-1}(b)$ for which $a_1 \neq a_2$ and $g(a_1) = g(a_2)$. Consequently, $f(a_1) = f(a_2)$, and so f is, also, not one-to-one.

In either case, if the statement holds for any set B with n elements, it also holds for any B with $n + 1$ elements. Thus, by PMI, the statement holds for any finite set B with $|B| > 0$. ∎

Examples of the pigeon-hole principle abound. If 11 shoes are chosen randomly from a box containing 10 pairs of shoes, at least one matched pair results. If $n \neq m$, then $\mathbb{N}_n \not\cong \mathbb{N}_m$.

Corollary 0.6.4.   If A is a finite set and B is a proper subset of A, then $A \not\cong B$.

Infinite sets come in two sizes, "large" and "much larger." We say that a set A is *denumerable* if $A \cong \mathbb{N}$. In this case we say that $|A| = \aleph_0$ (aleph null). A set is *countable* if it is either finite or denumerable.

The set $\mathbb{Z}$ is denumerable for the function $f: \mathbb{N} \to \mathbb{Z}$ defined by

$$f(n) = \begin{cases} \frac{n}{2}, & \text{if } n \text{ is even} \\ \frac{-(1+n)}{2}, & \text{if } n \text{ is odd} \end{cases}$$

is a bijection that maps 0 to 0, 1 to -1, 2 to 1, 3 to -2, and so on.

Theorem 0.6.5.   Let A be a denumerable set. If $B \subseteq A$ is an infinite set, then B is denumerable.

Proof.   Since A is denumerable, there is a bijection $f: \mathbb{N} \to A$. Suppose that we write $f(n) = a_n$ so that A may be enumerated as $A = \{a_0, a_1, \ldots\}$. Let n_0 be the smallest subscript for which $a_{n_0} \in B$. Let n_1 be the smallest subscript for which $a_{n_1} \notin B - \{a_{n_0}\}$. In general, let n_k be the smallest subscript for which $a_{n_k} \notin B - \{a_{n_0}, a_{n_1}, \ldots, a_{n_{k-1}}\}$. Since B is infinite, $B - \{a_{n_0}, a_{n_1}, \ldots, a_{n_{k-1}}\} \neq \emptyset$ for any k, and so we have constructed a one-to-one correspondence from $\mathbb{N}$ to B. Thus B is denumerable. ∎

Since finite sets are countable, we have that *any* subset of a countable set is countable.

Note that *every* infinite set contains a denumerable subset. To see this, let X be infinite. Then $X \neq \emptyset$, so we can pick an element in X, call it x_0. Again, since X is infinite, we have that $X - \{x_0\} \neq \emptyset$, and so we can choose $x_1 \in X - \{x_0\}$. Having defined each of the elements $x_0, x_1, \ldots, x_k$, we know that $X - \{x_0, x_1, \ldots, x_k\} \neq \emptyset$, and so we can pick some

$$x_{k+1} \in X - \{x_0, x_1, \ldots, x_k\}$$

The set $\{x_k \mid k = 0, 1, 2, \ldots\}$ is a denumerable subset of X.

We end this section by exhibiting an *uncountable* set. In showing that this set is uncountable, we give a powerful proof technique called *diagonalization*.

Theorem 0.6.6.   The set $2^{\mathbb{N}}$ is not countable.

Proof.   Suppose that $2^{\mathbb{N}}$ is countable. Since it is an infinite set, this must mean that $2^{\mathbb{N}}$ is denumerable and so we can enumerate it as $2^{\mathbb{N}} = \{A_0, A_1, \ldots\}$. Let $D = \{n \in \mathbb{N} \mid n \notin A_n\}$. Note that $D \subseteq \mathbb{N}$, and so $D = A_k$ for some k. Now consider k. If $k \in A_k$, then, since $A_k = D$, k cannot be in A_k. On the other hand, if $k \notin A_k$, then $k \notin D$, and so k must be in A_k. Both possibilities yield a contradiction. Consequently, the assumption that $2^{\mathbb{N}}$ is denumerable is incorrect. ∎

Since we know from Example 0.6.1 that the collection $\mathcal{F}$ of all functions from $\mathbb{N}$ into $\{0, 1\}$ is equivalent to $2^{\mathbb{N}}$, Theorem 0.6.6 assures us that $\mathcal{F}$ is uncountable.

The technique of diagonalization is useful in disproving many statements. In the preceding proof, it is not immediately clear where the "diagonal" part comes in. A classic example of diagonalization arises in showing that the open interval $(0, 1)$ is not countable. To see this, assume that $(0, 1)$ is countable so that we may write it as the set $\{a_0, a_1, \ldots\}$. We then represent each a_i in its decimal expansion, agreeing to use the nonterminating form for those numbers with both terminating and nonterminating forms.

Thus 0.25 would be represented as 0.24999.... Under this representation scheme, two numbers in (0, 1) are equal if and only if the corresponding digits in their representations are the same. We now list the a_i's as

$$a_0 = 0.d_{00}d_{01}d_{02}\ldots$$
$$a_1 = 0.d_{10}d_{11}d_{12}\ldots$$
$$\ldots$$
$$a_k = 0.d_{k0}d_{k1}d_{k2}\ldots d_{kk}\ldots$$
$$\ldots$$

For (0, 1) to fail to be countable, we must find a number $z \in (0, 1)$ for which $z \neq a_i$ for any i. Let $z = 0.z_0z_1\ldots$, where

$$z_k = \begin{cases} 5, & \text{if } a_{kk} \neq 5 \\ 2, & \text{if } a_{kk} = 5 \end{cases}$$

Note that z differs from each a_k in at least one decimal position. Also, $0 < z < 1$. Thus we have found the desired z, and so the a_i do not account for all of (0, 1).

In this proof the "diagonal" part of diagonalization is obvious.

Exercises for Section 0.6

0.6.1. Let A and B be sets. If A is finite, is $A \cap B$ finite?

0.6.2. Prove that if $A \subseteq B$ and A is infinite then B is infinite.

0.6.3. Give an example of each, if possible:

(a) An infinite subset of a finite set.
(b) A collection $\{A_i | i \in \mathbb{N}\}$ of finite sets whose union is finite.
(c) A collection $\{A_i | i \in \mathbb{N}\}$ of finite sets whose union is *not* finite.
(d) A finite collection of finite sets whose union is infinite.
(e) Finite sets A and B such that $|A \cup B| \neq |A| + |B|$.

0.6.4. Use the function $f: \mathbb{N} \times \mathbb{N} \to \mathbb{N}$ defined by $f(n, m) = 2^n 3^m$ together with Theorem 0.6.5 to show that $\mathbb{N} \times \mathbb{N}$ is countable.

0.6.5. Show that $\mathbb{N}^k$ is denumerable for any $k = 1, 2, \ldots$.

0.6.6. Show that $\mathbb{R}$ is not countable.

1

Alphabets and Languages

1.1 ALPHABETS, WORDS, AND LANGUAGES

The following all have at least two things in common:

> Computer programs written in some computer language, say Pascal.
>
> English words.
>
> The sequence of symbols that we usually use to represent an integer value.
>
> Sentences in some natural language such as English.

First, each is composed of sequences of symbols taken from some finite collection. In the case of English words, the finite collection of symbols is the set of alphabetic characters together with the few symbols that are used to compose words in English (such as the hyphen, apostrophe, and the like). Similarly, representations of integers are sequences from the set of digit characters $\{0, 1, 2, 3, 4, 5, 6, 7, 8, 9\}$. Computer programs written in Pascal and sentences in English are also composed of symbols taken from a finite collection. Here, however, the sets of symbols are somewhat different. In the case of Pascal programs, we may view the set of symbols as the collection of legal Pascal identifiers of length less than or equal to some constant, key and reserved words, special Pascal symbols, and white space symbols such as the carriage return, line-feed character, and the blank or space.

Second, note that in all cases the sequences of symbols that constitute the items in question are of finite length, although there is no limit to what that length may be.

The notion of a finite sequence of symbols is central to what we will be discussing in this text. We introduce notation and names for such sequences.

A finite nonempty set of symbols is called an *alphabet.* So, for example, the English alphabet consists of 26 symbols. In another setting we may have as our alphabet the collection of all legal English words or the collection of all legal Pascal symbols (the legal Pascal identifiers, key and reserved words, special characters, and so on). If Σ is any alphabet, we write $\sigma \in \Sigma$ to denote that σ is a symbol in Σ. Thus, if

$$\Sigma = \{0, 1, 2, 3, 4, 5, 6, 7, 8, 9\}$$

we may write $0 \in \Sigma$.

Note that since an alphabet is simply a nonempty finite set we have that, if Σ_1 and Σ_2 are alphabets, then so is $\Sigma_1 \cup \Sigma_2$. Moreover, any of $\Sigma_1 \cap \Sigma_2$, $\Sigma_1 - \Sigma_2$, and $\Sigma_2 - \Sigma_1$ that are nonempty are also alphabets.

A finite sequence of symbols from some alphabet is sometimes called a *word* over that alphabet. Thus, if the alphabet is the usual English alphabet, some words might be PROGRAM, DIGIT, MOON, and BLEAK. Moreover, our definition allows that BXWTEEMRE and JIPOQPY are also words. Our experience tends to identify the term word with the words of some natural language such as English. For this reason the term *string* is often used in place of word to avoid this preconception. We will use the terms string and word interchangeably throughout this text.

Note that if our underlying alphabet is the collection of all legal Pascal identifiers whose length is less than or equal to some constant, key and reserved words, Pascal special symbols and so on, any well-formed Pascal program constitutes a string. In the same manner that we formed garbage words from the English alphabet under our definition, we may also form garbage programs over this alphabet. Apparently, those strings over this alphabet that constitute well-formed Pascal programs have to meet certain restrictions just as "legal" English words are formed only in certain ways over the English alphabet.

Note that each symbol in an alphabet is a string over that alphabet. The *empty string*, which we shall denote by the symbol ε, is a word over *any* alphabet. The empty word is the empty sequence of symbols taken from whatever alphabet is in question. The empty string has certain properties, which we shall see shortly.

Any collection of words is called a *language.* Thus the collection $\{1, 12, 123, 1234, 12345, 123456\}$ is a language over the alphabet consisting of the digits. Similarly, the collection of all "real" English words is a language over the English alphabet. Note that if Σ is an alphabet then Σ is also a language—the language consisting of all single-symbol strings.

Languages may be quite large, as is the case for all "real" English words or the language $\{1, 11, 111, 1111, 11111, \ldots\}$ consisting of all strings of finitely many 1's. Note that this language is infinite (although each string in it is of finite length). Quite often, if a language is large, it is awkward to specify what words are in it. Specifying strings in languages is a central theme in this text, and we will spend considerable time on this problem.

Since a language is a collection of strings, we may have a language that consists of no strings—the *empty language.* Note that this is not the same as the language consisting of the empty string $\{\varepsilon\}$. The empty language is denoted the same way that we denote the empty set, $\emptyset$.

Suppose that Σ is any alphabet and that w is some string over Σ. If L is a language that consists of some strings over Σ and if w is a string in L, we write $w \in L$ and say that w *is an element of L*, or w is a member of L. Thus we have

$$121 \in \{1, 12, 121, 1212, 12121\}$$

It is often necessary to discuss the language consisting of *all* strings over some alphabet Σ. This is called the *star closure* or *universal language* of Σ and is denoted by Σ^*. For example, if we have the alphabet $\Sigma = \{1\}$, then

$$\Sigma^* = \{\varepsilon, 1, 11, 111, 1111, \ldots\}$$

Note that, for any alphabet, Σ^* is infinite (since alphabets are nonempty).

Exercises for Section 1.1

1.1.1. From what underlying set of symbols are English sentences derived?

1.1.2. Why is the empty language $\emptyset$ not the same as $\{\varepsilon\}$?

1.2 OPERATIONS ON STRINGS

If w is a string over some alphabet, we denote the *length* of w by the symbol $|w|$. The length of w is simply the number of symbols in the string. Thus, over the alphabet $\Sigma = \{1, 2\}$, if $w = 121$, then $|w| = 3$. Note that ε, the empty string, has no symbols, and so $|\varepsilon| = 0$.

If w and z are strings, the *concatenation* of w with z is the string that is obtained by appending the word z to the string w. For example, if $w = $ "banana" and $z = $ "rama," the concatenation of w with z is the string "bananarama." We denote concatenation of words w and z by wz or $w \cdot z$. Note that we must have

$$|wz| = |w| + |z|$$

Concatenation of the empty word ε with any word w leaves w unchanged. For this reason, ε is said to act as an *identity* with respect to the concatenation operation.

We may introduce the notion of *exponentiation* for words over an alphabet as follows. Let w be a word; for $n \in \mathbb{N}$, define

$$w^n = \begin{cases} \varepsilon, & \text{if } n = 0 \\ ww^{n-1}, & \text{if } n > 0 \end{cases}$$

Thus, over $\Sigma = \{1, 2\}$, if $w = 122$, we have

$$\begin{aligned} w^0 &= \varepsilon \\ w^1 &= 122 \\ w^2 &= 122122 \\ w^3 &= 122122122 \end{aligned}$$

and so on. We say that w^i is the *ith power of w*.

We have been using the $=$ symbol intuitively, without definition. For precision we define equality for strings as follows: If w and z are words, we say that w *is equal to z* if they have the same length and the same symbols at the same positions. We write $w = z$ to denote this.

The notions of *suffix* and *prefix* for strings over an alphabet are analogous to everyday usage. If w and x are words, we say that x is a *prefix* of w if, for some string y, we have that $w = xy$. For example, if w is the string 121, then the string $x = 12$ is a prefix of w, here $y = 1$. If, on the other hand, we consider $y = \varepsilon$, then for $w = xy$ we must have $w = x$, so any word can be viewed as a prefix of itself. We introduce the term *proper prefix* to denote a string that is a prefix of, but not equal to, another. Thus $x = 121$ is a prefix of the string $w = 121$, but x is *not* a proper prefix of w. Finally, note that the empty word ε is always a prefix of any word.

A string w is a *substring* or *subword* of another string z if there are strings x and y for which $z = xwy$.

The *reversal* or *transpose* of a word w is simply the mirror image of w. For example, if $w = $ "able" then its reversal is "elba." We denote the reversal of w by w^R. We may make this definition precise as follows:

$$
w^R = \begin{cases} w, & \text{if } w = \varepsilon \\ y^R a, & \text{if } w = ay \text{ for some } a \in \Sigma \text{ and } y \in \Sigma^* \end{cases}
$$

For example, suppose that $x = $ "able." Then, following the definition to form x^R, we have

$$
\begin{aligned}
x^R = (\text{able})^R &= (\text{ble})^R a \\
&= (\text{le})^R ba \\
&= (\text{e})^R lba \\
&= (\varepsilon)^R elba \\
&= \varepsilon elba \\
&= elba
\end{aligned}
$$

Consider the concatenation of the two words "*ab*" and "*cd*" to form *abcd* over the English alphabet. We know that $(abcd)^R = dcba$. Note that $dcba = (cd)^R(ab)^R$. That is, if w and y are strings and if $x = wy$, then $x^R = (wy)^R = y^R w^R$.

Reversal also "undoes" itself. Note that

$$
\begin{aligned}
((abcd)^R)^R &= (dcba)^R \\
&= abcd
\end{aligned}
$$

In general, we have $(x^R)^R = x$.

Exercises for Section 1.2

1.2.1. Let $\Sigma = \{1\}$. Is it the case that for each natural number n there is some word $w \in \Sigma^*$ for which $|w| = n$? If w is a string in Σ^* for which $|w| = n$, is it the only such string? How about if $\Sigma = \{1, 2\}$?

1.2.2. For a word w, is it the case that

$$|w^{i+j}| = |w^i| + |w^j|?$$

Find an expression for $|w^{i+j}|$ in terms of i, j, and $|w|$.

1.2.3. Is ε a proper prefix of itself?

1.2.4. Define the notions of *suffix* and *proper suffix* for strings over an alphabet.

1.2.5. For the word w = "bar" over the English alphabet, find all prefixes, suffixes, and subwords.

1.2.6. Prove formally that $(wy)^R = y^R w^R$.

1.3 OPERATIONS ON LANGUAGES

We may extend the ideas of concatenation, exponentiation, and reversal to entire languages. Let A and B be languages over some alphabet. We define the (language) *concatenation of A and B* as

$$A \cdot B = \{w \cdot x \mid w \in A \text{ and } x \in B\}$$

Thus $A \cdot B$ consists of all strings formed by taking each string in A and concatenating it with each string in B.

For example, if $A = \{bird, dog\}$ and $B = \{house\}$, then $A \cdot B$ would be the language $\{birdhouse, doghouse\}$.

Note that in forming the language concatenation $A \cdot B$ it is *not* necessary that A and B be over the same alphabet. If A is a language over Σ_1 and B is a language over Σ_2, then $A \cdot B$ is a language over $\Sigma_1 \cup \Sigma_2$. We often write AB in place of $A \cdot B$ when the meaning is unambiguous.

Since, for any word $x, x \cdot \varepsilon = x = \varepsilon \cdot x$, we have that, for any language $A, A \cdot \{\varepsilon\} = \{\varepsilon\} \cdot A = A$. That is, the language containing only the empty string acts as an *identity* for the operation of language concatenation.

As with strings, once we have defined the concatenation product for languages we may define *exponentiation*. Let A be any language over some alphabet Σ. We define

$$A^n = \begin{cases} \{\varepsilon\}, & \text{if } n = 0 \\ A \cdot A^{n-1}, & \text{if } n \geq 1 \end{cases}$$

Thus, if $A = \{ab\}$ over the English alphabet, we have

$$A^0 = \{\varepsilon\}$$
$$A^1 = A = \{ab\}$$
$$A^2 = A \cdot A^1 = \{abab\}$$
$$A^3 = A \cdot A^2 = \{ababab\}$$

Interestingly enough, from this definition we have $\emptyset^0 = \{\varepsilon\}$!

Since a language is a collection or set of strings, union, intersection, and sublanguage may be defined as with sets in general. If A and B are languages over some alphabet Σ, then the *union* of A and B, denoted $A \cup B$, consists of all words that appear in at least one of A or B. That is,

$$A \cup B = \{x \mid x \in A \text{ or } x \in B\}$$

The *intersection* of languages A and B is the language

$$A \cap B = \{x \mid x \in A \text{ and } x \in B \text{ or simultaneously}\}$$

That is, $A \cap B$ consists of only those words that appear in both A and B.

As an example, consider $\Sigma = \{0, 1\}$ and languages $A = \{\varepsilon, 0, 1, 10, 11\}$ and $B = \{\varepsilon, 1, 0110, 11010\}$. Then

$$A \cup B = \{\varepsilon, 0, 1, 10, 11, 0110, 11010\}$$

and

$$A \cap B = 1\{\varepsilon, 1\}$$

Before we look at the interaction of concatenation with intersection and union of languages, it will be convenient to formally define language equality and sublanguage. If A and B are languages over some alphabet Σ, and if all the strings in A are also strings in B, then A is said to be a *sublanguage* of B. Since this corresponds exactly to the set-theoretic concept of subset, we denote this by $A \subseteq B$.

Thus, for the languages $A = \{a, aa, aaa, aaaa, aaaaa\}$ and $B = \{a^n \mid n = 0, 1, 2, \ldots\}$, we have $A \subseteq B$. Note that any language L over an alphabet Σ is a sublanguage of Σ^*; that is, $L \subseteq \Sigma^*$.

Two languages A and B are said to be *equal* if they have exactly the same strings in them, that is, if they are equal as sets. We write $A = B$ to denote this. The following theorem relates sublanguages and equality.

Theorem 1.3.1.   Suppose that A and B are languages over some alphabet Σ. Then $A = B$ if and only if both $A \subseteq B$ and $B \subseteq A$.

Proof.   Suppose that $A = B$. We have to show that $A \subseteq B$ and $B \subseteq A$. Suppose that $x \in A$. Then, since A and B have exactly the same strings, we must have that $x \in B$. It follows that $A \subseteq B$. Similarly, if x is a string in B, then, since A and B have exactly the same strings, we must have that $x \in A$ and so $B \subseteq A$.

Conversely, suppose that both $A \subseteq B$ and $B \subseteq A$. Note that these conditions mean that every string in A is also a string in B, and vice versa. Thus A and B have exactly the same strings in them and so are equal.   ∎

Theorem 1.3.1 gives us a convenient way of determining if languages are equal. We first employ it to show that concatenation is distributive over union.

Theorem 1.3.2.   For languages A, B, and C over some alphabet Σ, the following hold:

    i. $A \cdot (B \cup C) = A \cdot B \cup A \cdot C$

    ii. $(B \cup C) \cdot A = B \cdot A \cup C \cdot A$

Proof.   (i) First we show that $A \cdot (B \cup C) \subseteq A \cdot B \cup A \cdot C$. To this end, let $x \in A \cdot (B \cup C)$. Then $x = w \cdot y$ for some strings $w \in A$ and $y \in B \cup C$. Since $y \in B \cup C$, we have that either $y \in B$ or $y \in C$. If $y \in B$, then $w \cdot y \in A \cdot B$, and so $w \cdot y \in A \cdot B \cup A \cdot C$. On the other hand, if $y \in C$, then $w \cdot y \in A \cdot C$, and again we have $w \cdot y \in A \cdot B \cup A \cdot C$. Thus, in either case we have that

$$A \cdot (B \cup C) \subseteq A \cdot B \cup A \cdot C$$

To show that $A \cdot B \cup A \cdot C \subseteq A \cdot (B \cup C)$, suppose that $x \in A \cdot B \cup A \cdot C$. Then either $x \in A \cdot B$ or else $x \in A \cdot C$. If $x \in A \cdot B$, then $x = u \cdot v$ for strings $u \in A$ and $v \in B$. Since $v \in B$, we have that $v \in B \cup C$, and so $uv \in A \cdot (B \cup C)$. On the other hand, if $x \in A \cdot C$, then $x = w \cdot y$ for strings $w \in A$ and $y \in C$. In this case, since $y \in C$, we have that $y \in B \cup C$, and so $w \cdot y \in A \cdot (B \cup C)$. Thus $A \cdot B \cup A \cdot C \subseteq A \cdot (B \cup C)$. It follows from Theorem 1.3.1 that $A \cdot (B \cup C) = A \cdot B \cup A \cdot C$.

The proof of part ii is similar and is left as an exercise. ■

Concatenation does not interact with intersection as nicely as it does with union. In general, concatenation does *not* distribute over intersection. To see this, suppose that $A = \{a, \varepsilon\}$, $B = \{\varepsilon\}$, and $C = \{a\}$. Note that $A \cdot B = \{a, \varepsilon\}$ and $A \cdot C = \{a^2, a\}$, so $A \cdot B \cap A \cdot C = \{a\}$. On the other hand, $B \cap C = \emptyset$, so $A \cdot (B \cap C) = \emptyset$.

If A is a language over some alphabet Σ, we define the *Kleene closure* or *star closure* of A to be $A^* = \bigcup_{n=0}^{\infty} A^n$. We also define the *positive* or *plus closure* of A to be $A^+ = \bigcup_{n=1}^{\infty} A^n$. Note that strings in the star closure consist of zero or more concatenations from the language, while those in the plus closure consist of one or more concatenations.

As an example, suppose that $A = \{a\}$ over the English alphabet. Then we have that $A^0 = \{\varepsilon\}$, $A^1 = \{a\}$, $A^2 = \{a^2\}$, and so on. Thus $A^* = \{\varepsilon, a, a^2, a^3, \ldots\}$. On the other hand, $A^+ = \{a, a^2, a^3, \ldots\}$.

Note that if Σ is any alphabet then Σ^* consists of all concatenations of 0 or more symbols from Σ. This is exactly the collection of strings that make up the universal language, which is also denoted by Σ^*. Thus our notation is consistent. Furthermore, note that any language over Σ is then necessarily a sublanguage of Σ^*. Moreover, if A is any language over Σ, we have that $A^n \subseteq \Sigma^*$ for all $n = 0, 1, 2, \ldots$, and so $A^* \subseteq \Sigma^*$ and $A^+ \subseteq \Sigma^*$. Note also that, since $A^n \subseteq A^*$ for all n, we must have that $A^+ \subseteq A^*$ as well. Finally, since $\emptyset^0 = \{\varepsilon\}$ and $\emptyset^n = \emptyset$ for all $n \geq 1$, we have that $\emptyset^* = \{\varepsilon\}$ and $\emptyset^+ = \emptyset$.

Example 1.3.1

Consider $\Sigma = \{0, 1, 2, 3, 4, 5, 6, 7, 8, 9\}$ and define A as the language consisting of all strings that do not contain any of the digits $2, 3, \ldots, 9$. Then $\varepsilon \in A, 0 \in A$, and $1 \in A$. So is $000101001 \in A$. Note that if $k > 1$ and $x \in A^k$ then $x = w_1 \cdot w_2 \cdots w_k$ for strings $w_i \in A$. Since each string w_i is a string that contains none of the digits $2, 3, \ldots, 9$, the string x also does not contain any of these digits. Thus we have that $x \in A$. That is, $A^k \subseteq A$ for $k \geq 1$.

On the other hand, if $x \in A$, then, since $\varepsilon \in A$, we may write

$$x = \varepsilon^{k-1} \cdot x$$

which is a string in A^k. Hence $A \subseteq A^k$ for $k \geq 1$, and so $A = A^k$ for $k \geq 1$. It follows that

$$A^+ = \bigcup_{k=1}^{\infty} A^k = \bigcup_{k=1}^{\infty} A = A$$

Also, since $A^0 = \{\varepsilon\} \subseteq A$, we have that $A^* = A^0 \cup A^+ = A^0 \cup A = A$. Thus in some cases we have that A^* and A^+ are the same.

If A and B are languages over Σ we define their *difference* to be

$$A - B = \{x \mid x \in A \text{ and } x \notin B\}$$

which is exactly the same as the set-theoretic difference.

Example 1.3.2

If A is as in Example 1.3.1 and B is the language of all strings of 0's, then $A - B$ is the language of all strings of 0's and 1's having *at least* one 1 in them.

We define the *complement of the language* A over the alphabet Σ to be

$$\overline{A} = \Sigma^* - A$$

which is also exactly analogous to the set-theoretic complement. Again appealing to Example 1.3.1, $\overline{A}$ is the language of all strings having *at least* one of the digits $2, 3, \ldots, 9$ in them.

Concatenation and language difference are incompatible in much the same manner that concatenation and intersection are. Specifically, $A(B - C) \neq AB \quad AC$ in general.

A useful identity that relates the closures A^+ and A^* is given in the next theorem. Although the result is intuitively obvious, we provide a rigorous proof of a portion of the theorem because such an argument is indicative of how such identities for languages are proved.

Theorem 1.3.3. $A^+ = A \cdot A^* = A^* A$.

Proof.   Let $x \in A^+$. Then, from the definition of the plus closure, we have that $x \in \bigcup_{k=1}^{\infty} A^k$, so for some $k_0 \geq 1$, we have $x \in A^{k_0}$.

Since $A^{k_0} = A \cdot A^{k_0 - 1}$, we have that $x \in A \cdot A^{k_0 - 1}$, and so

$$x \in \bigcup_{n=0}^{\infty} (A \cdot A^n) = A \cdot \bigcup_{n=0}^{\infty} A^n = A \cdot A^*$$

This shows that $A^+ \subseteq A \cdot A^*$.

Conversely, let

$$x \in A \cdot A^* = A \cdot \bigcup_{n=0}^{\infty} A^n = \bigcup_{n=0}^{\infty} (A \cdot A^n)$$

Then, for some $j \geq 0$, we have

$$x \in A \cdot A^j = A^{j+1} \subseteq \bigcup_{k=1}^{\infty} A^k = A^+$$

So $A \cdot A^* \subseteq A^+$.

The proof of $A^+ = A^* \cdot A$ is similar and is left to the reader. ■

Consider the language $A = \{ab\}$ over the English alphabet. We have that

$$A^+ = \{(ab)^i | i \geq 1\} = \{ab, abab, ababab, \ldots\}$$

We may then consider the language $(A^+)^i$ for various exponents i. For example, if $i = 2$, we have

$$(A^+)^2 = A^+ \cdot A^+ = \{ab \cdot ab, ab \cdot abab, ab \cdot ababab, \ldots,$$
$$abab \cdot ab, abab \cdot abab, abab \cdot ababab, \ldots\}$$

Since we may find each of the languages $(A^+)^i$, the language $(A^+)^+$ may be found as well. Moreover, since $(A^+)^0 = \{\varepsilon\}$, we may even determine $(A^+)^*$. It makes sense to ask what these languages, which are closures of closures, look like. The answers are surprisingly simple.

If x is a string in $(A^+)^+$, then, since $(A^+)^+ = \bigcup_{k=1}^{\infty}(A^+)^k$, we have that, for some $n \geq 1$, $x \in (A^+)^n$, and so $x = x_1 \cdot x_2 \cdot \cdots \cdot x_n$, where each $x_i \in A^+$. Since $x_i \in A^+ = \bigcup_{t=1}^{\infty} A^t$, there is some $t_i \geq 1$ for which $x_i \in A^{t_i}$. Thus each

$$x_i = y_{i,1} \cdot y_{i,2} \cdot \cdots \cdot y_{i,t_i}$$

where each $y_{i,j} \in A$. Thus we have

$$x = (y_{1,1}y_{1,2} \ldots y_{1,t_1}) \cdot (y_{2,1}y_{2,2} \ldots y_{2,t_2}) \cdot \cdots \cdot (y_{n,1}y_{n,2} \ldots y_{n,t_n})$$

But this is just a string in the language $A^{t_1+t_2+\cdots+t_n}$. Moreover, since $t_i \geq 1$ for each i, we have that

$$t_1 + t_2 + \cdots + t_n \geq 1$$

so this string is in A^+. Thus $(A^+)^+ \subseteq A^+$. On the other hand, since $A^+ = (A^+)^1 \subseteq \bigcup_{k=1}^{\infty}(A^+)^k = (A^+)^+$, we have that $A^+ \subseteq (A^+)^+$, and so $A^+ = (A^+)^+$.

It may be similarly shown that $(A^*)^* = A^*$. One interpretation of these phenomena is that no new strings are added to the languages A^* or A^+ by star- or plus-closing them any further. This is an intuitive indication of what the term *closure* means.

We may extend the ideas of reversal or transpose to languages as well. The *reversal of a language A* is

$$A^R = \{x^R \mid x \in A\}$$

For example, if $A = \{dog, bog\}$, then $A^R = \{god, gob\}$.

Note that, if we reverse all words in a language and then reverse them all again, we get the original language back again. Thus $(A^R)^R = A$.

Reversal is similarly well behaved for most other language operations, as Exercise 1.3.18 shows.

Reversal of concatenation reverses not only the strings in the languages being concatenated, but also the order of the concatenation of the languages, as shown in the following theorem.

Theorem 1.3.4. $(A \cdot B)^R = B^R \cdot A^R$.

Proof.   Let $x \in (AB)^R$. Then $x^R \in AB$, so $x^R = yz$ for some strings $y \in A$ and $z \in B$. Thus $x = (x^R)^R = (yz)^R = z^R \cdot y^R$. But $z \in B$, so $z^R \in B^R$. Similarly, $y \in A$, so $y^R \in A^R$, and thus we have $x \in B^R A^R$, which shows that $(AB)^R \subseteq B^R \cdot A^R$. Conversely, if $x \in B^R A^R$, then $x = uw$ for some words $u \in B^R$ and $w \in A^R$. But then $x^R = w^R u^R \in AB$, so $x^R \in AB$ and $x \in (AB)^R$. Thus $B^R A^R \subseteq (AB)^R$, and so $(AB)^R = B^R A^R$.   ∎

Exercises for Section 1.3

1.3.1. What is $A \cdot \emptyset$ for any language A?

1.3.2. Let $A = \{\text{the, my}\}$ and $B = \{\text{horse, house, hose}\}$ be languages over the English alphabet. Find $A \cdot B$, $A \cdot A$, and $A \cdot B \cdot B$.

1.3.3. Suppose that $A = \{\varepsilon, a\}$. Find A^n for $n = 0, 1, 2, 3$. How many elements does A^n have for *arbitrary* n? What are the strings in A^n for arbitrary n?

1.3.4. Suppose that $A = \{\varepsilon\}$. Find A^n for arbitrary n.

1.3.5. Let $A = \{\varepsilon, ab\}$ and $B = \{cd\}$. How many strings are in $A_j^n B$ for arbitrary n?

1.3.6. Let $A = \{a\}$ and $B = \{b\}$. Find $A^n B$, AB^n, and $(AB)^n$.

1.3.7. Let $A = \{\varepsilon\}$, $B = \{aa, ab, bb\}$, $C = \{\varepsilon, aa, ab\}$, and $D = \emptyset$ be the empty language. Find $A \cup B, A \cup C, A \cup D, B \cup D$ and $A \cap B, B \cap C, C \cap D, A \cap D$. Suppose that F is any language. Find $F \cup D$ and $F \cap D$.

1.3.8. Prove part ii of Theorem 1.3.2.

1.3.9. If A and B_i are languages over Σ for each $i = 1, 2, 3 \ldots$, show that

$$A \cdot \left(\bigcup_{i=1}^{\infty} B_i \right) = \bigcup_{i=1}^{\infty} (A \cdot B_i)$$

1.3.10. Under what conditions is it the case that $A^* = A^+$?

1.3.11. Note that for any language A we always have that $\varepsilon \in A^*$. Under what circumstances is $\varepsilon \in A^+$?

1.3.12. Show that $\{\varepsilon\}^* = \{\varepsilon\} = \{\varepsilon\}^+$.

1.3.13. In Examples 1.3.1 and 1.3.2, why is ε *not* in the languages $A - B$ and $\overline{A}$?

1.3.14. We have noted previously that $A^* = A^0 \cup A^+ = \{\varepsilon\} \cup A^+$. We might expect that $A^+ = A^* - \{\varepsilon\}$. Show that this is not the case in general. Under what circumstances *is* it the case that $A^+ = A^* - \{\varepsilon\}$?

1.3.15. Let A and B be languages over Σ. Show that $\overline{A \cap B} = \overline{A} \cup \overline{B}$ and that $\overline{A \cup B} = \overline{A} \cap \overline{B}$.

1.3.16. Find languages A, B, and C for which $A(B - C) \neq AB - AC$.

1.3.17. Show that $(A^*)^* = A^*$, $(A^*)^+ = A^*$, and $(A^+)^* = A^*$.

1.3.18. Show that, for languages A and B over an alphabet Σ, the following equalities hold:

    (a) $(A \cup B)^R = A^R \cup B^R$

    (b) $(A \cap B)^R = A^R \cap B^R$

    (c) $(\overline{A})^R = \overline{(A^R)}$

    (d) $(A^+)^R = (A^R)^+$

    (e) $(A^*)^R = (A^R)^*$

PROBLEMS

1.1. Let $\Sigma = \{a, b, \ldots, z\}$ be the English alphabet. Define the relation $<$ on Σ^* so that $x < y$ whenever x would precede y in alphabetical order (lexicographical ordering).

1.2. Let A be a language over some alphabet Σ. Is it the case that $\overline{\overline{A}} = A$?

1.3. Let $\Sigma = \{a, b, c\}$ and let $L = \{c^i x c^j | i, j \geq 0\}$, where x is restricted to $x = \varepsilon$, $x = aw$, or $x = wb$ for some $w \in \Sigma$. Is it the case that $L = \Sigma^*$? Is it the case that $L^2 = \Sigma^*$?

1.4. Let $\Sigma = \{a, b\}$. The following is a recursive definition of the language A:

    i. $\varepsilon \in A$.

    ii. If $x \in A$, then axb and bxa are in A.

    iii. If x and y are in A, then xy is in A.

    iv. Nothing else is in A.

    (a) Show that

$$A = \{w \in \Sigma^* \mid w \text{ has equal numbers of } a\text{'s and } b\text{'s}\}$$

    (b) If b and ε are in A, what other words are in A?

    (c) Give a recursive definition for $A \subseteq \{a, b\}^*$ consisting of all words containing twice as many a's as b's.

1.5. A *palindrome* is a string that reads the same backward as forward. For example, the word "a" is a palindrome, as is the string "radar." A more complicated example is the string (which *could* be attributed to Napoleon) "able was I ere I saw Elba." Give a recursive definition of a palindrome (note that ε is a palindrome).

1.6. Show that, for languages A and B, $(A \cup B)^* = (A^* B^*)^*$.

1.7. **McMillan's Inequality.** Although our definition of an alphabet as a finite set of symbols is mathematically correct, it presents problems when trying to apply it. For example, if $\Sigma = \{1, 11\}$, then $111 \in \Sigma^*$, yet it is not clear whether $111 = 1 \cdot 11$ or $111 = 1 \cdot 1 \cdot 1$ or $111 = 11 \cdot 1$. The problem is that, although from a theoretical point of view 11 is indivisible (is a single symbol and not a pair of 1's), we have no convenient way to represent this. Thus, while $w_1 = 1 \cdot 11$ and $w_2 = 11 \cdot 1$ look alike, they are *not* equal. For string equality we must have the same symbols at the same positions. In this problem we establish a condition for alphabets whose symbols are strings over other alphabets. This condition guarantees that we do not have the preceding problem with string equality. It is known as McMillan's inequality and is stated as follows:

McMillan's inequality: Let Σ be an alphabet consisting of r symbols. Let $a_1, a_2, \ldots, a_q$ be nonempty strings over Σ. If the set $\{a_1, a_2, \ldots, a_q\}$ is an alphabet, then

$$\sum_{i=1}^{q} r^{-|a_i|} \leq 1$$

The proof of McMillan's inequality is not hard, but does require insight about strings.

1. Noting that for strings w_1 and w_2, $|w_1| + |w_2| = |w_1 w_2|$, what does an arbitrary term in $(\sum_{i=1}^{q} r^{-|a_i|})^n$ look like after the product is expanded (but before any simplification takes place)?

2. Let
$$I_k = \{(i_1, i_2, \ldots, i_n) \mid k = |a_{i_1}| + \cdots + |a_{i_n}|\}$$

That is, I_k is just the collection of n-tuples of indexes of a_i's that can be used to form strings of length k. Let $M_k = |I_k|$, which is just the number of strings of a_i's giving strings of length k. Show that

$$\left(\sum_{i=1}^{q} r^{-|a_i|}\right)^n = \sum_{k=n}^{nt} r^{-k} M_k$$

where $t = \max\{|a_1|, |a_2|, \ldots, |a_n|\}$.

3. By part 2, since $M_k \leq r^k$ for all k, we have that

$$\left(\sum_{i=1}^{q} r^{-|a_i|}\right)^n \leq n(t-1) \leq nt$$

Show that if

$$\sum_{i=1}^{q} r^{-|a_i|} > 1$$

then a contradiction arises and thus McMillan's inequality holds.

McMillan's inequality can be used to derive a stronger result.

4. Let $l_1, l_2, \ldots, l_q$ be q natural numbers and Σ an alphabet with $r = |\Sigma|$. There exist q strings $a_1, a_2, \ldots, a_q$ in Σ^* of lengths $l_1, l_2, \ldots, l_q$, respectively, which form an alphabet if and only if

$$\sum_{i=1}^{q} r^{-|l_i|} \leq 1$$

1.8. Square-free and cube-free strings. Let Σ be an alphabet. A string $w \in \Sigma^*$ is said to be *square-free* if w is not of the form ux^2v for subwords u, x, and v, where $x \neq \varepsilon$. The definition of *cube-free* is similar. The string w is *strongly cube-free* if it contains no substring of the form x^2a, where $x \neq \varepsilon$ and a is the first symbol of x.

1. Show that no string of length greater than or equal to 4 over an alphabet of cardinality 2 can be square-free.

Let $w \in \Sigma^*$. A string $w' \in \Sigma^*$ for which $|w| = |w'|$ is an *interpretation of* w if the following condition is satisfied:

Let $1 \le i \le |w|$ and $1 \le j \le |w|$. If the ith and jth symbols of w are different, then the i and j symbols of w' are also different.

For example, if $w = aaabab$, then $cdefgh$ and $cdcece$ are interpretations of w, whereas $cdefgc$ is not.

2. Show that if w is square-free, cube-free, or strictly cube-free, then so is every interpretation of w.

An ω-string (omega string) is an infinite sequence of symbols over an alphabet. That is, ω-strings are strings of infinite length.

3. Let w be a square-free, cube-free, or strictly cube-free ω-string over Σ in which all symbols of Σ actually occur. Suppose that Σ' is an alphabet strictly containing Σ (that is, $\Sigma \subset \Sigma'$). Show that an ω-string can be constructed from w that is also square-free, cube-free, or strongly cube-free (as w is) and that contains all symbols of Σ'.

If a string or ω-string w is square-free, it still seems conceivable that w could contain two overlapping occurrences of some substring x, that is, a substring of the form $xy = zx$ for which $1 \le |y| = |z| < |x|$. Some simple trials suggest that constructing such a w is harder than first imagined. In fact, it is not even possible!

4. Show that if w is a string or ω-string that contains a substring xy such that $xy = zx$ and $1 \le |y| = |z| < |x|$, then w is not square-free.

2

Regular Languages

2.1 LANGUAGES OVER ALPHABETS

It is not coincidence that most of the languages we have considered so far have been rather trivial. With our present abilities the process of specifying what strings are in a language over some alphabet Σ is awkward and laborious except for Σ^* and some rather simple languages. Our concern for some time will be the business of defining languages—specifying exactly which strings make up a language. Since all languages over Σ are sublanguages of the universal language Σ^*, it makes sense to first determine just how many sublanguages Σ^* has for a particular alphabet Σ. We begin by investigating Σ^* itself.

By way of example consider the alphabet $\Sigma = \{a, b\}$. For any natural number n, there are only finitely many words over Σ of length n. (How many are there?) Moreover, we may *order* these strings *lexicographically*. By lexicographically, we mean in the same manner that they would be ordered in the dictionary. We agree to number ε as 0, number the words of length 1 next, and in general we number the words of length $n + 1$ after the words of length n. Thus we have

ε	0
a	1
b	2
aa	3
ab	4
ba	5
bb	6
aaa	7

and so on

In a more general situation, suppose that we have an arbitrary alphabet Σ. Since all alphabets are finite, we may assign some arbitrary order to the characters in Σ. Thus, without loss of generality, we may write

$$\Sigma = \{a_1, a_2, \ldots, a_n\}$$

We number the words in Σ^* in the same way as above.

$$
\begin{array}{cc}
\varepsilon & 0 \\
a_1 & 1 \\
a_2 & 2 \\
a_n & n \\
a_1 a_1 & n+1 \\
a_1 a_2 & n+2 \\
\text{and so on}
\end{array}
$$

This technique of assigning natural numbers to strings over an alphabet may be made more precise. Appealing to the original example, where $\Sigma = \{a, b\}$, we let each string over Σ denote a number in binary form using the digits 1 and 2 instead of 0 and 1. We let a be 1 and b be 2 and obtain

$$
\begin{array}{cc}
\varepsilon & 0 \\
a & 1 \\
b & 2 \\
aa & 11 = 3 \\
ab & 12 = 4 \\
abaa & 1211 = 19
\end{array}
$$

In this representation each word represents a unique integer. This would *not* be the case if we used the more intuitive representation of a as 0 and b as 1, for a^i would represent 0 for all $i \geq 0$.

Note that for any natural number m there is a unique base n representation of it. Thus we may find a string in Σ^* corresponding to m. For example, if $\Sigma = \{a, b\}$ and $m = 0$, we have that ε corresponds to m. If $m > 0$, then we first find the base 2 representation of m (using the digits 1 and 2 instead of 0 and 1). We then concatenate the characters that correspond to the digits in this representation of m. Thus, if $m = 32$, we first convert m to 11112 and then concatenate a's and b's to get $aaaab$.

In the preceding discussion we have shown a way to correspond strings in Σ^* with natural numbers in a manner that for every string there is a unique natural number and for every natural number there is a unique string. Since this essentially defines a function from $\mathbb{N}$ to Σ^*, we have in fact outlined the proof of the following theorem.

Theorem 2.1.1.   For any alphabet Σ, Σ^* is countably infinite.   ∎

Now that we know how large Σ^* is, we may determine how many sublanguages of Σ^* exist and, hence, how many languages there are over an alphabet Σ.

Theorem 2.1.2.   The collection of all languages over Σ is uncountable.

Proof. Suppose that the collection of all languages over Σ is countable. Let us call this collection $\mathbb{L}$. Since $\mathbb{L}$ is countable, we may enumerate it as $A_0, A_1, A_2, \ldots$. We use a diagonalization argument to derive a contradiction.

We know that Σ^* is countable and so may be enumerated as $w_0, w_1, \ldots$. Let $B = \{w_i \mid w_i \notin A_i\}$. That is, B consists of those words that do not appear in the language that has the same index as they do. Note that B is a set of strings over Σ and so is a language. Hence $B = A_k$ for some k. Note that if $w_k \in B$, then w_k is not in $A_k = B$. That is, w_k both is and is not in A_k, and we have a contradiction. On the other hand, if $w_k \notin B$, then, from the definition of B, w_k is a string in $A_k = B$ and so is in B. That is, w_k both is and is not in B, another contradiction. Since w_k must either be in B or not be in B, our assumption that the collection of all languages over Σ is countable is false. Thus the collection is uncountable. ∎

Theorem 2.1.2 provides some insight into the magnitude of the problem of specifying particular languages: there are uncountably many possible languages to specify for a particular alphabet. It turns out that no one language specification method is capable of defining *all* languages over an alphabet. In fact, the best we can do is to represent only countably many languages over an alphabet. This means that for a given language representation method there are languages that are unrepresentable. On the other hand, different methods have different expressive powers, that is, they define more languages than others. In investigating these methods of definition, we shall gain insight into the nature of computation itself.

Exercises for Section 2.1

2.1.1. For the alphabet $\Sigma = \{a, b\}$ and using the mapping $\Sigma^* \rightarrow \mathbb{N}$ given in this section, how many words are there of length 3? Of length 5? Of length k? What is the last number assigned to the words of length 2? Of length 5? Of length k?

2.1.2. In the general case where we have n characters in an alphabet Σ, how many words are there of length k? If we order the words of Σ in lexicographical order and assign numbers to them beginning with ε as 0, what is the number assigned to the last word of length k?

2.1.3. Using the digits 1 and 2 instead of 0 and 1, find the binary representation of (decimal) 22. Which word in $\Sigma^* = \{a, b\}^*$ corresponds to (decimal) 22?

2.1.4. We extend the preceding idea to $\Sigma = \{a, b, c\}$ using a *ternary* representation with the digits 1, 2, 3. Assuming that we associate a with 1, b with 2, and c with 3, which decimal integer corresponds to the word *abbacca* of Σ^*? Find the word in Σ^* that corresponds to (decimal) 20.

2.2   REGULAR LANGUAGES AND REGULAR EXPRESSIONS

The first language specification method that we will investigate defines the collection of languages called the *regular languages* over an alphabet. Regular languages are of practical interest because they may be used to specify the construction of lexical analyzers—programs that scan text and extract the lexemes (or lexical units) in it. For a given alphabet Σ, the regular languages over Σ are of theoretical interest because they form the smallest collection of languages over Σ that is closed under the operations of concatenation, star closure, and language union and that contains the empty language $\emptyset$ and the singleton languages $\{a\}$ for $a \in \Sigma$.

Definition 2.2.1. Let Σ be an alphabet. The collection of *regular languages* over Σ is defined recursively as follows:

    (a) $\emptyset$ is a regular language.

    (b) $\{\varepsilon\}$ is a regular language.

    (c) For each $a \in \Sigma$, $\{a\}$ is a regular language.

    (d) If A and B are regular languages, then $A \cup B$, $A \cdot B$, and A^* are regular languages.

    (e) No other languages over Σ are regular.

That is, the collection of regular languages over Σ consists of the empty language, all the singleton languages, including $\{\varepsilon\}$, and all languages formed by the language operations of concatenation, union, and star closure.

Example 2.2.1

        Let $\Sigma = \{a, b\}$ then the following are true:

        $\emptyset$ and $\{\varepsilon\}$ are regular languages.
        $\{a\}$ and $\{b\}$ are regular languages.
        $\{a, b\}$ is regular, being the union of $\{a\}$ and $\{b\}$.
        $\{ab\}$ is regular.
        $\{a, ab, b\}$ is regular.
        $\{a^i \mid i \geq 0\}$ is regular.
        $\{a^i b^j \mid i \geq 0 \text{ and } j \geq 0\}$ is regular.
        $\{(ab)^i \mid i \geq 0\}$ is regular.

Is the language of all strings over $\{a, b, c\}$ having no substring ac a regular language? To answer this question, let A be this language. If A is regular, then it can be written in the form indicated by the definition. Note that the basic building blocks are the languages $\{a\}$, $\{b\}$, $\{c\}$, $\emptyset$, and $\{\varepsilon\}$. Suppose that w is a word in A. Then w begins with 0 or more c's. If we remove them, we are left with a substring w' that does not begin with the character c. This substring is made up of a's, b's, and c's with any block of c's immediately following b's. Moreover, any block of c's does not occur at the beginning of w'. Thus we have

$$w' \in (\{a\} \cup \{b\}\{c\}^*)^*$$

and so

$$w \in \{c\}^*(\{a\} \cup \{b\}\{c\}^*)^*$$

which gives

$$A \subseteq \{c\}^*(\{a\} \cup \{b\}\{c\}^*)^*$$

Conversely, note that if u is a string having substring ac then

$$u \notin \{c\}^*(\{a\} \cup \{b\}\{c\}^*)^*$$

for there is no way that a c can immediately follow an a. Hence

$$\{c\}^*(\{a\} \cup \{b\}\{c\}^*)^* \subseteq A$$

We can somewhat simplify the specification of regular languages by introducing a kind of shorthand called *regular expressions*. We agree to write a in place of the singleton language $\{a\}$. Thus

$$
\begin{array}{lll}
a \cup b & \text{denotes} & \{a, b\} = \{a\} \cup \{b\} \\
ab & \text{denotes} & \{ab\} \\
a^* & \text{denotes} & \{a\}^*; \\
a^+ & \text{denotes} & \{a\}^+
\end{array}
$$

Furthermore, we agree that the order of precedence for the operators $*$, $\cup$, and $\cdot$ is $*$ first, $\cdot$ next, and $\cup$ last. This reduces our reliance on parentheses for grouping and makes such expressions easier to read. Thus, for example, an expression such as $(\{a\}^*\{b\}) \cup \{c\}$ reduces to the regular expression $a^*b \cup c$.

In terms of these notational conventions, we now define the *regular expressions* over the alphabet Σ recursively as follows:

1. $\emptyset$ and ε are regular expressions.
2. a is a regular expression for each $a \in \Sigma$.
3. If r and s are regular expressions, then so are $r \cup s$, $r \cdot s$, and r^*.
4. No other sequences of symbols are regular expressions.

Comparing this definition with the definition of regular languages, we see that each regular expression over Σ denotes a regular language over Σ.

For example, the language of all strings over $\{a, b, c\}$ having no substring ac is denoted by the regular expression $c^*(a \cup bc^*)^*$.

When necessary to distinguish between a regular expression r and the language that r denotes, we use $L(r)$ to denote the language. We also write $w \in r$ to mean $w \in L(r)$. If r and s are regular expressions over the same alphabet Σ and if $L(r) = L(s)$, then r and s are said to be *equivalent*. In case r and s are equivalent, we write $r = s$. We also write $r \subseteq s$ in the case that $L(r) \subseteq L(s)$. Note that establishing $r = s$ can thus be accomplished by showing $r \subseteq s \subseteq r$.

Note that, by the definition of the star-closure for languages, $\emptyset^* = \{\varepsilon\}$, and so in terms of regular expressions we have $\emptyset^* = \varepsilon$. Thus we *could* omit ε from the definition of regular expressions. It is as an abbreviation for $\emptyset^*$ that we include ε; that is, ε is included for convenience rather than necessity. Similarly, we may also abbreviate the expression rr^* by r^+.

Note that there may be many regular expressions denoting the same language. For example $(a^*b)^*$ and $\varepsilon \cup (a \cup b)^*b$ denote the same language: the language of all strings of 0 or more a's and b's that are either the empty string or have a b at the end. Thus $(a^*b)^* = \varepsilon \cup (a \cup b)^*b$. We may simplify regular expressions by replacing them with equivalent ones that are less complex. Thus, for example, the expression $ab \cup \varepsilon \cup (a \cup b)^*b$ could be replaced by $ab \cup (a^*b)^*$.

Numerous equivalencies for regular expressions exist and are based on the corresponding identities for languages. They are summarized in the following theorem.

Theorem 2.2.2.   Let r, s, and t be regular expressions over the same alphabet Σ. Then:

1. $r \cup s = s \cup r$.

2. $r \cup \emptyset = r = \emptyset \cup r$.

3. $r \cup r = r$.

4. $(r \cup s) \cup t = r \cup (s \cup t)$.

5. $r\varepsilon = \varepsilon r = r$.

6. $r\emptyset = \emptyset r = \emptyset$.

7. $(rs)t = r(st)$.

8. $r(s \cup t) = rs \cup rt$ and $(r \cup s)t = rt \cup st$.

9. $r^* = r^{**} = r^*r^* = (\varepsilon \cup r)^* = r^*(r \cup \varepsilon) = (r \cup \varepsilon)r^* = \varepsilon \cup rr^*$.

10. $(r \cup s)^* = (r^* \cup s^*)^* = (r^*s^*)^* = (r^*s)^*r^* = r^*(sr^*)^*$.

11. $r(sr)^* = (rs)^*r$.

12. $(r^*s)^* = \varepsilon \cup (r \cup s)^*s$.

13. $(rs^*)^* = \varepsilon \cup r(r \cup s)^*$.

14. $s(r \cup \varepsilon)^*(r \cup \varepsilon) \cup s = sr^*$.

15. $rr^* = r^*r$.

Many of these identities can be proved by *reparsing*. To illustrate, consider identity 11, $r(sr)^* = (rs)^*r$. If $w \in r(sr)^*$, then $w = r_0(s_1r_1) \ldots (s_nr_n)$ for some $n \geq 0$. Since concatenation is associative, we can reassociate or *reparse* the last expression and get $w = (r_0s_1)(r_1s_2) \ldots (r_{n-1}s_n)r_n \in (rs)^*r$. This gives us that $r(sr)^* \subseteq (rs)^*r$ [or $L(r(sr)^*) \subseteq L((rs)^*r)]$. We may similarly show that $(rs)^*r \subseteq r(sr)^*$ and establish the identity.

In proving identities we may also make use of previously known identities. For example, if $r = s^*t$, then we have

$$
\begin{aligned}
r = s^*t &= (\varepsilon \cup s^+)t &&\text{since } s^* = \varepsilon \cup s^+ \\
&= (\varepsilon \cup ss^*)t \\
&= \varepsilon t \cup ss^*t &&\text{from (8)} \\
&= t \cup sr &&\text{from (5)} \\
&= sr \cup t &&\text{from (1)}
\end{aligned}
$$

which proves that $r = s^*t$ implies that $r = sr \cup t$.

Exercises for Section 2.2

2.2.1. Verify by means of the definition of regular languages that the following are regular languages over $\Sigma = \{a, b\}$:

(a) $\{a^i \mid i > 0\}$.

(b) $\{a^i \mid i > n\}$ for some fixed $n \geq 0$.

(c) $\{w \in \Sigma^* \mid w \text{ ends with } a\}$.

2.2.2. Verify that the language of all strings of 0's and 1's having at least two consecutive 0's is a regular language.

2.2.3. Pascal identifiers are strings of arbitrary length composed of alphabetic characters and digits. Pascal identifiers must begin with an alphabetic character. Is this language a regular language?

2.2.4. Give a regular expression for the language of all Pascal identifiers.

2.2.5. (a) Show that $(r \cup \varepsilon)^* = r^*$.

(b) Show that $a^*b(a \cup ba^*b)^*$ and $(b \cup aa^*b) \cup (b \cup aa^*b)(a \cup ba^*b)^*(a \cup ba^*b)$ are equivalent.

2.2.6. Over $\Sigma = \{a, b, c\}$, are the regular expressions in each pair equivalent?

(a) $(a \cup b)^*a^*$ and $((a \cup b)a)^*$

(b) $\emptyset^{**}$ and ε

(c) $((a \cup b)c)^*$ and $(ac \cup bc)^*$

(d) $b(ab \cup ac)$ and $(ba \cup ba)(b \cup c)$

2.2.7. Simplify:

(a) $\emptyset^* \cup a^* \cup b^* \cup (a \cup b)^*$

(b) $((a^*b^*)^* \cdot (b^*a^*)^*)^*$

(c) $(a^*b)^* \cup (b^*a)^*$

(d) $(a \cup b)^*a(a \cup b)^*$

2.2.8. Show that $(aa)^*a = a(aa)^*$.

2.2.9. Simplify the following regular expressions.

(a) $(\varepsilon \cup aa)^*$

(b) $(\varepsilon \cup aa)(\varepsilon \cup aa)^*$

(c) $a(\varepsilon \cup aa)^*a \cup \varepsilon$

(d) $a(\varepsilon \cup aa)^*(\varepsilon \cup aa) \cup a$

(e) $(a \cup \varepsilon)a^*b$

(f) $(\varepsilon \cup aa)^*(\varepsilon \cup aa)a \cup a$

(g) $(\varepsilon \cup aa)(\varepsilon \cup aa)^*(\varepsilon \cup aa) \cup (\varepsilon \cup aa)$

(h) $(\varepsilon \cup aa)(\varepsilon \cup aa)^*(ab \cup b) \cup (ab \cup b)$

(i) $(a \cup b)(\varepsilon \cup aa)^*(\varepsilon \cup aa) \cup (a \cup b)$

(j) $(aa)^*a \cup (aa)^*$

(k) $a^*b((a \cup b)a^*b)^* \cup a^*b$

(l) $a^*b((a \cup b)a^*b)^*(a \cup b)(aa)^* \cup a(aa)^* \cup a^*b((a \cup b)a^*b)^*$

2.3 DETERMINISTIC FINITE AUTOMATA

Consider the regular language A given by $c^*(a \cup bc^*)^*$. If we are given a particular string w and asked if w is in A, we must analyze not only the characters that make up w but also their relative positions. For example, the string abc^5c^3ab is in A, whereas $cabac^3bc$ is not. We may construct a diagram to assist us in determining membership. Such a diagram is of the form of a directed graph with certain additional information incorporated into it and is called a *transition diagram*. The nodes of the graph are called *states* and act as place markers for the portion of the string that we have analyzed so far. The edges of the graph are labeled with characters from the alphabet and are called *transitions*. If the next character in the string matches the label of some transition from the current state, we go to the state that that transition leads to. Of course, we must start in some *initial state*, and when we have considered all characters in the string, we need some way of knowing if we have found a "legal" string. Thus we mark certain states as *accepting states*. If we end up in an accepting state when the entire string has been considered, we have a "legal" string. We mark the initial state with an arrow ($\rightarrow$) and draw a circle around the accepting states.

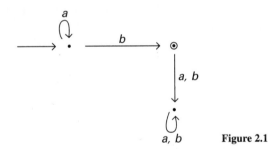

Figure 2.1

For example, the transition diagram in Figure 2.1 accepts all strings consisting of 0 or more a's followed by a single b. Note that for any string of the form $a^k b$, with $k \geq 0$, traversal of the diagram ends up in the accepting state. Traversal with any other string of a's and b's (including the empty string) ends up in some state other than the accepting state.

Consider the language $A = \{(ab)^i \mid i \geq 1\}$, which is given by the regular expression $(ab)^+$. Note that in a string in this language we must have at least *one* copy of ab. Thus, in building a transition diagram for this language, the initial state cannot be an accepting state. Moreover, encountering the character b in the initial state signals an unacceptable string. Thus there are two transitions from the initial state, one for a and one for b. The a transition leads to a state in which we expect to see a b as the next character. If b is encountered, we move to an accepting state. That is, if there are no more characters to consider, we have identified a legal string. If we have not exhausted the string, we take some appropriate transition out of this state. The transition diagram for A is shown in Figure 2.2.

Note that we have a single accepting state. If analysis terminates in any other state, the string is not correctly formed. Note, too, that once an incorrectly formed prefix is identified, we move to a nonaccepting state and stay there.

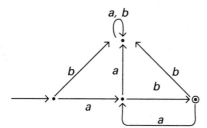

Figure 2.2

Consider the language $(ab)^*$. In this case the empty string *is* acceptable. Thus we may accept in the initial state. The corresponding transition diagram is shown in Figure 2.3.

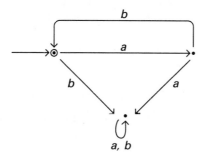

Figure 2.3

Let us label the states in the transition diagram of the last example by the letters q_i, for $i = 0, 1, 2$. Thus we have Figure 2.4.

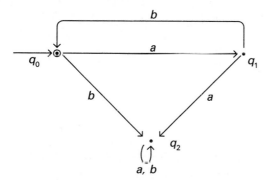

Figure 2.4

We may represent this diagram by a table that indicates the next state for a particular current state and input combination (Figure 2.5).

Note that the table for our transition diagram has a unique next state for each current state–input pair. Thus, for any current state and input, we may determine what the next state will be. We may think of the diagram as representing the action of some

State\Input	a	b
q_0	q_1	q_2
q_1	q_2	q_0
q_2	q_2	q_2

Figure 2.5

machine. This machine can exist in any one of a number of different states. It changes state depending on an input and its current state. Such a machine is called a *finite automaton*, a simple idealized computer. Finite automata are defined in terms of their states, the inputs that they allow, and their reaction to the inputs. Finite automata come in two types, deterministic and nondeterministic, depending on how well defined the ability to change states is. The automaton corresponding to Figure 2.5 for $(ab)^*$ is deterministic.

Formally, a *deterministic finite automaton M* is a collection of five things.

1. An input alphabet Σ.
2. A finite collection of states Q.
3. A special start state s.
4. A collection of final or accepting states F.
5. A function $\delta : Q \times \Sigma \to Q$ that determines a unique next state for each pair (q_i, σ) of current state and input.

We generally abbreviate the term *deterministic finite automaton* by *dfa*. We write $M = (Q, \Sigma, s, F, \delta)$ to indicate the collection of states, the alphabet, the start state, the collection of accepting states, and the function associated with the dfa M.

For example, the dfa corresponding to the previous example is given by $M = (Q, \Sigma, s, F, \delta)$, where

$$Q = \{q_0, q_1, q_2\}$$
$$\Sigma = \{a, b\}$$
$$s = q_0$$
$$F = \{q_0\}$$

δ as defined in the table in Figure 2.6.

δ	a	b
q_0	q_1	q_2
q_1	q_2	q_0
q_2	q_2	q_2

Figure 2.6

The most crucial aspect of a dfa is that δ is a *function*. As a function, δ must be defined for all pairs (q_i, σ) in $Q \times \Sigma$. This means that, no matter what the current state is or what the input character is, there is *always* a next state and that next state is unique. Thus for a pair (q_i, σ) there is *one and only one* functional value (next state), $\delta(q_i, \sigma)$.

In other words, the next state is fully determined by the information present in the pair (q_i, σ).

We may create a transition diagram immediately from the definition of a dfa. First, create and label a node for each state. Then for each entry q_j in the row corresponding to a state q_i draw an edge from q_i to q_j labeled with the input character associated with q_j. Finally, indicate the node s by an arrow, and circle all nodes in F indicating accepting states. Thus the transition diagram for the dfa $M = (Q, \Sigma, s, F, \delta)$, where

$$Q = \{q_0, q_1\}$$
$$\Sigma = \{a, b\}$$
$$F = \{q_0\}$$
$$s = q_0$$

and δ given by Figure 2.7

δ	a	b
q_0	q_0	q_1
q_1	q_1	q_0

Figure 2.7

is shown in Figure 2.8.

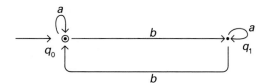

Figure 2.8

As another example, consider the dfa $M = \{Q, \Sigma, s, F, \delta\}$ given by

$$Q = \{q_0, q_1, q_2, q_3\}$$
$$\Sigma = \{a, b\}$$
(*) $\quad s = q_0$
$$F = \{q_0, q_1, q_2\}$$

and δ given by the table in Figure 2.9.

δ	a	b
q_0	q_0	q_1
q_1	q_0	q_2
q_2	q_0	q_3
q_3	q_3	q_3

Figure 2.9

The corresponding transition diagram is shown in Figure 2.10.

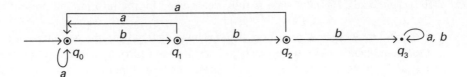

Figure 2.10

Exercises for Section 2.3

2.3.1. Find a regular expression for the language of all strings over $\{a, b\}$ that have an even number of b's. Construct a transition diagram for this language.

2.3.2. Construct a transition diagram for the regular language given by $c^*(a \cup bc^*)^*$. Convert your diagram into a table, as in Figure 2.5, labeling the states $q_0, q_1, \ldots$.

2.3.3. Let $M = \{Q, \Sigma, s, F, \delta\}$ be given by

$$Q = \{q_0, q_1, q_2, q_3\}$$
$$\Sigma = \{0, 1\}$$
$$F = \{q_0\}$$
$$s = q_0$$

and δ given by the table in Figure 2.11.

δ	0	1
q_0	q_2	q_1
q_1	q_3	q_0
q_2	q_0	q_3
q_3	q_1	q_2

Figure 2.11

Construct the transition diagram. Give the sequence of states in accepting the string 110101 (the leftmost character is the first to be analyzed).

2.3.4. Is Figure 2.12 the transition diagram of a dfa? Why or why not?

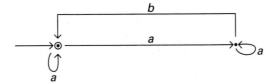

Figure 2.12

2.4 DFAs AND LANGUAGES

Certain definitions and notation are useful when working with dfa's. If M is a dfa, then the *language accepted by M* is

$$L(M) = \{w \in \Sigma^* \mid w \text{ is accepted by } M\}$$

That is, $L(M)$ is just the collection of strings that move M from its initial state to an accepting state.

For example, the language accepted by the dfa in (*) at the end of the last section is

$$L(M) = \{w \in \{a, b\}^* \mid w \text{ does not contain three consecutive } b\text{'s}\}$$

It is worth emphasizing that $L(M)$ consists of *all* strings accepted by M, not just any set of strings all of which are accepted by M.

For each (q_i, σ) in $Q \times \Sigma$, $\delta(q_i, \sigma)$ is some state in Q and so itself may be paired with input. This pair in turn is mapped by δ to some new state in Q. In particular, if q_0 is the initial state of M and we have as input the string $\sigma_1\sigma_2\sigma_3$, we have a resulting state of $\delta(\delta(\delta(q_0, \sigma_1), \sigma_2), \sigma_3)$. For example, for the dfa (*) of the last section, we have, for the string $bbab$, $\delta(\delta(\delta(\delta(q_0, b), b), a), b) = q_1$. Note the recursiveness of the application of M to the string. Note, too, that writing this expression is quite laborious. We agree to write $\delta(q_0, bbab)$ as an abbreviation for $\delta(\delta(\delta(\delta(q_0, b), b), a), b)$. To be precise, if $q_i \in Q$ and w is a string of the form $a_i w'$ for some $a_i \in \Sigma$ and substring w', we define $\delta(q_i, w)$ to be $\delta(\delta(q_i, a_i), w')$.

We say that two dfa's M_1 and M_2 are *equivalent* if $L(M_1) = L(M_2)$. For example, over the alphabet $\Sigma = \{a\}$, let M_1 and M_2 be given by the transition diagrams

Both accept the language a^+ and thus are equivalent. On the other hand M_3 given by the diagram

is not equivalent to either M_1 or M_2 (why?). Note that M_4 given by the transition diagram

is equivalent to M_3 and is "simpler" in the sense that it has fewer states. Problems at the end of the chapter investigate the problems of determining if two dfa's are equivalent and of transforming a dfa into an equivalent one that is simpler.

Exercises for Section 2.4

2.4.1. Let M be a dfa. When is ε in $L(M)$?

2.4.2. Construct dfa's that accept each of the following languages over $\{a, b\}$:

    (a) $\{w \mid$ each a in w is between two b's$\}$

    (b) $\{w \mid w$ has $abab$ as a substring$\}$

    (c) $\{w \mid w$ has neither aa or bb as a substring$\}$

    (d) $\{w \mid w$ has an odd number of a's and an even number of b's$\}$

    (e) $\{w \mid w$ has both ab and ba as substrings$\}$.

2.4.3. Let S be the collection of all dfa's over an alphabet Σ. Let $R \subseteq S \times S$ be the relation defined by (M_1, M_2) is in R if and only if M_1 is equivalent to M_2 (as finite automata). Show that R is an equivalence relation on S (and thus that the definition of equivalence for dfa's is consistent with the normal mathematical use of the term).

2.5 NONDETERMINISTIC FINITE AUTOMATA

If we allow zero, one, or more transitions from a state on the same input symbol, our finite automaton is said to be *nondeterministic*. Nondeterministic finite automata (nfa) can be much more convenient to design than deterministic ones. Consider the relatively simple regular language $a^*b \cup ab^*$. Strings in this language consist of either some a's followed by a b or an a followed by some b's. A dfa accepting A is given by the transition diagram in Figure 2.13.

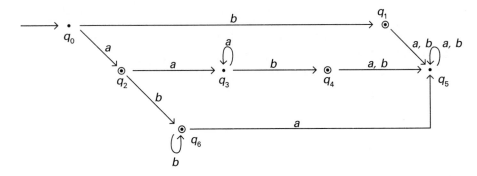

Figure 2.13

Although this is a relatively simple language it takes a few moments to determine that this transition diagram corresponds to a dfa for A. We must first check that it identifies only those strings in A and, second, that it actually shows a dfa. To do this, we must check that the transition rule is a function, that each state has one and only one transition from it for every symbol in the alphabet.

Consider now the transition diagram in Figure 2.14. Note that this diagram accepts only strings in A. Note, too, that the transition rule is certainly not a function from $Q \times \Sigma$ to Q because it assigns no next state to the input–state pairs (q_4, a), (q_3, a), (q_3, b), (q_2, a), and (q_2, b). Moreover, there is more than one next state corresponding to the pair (q_0, a). This transition diagram is that of an nfa. Finally, note that we can determine the language accepted by this nfa somewhat easier than for the previous dfa's diagram.

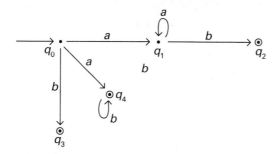

Figure 2.14

If we attempt to define the term nondeterministic finite automaton formally, we see that much of the definition for dfa carries over. That is, we have a finite set of states Q, an input alphabet Σ, a designated initial or start state s, a collection of accepting states F, and a transition rule. The only real difference is in the transition rule. For nfa's the rule associates pairs (q, σ) with *zero or more next states*. We might say that the rule *relates* pairs (q, σ) with collections of states. This just means that the rule is a relation between $Q \times \Sigma$ and Q, or on $(Q \times \Sigma) \times Q$. Thus we define a *nondeterministic finite automaton M* as a collection of five objects $(Q, \Sigma, s, F, \Delta)$, where

1. Q is a finite set of states.
2. Σ is an input alphabet.
3. s is one of the states in Q designated as a start state.
4. F is a collection of accepting or final states.
5. Δ is a relation on $(Q \times \Sigma) \times Q$ and is called the *transition relation*.

Note that, since Δ is a relation for any pair (q, σ) consisting of a current state and an input symbol, $\Delta(q, \sigma)$ is a collection of zero or more states [that is, $\Delta(q, \sigma) \subseteq Q$]. This reflects that from any state q we may have zero or more choices for the next state, all for the same input symbol.

For example, the nfa described earlier for $A = a^*b \cup ab^*$ is given by

$$Q = \{q_0, q_1, q_2, q_3, q_4\}$$
$$F = \{q_2, q_3, q_4\}$$
$$s = q_0$$
$$\Sigma = \{a, b\}$$

and Δ is given by the table in Figure 2.15.

Note that in the table for the transition relation the entries are sets. The presence of $\emptyset$ as a table entry indicates that no transition from that particular state on the corresponding input exists. The presence of more than one possible next state for a current state–input pair indicates that we may choose among the possibilities. The choice is *not determined* by anything in the model. For this reason, the behavior of the automaton is referred to as *nondeterministic*.

Δ	a	b
q_0	$\{q_1, q_4\}$	$\{q_3\}$
q_1	$\{q_1\}$	$\{q_2\}$
q_2	$\emptyset$	$\emptyset$
q_3	$\emptyset$	$\emptyset$
q_4	$\emptyset$	$\{q_4\}$

Figure 2.15

As another example, consider the nfa $M = (Q, \Sigma, s, F, \Delta)$ given by

$$Q = \{q_0, q_1, q_2\}$$
$$\Sigma = \{a, b\}$$
$$F = \{q_0\}$$
$$s = q_0$$

and Δ given by the table in Figure 2.16. This nfa has the corresponding transition diagram shown in Figure 2.17.

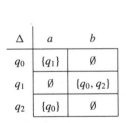

Δ	a	b
q_0	$\{q_1\}$	$\emptyset$
q_1	$\emptyset$	$\{q_0, q_2\}$
q_2	$\{q_0\}$	$\emptyset$

Figure 2.16

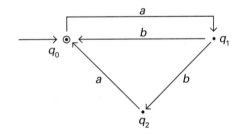

Figure 2.17

This nfa accepts the language $(ab \cup aba)^*$. Notice that when in state q_1 with input b there are two possible next states. We may choose to go to either one of these next states. Again, the choice of a next state is not determined by the model. In consuming the string aba, a choice of q_2 as the next state for the pair (q_1, b) leads to an accepting state, whereas choosing q_0 as the next state does not. Some quesswork seems to be involved in analyzing strings with nfa's. This is a characteristic of nondeterminism: at some point when a choice must be made and the choice cannot be determined from the model, we must guess correctly. In a nondeterministic model of computation (of which nfa's are one kind), we assume that the correct guess is always made.

As with dfa's, if M is an nfa, we define the *language accepted* by M to be

$$L(M) = \{w \mid w \text{ is a string accepted by } M\}$$

where a string w is accepted by M when w takes M from its initial state to some final or accepting state (as w is exhausted).

To determine if a particular string is in $L(M)$, we may traverse the transition diagram corresponding to M. We must find a path that terminates in an accepting state when the string is consumed. In this traversal we must nondeterministically choose one transition from a state over another when more than one exists for the same symbol. To determine if the string is *not* in $L(M)$, we must exhaust all possible paths through the transition diagram for the string. For even simple transition diagrams, this can be a very time consuming problem. The next example indicates an approach to this problem other than exhaustively searching the diagram.

Example 2.5.1

The transition diagram in Figure 2.18 corresponds to an nfa that accepts the language

$$(a^*b^*)^*(aa \cup bb)(a^*b^*)^*$$

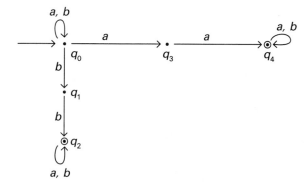

Figure 2.18

The table for Δ is given in Figure 2.19.

Δ	a	b
q_0	$\{q_0, q_3\}$	$\{q_0, q_1\}$
q_1	$\emptyset$	$\{q_2\}$
q_2	$\{q_2\}$	$\{q_2\}$
q_3	$\{q_4\}$	$\emptyset$
q_4	$\{q_4\}$	$\{q_4\}$

Figure 2.19

The recursive nature of string analysis that we saw with respect to dfa's can be retained in nfa's if we are careful in defining our notation. If $X \subseteq Q$, let us interpret $\Delta(X, \sigma)$ to be the set of states $\{p \mid q \in X \text{ and } p \in \Delta(q, \sigma)\}$. That is, $\Delta(X, \sigma)$ is just the set of all next states reachable from states in X on input σ. Note that $\Delta(X, \sigma) = \bigcup_{q \in X} \Delta(q, \sigma)$ [remember that $\Delta(q, \sigma)$ is a set for any state q].

Thus, in the preceding example,

$$\Delta(\{q_0, q_2, q_3\}, b) = \{q_0, q_1\} \cup \{q_2\} \cup \emptyset = \{q_0, q_1, q_2\}$$

Now note that, for the string $abaab$, we have $\Delta(q_0, a) = \{q_0, q_3\}$, so that

$$\begin{aligned} \Delta(\{q_0, ab) &= \Delta(\Delta(q_0, a), b) \\ &= \Delta(\{q_0, q_3\}, b) \\ &= \{q_0, q_1\} \cup \emptyset \\ &= \{q_0, q_1\} \end{aligned}$$

We may thus extend our notation from dfa's to nfa's and write $\Delta(q_0, abaab)$ as an abbreviation for $\Delta(\Delta(\Delta(\Delta(\Delta(q_0, a), b), a), a), b)$.

In Example 2.5.1 we have $\Delta(q_0, abaab) = \{q_0, q_1, q_4\}$. The collection $\Delta(q_0, abaab)$ is simply the set of all states that we can reach in M when analyzing the string $abaab$. This collection accounts for all possible paths or traversals of M with this input string. That $\Delta(q_0, abaab)$ contains at least one accepting state, q_4, indicates that some traversal of this transition diagram on the input string $abaab$ terminates in an accepting state. Thus $abaab$ is in the language accepted by this nfa.

Exercises for Section 2.5

2.5.1. Construct a dfa and associated transition diagram that accepts the language $(ab \cup aba)^*$. Compare with the nfa of Example 2.5.1.

2.5.2. Find an nfa (which is *not* a dfa) that accepts the language $ab^* \cup ab^*a$.

2.5.3. Use the preceding technique to determine if the strings $babba$ and $aabaaba$ are accepted by the nfa of Example 2.5.1.

2.5.4. Let the nfa M be given by $Q = \{q_0, q_1\}$, $\Sigma = \{a, b\}$, $s = q_0$, $F = \{q_1\}$, and Δ given as in Figure 2.20. Determine if a^2b, ba, and b^2a are in $L(M)$. Draw a transition diagram for M.

Δ	a	b
q_0	$\{q_0, q_1\}$	$\{q_1\}$
q_1	$\emptyset$	$\{q_0, q_1\}$

Figure 2.20

2.6 EQUIVALENCE OF NFA AND DFA

We have defined equivalence for dfa's. We extend this definition to the class of all finite automata (both dfa's and nfa's) by defining automaton M to be *equivalent* to automaton M' whenever $L(M) = L(M')$.

Example 2.6.1

The automata depicted in Figure 2.21 are equivalent. Note that one is deterministic and one is nondeterministic. Both, however, accept the same language, $a(a \cup b)^*$.

Since a function is a special case of relation (that is, functions are relations that have further requirements), the functions in dfa's certainly qualify as relations in nfa's.

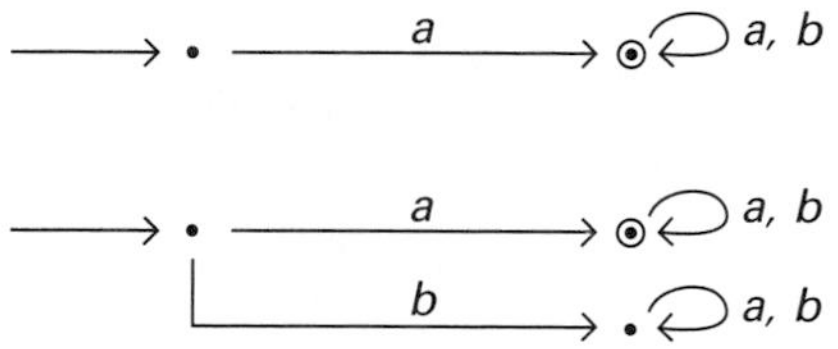

Figure 2.21

Hence every dfa is an nfa. Thus the collection of languages accepted by nfa's includes all languages accepted by dfa's. It turns out that nfa's do not accept any languages other than those accepted by dfa's. Thus nfa's are no more powerful than dfa's in terms of the languages they accept. To establish this fact, we need to show that any language accepted by an nfa can also be accepted by some dfa.

Let $M = (Q, \Sigma, s, F, \Delta)$ be any nfa. In the previous section we presented a way of traversing M, which gave us the collection of all states attainable from the start state at each step in analyzing a string. This technique provides the basis for constructing a dfa $M' = (Q', \Sigma', s', F', \delta)$ that accepts the same language as M. Essentially, what we do is let each state in Q' correspond to a set of states from Q. In analyzing a string with M, we accept when the final collection of states contains at least one of the accepting states from F. Thus we let F' be that collection of states in Q' that corresponds to sets of states (from Q) containing a state in F. We let s' correspond to the set $\{s\}$, $\Sigma' = \Sigma$, and define δ so that it moves us from one collection of M states to another, as Δ does.

Example 2.6.2

Consider the nfa M that accepts $a \cup (ab)^+$ as given by the transition diagram in Figure 2.22. For this nfa, we have

$$\Delta(q_0, a) = \{q_1, q_2\}$$
$$\Delta(q_0, b) = \emptyset$$
$$\Delta(\{q_1, q_2\}, a) = \emptyset$$
$$\Delta(\{q_1, q_2\}, b) = \{q_3\}$$
$$\Delta(\emptyset, a) = \Delta(\emptyset, b) = \emptyset$$
$$\Delta(q_3, a) = \{q_2\}$$
$$\Delta(q_3, b) = \emptyset$$
$$\Delta(q_2, a) = \emptyset$$
$$\Delta(q_2, b) = \{q_3\}$$

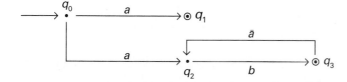

Figure 2.22

Thus the transition diagram corresponding to the dfa M' that is equivalent to M is as given in Figure 2.23. Note that each state in M' corresponds to a set of states from M. Accepting states in M' correspond to sets of states from M that contain accepting states.

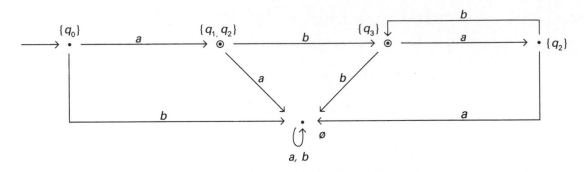

Figure 2.23

It is easy to verify that the transition rule is a function. Thus we may give $M' = (Q', \Sigma', s', F', \delta)$ as

$$Q' = \{\emptyset, \{q_0\}, \{q_2\}, \{q_3\}, \{q_1, q_2\}\}$$
$$\Sigma' = \Sigma$$
$$s' = \{q_0\}$$
$$F' = \{\{q_3\}, \{q_1, q_2\}\}$$

and δ as given by the table in Figure 2.24.

δ	a	b
$\emptyset$	$\emptyset$	$\emptyset$
$\{q_0\}$	$\{q_1, q_2\}$	$\emptyset$
$\{q_2\}$	$\emptyset$	$\{q_3\}$
$\{q_3\}$	$\{q_2\}$	$\emptyset$
$\{q_1, q_2\}$	$\emptyset$	$\{q_3\}$

Figure 2.24

We now give formal proof that any language accepted by an nfa is also accepted by a dfa, thus proving that nfa languages and dfa languages comprise the same collection of languages.

Theorem 2.6.1. Let $M = (Q, \Sigma, s, F, \Delta)$ be an nfa. Then there exists a dfa $M' = (Q', \Sigma', s', F', \delta)$ that is equivalent to M.

Proof. Define $M' = (Q', \Sigma', s', F', \delta)$ as follows: let $s' = \{s\}$, $\Sigma' = \Sigma$, $Q' = 2^Q$ (that is, the collection of *all* subsets of Q), and F' is the collection of all subsets in Q' that contain states in F. Note that we have included in Q' and F' rather more objects than we did in the previous example. This will not alter the construction of M', however. For each set $\{q_{i_1}, q_{i_2}, \dots, q_{i_n}\}$ in Q' and each input symbol σ in Σ, we define δ as

$$\delta(\{q_{i_1}, q_{i_2}, \dots, q_{i_n}\}, \sigma) = \{p_1, p_2, \dots, p_k\}$$

if and only if

$$\Delta(\{q_{i_1}, q_{i_2}, \ldots, q_{i_n}\}, \sigma) = \{p_1, p_2, \ldots, p_k\}$$

Note that δ so defined is a function from $Q' \times \Sigma'$ to Q' since it is well defined everywhere on $Q' \times \Sigma'$.

To establish that $L(M) = L(M')$, we must show that, for any string w, $\delta(s', w) = \{p_1, p_2, \ldots p_j\}$ if and only if $\Delta(s, w) = \{p_1, p_2, \ldots, p_j\}$ so that M' accepts w if and only if M accepts w. We prove this by induction on the length of w. If the length of w is 0 (that is, $w = \varepsilon$), then

$$\Delta(s, w) = \Delta(s, \varepsilon) = \{s\} = \delta(s', w)$$

Now suppose that for any string w of length less than or equal to m we have $\Delta(s, w) = \delta(s', w)$. Suppose that u is a string of length $m + 1$. Then, for some $\sigma \in \Sigma$, we have $u = w\sigma$, where w is a string of length m. In this case, $\delta(s', w\sigma) = \delta(\delta(s', w), \sigma)$. Now, by our induction hypothesis, since w has length m, $\delta(s', w) = \{p_1, p_2, \ldots, p_j\}$ if and only if $\Delta(s, w) = \{p_1, p_2, \ldots, p_j\}$. But from the way we've defined δ, we have that

$$\delta(\{p_1, p_2, \ldots, p_j\}, \sigma) = \{r_1, r_2, \ldots, r_k\}$$

if and only if

$$\Delta(\{p_1, p_2, \ldots, p_j\}, \sigma) = \{r_1, r_2, \ldots, r_k\}$$

Thus $\delta(s', w\sigma) = \{r_1, r_2, \ldots, r_k\}$ if and only if $\Delta(s, w\sigma) = \{r_1, r_2, \ldots, r_k\}$. That is, the equality holds for strings of length $m + 1$ when it holds for strings of length m. Now from the preceding we have that $\delta(s', w)$ is a state in F' if and only if $\Delta(s, w)$ contains a state in F. Thus M' accepts w if and only if M accepts w. ■

Note that in the proof the dfa M' corresponding to the nfa M is likely to contain many states that are not accessible from the start state. In practice it is a good idea to start with s' and add states only when they are the result of a transition from a previously added state.

Exercises for Section 2.6

2.6.1. Construct a dfa corresponding to the nfa given by Figure 2.25. What language is accepted by these automata?

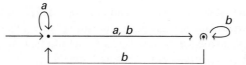

Figure 2.25

2.6.2. Find an nfa accepting $(ab \cup aab \cup aba)^*$. Convert this nfa into a dfa.

2.6.3. Find an nfa for $(a \cup b)^* aabab$. Convert it into a dfa.

2.6.4. Suppose that M is an nfa that is already deterministic. What results when the construction of Theorem 2.6.1 is applied to M?

2.7 ε-TRANSITIONS

We may extend the definition of a nondeterministic finite automaton to include transitions from one state to another that do not depend on any input. Such transitions are called *ε-transitions* because they consume no input when they occur. For example, the nfa's of Figures 2.26 and 2.27 contain ε-transitions.

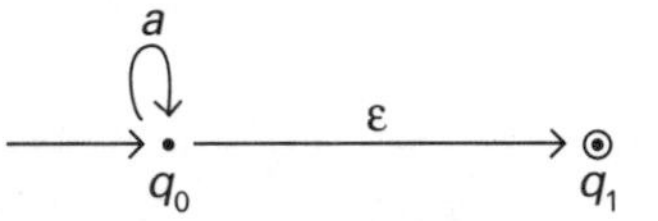

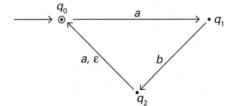

Figure 2.26

In the nfa of Figure 2.26, the automaton can change its state from q_0 to q_1 without consuming any input. Note that q_1 is the single accepting state of this nfa. If w is any string of 0 or more a's, this automaton loops at q_0 as it consumes a's. Once the string of a's is exhausted, it moves to q_1 and accepts.

The nfa of Figure 2.27 can choose to move from state q_2 to state q_0 without consuming any input. In both nfa's the decision to follow an ε-transition occurs in the same way that any other multiple-choice transition of an nfa occurs—based on something not determined by the model. Thus ε-transitions are consistent with the nondeterministic flavor of our previous version of nfa.

Figure 2.27

If ε-transitions are present in an nfa, the transition relation Δ associates pairs in $Q \times (\Sigma \cup \{\varepsilon\}) \times Q$ with subsets of Q. That is, Δ is a relation on $Q \times (\Sigma \cup \{\varepsilon\}) \times Q$. We can include a column in the table for Δ to accommodate pairs of the form (q_i, ε). When ε-transitions are present in an nfa, it will be convenient to assume that *each* state has an ε-transition that loops at that state. We will use this to systematize computation by such nfa's. Thus the nfa of Figure 2.27 would have the transition table given by Figure 2.28.

In attempting to calculate the set of next states for an nfa that contains ε-transitions we must take into account ε-transitions both "before" and "after" transitions directly on σ. For example, consider the nfa M given by Figure 2.29.

We have that the set of next states for current state q_0 on input a is the set $\{q_1, q_4\}$ due to an ε-transition after the transition on a. Similarly, the set of next states for current state q_1 on input b is the set $\{q_0, q_2, q_5\}$ due to an ε-transition before those directly on b. Note that $\Delta(q_0, ababbb) = \{q_0, q_5\}$ so that $ababbb$ is accepted by M.

Δ	a	b	$ε$
q_0	$\{q_1\}$	$\emptyset$	$\emptyset$
q_1	$\emptyset$	$\{q_2\}$	$\emptyset$
q_2	$\{q_0\}$	$\emptyset$	$\{q_0\}$

Figure 2.28

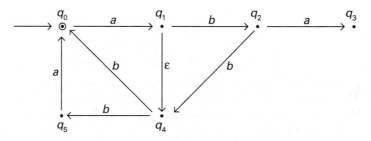

Figure 2.29

We may systematize the process of calculating the sets of next states for an nfa with ε-transitions as follows. For any state $q \in Q$, define the *ε-closure of q* to be

$$ε\text{-}cl(q) = \{p \mid p \text{ is accessible from } q \text{ without consuming input}\}$$

We extend this definition to an entire collection of states as

$$ε\text{-}cl(\{q_{i_1}, q_{i_2}, \ldots, q_{i_n}\}) = \bigcup_{k=1}^{n} ε\text{-}cl(q_{i_k})$$

For example, for the nfa given by Figure 2.30, we have

$$ε\text{-}cl(q_3) = \{q_3\}$$

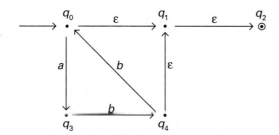

Figure 2.30

since each state is accessible from itself without consuming any input. We also have

$$ε\text{-}cl(q_0) = \{q_0, q_1, q_2\}$$

and

$$ε\text{-}cl(q_4) = \{q_1, q_2, q_4\}$$

For $q \in Q$ and $\sigma \in \Sigma$, define

$$d(q, \sigma) = \{p \mid \text{there is a transition from } q \text{ to } p \text{ labeled } \sigma\}$$

The collection $d(q, \sigma)$ is the collection of states directly "next" to q via a transition on σ. We extend the definition of d to sets as

$$d(\{q_{i_1}, q_{i_2}, \ldots, q_{i_n}\}, \sigma) = \bigcup_{k=1}^{n} d(q_{i_k}, \sigma)$$

Thus in the preceding example we have

$$d(q_0, a) = \{q_3\}$$
$$d(q_0, b) = \emptyset$$
$$d(\{q_3, q_4\}, b) = \{q_0, q_4\}$$

Note that $\varepsilon\text{-}cl(d(q, \sigma))$ is the set of all states that are accessible from q by a transition first on σ and then one or more ε-transitions. On the other hand, $d(\varepsilon\text{-}cl(q), \sigma)$ is the set of all states accessible from q by first taking one or more ε-transitions and then a transition on σ.

Finally, note that $\varepsilon\text{-}cl(d(\varepsilon\text{-}cl(q), \sigma))$ is the set of all states accessible from q by first taking one or more ε-transitions, then a transition on σ, and then one or more ε-transitions. Keep in mind that staying at a state can be viewed as taking an ε-transition. Thus $\varepsilon\text{-}cl(d(\varepsilon\text{-}cl(q), \sigma))$ is the set of next states for current state q on input σ. This systematizes the calculation of sets of next states. We first find $\varepsilon\text{-}cl(q)$, then calculate $d(\varepsilon\text{-}cl(q))$, and then find the ε-closure of the resulting set of states.

Example 2.7.1

Consider the nfa with ε-transitions given by Figure 2.31. Using the preceding formula, we find the set of next states on input a for current state q_0 as follows:

$$\varepsilon\text{-}cl(q_0) = \{q_0, q_1\}$$
$$d(\varepsilon\text{-}cl(q_0), a) = \{q_3, q_4\}$$
$$\varepsilon\text{-}cl(\{q_3, q_4\}) = \{q_1, q_3, q_4, q_5\}$$

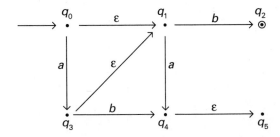

Figure 2.31

Thus on input a the set of next states is $\{q_1, q_3, q_4, q_5\}$. That is, $\Delta(q_0, a) = \{q_1, q_3, q_4, q_5\}$.

For an nfa $M = (Q, \Sigma, s, F, \Delta)$ that has ε-transitions, we may construct an nfa without ε-transitions that accepts the same language. Define $M' = (Q, \Sigma, s, F', \Delta')$ by

$$F' = F \cup \{q \mid \varepsilon\text{-}cl(q) \cap F \neq \emptyset\}$$

and $\Delta'(q, \sigma) = \varepsilon\text{-}cl(d(\varepsilon\text{-}cl(q), \sigma))$, as before.

Note that the transformed automaton M' contains no ε-transitions.

Example 2.7.2

The nfa of Figure 2.31 is transformed into the nfa of Figure 2.32, when all ε-transitions are removed by the preceding process.

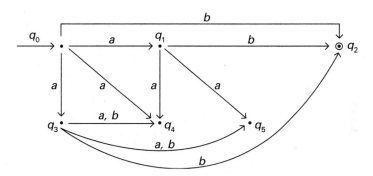

Figure 2.32

We now have that the collection of languages accepted by nfa with ε-transitions is exactly the same as the collection of languages accepted by nfa without ε-transitions. The converse is easily seen to be true, too. Thus all our automata accept the same collection of languages. In constructing an automaton to accept a language, we thus have three alternatives to choose from. The use of ε-transitions is convenient for combining finite automata, as we shall see later.

Exercises for Section 2.7

2.7.1. Calculate $\Delta(q_0, abb)$ and $\Delta(q_0, aba^2b)$ for the nfa of Figure 2.29.

2.7.2. Find $\varepsilon\text{-}cl(\{q_1, q_4\})$ for the nfa of Figure 2.30.

2.7.3. Find $\varepsilon\text{-}cl(d(q_3, b))$ in the nfa of Figure 2.30.

2.7.4. Use the given technique to calculate $\Delta(q_3, b)$ for Example 2.3.1.

2.7.5. For the nfa given by Figure 2.33; (a) find a transition table for Δ, (b) find the ε-closure(q_i) for $i = 0, 1, 2$, and (c) calculate $\Delta(q_0, a)$, $\Delta(q_0, b)$, and $\Delta(q_0, c)$ in Figure 2.33.

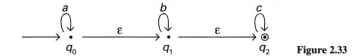

Figure 2.33

2.7.6. For the nfa of Exercise 2.7.5, find the transformed nfa with ε-transitions removed. Give the table for Δ'.

2.8 FINITE AUTOMATA AND REGULAR EXPRESSIONS

Thus far we have treated the relationship between finite automata and regular expressions only intuitively. In this section we formalize that relationship in Kleene's theorem (Theorem 2.8.4). For the moment, let us look at various properties of the languages accepted by finite automata.

For an alphabet Σ we can construct nfa's (and hence dfa's) to accept the singleton words. For example, the nfa of Figure 2.34 accepts the singleton language $\{a\}$. For that matter we may even construct an nfa to accept $\emptyset$, the empty language. Such an nfa is shown in Figure 2.35. Note that no strings are accepted by this nfa.

Figure 2.34   **Figure 2.35**

Suppose that $M_1 = (Q_1, \Sigma_1, s_1, F_1, \Delta_1)$ and $M_2 = (Q_2, \Sigma_2, s_2, F_2, \Delta_2)$ are nfa's. We can combine M_1 and M_2 into a new nfa that accepts $L(M_1) \cup L(M_2)$ by adding a new start state s and two new ε-transitions, one from s to s_1 and one from s to s_2. The formal construction of the new nfa $M = (Q, \Sigma, s, F, \Delta)$ is given by $\Sigma = \Sigma_1 \cup \Sigma_2$, $F = F_1 \cup F_2$, and $Q = Q_1 \cup Q_2 \cup \{s\}$, where s is the new initial state, and Δ is defined to include all transitions given by Δ_1 and Δ_2 *and* the two new ε-transitions from s to s_1 and s_2. In this case it is convenient to think of the transition relations Δ_1 and Δ_2 as collections of ordered triples from $Q_1 \times \Sigma \times Q_1$ and $Q_2 \times \Sigma \times Q_2$, where (q, σ, p) means that a transition from q to p exists on input character σ (that is, $p \in \Delta_i(q, \sigma)$). Using this notation, we can define

$$\Delta = \Delta_1 \cup \Delta_2 \cup \{(s, \varepsilon, s_1), (s, \varepsilon, s_2)\}$$

For example, the nfa's in Figure 2.36, which accept ab^* and $(ab)^*$, respectively, may be combined into the nfa with ε-transitions in Figure 2.37, which accepts $ab^* \cup (ab)^*$.

Let $M_1 = (Q_1, \Sigma_1, s_1, F_1, \Delta_1)$ and $M_2 = (Q_2, \Sigma_2, s_2, F_2, \Delta_2)$ be nfa's. We may combine them to form an nfa that accepts $L(M_1)L(M_2)$. We need an nfa that recognizes a string in $L(M_1)$ and then recognizes one in $L(M_2)$. That is, a traversal to an accepting state for the entire string must first encounter an accepting state of M_1 and then encounter (and terminate in) an accepting state of M_2. We do this by nondeterministically moving from each final state of M_1 to the initial state of M_2 via an ε-transition.

For example, the nfa's in Figure 2.38 accept the languages $\{a\}$ and $\{b\}$, respectively. Combining as indicated, we get an nfa that accepts the language $\{ab\}$ (see Figure 2.39).

Note that the automaton that results has as its initial state the initial state of M_1 and as its final state(s) the final state(s) of M_2. Thus the nfa $M = (Q, \Sigma, s, F, \Delta)$ that accepts $L(M_1)L(M_2)$ is given as

$$Q = Q_1 \cup Q_2$$
$$s = s_1$$
$$F = F_2$$
$$\Delta = \Delta_1 \cup \Delta_2 \cup (F_1 \times \{\varepsilon\} \times \{s_2\})$$

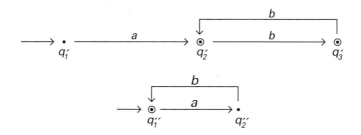

Figure 2.36

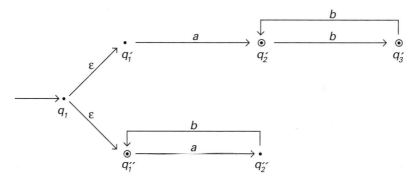

Figure 2.37

The transition relation Δ includes all transitions present in the two nfa's together with all triples of the form (q, ε, s_2), where q is an accepting state from M_1. That is, $s_2 \in \Delta(q, \varepsilon)$ for all $q \in F_1$.

We may derive a procedure for constructing an nfa accepting $L(M)^*$ for the nfa $M = (Q, \Sigma, s, F, \Delta)$ as follows. First, add a new initial state s'; make this state also an accepting state so that ε is accepted. Then allow an ε-transition from s' to the old initial state s. Thus M may be begun once M' has been started in s'. From all accepting states of M, allow an ε-transition back to s'. Once a string in $L(M)$ has been exhausted, computation can either resume in the initial state of M or terminate in s'. The resulting

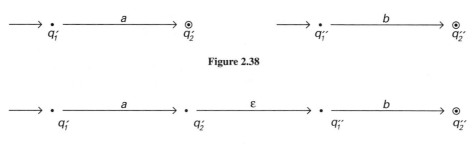

Figure 2.38

Figure 2.39

automaton is $M' = (Q', \Sigma, s', F', \Delta')$, where

$$Q' = Q \cup \{s'\}$$
$$F' = \{s'\}$$
$$\Delta' = \Delta \cup \{(s', \varepsilon, s)\} \cup (F \times \{\varepsilon\} \times \{s'\})$$

Note that Δ' thus defined includes the necessary ε-transitions as well as the transitions of the original nfa M.

The previous discussion establishes the following theorem.

Theorem 2.8.1.   The collection of languages accepted by finite automata over some alphabet Σ contains $\emptyset$ and the singleton languages $\{a\}$ for each $a \in \Sigma$. This collection is closed with respect to union, concatenation, and star closure.

Given a regular expression r to construct an nfa (with ε-transitions in the case of all but the trivial regular expressions), we apply the preceding techniques to the terms in the regular expression. Thus any regular language is accepted by a finite automaton. As will be shown in Lemma 2.8.3, the converse is also true. That is, any language accepted by a finite automaton is also a regular language. Consequently, the collection of regular languages is exactly the same as the collection of languages accepted by finite automata (Theorem 2.8.4).

Consider a finite automaton $M = (Q, \Sigma, s, F, \Delta)$ and assume that $s = q_0$ is the start state. For each state q_i, let

$$A_i = \{w \in \Sigma^* \mid \Delta(q_i, w) \cap F \neq \emptyset\}$$

That is, A_i is just that set of strings over Σ that move M from q_i to some accepting state. We say that A_i is the set of strings *accepted by the state* q_i. Note that $A_0 = L(M)$. Also, notice that it is possible that $A_i = \emptyset$. If $q_i \in F$, then we have that $\varepsilon \in A_i$.

As an example, consider the finite automaton of Figure 2.40. Here we have

$$A_5 = \emptyset, \qquad A_2 = \varepsilon$$
$$A_4 = \varepsilon, \qquad A_1 = b$$
$$A_3 = a, \qquad A_0 = ab \cup ba$$

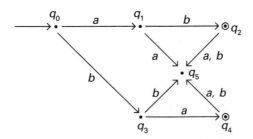

Figure 2.40

Suppose that $q_j \in \Delta(q_i, \sigma)$. Then A_i contains σA_j. In fact, we have

$$A_i = \cup\{\sigma A_j \mid q_j \in \Delta(q_i, \sigma)\}$$

This observation provides the basis of a recursive technique for deriving a regular expression from a finite automaton. To illustrate consider, the preceding example. Note that

$$A_0 = aA_1 \cup bA_3, \qquad\qquad A_3 = aA_4 \cup bA_5$$
$$A_1 = bA_2 \cup aA_5, \qquad\qquad A_4 = \varepsilon \cup aA_5 \cup bA_5$$
$$A_2 = \varepsilon \cup aA_5 \cup bA_5, \qquad\quad A_5 = \emptyset$$

Thus we have a set of equations that hold for $L(M)$. We can solve them by substitution, giving $L(M) = ab \cup ba$.

Although the preceding technique appears to work well, a problem quickly arises. Consider the finite automaton given by Figure 2.41. Here we have

$$A_0 = aA_0 \cup bA_1$$
$$A_1 = \varepsilon$$

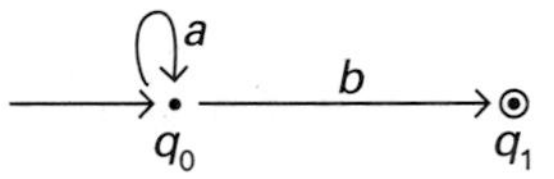

Figure 2.41

Solving by substitution, we get $A_0 = aA_0 \cup b$ and are unable to simplify further. The following lemma shows how to deal with this circumstance so that we get $A_0 = a^*b$ (as we expect by inspection of the transition diagram).

Lemma 2.8.2.   (Arden's Lemma) An equation of the form $X = AX \cup B$, where $\varepsilon \notin A$, has unique solution $X = A^*B$.

Proof. Note that $A^*B = (A^+ \cup \varepsilon)B = A^+B \cup B = A(A^*B) \cup B$. Thus A^*B is contained in any solution. Suppose that $X = A^*B \cup C$ is a solution, where $C \cap A^*B = \emptyset$. If we substitute this into the equation $X = AX \cup B$, we get

$$\begin{aligned} A^*B \cup C &= A(A^*B \cup C) \cup B \\ &= A^+B \cup AC \cup B \\ &= A^+B \cup B \cup AC \\ &= (A^+ \cup \varepsilon)B \cup AC \\ &= A^*B \cup AC \end{aligned}$$

Intersecting both sides with C gives $C = AC \cap C$ (all other terms are $\emptyset$). Thus $C \subseteq AC$. But, since $\varepsilon \notin A$, the shortest string in AC must be longer than the shortest string in C. This contracts $C \subseteq AC$ unless $C = \emptyset$. Thus we must have $C = \emptyset$, and so A^*B is the unique solution. ∎

Consider the finite automaton given by Figure 2.42. Here we have

$$A_0 = aA_1$$
$$A_1 = aA_2 \cup bA_4$$
$$A_2 = aA_3 \cup bA_4$$
$$A_3 = \varepsilon \cup aA_3 \cup bA_4$$

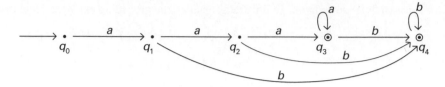

Figure 2.42

Substituting and applying Arden's lemma as necessary, we get

$$
\begin{aligned}
A_4 &= b^* \\
A_3 &= aA_3 \cup b^+ \cup \varepsilon \\
    &= a^*b^* \\
A_2 &= a^+b^* \cup b^+ \\
A_1 &= a(a^+b^* \cup b^+) \cup b^+ \\
    &= aa^+b^* \cup ab^+ \cup b^+ \\
A_0 &= aA_1 \\
    &= a^2a^+b^* \cup a^2b^+ \cup ab^+
\end{aligned}
$$

We then have the following lemma.

Lemma 2.8.3.   Let M be any finite automaton. Then there exists a regular expression r for which $L(r) = L(M)$.

Combining Lemma 2.8.3 with the remarks that preceded Theorem 2.8.1 we have Kleene's theorem.

Theorem 2.8.4.   (Kleene)   A language is regular if and only if it is accepted by a finite automaton.

Exercises for Section 2.8

2.8.1. Find an nfa that accepts ε.

2.8.2. Give an nfa to accept $\{a\}$. Give an nfa to accept $\{b\}$. Use the technique of this section to combine these nfa's into one that accepts the language $\{a, b\}$.

2.8.3. Find an nfa that accepts $(a \cup b)^* \cup (aba)^+$.

2.8.4. Find an nfa that accepts all strings of the form $bowwow, bowwowwow, bowwowwowwow, \ldots$. Find an nfa that accepts all strings of the form $ohmy, ohmyohmy, ohmyohmyohmy, \ldots$. Combine the two nfa's to accept the union of the languages. Note that the symbols in an alphabet need not be single characters.

2.8.5. Let M_1 be given by Figure 2.43 and M_2 be given by Figure 2.44. Give an nfa that accepts $L(M_1)L(M_2)$. Give an nfa that accepts $L(M_2)L(M_1)$.

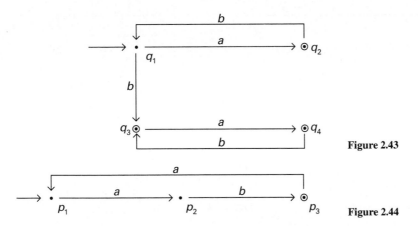

Figure 2.43

Figure 2.44

2.8.6. Let $M_1 = (\{q_1, q_2, q_3\}, \{a, b\}, \{q_1\}, \{q_1\}, \Delta_1)$ and $M_2 = (\{p_1, p_2, p_3, p_4\}, \{0, 1\}, \{p_1\},$ $\{p_1, p_2\}, \Delta_2)$, where Δ_1 and Δ_2 are given in the tables in Figure 2.45. Give an nfa that accepts $L(M_1)L(M_2)$. Give an nfa that accepts $L(M_2)L(M_1)L(M_1)$. Give an nfa that accepts $(L(M_1))^2 \cup L(M_1)$.

Δ_1	a	b
q_1	$\{q_2, q_3\}$	$\emptyset$
q_2	$\emptyset$	$\{q_1\}$
q_3	$\{q_3\}$	$\{q_3\}$

Δ_2	0	1
p_1	$\{p_2\}$	$\emptyset$
p_2	$\emptyset$	$\{p_3, p_4\}$
p_3	$\{p_2\}$	$\emptyset$
p_4	$\{p_3\}$	$\emptyset$

Figure 2.45

2.8.7. Find an nfa for $(ab)^*$ from the nfa's for $\{a\}$ and $\{b\}$.

2.8.8. Find an nfa for $(aa \cup b)^*(bb \cup a)^*$ from the nfa's for $\{a\}$ and $\{b\}$.

2.8.9. Find an nfa for
$$((a \cup b)(a \cup b))^* \cup ((a \cup b)(a \cup b)(a \cup b))^*$$
from the nfa's for $\{a\}$ and $\{b\}$.

2.8.10. If $M = (Q, \Sigma, s, F, \delta)$ is a *deterministic* finite automaton, then the complement of $L(M)$ [that is, $\Sigma^* - L(M)$] is accepted by the finite automaton $M' = (Q, \Sigma, s, Q - F, \delta)$. Is M' a dfa or an nfa? Find a dfa that accepts ab^*ab. Find a finite automaton that accepts $\{a, b\}^* - ab^*ab$.

2.8.11. Prove that $A_i = \bigcup_\sigma \{\sigma A_j \mid q_j \in \Delta(q_i, \sigma)\}$.

2.8.12. Give a regular expression for the languages accepted by the finite automaton of Figure 2.46.

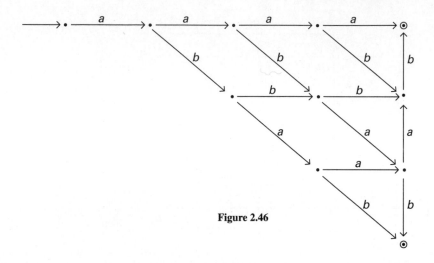

Figure 2.46

2.8.13. Find a regular expression for the dfa of Figure 2.47.

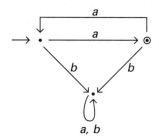

Figure 2.47

2.8.14. For each of the automata in Figure 2.48, find a regular expression for the language that is accepted.

a.)

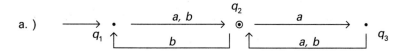

b.)

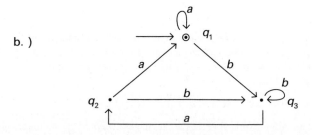

Figure 2.48

c.)

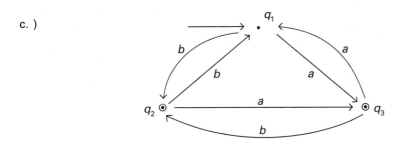

d.)

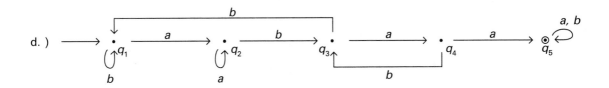

e.)

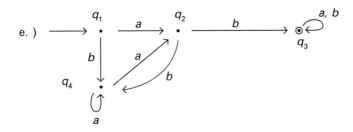

Figure 2.48 *(continued)*

2.9 PROPERTIES OF REGULAR LANGUAGES

The results of the last section establish the important connection between finite automata and regular expressions. Any statement true of regular languages is also true of the languages accepted by finite automata, and vice versa. Thus, for example, the collection of regular languages is closed with respect to concatenation, union, and star closure because the languages accepted by finite automata are (Theorem 2.8.1).

An important question that we can ask about regular languages is, given a language L, is L regular? Certainly, if L is finite, it is regular, for we may construct a regular expression or a finite automaton for it in a straightforward manner. Also, if L is specified either by a finite automaton or a regular expression, the answer is obvious. Unfortunately, relatively few languages are regular, and in the case of an infinite language, searching exhaustively for a regular expression or a finite automaton for it may be futile. In this case we need some property that all infinite regular languages share that is *not* present in any nonregular language.

Suppose a language is regular and so is accepted by some dfa $M = (Q, \Sigma, s, F, \delta)$, where Q contains n states. If $L(M)$ is infinite, we may find strings of length greater than n. Suppose that $w = a_1 a_2 \ldots a_{n+1}$ is one such string of length $n + 1$ in $L(M)$. If we let

$$q_1 = \delta(s, a_1)$$
$$q_2 = \delta(q_1, a_2)$$

and so on, we will account for $n+1$ states, $q_1, q_2, \ldots, q_{n+1}$. Since Q contains only n states, not all the q_i can be distinct. Hence for some indexes j and k, with $1 \le j < k \le n + 1$, we must have that $q_j = q_k$. Thus we have a cycle in the path from s to an accepting state of the form given in Figure 2.49.

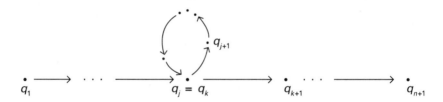

Figure 2.49

Since $j < k$, we have that the "middle part," that is, $a_{j+1} \ldots a_k$, has length *at least* 1. Also note that the string $w' = a_1 \ldots a_j a_{k+1} \ldots a_{n+1}$ must also be a string in $L(M)$. For that matter, we may go around the cycle any number of times so that $a_1 \ldots a_j (a_{j+1} \ldots a_k)^m a_{k+1} \ldots a_{n+1}$ is in $L(M)$ for any $m \ge 0$. That is, we may "pump" the middle part zero or more times and still have a string that is acceptable to the automaton. We formalize this in the following *pumping lemma*.

Lemma 2.9.1. Let L be an infinite regular language. Then there is a constant n with the property that, if w is any string in L of length greater than or equal to n, then we may write $w = uvx$ in such a way that $uv^i x \in L$ for all $i \ge 0$, with $\mid v \mid \ge 1$ and $\mid uv \mid \le n$.

The pumping lemma identifies a property that any regular language must possess and so gives us a way of determining if a language is not regular. To show that an infinite language is not regular, we show that for any large enough value of n at least one string having length n or greater fails to be "pumpable."

For example, consider the language

$$L = \{a^{i^2} \mid i \ge 1\}$$

Any string in L must have length that is a perfect square. Suppose that L is regular and let n be the constant given by the pumping lemma. Note that $a^{n^2} \in L$, and so by the pumping lemma we may write $a^{n^2} = uvx$ in some manner so that $1 \leq |v| \leq n$ and $uv^i x \in L$ for all $i \geq 1$. Then we have

$$
\begin{aligned}
n^2 &= |uvx| \\
&< |uv^2x| \\
&\leq n^2 + n \\
&< (n+1)^2
\end{aligned}
$$

That is, the length of uv^2x lies strictly between consecutive perfect squares and so is not a perfect square. Thus uv^2x cannot be in L. That is, L cannot be regular.

Example 2.9.1

As another example, consider the language $L = \{a^m b^m \mid m \geq 0\}$. L is clearly infinite, and so if L is regular we can apply the pumping lemma. Let n be the constant given by the lemma and consider $a^n b^n$, whose length is certainly greater than n. We may thus write $a^n b^n = uvx$ for some strings u, v, and x with $|v| \geq 1$ and $|uv| \leq n$. We concentrate on v, noting that $|uv| \leq n$ forces v to consist of only a's. Suppose that $v = a^s$ for $s \geq 1$. Then, if $u = a^r$, we have $x = a^{n-(r+s)} b^n$. It follows that $uv^2 x = a^r a^{2s} a^{n-(r+s)} b^n = a^{n+s} b^n$. Since $s \geq 1$, this string cannot be in L. Thus L cannot be regular since it fails to satisfy the pumping lemma.

That $\{a^n b^n \mid n \geq 0\}$ is not regular and so is not accepted by a finite automaton brings to light a common property of all regular languages. In scanning a string with a finite automaton, we have only the current symbol and the current state at our disposal. When scanning the b's, we do not have access to any information about how many a's were scanned.

Another way of saying this is that the amount of memory needed to accept or reject a string must be bounded. If we think of the states as memory, the finiteness of the collection of states forces the bounding. We could certainly construct a *nonfinite* state automaton to accept this language. It would consist of a start state that is also an accepting state, together with a path for *each* $a^n b^n$ for all $n > 0$. See Figure 2.50. Note that there are infinitely many states, so the memory is not bounded in this kind of automaton.

In addition to providing a tool for determining if a language is regular, the pumping lemma provides a means for determining if a finite automaton accepts *any* nonempty language at all and if the language it accepts is finite or infinite.

Theorem 2.9.2.   Let M be a finite automaton with k states.

1. $L(M) \neq \emptyset$ if and only if M accepts a string of length less than k.

2. $L(M)$ is infinite if and only if M accepts a string of length n, where $k \leq n < 2k$.

Proof.   **1.** If M accepts a string of length less than k, then certainly $L(M) \neq \emptyset$. Conversely, suppose that $L(M) \neq \emptyset$. Then there exists some $w \in L(M)$. We need to show that $L(M)$ contains a string of length less than k. If $|w| < k$, we are done. Suppose, instead, that $|w| \geq k$. From the discussion preceding Lemma 2.9.1, we know that there must be a

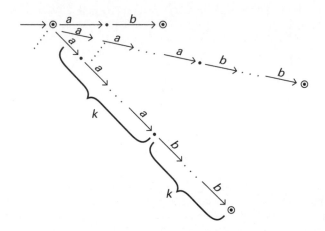

Figure 2.50

cycle in an accepting path for w, and so we may write $w = uvx$ for some strings u, v, and x, where u is the portion before the cycle, v is the portion *in* the cycle, and x is the portion *after* the cycle. Thus $|v| \geq 1$, and we must have $uv^i x \in L(M)$ for all $i \geq 0$. In particular, $ux \in L(M)$. If $|ux| < k$, we are done. Otherwise, apply the preceding process to ux. Note that $|ux| < |uvx|$, so repeated application of the preceding process, each time removing the "middle" subword, while still producing a string in $L(M)$, eventually yields a string of length less than k in $L(M)$.

2. Suppose that $w \in L(M)$ with $k \leq |w| < 2k$. In the discussion preceding Lemma 2.9.1, we established that M must have a cycle in its path that accepts w and thus that $w = uvx$ for some strings u, v, x with $|v| \geq 1$. Thus $uv^i x \in L(M)$ for all $i \geq 0$, and so $L(M)$ is infinite. Conversely, suppose that $L(M)$ is infinite. Then not all strings can have length less than k, and so some string $w \in L(M)$ has length at least k. If $|w| < 2k$, we are done. If not, then apply the construction from the discussion preceding Lemma 2.9.1 to w to get $w = uvx$, where $|v| \geq 1$ and $|uv| \leq k$ so that $|v| \leq k$. Now $|w| \geq 2k$ and $|v| \leq k$, forcing $|ux| \geq k$. As in Part 1, if $|ux| < 2k$, we are done. Otherwise, apply this process to ux repeatedly until a string of length between k and $2k - 1$ is found. ■

Theorem 2.9.2 provides us with procedures for deciding if $L(M)$ is empty and if $L(M)$ is finite or infinite. Since alphabets are finite collections, we may perform these procedures in finite time, and so we may assert that the procedures give algorithms for these problems. These algorithms are not particularly efficient, however. Faster determinations may be made for dfa's by removing all states not reachable from the initial state on *any* input. $L(M)$ is then nonempty if any final states remain. If we then delete all nonfinal states from which no final state can be reached and check for cycles, we may determine the finiteness or infiniteness of $L(M)$.

Problems at the end of the chapter explore another decision problem, the equivalence of regular languages.

Once we know some examples of nonregular languages, there are other techniques to check for regularity in addition to using the pumping lemma.

Suppose that L and K are some languages over Σ. From De Morgan's laws for sets we have that

$$(\Sigma^* - L) \cup (\Sigma^* - K) = \Sigma^* - (L \cap K)$$

Thus we have

$$
\begin{aligned}
L \cap K &= \Sigma^* - (\Sigma^* - (L \cap K)) \\
&= \Sigma^* - ((\Sigma^* - L) \cup (\Sigma^* - K))
\end{aligned}
$$

Now from Exercise 2.8.10 we know that, if L and K are accepted by a dfa, then $\Sigma^* - L$ and $\Sigma^* - K$ are also. Thus, if L and K are regular, then so are $\Sigma^* - L$ and $\Sigma^* - K$. We also know that the union of regular languages is regular so that $(\Sigma^* - L) \cup (\Sigma^* - K)$ is regular, and hence its complement $\Sigma^* - ((\Sigma^* - L) \cup (\Sigma^* - K))$ is regular. Thus $L \cap K$ is regular when L and K are.

Intersection is a useful tool in determining regularity for languages. For example, let $\Sigma = \{0, 1, 2, 3, 4, 5, 6, 7, 8, 9\}$. Then the language of nonnegative integers is given by $L_1 = 0 \cup \{1, 2, \ldots, 9\}\Sigma^*$. The language of all strings of digits ending in 0, 2, 4, 6, or 8 is given by $L_2 = \Sigma^*\{0, 2, 4, 6, 8\}$. Note that both L_1 and L_2 are regular. The language of all nonnegative integers divisible by 2 is given by $L = L_1 \cap L_2$ and so is regular, too.

Example 2.9.2

Let $\Sigma = \{a, b\}$. We will use intersection to show that the language $L = \{ww^R | w \in \Sigma^*\}$ is not regular. First, we note that by the pumping lemma $L_1 = \{a^n b^{2k} a^n | n, k \geq 0\}$ is not regular. Second, $L_2 = \{a^k b^n a^m | k, n, m \geq 0\}$ is regular (it is denoted by the regular expression $a^*b^*a^*$). Finally, note that $L_2 \cap L = L_1$. If L were regular, then L_1 would necessarily also be regular. Hence L cannot be regular.

Exercises for Section 2.9

2.9.1. Show that $\{a^p | p \text{ is prime}\}$ is not a regular language.

2.9.2. Show that $\{a^n ba^m ba^{n+m} | n, m \geq 1\}$ is not a regular language.

2.9.3. Determine if the following are regular languages or not and show or tell why or why not.

    (a) $\{a^i b^{2i} | i \geq 1\}$

    (b) $\{(ab)^i | i \geq 1\}$

    (c) $\{a^{2n} | n \geq 1\}$

    (d) $\{a^n b^m a^{n+m} | n, m \geq 1\}$

    (e) $\{a^{2^n} | n \geq 0\}$

    (f) $\{w | w = w^r \text{ for } w \in \{a, b\}^*\}$

    (g) $\{wxw^r | w, x \in \{a, b\}^+\}$

2.9.4. Use the procedure indicated in Theorem 2.9.2 to decide if $L(M)$ is finite or infinite for the finite automaton given by Figure 2.51.

2.9.5. Use the remarks following Theorem 2.9.2 to determine if the dfa given by Figure 2.52 accepts a nonempty language. If the language is nonempty, determine if the language it accepts is finite or infinite.

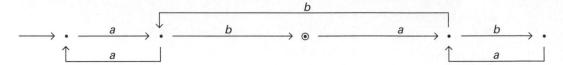

Figure 2.51

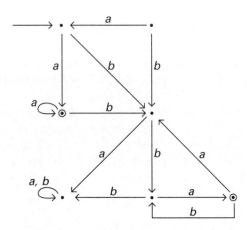

Figure 2.52

2.9.6. Let $\Sigma = \{a, b\}$.

(a) Construct dfa's for a^*b and ab^*.

(b) From the dfa's in part (a), construct dfa's that accept $\Sigma^* - a^*b$ and $\Sigma^* - ab^*$.

(c) From the dfa's in part (b), construct a *dfa* that accepts the union $(\Sigma^* - a^*b) \cup (\Sigma^* - ab^*)$.

(d) Use the result of part (c) to construct a dfa that accepts the language $a^*b \cap ab^*$.

2.9.7. The construction in Exercise 2.9.6, while effective, is not particularly efficient. In part (c) an nfa results from the union and must be transformed into a dfa before continuing. As a practical matter, we can directly construct the required dfa for the intersection of regular languages over the same alphabet by making use of Cartesian products. Let $M_1 = (Q_1, \Sigma, s_1, F_1, \delta_1)$ and $M_2 = (Q_2, \Sigma, s_2, F_2, \delta_2)$ be two dfa's. Define $M = (Q_1 \times Q_2, \Sigma, (s_1, s_2), F_1 \times F_2, \delta)$, where (s_1, s_2) denotes the ordered pair of states. The transition function δ is defined for all ordered pairs $(q_i, p_j) \in Q_1 \times Q_2$ and all $\sigma \in \Sigma$ by

$$\delta((q_i, p_j), \sigma) = (\delta_1(q_i, \sigma), \delta_2(p_j, \sigma))$$

(a) Construct dfa's for a^*b and ab^* over $\Sigma = \{a, b\}$.

(b) Use this technique to directly construct a dfa that accepts $a^*b \cap ab^*$.

2.9.8. Use the pumping lemma to show that L_1 of Example 2.9.2 is not regular.

2.9.9. Show $\{ww \mid w \in \{a, b\}^*\}$ is not regular.

2.10 APPLICATIONS OF REGULAR EXPRESSIONS AND FINITE AUTOMATA

Finite automata are frequently applied to problems involving analysis of strings of characters. Such problems include searching and identification problems, such as searching a file for an occurrence of a string or recognizing strings of input satisfying certain criteria. A finite automaton itself is a model of a procedure for recognizing a string given by the associated regular expression. Thus, in searching a file for a string, we systematically apply the finite automaton to the strings of the file until either it accepts a string or we exhaust the file.

A common problem in computer programming is that of ensuring that the data input to a program is correct. For example, if an unsigned integer input is expected and the user inadvertently miskeys one of the digits as a nondigit character, all levels of inappropriate results can occur from an abnormal termination to the calculation of incorrect results (garbage in garbage out). Careful programming attempts to "bulletproof" a program by including input routines that analyze the data as the user enters them and in some manner prevents the program from being applied to incorrect data. If we can construct a finite automaton that accepts only the strings that represent correct data, we then have a model for such an input analysis routine. Since finite automata correspond to regular expressions, the problem reduces to specifying correct data as regular expressions.

In the case of unsigned integer input, the language is given by $I = \{1, 2, 3, 4, 5, 6, 7, 8, 9\} \cdot \{0, 1, 2, 3, 4, 5, 6, 7, 8, 9\}^*$. Constructing a finite automaton that accepts I is straightforward (see Figure 2.53).

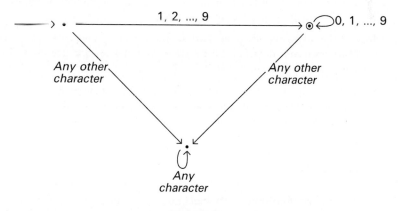

Figure 2.53

Translating the finite automaton into code in a programming language is also straightforward; we need only keep track of the current position in the string and the current state. As we move through the string, we change states accordingly, and when the string is exhausted, we check the terminating state and accept or reject the string.

Regular expressions can be used to specify the lexical units in a programming language. The associated finite automatons can be used to recognize these units (called

tokens). Such analysis is an important step in compiling a computer program. For example, let Σ be the character set of some computer language, that is, all characters that a compiler for that language must recognize. Let $L \subset \Sigma$ be the subcollection of all the letters and $D \subset \Sigma$ the subcollection of all the digits. Suppose that a comment in the language is begun by the characters "- -" and terminated by the end of line symbol, which we will denote eol. Then a regular expression for the token known as *comment* is
- -$(\Sigma$-eol$)^*$eol.

Similarly, the identifiers of the language may be composed of letters, digits, and underscores, must begin with a letter, and must end with a letter or a digit. A regular expression for these tokens can be given as $L(L \cup D \cup \_)^*(L \cup D)$. We can certainly construct a finite automaton to recognize this regular language and so can write appropriate code to recognize identifiers.

A concern in the lexical analysis phase of a compiler that was not present in the example of integer input is that in attempting to recognize a lexeme we usually have several different possibilities. For example, if the current string fails as a comment, we still would like to check it as an identifier and possibly as other tokens if it fails there. Generally, in a compiler the finite automata for all the tokens are ordered in some manner and systematically applied to the current string until one succeeds in accepting it, or all fail. If all fail, the string is not part of a correctly formed program.

Exercises for Section 2.10

2.10.1. Write code in your favorite programming language to implement the finite automaton of Figure 2.53.

2.10.2. Write code in your favorite programming language to implement a finite automaton that accepts only signed and unsigned integers.

2.10.3. Write a routine in your favorite programming language that identifies signed and unsigned *real* numbers (for simplicity you may assume that the real numbers are not in exponentiated form, that is, 1.23e–9).

2.10.4. Write a routine in your favorite programming language that will identify a string as a signed or unsigned integer, a signed or unsigned real number, a comment, or an identifier (see the example preceding the exercises).

PROBLEMS

2.1. The Moore algorithm. We know that if L_1 and L_2 are regular languages over Σ, then $\Sigma^* - L_1$ and $\Sigma^* - L_2$ are regular languages and consequently so are $L_1 \cap (\Sigma^* - L_2)$ and $L_2 \cap (\Sigma^* - L_1)$.

Let $L = (L_1 \cap (\Sigma^* - L_2)) \cup (L_2 \cap (\Sigma^* - L_1))$ and note that since L is regular it so is accepted by a dfa M. By Theorem 2.9.2, we can determine if M accepts any string (that is, if $L = \emptyset$ or not). But note that if M accepts a string then L contains a string and so not both of $L_1 \cap (\Sigma^* - L_2)$ and $L_2 \cap (\Sigma^* - L_1)$ can be empty.

Suppose that we have $L_1 \cap (\Sigma^* - L_2) \neq \emptyset$. Then some string is in L_1 and not in L_2, and so $L_1 \neq L_2$. In the same manner, if $L_2 \cap (\Sigma^* - L_1) \neq \emptyset$, we also determine that $L_1 \neq L_2$. On the other hand, if M accepts no string, then $L = \emptyset$, and so both $L_1 \cap (\Sigma^* - L_2)$

and $L_2 \cap (\Sigma^* - L_1)$ are empty. That is, there is no string in L_1 that is not in L_2, and vice versa, and so $L_1 = L_2$.

We have shown that there is an algorithm to determine if two regular languages are the same. Our algorithm is not particularly efficient, however, for we first have to form the language L, find a dfa for it, and then determine if that dfa accepts a string. A much less complex algorithm, due to Moore, is given next.

Suppose that M and M' are two dfa's over the alphabet Σ. To keep the presentation as simple as possible, assume that $\Sigma = \{a, b\}$. We first rename the states of M and M' so that all states are distinct. Suppose that q_1 and q_1' are the initial states of M and M', respectively.

We construct a comparison table consisting (in this case) of three columns. Entries in each column are pairs of states (q, q'), one from M and one from M'. The entry in column 1 simply names the pair of states that this row of the table deals with. The entry in column 2 is the pair of states that follows those in column 1 on an a transition. Likewise, the pair in column 3 is the next states on a b transition.

Thus, if (q, q') is an entry in column 1 and (p, p') and (r, r') are the entries in columns 2 and 3 of that row, then $\delta(q, a) = p$, $\delta'(q', a) = p'$, $\delta(q, b) = r$, and $\delta'(q', b) = r'$ are all transitions in M and M'. We construct the table a row at a time, starting with (q_1, q_1') as the entry in column 1 of the first row. In general if (q, q') is in column 1 of any row, we fill in column 2 and column 3 appropriately. If either of the entries in column 2 or 3 do not already appear in column 1, we add them before we proceed to the next row.

If we ever reach a pair (p, p') in the table (in any column) for which p is a final state of M, but p' is not a final state for M' (or vice versa), we stop the process, for we have found that M and M' are not equivalent. Otherwise, the process stops when there are no uncompleted rows. In this case, M and M' are equivalent.

For example, the dfa's in Figure 2.54 are not equivalent because their table is (partially) as follows:

| | a Transition | b Transition |
Column 1	Column 2	Column 3
(q_1, q_1')	(q_1, q_1')	(q_2, q_2')
(q_2, q_2')	(q_3, q_4')	(q_1, q_3')

Although the table is not complete, we terminate the process because q_1 is a final state of the first dfa, but q_3' is not a final state of the second. Thus these dfa's are not equivalent.

The Moore algorithm extends appropriately to any alphabet Σ. We simply include a column for each symbol of Σ.

1. Are the dfa's of Figure 2.55 on page 76 equivalent?

2. Are the dfa's of Figure 2.56 on page 77 equivalent?

2.2. Consider the dfa given by Figure 2.57 on page 77. Note that certain states behave the same way for all input strings. For example, if we are in q_2 or q_8 and scan any nonempty input string, we wind up in the same resulting state. In some sense the presence of both q_2 and q_8 in this dfa is redundant.

It is often convenient to find a dfa for a language that is a *minimal* dfa in the sense that it has a minimum number of states. Essentially, what we do is eliminate all redundant (in the preceding sense) states.

Let $M = (Q, \Sigma, s, F, \delta)$ be a dfa. States p and q are *distinguishable* if for some string x in Σ^* we have $\delta(p, x) \in F$ and $\delta(q, x) \notin F$, or vice versa. If all pairs of states

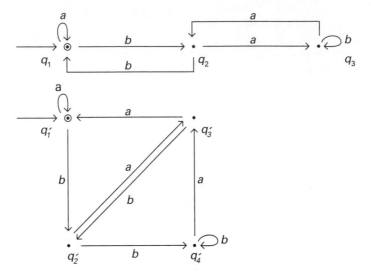

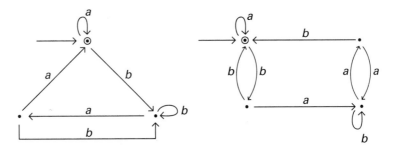

Figure 2.54

Figure 2.55

are distinguishable, M has no redundant states and so is already a minimum state dfa. On the other hand, if M contains one or more collections of indistinguishable states, we may eliminate redundancy by replacing each such collection by a single state.

We can find pairs of equivalent (indistinguishable) states by means of a table in which each row and column corresponds to a state. We initially mark all entries corresponding to a final and a nonfinal state as distinguishable. Then, for each pair of states p and q not known to be distinguishable, we consider $p_a = \delta(p, a)$ and $q_a = \delta(q, a)$ for each $a \in \Sigma$. If p_a and q_a are distinguishable by means of the string x, then p and q are distinguishable by means of the string ax.

Thus, if the entry corresponding to p_a and q_a is marked for some a, we mark the entry for p and q. If for every $a \in \Sigma$ the entry for p_a and q_a is unmarked, we place (p, q) on a list associated with (p_a, q_a) for all a. At some future time, if p_a and q_a are found to be distinguishable, we then mark the entry for p and q as well. We need less than half of the table because entries symmetric about the diagonal correspond to the same pairs of states. Moreover, entries on the diagonal are known to be indistinguishable.

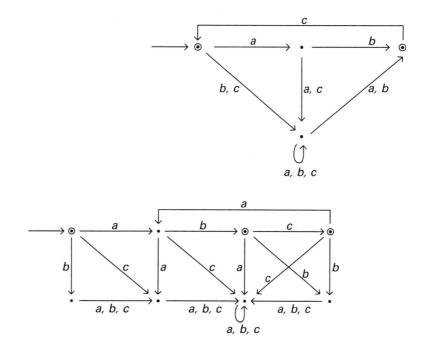

Figure 2.56

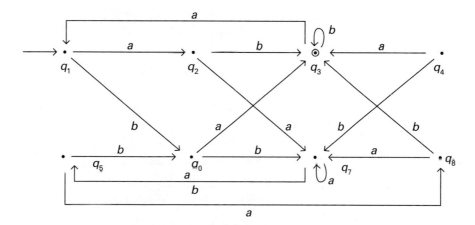

Figure 2.57

For the dfa of the preceding example, the table is as follows:

q_2	x					
q_3	x	x				
q_4	x	x	x			
q_5		x	x	x		
q_6	x	x	x		x	
q_7	x	x	x	x	x	x
q_8	x		x	x	x	x	x
	q_1	q_2	q_3	q_4	q_5	q_6	q_7

The collections of indistinguishable states are $\{q_1, q_5\}$, $\{q_2, q_8\}$, $\{q_4, q_6\}$, $\{q_3\}$, and $\{q_7\}$. In the reduced dfa that results, we replace each collection of indistinguishable states by a single state. Thus the reduced dfa for our example is given by Figure 2.58.

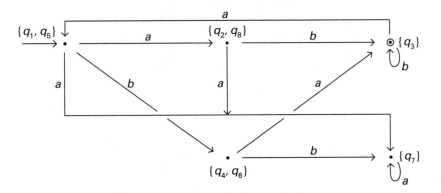

Figure 2.58

1. Find minimum state dfa's corresponding to the dfa's of Figure 2.59.

2.3. Let $\Sigma = \{(a, b, c) \mid a, b, c \in \{0, 1\}\}$ be the alphabet consisting of all 3-tuples of 0's and 1's. Let us view each 3-tuple as a column vector, that is, $\begin{pmatrix} 0 \\ 1 \\ 0 \end{pmatrix}$. Then a binary addition such as

$$
\begin{array}{r}
0011 \\
+ \quad 0101 \\
\hline
1000
\end{array}
$$

could be viewed as the string $\begin{pmatrix} 0 \\ 0 \\ 1 \end{pmatrix} \begin{pmatrix} 0 \\ 1 \\ 0 \end{pmatrix} \begin{pmatrix} 1 \\ 0 \\ 0 \end{pmatrix} \begin{pmatrix} 1 \\ 1 \\ 0 \end{pmatrix}$ over Σ.

1. Show that the language L_1 over Σ, which consists of all strings that represent "correct" binary additions, is a regular language.

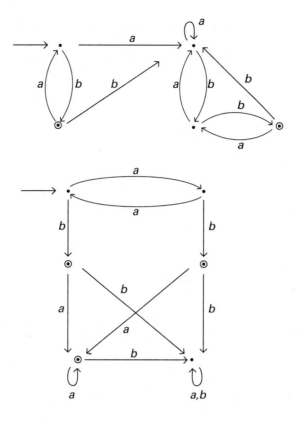

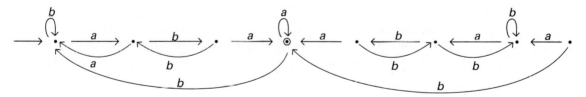

Figure 2.59

2. Use the pumping lemma (Lemma 2.9.1) to prove that the language L_2 consisting of all strings that represent correct binary multiplications is not regular.

There are a number of ways in which we may treat addition. When we perform addition, we generally add corresponding pairs of digits and carry-in values to generate a result digit and a carry-out value. Consider binary addition where the carry-in value is either 0 or 1. If the carry-in value is 0, then a carry-out is generated only if the pair of corresponding digits consists of two 1's. If the carry-in value is 1, then the only way that the carry out is *not* 1 is if the pair of corresponding digits from the addends is two 0's.

Let us use notation $(x, y)/z$ to denote the pair of digits (x, y) from the addends, and z denotes the digit that results on adding $x + y + $ (existing carry). Then binary addition may be represented by the diagram in Figure 2.60. Note that this diagram very closely resembles a transition diagram for a finite automaton. In fact, we have two distinct states corresponding to the carry value, transitions between states that depend on the digits to be added (input) as well as the current carry value (state), and a distinct start state (the carry is initially 0). The only real difference between this diagram and the transition diagram of a finite automaton is that here we have represented an "output" in the form of a result of the addition.

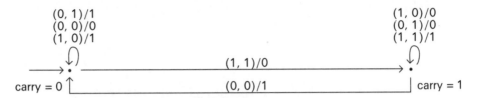

Figure 2.60

A *deterministic finite state transducer* is a 6-tuple $M = (Q, \Sigma, \Gamma, s, \delta, \tau)$, where Q is a finite set of states containing a distinguished start state s; Σ and Γ are alphabets with Σ the *input* alphabet and Γ the *output* alphabet; δ is the transition function, where $\delta : Q \times \Sigma \to Q$; and τ is the *output* function, where $\tau : Q \times \Sigma \to \Gamma$.

Note that, as with the finite automata of the chapter, δ depends on the current state and the current input symbol. τ also depends on the current state and input and tells what the output is.

An important observation is that there is no set of final states. Transducers are not concerned with accepting their input, but rather with transforming it into an output. In this sense a transducer maps input strings to output strings. That is, it computes a *string function* from Σ^* to Γ^*.

3. Consider a vending machine that sells cans of soda. For simplicity, assume that there is one selection button and that soda costs $0.30. Also assume that, once $0.30 has been put into the machine, any additional coins that are inserted will be returned. Devise a deterministic finite state transducer that models the vending machine's behavior.

4. How might a deterministic finite state transducer be constructed to *accept* a language?

2.4. Characterization of regular languages. $L \subseteq a^*$. In Section 2.9 and its exercises, we saw a number of nonregular languages of the form

$$\{a^i \mid i \text{ satisfies some condition}\}$$

On the other hand, many languages of this form *are* regular, for example, the languages $L_k = \{a^{k+i} \mid i \geq 0\}$ for $k = 0, 1, \ldots$. A reasonable question to ask is under what conditions a language of this form is regular. In this problem we establish a result that answers this question.

An *arithmetic progression* is a sequence of equally spaced natural numbers. For example, $\{4, 7, 10, \ldots\}$ is an arithmetic progression. Each arithmetic progression has two parameters that completely determine it; the starting point p and the common difference q. We may define an arithmetic progression in terms of these two parameters:

$$A_{pq} = \{x \mid x = p + nq \text{ for some } n \in \mathbb{N}\}$$

Note that under this definition a set containing a single natural number is an arithmetic progression with $q = 0$. Thus, for example, $\{3\}$ is the arithmetic progression A_{30}.

1. Let A_{pq} be an arithmetic progression. Show that the language L is regular where

$$L = \{a^i | i \in A_{pq}\}$$

A set of natural numbers X is said to be *ultimately periodic* if X is either finite or if there are two natural numbers $n_0 \geq 0$ and $t \geq 1$ for which, if $x \geq n_0$, then $x \in X$, if and only if $x + t \in X$. For example, the set $\{2, 3, 7, 14, 103, 109, 115, 121, \ldots\}$ is ultimately periodic with $n_0 = 103$ and $t = 6$. Note that any arithmetic progression A_{pq} is ultimately periodic since, if $x > p$, then $x \in A_{pq}$ if and only if $x = p + nq$ for some n, if and only if $x + q = p + (n + 1)q \in A_{pq}$. That is, we can take $n_0 = p$ and $t = q$.

2. Show that the union of two arithmetic progressions is an ultimately periodic set.

3. Show that the union of an ultimately periodic set X with an arithmetic progression A_{pq} is an ultimately periodic set.

Note that exercises 2 and 3 imply that any finite union of arithmetic progressions is an ultimately periodic set.

4. Show that any ultimately periodic set X is the union of finitely many arithmetic progressions. *Hints:* Obviously, if X is finite you are done. Assume that X is infinite. The set $\{x | x < n_0\}$ is finite. What relationship exists between the finite set $\{x | n_0 \leq x < n_0 + t\}$ and the set $\{x | x \geq n_0 + t\}$?

The result of exercises 3 and 4 is that a set X is ultimately periodic if and only if it is a union of finitely many arithmetic progressions.

5. Show that, if $L \subseteq a^*$ and $\{i \mid a^i \in L\}$ is ultimately periodic, then L is regular.

6. Show that if $L \subseteq a^*$ is regular, then $\{i \mid a^i \in L\}$ is ultimately periodic. *Hint:* Apply exercise 4 and the pumping lemma.

7. Use exercises 5 and 6 to show that the language

$$L = \{a^{n^2} \mid n \geq 1\}$$

is not regular. *Hint:* Consider the set

$$X = \{n^2 \mid n \geq 1\}$$

Is this set ultimately periodic?

8. Apply exercises 5 and 6 to show that the following languages are not regular:

(a) $\{a^{2^n} \mid n \geq 1\}$

(b) $\{a^p \mid p \text{ is a prime}\}$

(c) $\{a^{n!} \mid n \geq 1\}$

2.5. Homomorphisms and Substitution. Theorem 2.8.1 establishes certain closure properties of regular languages: the collection of regular languages is closed with respect to union, concatenation, and star closure. In this problem we investigate two other closure properties of this class of languages.

Let Σ_1 and Σ_2 be alphabets. A *substitution* associates each symbol $a \in \Sigma_1$ with a language $S \subseteq \Sigma_2^*$. Formally, we may define a substitution as a function $f \colon \Sigma_1 \to 2^{\Sigma_2^*}$ so that $f(a_i) = S_i$, where $a_i \in \Sigma_1$ and $S_i \subseteq \Sigma_2^*$. We extend substitution to strings and languages over Σ_1 by

$$f(\varepsilon) = \varepsilon$$
$$f(wa) = f(w)f(a)$$

where $w \in \Sigma_1^*$ and $a \in \Sigma_1$.

As an example, let $\Sigma_1 = \{a, b\}$ and $\Sigma_2 = \{0, 1\}$. Define $f(a) = \{011\}^*$ and $f(b) = \{1001, 01101\}$. Then

$$f(aba) = \{011\}^*\{1001, 01101\}\{011\}^*$$

$$f(ab^*) = \bigcup_{i=0}^{\infty} f(ab^i) = \bigcup_{i=0}^{\infty} f(a)f(b^i) = \bigcup_{i=0}^{\infty}\{011\}^*\{1001, 01101\}^i$$

$$= \{011\}^* \bigcup_{i=0}^{\infty}\{1001, 01101\}^i = \{011\}^*\{1001, 01101\}^*$$

1. Let Σ_1 and Σ_2 be alphabets and f a substitution, where, for each $a \in \Sigma_1$, $f(a) = R_a \subseteq \Sigma_2^*$ is a regular language. Let a and b be in Σ_1.

   (a) Show that $f(a \cup b) = f(a) \cup f(b)$.

   (b) Show that $f(a^*) = f(a)^*$.

   (c) Let $R \subseteq \Sigma_1$ be a regular language. Show that $f(R)$ is a regular language. *Hint:* Induct on the number of operators in a regular expression for R.

Suppose that f is a substitution in which, for each $a \in \Sigma_1$, $f(a)$ contains only one string. Such a substitution is called a *homomorphism*. If $L \subseteq \Sigma_1^*$, we say that $f(L)$ is the *homomorphic image* of the language L. If $L \subseteq \Sigma_2^*$, we say that $f^{-1}(L)$ is the *inverse homomorphic image* of the language L.

For example, let $f: \{a, b, c\} \rightarrow \{a, b\}^*$ be defined as $f(a) = a$, $f(b) = ba$, and $f(c) = a$. Then, if $L_1 = a^*(b \cup c)^*$, we have $f(L_1) = a^*(ba \cup a)^*$. If $L_2 = (aba \cup a)^*$, then $f^{-1}(L_2) = ((a \cup c)a \cup (a \cup c))^*$. [Note that $f(a) = f(c) = a$ so that $f^{-1}(a) = a \cup c$.] Here L_2 is a regular language and $f^{-1}(L_2)$ is also a regular language. This is no coincidence, as exercise 2 will show.

2. Show that, if L is a regular language and f is a homomorphism, then $f^{-1}(L)$ is a regular language.

The statement in exercise 2 can actually be made more general. If f is a substitution, then $f^{-1}(L)$ is regular if L is regular. Combining exercises 1 and 2, we have that the class of regular languages is closed with respect to homomorphic image and inverse homomorphic image.

Since homomorphisms and their inverses "preserve" regularity, we may use them to determine if a language is regular or not. The idea here is to take a language whose regularity is unknown and try to transform it into a known regular or nonregular language by means of homomorphisms.

For example, the language $\{a^n b^n | n \geq 1\}$ is known to be not regular. Consider the language $L = \{a^n b a^n | n \geq 1\}$. While the pumping lemma could be applied to deduce that L is not regular, we can arrive at the same conclusion by means of homomorphism. Suppose that L *is* regular. Let $f: \{a, b, c\} \rightarrow \{a, b\}^*$ be the homomorphism defined previously, and consider $L_1 = f^{-1}(L) = f^{-1}(\{a^n b a^n | n \geq 1\})$. Since $f^{-1}(a) = a \cup c$, we have that

$$f^{-1}(a^n b a^n) = \{a^i c^j a^k c^l b a^r c^s a^t c^u \mid i + j + k + l = n \text{ and } r + s + t + u + 1 = n\}$$

Thus

$$f^{-1}(L) = \{a^i c^j a^k c^l b a^r c^s a^t c^u | i + j + k + l = r + s + t + u + 1\}$$

Then

$$f^{-1}(L) \cap a^* b c^* = \{a^n b c^{n-1} | n \geq 1\}$$

Since a^*bc^* is clearly regular and since we are assuming that L is regular and hence $f^{-1}(L)$ is regular, we must have that $\{a^n bc^{n-1}|n \geq 1\}$ is also regular. Now let $g : \{a, b, c\} \to \{a, b\}^*$ be the homomorphism defined by $g(a) = a$ and $g(b) = g(c) = b$. Then we have

$$g(f^{-1}(L) \cap a^*bc^*) = g(\{a^n bc^{n-1}|n \geq 1\}) = \{a^n b^n |n \geq 1\}$$

Since g is a homomorphism, we must have that $\{a^n b^n |n \geq 1\}$ is regular, a contradiction. Thus it cannot be the case that $\{a^n ba^n |n \geq 1\}$ is regular.

3. Show that $\{a^i b^j c^i |i \geq j \geq 1\}$ is not regular.

4. Show that $\{a^i ba^j |i \neq j$ and $i, j \geq 1\}$ is not regular.

3

Context-free Languages

3.1 REGULAR GRAMMARS

Regular expressions and finite automata provide us with two means of specifying or defining languages. Regular expressions provide us with a template or pattern for the strings of the language. All strings matching a particular pattern, and only those strings, constitute that particular regular language. Similarly, a finite automaton specifies a language as the set of all strings that move it from its initial state to one of its accepting states. We might also view a finite automaton as a generator of strings in the language in the following sense. A symbol is *generated* by traversing the path labeled by that symbol from the current state to the next. We begin with the empty string and end up with a string in the language when the traversal ends in an accepting state.

As an example, consider the finite automaton given by the transition diagram in Figure 3.1. This finite automaton accepts the regular language $a(a^* \cup b^*)b$. Think of starting in the initial state and traversing this diagram in some manner. When a path is taken from one state to another, "output" the symbol labeling that path. Thus we could output the string aa^2b by moving from state q_1 to q_2 to q_3 to q_3 to q_3 to q_5. It is easy to see that such strings generated in this manner are strings accepted by this finite automaton. Moreover, any string accepted by this finite automaton may be generated by this method.

Note that any strings in the preceding language consist of an a followed by some "end part." If we let E stand for the end part, we may symbolically represent this observation by $S \rightarrow aE$. The arrow $\rightarrow$ might be read as "can be" or "consists of." The end part of such a string consists of one of two arrangements of a's and b's. Thus we may write $E \rightarrow A$ and $E \rightarrow B$ to indicate the multiple possibilities for E. The two

84

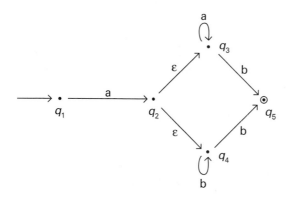

Figure 3.1

arrangements of a's and b's may be expressed as $A \rightarrow aA$ together with $A \rightarrow b$ to indicate a string of a's followed by a b or as $B \rightarrow bB$ together with $B \rightarrow b$, indicating a string of b's followed by another b.

Summarizing, we have the expressions

$$S \rightarrow aE$$
$$E \rightarrow A$$
$$E \rightarrow B$$
$$A \rightarrow b$$
$$A \rightarrow aA$$
$$B \rightarrow b$$
$$B \rightarrow bB$$

These expressions may be viewed as *replacement rules* when generating strings. The symbol on the left of the arrow may be replaced by the string on the right.

For example, we may generate aab by starting with S, replacing it by aE, replacing the E by aA, and finally replacing the A by b. We have a sequence of strings beginning with S and ending with aab. At each step the uppercase letters (S, E, and A) represent the, as yet, ungenerated part of the final string. Under these circumstances it makes sense to interpret the arrow in the preceding expressions as "is replaced by."

Finally, let us introduce the symbol | to be read as "or." Using this symbol, the two rules $E \rightarrow A$ and $E \rightarrow B$ can be combined as $E \rightarrow A|B$, as can other rules. The preceding collection of rules for generating strings may then be rewritten as follows:

1. $S \rightarrow aE$
2. $E \rightarrow A \mid B$
3. $A \rightarrow aA \mid B$
4. $B \rightarrow bB \mid b$

The string a^3b may be generated from S by first applying rule 1 to get aE, then rule 2 to get aA, and then rule 3 to get aaA and $aaaA$; finally, the second part of rule 3 can be applied to get $aaab$. We write a description of this process of generation as

$$S \Rightarrow aE \Rightarrow aA \Rightarrow aaA \Rightarrow aaaA \Rightarrow aaab$$

where the double arrow $\Rightarrow$ is read as "derives," "produces," or "generates." We use the notation $S \stackrel{*}{\Rightarrow} w$ to indicate that the string w is derivable from S in 0 or more steps.

Notice that in this model we have introduced a collection of new symbols to represent ungenerated portions of strings. When strings are fully generated, they consist totally of symbols from the alphabet Σ, but before that time they are strings of both alphabet symbols and these new symbols. The new symbols are called *nonterminals*, reflecting the fact that they must be replaced by some string of alphabet symbols before a string in the language has been completely generated. Alphabet symbols from Σ, on the other hand, are called *terminals*, reflecting that for them replacement is impossible. Also, note that the symbol used to represent a completely ungenerated string in the language is necessarily a nonterminal. Finally, notice that we have generated strings in the language from left to right—we must only have nonterminals as the rightmost symbol in the replacement strings for the replacement rules given. This reflects the way in which a finite automaton would recognize a language string.

We make the following definition:

Definition 3.1.1.   A *regular grammar* G is a 4-tuple $G = (\Sigma, N, S, P)$, where Σ is an alphabet, N is a collection of nonterminal symbols, S is some particular nonterminal called the *start symbol*, and P is a collection of replacement rules, called *productions*, of the form $A \rightarrow w$, where $A \in N$ and w is some string over $\Sigma \cup N$ satisfying:

1. w contains at most one nonterminal.

2. If w contains a nonterminal, then it appears as the rightmost symbol of w.

The *language generated* by the regular grammar G is denoted $L(G)$.

For example, consider the regular grammar $G = (\Sigma, N, S, P)$, where

$$\begin{aligned}
\Sigma &= \{a, b\} \\
N &= \{S, A\} \\
P : S &\rightarrow bA \\
A &\rightarrow aaA \,|\, b \,|\, \varepsilon
\end{aligned}$$

Note that $L(G)$ contains all strings of the form $ba^{2n}b$ and ba^{2n}. That is, $L(G) = b(a^2)^*(b \cup \varepsilon)$. This may be proved by using induction on n to show that any string of the form $ba^{2n}b$ or ba^{2n} is in $L(G)$ and then inducting on the length of a derivation to show that $L(G)$ is contained in $b(a^2)^*(b \cup \varepsilon)$. (Note that the basis step is for a derivation of length 2.)

From the definition we must have that the right-hand side of any production is a string in $\Sigma^*(N \cup \varepsilon)$. Note that ε is therefore a legitimate right-hand side for a production. In the preceding example, the production $A \rightarrow \varepsilon$ ends the generation of a string (as does the production $A \rightarrow b$) because the nonterminal A is "erased."

Since productions pair nonterminals in N with strings in $\Sigma^*(N \cup \varepsilon)$, it is often convenient to represent them as ordered pairs in $N \times \Sigma^*(N \cup \varepsilon)$. Thus the pair (x, y) in

$N \times \Sigma^*(N \cup \varepsilon)$ represents the production $x \to y$. The productions in P of the previous example could be given as

$$P = \{(S, bA), (A, aaA), (A, b), (A, \varepsilon)\}$$

If we agree to write nonterminals as uppercase letters and terminals as lowercase letters and further agree to use S uniformly as the start symbol, we may then specify a regular grammar completely in terms of its productions. Thus, for example, $S \to aS|b$ completely specified the regular grammar that generates the language a^*b.

Exercises for Section 3.1

3.1.1. Use the rules of Figure 3.1 to derive ab, ab^3, aa^3b. Is it possible to derive $abab$?

3.1.2. Suppose that we have the rules $S \to aS|bT$ and $T \to aa$. Give a derivation for $abaa$, $aabaa$, and $aaabaa$. Show how to derive a^kba^2 for $k \geq 1$. Is it possible to derive the strings $baa, b,$ or aa?

3.1.3. Find a regular grammar for the following languages:

(a) $a^*b \cup a$

(b) $a^*b \cup b^*a$

(c) $(a^*b \cup b^*a)^*$

3.1.4. The regular grammar given by

$$S \to bA|aB|\varepsilon$$
$$A \to abaS$$
$$B \to babS$$

generates a regular language. Give a regular expression for this language.

3.1.5. In our definition of regular grammars, the right-hand sides of productions can contain a nonterminal in only the rightmost position (when any nonterminal is present). This corresponds to generating strings from left to right. For this reason, what we have termed regular grammar may also be called a *right-regular grammar*. A *left-regular grammar* is one in which the strings are generated from the right; that is, the productions are pairs from $N \times (N \cup \Sigma)\Sigma^*$.

(a) Find a left-regular grammar for the language $\{a^nbaa|n \geq 0\}$.

(b) Find both a left- and a right-regular grammar for

$$\{w \in \{a, b, c\}^*|w \text{ ends in } b \text{ and every} c \text{ is immediately followed by an } a\}$$

(c) For any (left or right) regular grammar $G = (\Sigma, N, S, P)$, we can define the *reverse* of G as $G^R = (\Sigma, N, S, P')$, where

$$P' = \{(A, x^R)|(A, x) \in P\}$$

Thus, if $A \to aB$ is a production in G, then $A \to Ba$ is a production in G^R. Suppose that G is a right-regular grammar.

i. Show that G^R is a left-regular grammar.

ii. Show that $w \in L(G)$ if and only if $w^R \in L(G^R)$ by inducting on the number of productions used to produce w.

As a result of part (c), we may conclude that the class of languages generated by left-regular grammars is the same as the class of languages generated by right-regular grammars. For this reason, the term *regular grammar* is often applied to any grammar that is either left or right regular.

3.2 REGULAR GRAMMARS AND REGULAR LANGUAGES

Suppose L is a regular language. We may find a regular grammar that generates L by working with any dfa $M = (Q, \Sigma, s, F, \delta)$ for which $L = L(M)$. We define $G = (N, \Sigma, S, P)$ by

$$N = Q$$
$$\Sigma = \Sigma$$
$$S = s$$
$$P = \{(q, ap)|\delta(q, a) = p\} \cup \{(q, \varepsilon)|q \in F\}$$

That is, $q \to ap$ whenever $\delta(q, a) = p$, and $q \to \varepsilon$ if q is an accepting state of the dfa.

For example, the dfa given by Figure 3.2 accepts the language a^*b. The corresponding regular grammar has productions

$$q_1 \to aq_1 \mid bq_2$$
$$q_2 \to aq_3 \mid bq_3 \mid \varepsilon$$
$$q_3 \to aq_3 \mid bq_3$$

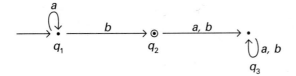

Figure 3.2

In this grammar the q_i are nonterminals (a break with our usual notation, which can be easily fixed by renaming the q_i and q_1 as the start symbol).

Note that $w \in L(M)$ for $w = \sigma_1\sigma_2\ldots\sigma_n$ means that

$$\delta(s, \sigma_1\sigma_2\ldots\sigma_n) = p$$

for some $p \in F$. If we write $q_{i+1} = \delta(q_i, \sigma_i)$ with $q_1 = s$, then we have

$$\begin{aligned}
\delta(s, \sigma_1\sigma_2\ldots\sigma_n) &= \delta(q_1, \sigma_1\sigma_2\ldots\sigma_n) \\
&= \delta(q_2, \sigma_2\ldots\sigma_n) \\
&= \delta(q_3, \sigma_3\ldots\sigma_n) \\
&\quad\ldots \\
&= \delta(q_n, \sigma_n) \\
&= p \in F
\end{aligned}$$

Now, since $q_{i+1} = \delta(q_i, \sigma_i)$, we have $q_i \to \sigma_i q_{i+1}$ in G, and so (since $s = q_1$)

$$
\begin{aligned}
s = q_1 &\Rightarrow \sigma_1 q_2 \\
&\Rightarrow \sigma_1 \sigma_2 q_3 \\
&\cdots \\
&\Rightarrow \sigma_1 \sigma_2 \ldots \sigma_n p \\
&\Rightarrow \sigma_1 \sigma_2 \ldots \sigma_n
\end{aligned}
$$

So $w \in L(M)$ gives that w is generated by G; that is, $L(M) \subseteq L(G)$.

Conversely, if w is generated by G, say by the derivation

$$
\begin{aligned}
q_1 &\Rightarrow \sigma_1 q_2 \\
&\Rightarrow \sigma_1 \sigma_2 q_3 \\
&\cdots \\
&\Rightarrow \sigma_1 \sigma_2 \ldots \sigma_n p \\
&\Rightarrow \sigma_1 \sigma_2 \ldots \sigma_n
\end{aligned}
$$

then we must have, in M,

$$
\begin{aligned}
\delta(s, \sigma_1 \sigma_2 \ldots \sigma_n) &= \delta(q_1, \sigma_1 \sigma_2 \ldots \sigma_n) \\
&= \delta(q_2, \sigma_2 \ldots \sigma_n) \\
&= \delta(q_3, \sigma_3 \ldots \sigma_n) \\
&\cdots \\
&= \delta(q_n, \sigma_n) \\
&= p \in F
\end{aligned}
$$

(since $s = q_1$). Thus $w \in L(G)$ forces $w \subset L(M)$, and we have $L(G) \subseteq L(M)$. It follows then that $L(G) = L(M)$.

It is also possible to start with a regular grammar G and construct an nfa M so that $L(G) = L(M)$. Let $G = (N, \Sigma, S, P)$ be a regular grammar and define $M = (Q, \Sigma, s, F, \Delta)$ by

$$
\begin{aligned}
Q &= N \cup \{f\}, \quad \text{where } f \text{ is a new symbol} \\
s &= S \\
F &= \{f\}
\end{aligned}
$$

and Δ is constructed from the productions in P as follows:

1. If $A \to \sigma_1 \ldots \sigma_n B$ is a production in P with nonterminals A and B, then add to Q new states $q_1, q_2, \ldots, q_{n-1}$ and transformations so that

$$
\Delta(A, \sigma_1 \ldots \sigma_n) = \Delta(q_1, \sigma_2 \ldots \sigma_n) = \cdots = \Delta(q_{n-1}, \sigma_n) = B
$$

2. If $A \to \sigma_1 \ldots \sigma_n$ is a production in P, then add to Q new states $q_1, \ldots, q_{n-1}$ and transitions to Δ so that

$$
\Delta(A, \sigma_1 \ldots \sigma_n) = \Delta(q_1, \sigma_2 \ldots \sigma_n) = \cdots = \Delta(q_{n-1}, \sigma_n) = f
$$

The construction of Δ may be thought of as labeling edges in the transition diagram for M by strings and then adding in states to accommodate each symbol in the string. Thus, if $A \to \sigma_1 \ldots \sigma_n B$, we would first label the edge between states A and B by $\sigma_1 \ldots \sigma_n$ and then add in $n - 1$ new states, resulting in an edge:

$$\underset{A}{\bullet} \xrightarrow{\sigma_1} \bullet \xrightarrow{\sigma_2} \bullet \; \cdots \cdots \; \xrightarrow{\sigma_n} \underset{B}{\bullet}$$

For example, the regular grammar

$$S \to aB|bA|\varepsilon$$
$$A \to abaS$$
$$B \to babS$$

would give the nfa whose transition diagram is shown in Figure 3.3.

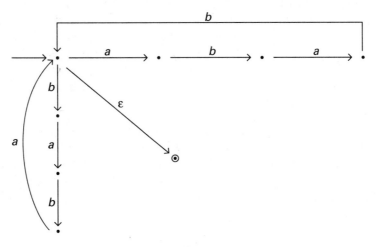

Figure 3.3

If G is a regular grammar and $w \in L(G)$ with $w = \sigma_1 \ldots \sigma_n$, then for some nonterminals $A_1, A_2, \ldots, A_{n-1}$ we have the derivation

$$S \Rightarrow \sigma_1 A_1 \Rightarrow \cdots \Rightarrow \sigma_1 \ldots \sigma_{n-1} A_{n-1} \Rightarrow \sigma_1 \ldots \sigma_n$$

and so in the nfa resulting from this construction we have

$$\Delta(s, \sigma_1 \ldots \sigma_n) = \Delta(A_1, \sigma_2 \ldots \sigma_n) = \cdots = \Delta(A_{n-1}, \sigma_n) = f$$

Thus $w \in L(M)$. Conversely, if $\Delta(s, \sigma_1 \ldots \sigma_n) = f$, then $S \overset{*}{\Rightarrow} \sigma_1 \ldots \sigma_n$, so $w \in L(G)$. Hence $L(G) = L(M)$.

While we have demonstrated useful construction techniques here, we have actually shown much more:

Theorem 3.2.1. L is a regular language if and only if it is generated by a regular grammar.

Thus we now have three general methods of specifying regular languages: regular expressions, finite automata, and regular grammars.

Exercises for Section 3.2

3.2.1. Construct a regular grammar for the regular language accepted by the finite automaton in Figure 3.4.

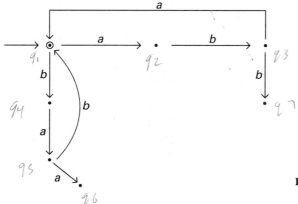

Figure 3.4

3.2.2. Construct an nfa for the regular grammar

$$S \rightarrow aS \mid bB \mid b$$
$$B \rightarrow cC$$
$$C \rightarrow aS$$

3.2.3. Construct an nfa for the regular grammar

$$S \rightarrow abA \mid B \mid baB \mid \varepsilon$$
$$A \rightarrow bS \mid b$$
$$B \rightarrow aS$$

3.2.4. Find a regular grammar for the language

$$L = \{w \in \{a, b\}^* \mid w \text{ does not contain the substring } aa\}$$

3.2.5. Find a regular grammar for $L = \{a^n b^n \mid n \geq 0\}$?

3.2.6. A *left-regular production* is one of the form $A \rightarrow Bw$ where A and B are nonterminals and w is a string of terminals. A *right-regular production* is one of the form $A \rightarrow wB$. Thus left-regular grammars (see Exercise 3.1.5) and right-regular grammars contain only left-regular productions and right-regular productions, respectively. Show that a regular grammar cannot contain both left- and right-regular productions.

3.3 CONTEXT-FREE GRAMMARS

Recall that in our definition of regular grammars we required that the right side of all productions contain at most one nonterminal. Moreover, when a nonterminal is present, it *must* occur at the end of the string (left or right end depending on left- or right-regular grammar). This is made formal by requiring that the productions P satisfy $P \subseteq N \times \Sigma^*(N \cup \varepsilon)$ (or, in the case of left regularity, $P \subseteq N \times (N \cup \varepsilon)\Sigma^*$). This requirement heavily restricts the way in which productions may be formed and consequently restricts the class of languages that we may specify.

Suppose we allow $P \subseteq N \times (N \cup \Sigma)^*$ so that productions may have zero, one, or more nonterminals occurring anywhere within their right-hand sides. For example, the grammar given by

$$S \rightarrow aB \mid bA$$
$$A \rightarrow a \mid aS \mid bAA$$
$$B \rightarrow b \mid bS \mid aBB$$

is a grammar of this type. Note that such a grammar is definitely *not* a regular grammar. On the other hand, all regular grammars satisfy this new requirement for the way in which productions are formed and so are grammars of this type. Thus we have a more general type of grammar.

Definition 3.3.1.   A *context-free grammar* (*cfg*) is a 4-tuple,

$$G = (N, \Sigma, S, P)$$

where N is a finite collection of nonterminals, Σ is an alphabet (also known as a set of terminals), S is a specific nonterminal called the start symbol, and $P \subseteq N \times (N \cup \Sigma)^*$ is a set of productions.

The *language generated by the cfg G* is denoted $L(G)$ and is called a *context-free language* (*cfl*).

For example, since any regular grammar is a cfg, we have that any regular language is a cfl.

Like a regular grammar, a cfg is a way of showing how to generate strings in a language. As with regular grammars, we use the notation $\Rightarrow$ to indicate the act of generation as opposed to $\rightarrow$, which is part of a production rule. When deriving a string, the nonterminals still represent ungenerated portions of the string. In the case of regular grammars, that ungenerated portion always occurs at one end. In cfg's that are not regular grammars, there may be more than one ungenerated portion and they may occur anywhere within the string. When the derivation is complete, all ungenerated portions have been replaced by strings (possibly empty) of terminal symbols.

Consider the cfg given by

$$S \rightarrow aSb \mid \varepsilon$$

An easy induction on n shows that this context-free grammar generates the context-free language $\{a^n b^n \mid n \geq 0\}$. From Chapter 2 we know that this language is *not* regular. Thus there are context-free languages that are not regular languages. That is, the collection of context-free languages properly contains the collection of regular languages.

We will spend considerable time investigating context-free grammars and context-free languages. Before continuing, however, it is appropriate to mention other ways in which we might generalize from regular grammars. In the generalization to context-free grammars, we removed all restrictions on the right side of production rules, allowing the right side of productions to be formed from any string over $N \cup \Sigma$. The only place left to generalize is on the left side of the production rules. A *phrase-structured grammar* is one in which the left sides of the production rules may be formed from any nonempty string over $N \cup \Sigma$, which contains some nondeterminal. Thus, for a phrase-structured grammar, the collection of production rules P satisfies

$$P \subseteq (N \cup \Sigma)^* N (N \cup \Sigma)^* \times (N \cup \Sigma)^*$$

Phrase-structured grammars are also known as *type 0* or *unrestricted* grammars.

The term context free, when applied to grammars, suggests that there should be grammars in which context is sensitive. *Context-sensitive grammars* are phrase-structured grammars in which we restrict productions $\alpha \to \beta$ so that $|\alpha| \leq |\beta|$. There is a normal form for these grammars in which each production is of the form $\alpha_1 A \alpha_2 \to \alpha_1 \beta \alpha_2$ with $\beta \neq \varepsilon$. Such productions permit the replacement of the nonterminal A by the string β only when A occurs in the "context" of α_1 and α_2.

Context-sensitive grammars cannot generate as many languages as phrase-structured grammars, but they allow derivations to proceed in a predictable manner. Note, however, that since $|S| = 1$ and since $|\varepsilon| = 0$, it is impossible to derive the empty string in a true context-sensitive grammar. Programming languages are often designed to be context sensitive as a means for simplifying the process of compilation.

Exercises for Section 3.3

3.3.1. For the context-free grammar given by

$$S \to AA$$
$$A \to AAA \mid a \mid bA \mid Ab$$

(a) Give a derivation for the string $b^2 aba^2 ba$.

(b) Show how a derivation for $b^{m_1} ab^{m_2} a \dots b^{m_{2n}} ab^{m_{2n+1}}$ can be performed for any $n > 0$ and $m_1, m_2, \dots, m_{2n+1} \geq 0$.

3.3.2. The context-free grammar G given by

$$S \to aSb \mid aSa \mid bSa \mid bSb \mid \varepsilon$$

is not a regular grammar, yet $L(G)$ *is* a regular language! Find a regular grammar G' such that $L(G') = L(G)$.

3.3.3. Give a context-free grammar for each of the following context-free languages:

(a) $\{a^m b^n \mid m \geq n\}$

(b) $\{w \in \{a, b\}^* \mid w$ has twice as many a's as b's$\}$

(c) $\{a^m b^n \mid n \leq m \leq 2n\}$

(d) $\{a^m b^n c^p d^q \mid m + n \geq p + q\}$

3.4 DERIVATION OR PARSE TREES AND AMBIGUITY

As a string is derived from a context-free grammar, the start symbol is replaced by some string. Each nonterminal in this string is, in turn, replaced by another string, and so on, until a string consisting only of terminal symbols remains. No further replacement may occur because there are no nonterminals to be replaced. It is sometimes useful to have a picture of the derivation, one that indicates the contribution of each nonterminal to the final string of terminals. Such a picture takes the form of a tree and is called a *derivation tree* (or *parse tree*).

A derivation tree for a derivation is constructed by creating a root node and labeling it with the start symbol. The root node has as children one node for each symbol in the right side of the production used to replace the start symbol. Any node labeled by a nonterminal also has as children nodes labeled by each symbol in the right side of the production used to replace that nonterminal. Nodes that have no children must necessarily be labeled with terminal symbols.

Consider the context-free grammar

$$S \rightarrow AB$$
$$A \rightarrow aA \mid a$$
$$B \rightarrow bB \mid b$$

The string *aabbb* may be derived by

$$S \Rightarrow AB \Rightarrow AbB \Rightarrow AbbB \Rightarrow Abbb \Rightarrow aAbbb \Rightarrow aabbb$$

A derivation tree for this derivation looks like Figure 3.5. We begin at the root S and generate children A and B. Each of A and B root a subtree corresponding to the portion of the final string that they generate. Note that all leaf nodes are labeled by terminal symbols. Reading the leaves from left to right yields the string *aabbb*.

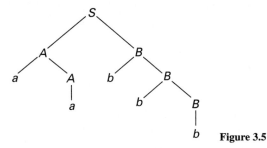

Figure 3.5

Finally, note that there are many possible derivations for *aabbb*, which all have this derivation tree. For example,

$$S \Rightarrow AB \Rightarrow aAB \Rightarrow aaB \Rightarrow aabB \Rightarrow aabbB \Rightarrow aabbb$$

and

$$S \Rightarrow AB \Rightarrow aAB \Rightarrow aAbB \Rightarrow aAbbB \Rightarrow aAbbb \Rightarrow aabbb$$

For this string and this grammar, every derivation of *aabbb* has the same derivation tree. This need not be the case, however. To see this, consider the grammar

$$S \rightarrow SbS \mid ScS \mid a$$

We may derive the string *abaca* in two different ways as follows:

1. $S \Rightarrow SbS \Rightarrow SbScS \Rightarrow SbSca \Rightarrow Sbaca \Rightarrow abaca$
2. $S \Rightarrow ScS \Rightarrow SbScS \Rightarrow abScS \Rightarrow abacS \Rightarrow abaca$

The derivation tree for derivation 1 is

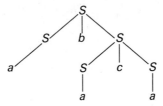

while the tree for derivation 2 is

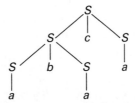

Note that the two trees are distinct, yet the strings produced are the same. (The string derived corresponds to the leaf nodes and is called the *yield* of the derivation tree.)

A grammar is said to be *ambiguous* if two or more distinct derivation trees exist for some string. A grammar in which for any string *w* all derivations of *w* have the same derivation tree is *unambiguous*.

Ambiguity can be a problem for certain languages if meaning depends in part on structure, as is usually the case with natural and programming languages. If a language structure has more than one decomposition and if construction partially determines meaning, then the meaning is ambiguous. Consider the sentence "John saw a man with a telescope." The meaning of this sentence is ambiguous for the phrase "with a telescope" may describe either the man that John saw or the technique John employed to see the man.

As another example of ambiguity obscuring meaning, consider the following grammar for simple assignment statements:

$$A \rightarrow I := E$$
$$I \rightarrow \underline{a} \mid \underline{b} \mid \underline{c}$$
$$E \rightarrow E \underline{+} E \mid E \underline{*} E \mid \underline{(E)} \mid I$$

Here the terminal symbols have been underlined.

The string $a := b + c * a$ is a string in this language of assignment statements. There are two distinct derivation trees for it, however (see Figure 3.6).

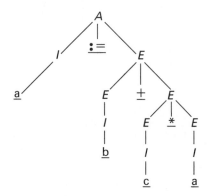

Figure 3.6

If we attempt to determine how the value on the right of the assignment operator (the := symbol) is computed, there are two possible results, $b + (c * a)$ or $(b + c) * a$. These results are not, in general, equal.

In some cases, if a grammar is ambiguous, another grammar producing the same language can be found that is unambiguous. For example, the grammar

$$S \rightarrow A \mid B$$
$$A \rightarrow a$$
$$B \rightarrow a$$

is ambiguous, having two distinct derivation trees for the string a. An equivalent unambiguous grammar might be

$$S \rightarrow a$$

If all context-free grammars for a language are ambiguous, the language itself is said to be an *inherently ambiguous context-free language*. The language

$$L = \{a^i b^j c^k \mid i = j \text{ or } j = k\}$$

is inherently ambiguous. Intuitively, any grammar for L must have one kind of derivation tree to generate strings for which $i = j$ and another for strings in which $j = k$. If a string has $i = j = k$, it will have two derivations.

We observed earlier that a given string may have more than one derivation even in context-free grammars that are unambiguous. Different derivations correspond to selecting different nonterminals to expand. By convention, two ways of generating a string are singled out. In a *leftmost derivation* the leftmost nonterminal is always expanded. Thus for the grammar

$$S \rightarrow SbS \mid ScS \mid a$$

a leftmost derivation of *abaca* might be

$$S \Rightarrow ScS \Rightarrow SbScS \Rightarrow abScS \Rightarrow abacS \Rightarrow abaca$$

A *rightmost derivation* is one in which the rightmost nonterminal is always expanded. Thus

$$S \Rightarrow ScS \Rightarrow Sca \Rightarrow SbSca \Rightarrow Sbaca \Rightarrow abaca$$

is a rightmost derivation of the string. Note that these two derivations have the same derivation tree:

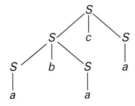

Several other derivations share this derivation tree as well. In this particular grammar,

$$S \Rightarrow SbS \Rightarrow abS \Rightarrow abScS \Rightarrow abacS \Rightarrow abaca$$

is a leftmost derivation distinct from the preceding one. The presence of two distinct leftmost derivations corresponds to the existence of two distinct derivation trees. Thus we can characterize an ambiguous grammar as one having two (or more) distinct leftmost derivations for the same string.

As a final observation, note that for regular grammars any derivation is at once both a leftmost and a rightmost derivation, regardless of whether we have a left-regular or a right-regular grammar.

Exercises for Section 3.4

3.4.1. Show that the following grammar is ambiguous,

$$S \rightarrow bA \mid aB$$
$$A \rightarrow a \mid aS \mid bAA$$
$$B \rightarrow b \mid bS \mid aBB$$

3.4.2. Find an unambiguous grammar for the grammar in Exercise 3.4.1.

3.4.3. Find a rightmost derivation for *abaca* distinct from the rightmost derivation

$$S \Rightarrow ScS \Rightarrow Sca \Rightarrow SbSca \Rightarrow Sbaca \Rightarrow abaca$$

for the *cfg* $S \rightarrow SbS \mid ScS \mid a$.

3.4.4. Is it possible to have ambiguous regular grammars? If yes, give an example. If no, prove your answer.

3.5 SIMPLIFYING CONTEXT-FREE GRAMMARS

As it stands, our definition of context-free grammar provides very little control over the kinds of productions allowed. This, in turn, allows us to construct grammars in which the derivation trees are almost uncontrollably bushy, as with, say,

$$S \rightarrow abcdefgS \mid abcdefg$$

or pointlessly tall and narrow, as with

$$
\begin{aligned}
S &\rightarrow A \\
A &\rightarrow B \\
B &\rightarrow C \\
C &\rightarrow D \\
D &\rightarrow a \mid A
\end{aligned}
$$

We would like to place restrictions on the way that productions can be formed so that the resulting derivation trees are not needlessly complex or pointlessly simple. At the same time, we do not want to constrain production formation to the point that some context-free languages cannot be generated by production sets that meet the restrictions. We seek some well-behaved standard forms (or *normal* forms) for productions.

As a first step toward the development of such forms, we will need to clean up grammars by eliminating useless productions and symbols. Consider the context-free grammar G of the following example:

Example 3.5.1

$$
\begin{aligned}
S &\rightarrow Aa \mid B \mid D \\
B &\rightarrow b \\
A &\rightarrow aA \mid bA \mid B \\
C &\rightarrow abd
\end{aligned}
$$

Note that C is never part of a derivation beginning at the start symbol; that is, it is not the case that $S \overset{*}{\Rightarrow} \alpha C \beta$ for any strings α and β in $(N \cup \Sigma)^*$. Consequently, the symbol C and the production

$$C \rightarrow abd$$

are useless in the sense that they can never contribute to the generation of a string in $L(G)$. The symbol D can be produced from S, but D itself never derives any string of terminal symbols and so never is part of a derivation of a string of terminals. Thus D is also useless, although for a different reason than C. The symbol B is, in some sense, redundant. It derives only a single terminal; thus the derivations $S \Rightarrow B \Rightarrow b$ and $A \Rightarrow B \Rightarrow b$ could be shortened to $S \Rightarrow b$ and $A \Rightarrow b$, eliminating B entirely. Finally, note that if the production $C \rightarrow abd$ is eliminated then the terminal symbol d can never appear in a string of terminals generated by the resulting grammar.

We have identified a number of different areas in which context-free grammars might be cleaned up. Each of these problems may be eliminated without affecting the generative ability of the grammar. We will first eliminate nonterminals that do not derive strings of terminals, such as D in Example 3.5.1.

Let $G = (N, \Sigma, S, P)$ be a context-free grammar. We convert G into $G' = (N', \Sigma, S, P')$ so that $L(G) = L(G')$, and for all $A \in N'$ we have that $A \stackrel{*}{\Rightarrow} w$ for some $w \in \Sigma^*$. To do this, we iteratively construct the new set of nonterminals N' and the new set of productions P' as follows:

Algorithm 3.5.1.

1. Initialize N' to all nonterminals A for which $A \to w$ is a production in G with $w \in \Sigma^*$.

2. Initialize P' to all productions $A \to w$ for which $A \in N'$ and $w \in \Sigma^*$.

3. Repeat

   Add to N' all nonterminals A for which $A \to w$ for some $w \in (N' \cup \Sigma)^*$ is a production in P and add that production to P'.

   until no more nonterminals are added to N'.

Note that the loop in step 3 eventually terminates since N and P are finite. Essentially, what we are doing is working backward from terminal strings through all possible parse trees, noting the nonterminals (and productions) involved. Any nonterminal (and production) that doesn't eventually appear in N' never contributes a terminal substring to a "finished" string of terminal symbols generated by the grammar. Consequently, its elimination does not alter the language generated.

For example in the grammar of Example 3.5.1 we should hope to eliminate the nonterminal D. After applying Algorithm 3.5.1 to this grammar, the following grammar results:

$$S \to Aa \mid B$$
$$A \to aA \mid bA \mid B$$
$$B \to b$$
$$C \to abd$$

We have defined context-free grammars to allow the possibility of ε occurring as the right-hand side of a production. Algorithm 3.5.1 must treat ε as a terminal string. Thus, for example, in transforming the grammar

$$S \to aA \mid \varepsilon$$
$$A \to aA \mid bB \mid \varepsilon$$
$$B \to bB$$

the resulting grammar will be

$$S \to aA \mid \varepsilon$$
$$A \to aA \mid \varepsilon$$

Productions of the form $A \rightarrow \varepsilon$ are called ε *productions*. They are sometimes necessary and at other times unnecessary and undesirable in a grammar. Eventually, we will be able to eliminate them when they actually are unnecessary.

Even after transforming the grammar in Example 3.5.1, we are left with the useless production $C \rightarrow abd$. This production ended up in the transformed grammar because its application results in a string of terminals. Its presence is undesirable, however, because we can never derive a string that includes the nonterminal C by starting with the start symbol S. Moreover, since the terminal symbol d only appears in a string by means of this production, we can actually reduce the size of the alphabet by removing d, while not altering the language generated. The following algorithm eliminates nonterminals and terminals that do not appear in any strings derivable from S. The resulting transformed grammar guarantees that a symbol X appears as a terminal or nonterminal only if $S \overset{*}{\Rightarrow} \alpha X \beta$ for some strings α and β over $(N \cup \Sigma)^*$.

Let $G = (N, \Sigma, S, P)$ be a context-free grammar. We convert G into the grammar $G' = (N', \Sigma', S, P')$ so that $L(G) = L(G')$, and for all $X \in N' \cup \Sigma'$ we have that $S \overset{*}{\Rightarrow} \alpha X \beta$ for α and β strings in $(N' \cup \Sigma')^*$. To do this, we iteratively construct the new sets of terminals, nonterminals, and productions as follows:

Algorithm 3.5.2.

1. Initialize N' to contain the start symbol S, and initialize P' and Σ^* to $\emptyset$.

2. Repeat
   For $A \in N'$, if $A \rightarrow w$ is a production in P then:
   1. Put $A \rightarrow w$ in P'.
   2. For any nonterminal B in w, put B in N'.
   3. For any terminal σ in w, put σ in Σ'.
   until no new productions are added.

Note that, since P, N and Σ are finite, the loop in step 2 eventually terminates. What the algorithm does is to account for all terminals and nonterminals reachable from S. If a terminal or nonterminal is never reached from S, it is never included in N' or Σ'. If it is an unreachable nonterminal, then all productions with it on the left side are excluded.

Consider the grammar from Example 3.5.1 transformed by Algorithm 3.5.1 into

$$S \rightarrow Aa \mid B$$
$$B \rightarrow b$$
$$A \rightarrow aA \mid bA \mid B$$
$$C \rightarrow abd$$

The grammar that results after applying Algorithm 3.5.2 is

$$S \rightarrow Aa \mid B$$
$$A \rightarrow aA \mid bA \mid B$$
$$B \rightarrow b$$

Note that the production $C \rightarrow abd$ has been eliminated, along with the nonterminal C and the terminal d.

Note that the order in which the preceding two algorithms are applied to a grammar is important. Consider the grammar

$$S \rightarrow AB \mid a$$
$$A \rightarrow a$$

We get different results by applying Algorithm 3.5.1 before Algorithm 3.5.2 than we do by applying Algorithm 3.5.2 before Algorithm 3.5.1.

$$\left.\begin{array}{l} S \rightarrow AB \mid a \\ A \rightarrow a \end{array}\right\} \xrightarrow{\text{Alg. 3.5.1}} \left.\begin{array}{l} S \rightarrow a \\ A \rightarrow a \end{array}\right\} \xrightarrow{\text{Alg. 3.5.2}} \quad S \rightarrow a$$

$$\left.\begin{array}{l} S \rightarrow AB \mid a \\ A \rightarrow a \end{array}\right\} \xrightarrow{\text{Alg. 3.5.2}} \left.\begin{array}{l} S \rightarrow AB \mid a \\ A \rightarrow a \end{array}\right\} \xrightarrow{\text{Alg. 3.5.1}} \begin{array}{l} S \rightarrow a \\ A \rightarrow a \end{array}$$

We now direct our attention to the ε productions, those productions of the form $A \rightarrow \varepsilon$. Certainly, if $\varepsilon \in L(G)$, we cannot eliminate all such productions, for ε must be generated by the grammar. It turns out that, if ε is *not* in $L(G)$, we can remove all ε productions.

A nonterminal A is said to be *nullable* if $A \overset{*}{\Rightarrow} \varepsilon$. The ability to identify all nullable nonterminals is crucial to the elimination of ε productions. The following algorithm identifies the set of all nullable nonterminals $\mathcal{N}$ for a context-free grammar $G = (N, \Sigma, S, P)$.

Algorithm 3.5.3.

1. Initialize $\mathcal{N}$ to all nonterminals A for which an ε production, $A \rightarrow \varepsilon$, exists.

2. Repeat:
   If $B \rightarrow w$ for some $w \in (N \cup \Sigma)^*$ and all symbols of w are in $\mathcal{N}$, then add B to $\mathcal{N}$.
   until no more nonterminals are added to $\mathcal{N}$.

For the moment we will concern ourselves only with context-free grammars $G = (N, \Sigma, S, P)$ for which $L(G)$ does not contain ε. Once the nullable nonterminals have been identified, we modify the production rules to eliminate ε productions. This is accomplished by replacing productions of the form $B \rightarrow X_1 X_2 \ldots X_n$ by all productions formed by removing some subset of the X_i's that are nullable. We are careful to *not* include $B \rightarrow \varepsilon$, even if all X_i's are nullable.

We create the new set of productions P' as follows:

If $B \rightarrow X_1 X_2 \ldots X_n$ is a production in P, then put into P' all productions of the form $B \rightarrow Y_1 Y_2 \ldots Y_n$, where the Y_i's satisfy:

$Y_i = X_i$ if X_i is *not* nullable.

$Y_i = $ either X_i or ε if X_i is nullable.

Y_i is not ε for all i (that is, no productions of the form $B \rightarrow \varepsilon$ are placed in P').

It is important to note that from one production $B \rightarrow X_1 X_2 \ldots X_n$ in P we may gain a number of new productions in P'. For example, if $B \rightarrow X_1 X_2$ and both of X_1 and X_2 are nullable, we would get the productions

$$B \rightarrow X_1 \mid X_2 \mid X_1 X_2$$

Consider the grammar G:

$$S \rightarrow aA$$
$$A \rightarrow aA \mid \varepsilon$$

Note that A is the only nullable nonterminal [and that $\varepsilon \notin L(G)$]. In considering the production $S \rightarrow aA$, we would have $X_1 = a$ and $X_2 = A$. Thus we include the productions $S \rightarrow a \mid aA$ in the new collection. The resulting grammar, after considering all the original productions, is

$$S \rightarrow aA \mid a$$
$$A \rightarrow aA \mid a$$

Note that the ε production $A \rightarrow \varepsilon$ has been eliminated.

For a context-free grammar G, if $L(G)$ *does* contain ε, it is still possible to eliminate all but one ε production from G. First, eliminate all ε productions from G. This transforms G into the G' for which $L(G') = L(G) - \{\varepsilon\}$. We then add the production $S \rightarrow \varepsilon$, which restores ε to the language generated.

Productions of the form $A \rightarrow B$, where both A and B are nonterminals, are called *unit* or *nongenerative* productions. The presence of unit productions does not necessarily indicate that a symbol is useless. Unit productions *do* make the context-free grammar unnecessarily complex, however.

For example, applying a production of the form $A \rightarrow B$ simply renames a nonterminal and adds a step to the length of the derivation. Any string derivable from the nonterminal B is derivable from A also. Thus we may eliminate the extra step by skipping over B. For example, if the productions for A and B are

$$A \rightarrow B$$
$$B \rightarrow w_1 \mid C$$

where $C \in N$ and $w_1 \in (N \cup \Sigma)^*$, we may eliminate the production $A \rightarrow B$ and include the productions $A \rightarrow w_1 \mid C$. Note that, while we eliminated the unit production $A \rightarrow B$, we introduced the unit production $A \rightarrow C$. We could continue this process until unit productions no longer appear in the grammar, but we will take a different approach, which will eliminate the circular aspect of this process.

Note that in the preceding example the unit production $A \rightarrow C$ appears as the result of the productions $A \rightarrow B$ and $B \rightarrow C$ in the original grammar. If we know all nonterminals X such that $A \overset{*}{\Rightarrow} X$ by means of only unit productions, then we can avoid repeatedly introducing and then having to eliminate these unit productions one by one. To see how this may be accomplished, suppose that we have the productions

$$A \rightarrow B$$
$$B \rightarrow C \mid w_1$$
$$C \rightarrow D$$
$$D \rightarrow w_2$$

We then have that $A \Rightarrow B \Rightarrow C \Rightarrow D$. We observe that the productions $A \rightarrow w_1 \mid w_2$ allow A to derive the same strings as the original five productions. The new productions are taken from the nonunit productions of the original production set by making a production $A \rightarrow y$ for each nonunit production $X \rightarrow y$, where $X \in \{B, C, D\}$. We now make this technique precise.

First, for $A \in N$ define

$$\text{Unit}(A) = \{B \in N \mid A \overset{*}{\Rightarrow} B \text{ using only unit productions}\}$$

[Note $A \in \text{Unit}(A)$ since $A \overset{*}{\Rightarrow} A$ by means of 0 productions.] Now let $G = (N, \Sigma, S, P)$ be a context-free grammar having no ε productions. We construct an equivalent context-free grammar $G' = (N, \Sigma, S, P')$ in which P' contains no unit productions as follows:

1. Initialize P' to contain all of P.
2. For each $A \in N$, find the set Unit (A).
3. For each A for which Unit $(A) \neq \{A\}$
   For each $B \in \text{Unit}(A)$
     For each nonunit production $B \rightarrow w$ in P
       add $A \rightarrow w$ to P'.
4. Remove all unit productions from P'.

For example, in the grammar

$$S \rightarrow A \mid Aa$$
$$A \rightarrow B$$
$$B \rightarrow C \mid b$$
$$C \rightarrow D \mid ab$$
$$D \rightarrow b$$

we have

$$\text{Unit}(S) = \{S, A, B, C, D\}$$
$$\text{Unit}(A) = \{A, B, C, D\}$$
$$\text{Unit}(B) = \{B, C, D\}$$
$$\text{Unit}(C) = \{C, D\}$$
$$\text{Unit}(D) = \{D\}$$

The algorithm first introduces the new productions

$$S \rightarrow b \mid ab$$
$$A \rightarrow b \mid ab$$
$$B \rightarrow ab \mid b$$
$$C \rightarrow b \mid ab$$

and then eliminates the productions $S \rightarrow A$, $A \rightarrow B$, $B \rightarrow C$, and $C \rightarrow D$. The resulting grammar is

$$S \rightarrow b \mid ab \mid Aa$$
$$A \rightarrow b \mid ab$$
$$B \rightarrow ab \mid b$$
$$C \rightarrow b \mid ab$$
$$D \rightarrow b$$

Note that this grammar can be further simplified by means of our other techniques.

In the preceding we have managed to eliminate certain bothersome forms of productions in context-free grammars. As a final step in simplifying context-free grammars, we present a standard or *normal* form for productions. A context-free grammar is said to be in *Chomsky normal form* if it contains no ε productions and if all productions are of the form either $A \rightarrow a$, for $a \in \Sigma$, or of the form $A \rightarrow BC$, where B and C are nonterminals. That is, in Chomsky normal form the right-hand side of each production is either a single terminal or a pair of nonterminals. Note that for a grammar in Chomsky normal form the derivation tree of any derivation is quite well behaved—except at the leaves, the tree is binary!

If G is a context-free grammar and $\varepsilon \notin L(G)$, we can transform G into a context-free grammar in Chomsky normal form. To do this, we first eliminate all ε productions, useless symbols, and unit productions from G. Note that once this has been done, if $A \rightarrow w$ is a production in G, then we may be assured that $|w| \geq 1$. Moreover, if $|w| = 1$, then w is a terminal symbol from Σ, since there are no unit productions. On the other hand, if $|w| > 1$, then w may contain both terminals and nonterminals. We now transform G by converting such w's into strings containing only nonterminals.

Suppose that we have a production of the form $A \rightarrow w$, where $w = X_1 X_2 \ldots X_n$. If X_i is a terminal symbol, say σ, we replace X_i by the new nonterminal C_σ and add the production $C_\sigma \rightarrow \sigma$. Once this conversion is applied to G, all productions are of the form $A \rightarrow w$, where w is either a single terminal symbol or else a string consisting of only nonterminals.

The final step in transforming G into Chomsky normal form is to eliminate strings of more than two nonterminals on the right-hand side of any production. To do this, if $A \rightarrow B_1 B_2 \ldots B_n$ is such a production with $n \geq 2$, we replace it by the $n - 1$ productions

$$A \rightarrow B_1 D_1$$
$$D_1 \rightarrow B_2 D_2$$
$$\vdots$$
$$D_{n-2} \rightarrow B_{n-1} B_n$$

Here the D_i are new nonterminals.

In the transformed grammar that results, the right side of each production consists of either a single terminal or else a string of two nonterminals. Consequently, any context-free language not containing ε can be generated by a context-free grammar in Chomsky normal form.

For example, consider the cfg

$$S \rightarrow bA \mid aB$$
$$A \rightarrow bAA \mid aS \mid a$$
$$B \rightarrow aBB \mid bS \mid b$$

Note that this grammar contains no ε productions, unit productions, or useless symbols. After the first transformation, this grammar becomes

$$S \rightarrow C_b A \mid C_a B$$
$$A \rightarrow C_b AA \mid C_a S \mid a$$
$$B \rightarrow C_a BB \mid C_b S \mid b$$
$$C_a \rightarrow a$$
$$C_b \rightarrow b$$

Note that in this version of the grammar all right-hand sides of productions consist of either a single terminal symbol or a string of two or more nonterminals. After the final conversion, the Chomsky normal form of the grammar is

$$S \rightarrow C_b A \mid C_a A$$
$$A \rightarrow C_b D_1 \mid C_a S \mid a$$
$$D_1 \rightarrow AA$$
$$B \rightarrow C_a D_2 \mid C_b S \mid b$$
$$D_2 \rightarrow BB$$

If L is a context-free language that contains ε, then we may find a context-free grammar in Chomsky normal form for $L - \{\varepsilon\}$ and then add the production $S \rightarrow \varepsilon$ to it. The resulting grammar is in Chomsky normal form except for the single ε production.

Exercises for Section 3.5

3.5.1. Apply Algorithm 3.5.1 to the following grammars:

(a)

$$S \rightarrow aAb \mid cEB \mid CE$$
$$A \rightarrow dBE \mid eeC$$
$$B \rightarrow ff \mid D$$
$$C \rightarrow gFB \mid ae$$
$$D \rightarrow h$$

(b)

$$S \rightarrow aB$$
$$A \rightarrow bcCCC \mid dA$$
$$B \rightarrow e$$
$$C \rightarrow fA$$
$$D \rightarrow Dgh$$

3.5.2. Apply Algorithm 3.5.1 to the following grammar:

$$S \rightarrow a \mid aA \mid B \mid C$$
$$A \rightarrow aB \mid \varepsilon$$
$$B \rightarrow Aa$$
$$C \rightarrow bCD$$
$$D \rightarrow ccc$$

3.5.3. Apply Algorithm 3.5.2 to the context-free grammar

$$s \rightarrow aAb$$
$$A \rightarrow ccC$$
$$B \rightarrow dd \mid D$$
$$C \rightarrow ae$$
$$D \rightarrow f$$
$$U \rightarrow gW$$
$$W \rightarrow h$$

3.5.4. Apply Algorithm 3.5.2 to the context-free grammar

$$S \rightarrow a \mid aA \mid B$$
$$A \rightarrow aB \mid \varepsilon$$
$$B \rightarrow Aa$$
$$D \rightarrow ddd$$

3.5.5. Remove useless symbols from the following grammar by means of Algorithms 3.5.1 and 3.5.2:

$$S \rightarrow A \mid AA \mid AAA$$
$$A \rightarrow ABa \mid ACa \mid a$$
$$B \rightarrow ABa \mid Ab \mid \varepsilon$$
$$C \rightarrow Cab \mid CC$$
$$D \rightarrow CD \mid Cd \mid CEa$$
$$E \rightarrow b$$

3.5.6. Find the collection of nullable nonterminals for the following grammar:

$$S \rightarrow aA \mid bA \mid a$$
$$A \rightarrow aA \mid bAb \mid \varepsilon$$

3.5.7. Find the collection of nullable nonterminals for the following grammar:

$$S \rightarrow ABaC$$
$$A \rightarrow AB$$
$$B \rightarrow b \mid \varepsilon$$
$$C \rightarrow D \mid \varepsilon$$
$$D \rightarrow d$$

3.5.8. Eliminate ε productions in the grammar

$$S \rightarrow aA \mid bA \mid a$$
$$A \rightarrow aA \mid bAb \mid \varepsilon$$

3.5.9. Eliminate ε productions from the grammar

$$S \rightarrow AB$$
$$A \rightarrow aA \mid abB \mid aCa$$
$$B \rightarrow bA \mid BB \mid \varepsilon$$
$$C \rightarrow \varepsilon$$
$$D \rightarrow dB \mid BCB$$

3.5.10. Eliminate ε productions from the grammar

$$S \rightarrow a \mid aA \mid B$$
$$A \rightarrow aB \mid \varepsilon$$
$$B \rightarrow Aa$$

3.5.11. Eliminate ε productions in the grammar

$$S \rightarrow ABaC$$
$$A \rightarrow AB$$
$$B \rightarrow b \mid \varepsilon$$
$$C \rightarrow D \mid \varepsilon$$
$$D \rightarrow d$$

3.5.12. Simplify the following grammar as much as possible:

$$S \rightarrow aB \mid aaB$$
$$A \rightarrow \varepsilon$$
$$B \rightarrow bA$$
$$B \rightarrow \varepsilon$$

3.5.13. The language associated with the following context-free grammar contains ε. Remove all ε productions except $S \rightarrow \varepsilon$.

$$S \rightarrow AB \mid aB \mid \varepsilon$$
$$A \rightarrow BBB \mid aB \mid a \mid \varepsilon$$
$$B \rightarrow a \mid aA \mid \varepsilon$$

3.5.14. Give an algorithm that constructs Unit (A) for nonterminals A in a cfg.

3.5.15. Remove all unit productions from the context-free grammar

$$S \rightarrow CBa \mid D$$
$$A \rightarrow bbC$$
$$B \rightarrow Sc \mid ddd$$
$$C \rightarrow eA \mid f \mid C$$
$$D \rightarrow E \mid SABC$$
$$E \rightarrow gh$$

3.5.16. Remove all unit productions from the context-free grammar G given by

$$S \rightarrow Aa \mid Ba \mid B$$
$$A \rightarrow Aa \mid \varepsilon$$
$$B \rightarrow aA \mid BB \mid \varepsilon$$

[Note that $\varepsilon \in L(G)$.]

3.5.17. Convert the following to Chomsky normal form:

(a)
$$S \to AB \mid CA$$
$$A \to a$$
$$B \to BC \mid AB$$
$$C \to aB \mid b$$

(b)
$$S \to aAb \mid cHB \mid CH$$
$$A \to dBH \mid eeC$$
$$B \to ff \mid D$$
$$C \to gFB \mid ah$$
$$D \to i$$
$$E \to jF$$
$$F \to dcGGG \mid cF$$
$$G \to kF$$
$$H \to Hlm$$

3.5.18. Show that conversion to Chomsky normal form can square the number of productions in a context-free grammar.

3.6 PROPERTIES OF CONTEXT-FREE LANGUAGES

Grammars in Chomsky normal form enable us to find an exact relationship between the length of a string and the number of steps in its derivation. If ε can be derived, it results from a single rule application, $S \to \varepsilon$. A simple inductive argument shows that if w can be derived and $|w| > 0$ then the derivation has exactly $2|w|$ steps. By *step*, we mean a replacement. Thus writing down the start symbol is a step, as is replacing it or any other nonterminal by the right-hand side of a production.

Suppose that G is a context-free grammar in Chomsky normal form and consider the derivation tree of any string in $L(G)$. If a node has two children, then the child nodes are labeled by nonterminals and may have at most two children of their own. (This is because G is in Chomsky normal form.) That is, the root node can have two children, each of its children can have two children, and so on. At each level we can double the number of nodes at the previous level. Thus at level k we could have 2^k nodes. (Level 0 is the level of the root node.)

On the other hand, if a node has only one child, then that child node is labeled by a terminal symbol, again because the grammar is in Chomsky normal form. Thus every terminal symbol labeling a leaf node actually corresponds to two nodes, the leaf and its parent.

Now suppose that the longest path from the root to a leaf consists of $m + 2$ nodes (and $m + 1$ arcs). The derivation tree then has $m + 2$ levels (that is, levels $0, 1, \ldots, m + 1$), and the nodes at the last level (the leaves) are single children of their parent nodes. The parent nodes occur at level m and there are at most 2^m of them. Thus, if the longest path in a derivation tree consists of $m + 2$ nodes, then the maximum length of the derived string is 2^m. Another way of saying this is that, if the derived string has length greater than 2^m, then its longest path must contain more than $m + 2$ nodes.

Now, each node in the derivation tree of a string corresponds to the application of a production. Consequently, this relationship between the number of production steps involved and the length of the resulting terminal string suggests that context-free grammars in Chomsky normal form generate an average of one terminal for every two productions.

Knowledge about the relationship between the length of a string and its derivation in a context-free grammar allows us to prove the following *pumping lemma* for context-free languages.

Lemma 3.6.1.   Let L be a context-free language that does not contain ε. Then there is an integer k for which, if $z \in L$ and $|z| > k$, then z may be rewritten as $z = uvwxy$ with the properties that:

1. $|vwx| \le k$.

2. At least one of v or x is not ε. $|vx| \ge 1$

3. $uv^i wx^i y \in L$ for all $i \ge 0$.

Proof.   Suppose that $G = (N, \Sigma, S, P)$ is a context-free grammar in Chomsky normal form with $L = L(G)$. Let n be the number of nonterminals in N and let $k = 2^n$. Suppose that $z \in L$ with $|z| > k$.

Let us consider the longest path in z's derivation tree. Since $|z| > 2^n$, this path must contain more than $n + 2$ nodes. Of the last $n + 2$ nodes in this path, the very last node corresponds to a terminal. Hence $n + 1$ of the nodes are labeled by nonterminals. Since there are only n nonterminals in N, some nonterminal is repeated. Suppose that A is repeated in this path. Then we have

$$S \overset{*}{\Rightarrow} uAy \overset{*}{\Rightarrow} uvAxy \overset{*}{\Rightarrow} uvwxy = z$$

for some substrings $u, v, w, x,$ and y. Now, since we were only considering the last $n + 2$ nodes of this path, the path from A to vwx can have at most $n + 2$ nodes in it. Thus

$$|vwx| \le 2^n$$

by the remarks preceding this theorem.

Also, since $A \overset{*}{\Rightarrow} vAx$, we must have that $A \overset{*}{\Rightarrow} v^i Ax^i$ for any $i \ge 0$. Thus $S \overset{*}{\Rightarrow} uv^i wx^i y$ for all $i \ge 0$.

Finally, note that since $A \overset{*}{\Rightarrow} vAx$ and since G is in Chomsky normal form we must have that

$$A \Rightarrow BC \overset{*}{\Rightarrow} vAx \overset{*}{\Rightarrow} vwx$$

for some nonterminals B and C. Now either $B \overset{*}{\Rightarrow} v$ and $C \overset{*}{\Rightarrow} Ax$ or else $B \overset{*}{\Rightarrow} vA$ and $C \overset{*}{\Rightarrow} x$. Since v and x are strings of terminals and there are no ε productions, the first case ensures that $|v| \ge 1$ so that $v \ne \varepsilon$, and the second case ensures that $|x| \ge 1$ so that $x \ne \varepsilon$. In either case at least one of v or x is not ε.   ■

As with the pumping lemma for regular languages, the pumping lemma for context-free languages gives us the ability to show that certain languages are not context-free. To do this, we take essentially the same approach as in the case of regular languages.

For example, the language $L = \{a^i b^j | j = i^2\}$ is not context-free. To see this, suppose that L actually *is* context-free. We will show that this is impossible. If L is context-free, then the pumping lemma applies, and so there is a k satisfying the conditions of Lemma 3.6.1. Consider $z = a^k b^{k^2}$. Certainly, $z \in L$ and $|z| > k$. Thus we may decompose z into

$$z = uvwxy$$

and be assured that $uv^i wx^i y \in L$ for all $i \geq 0$, that $|vx| \geq 1$, and that $|vwx| \leq k$. Note that, if $v = a^r b^s$ for some r and s then $v^i = (a^r b^s)^i$, and so $uv^i wx^i y$ has b's before a's and thus cannot be in L. Similarly, if $x = a^r b^s$, we cannot "pump" either. Thus we must have either

$$v = a^r \text{ and } x = a^s$$

or

$$v = b^r \text{ and } x = b^s$$

or else

$$v = a^r \text{ and } x = b^s$$

for some values of r and s. In the first case we have

$$uv^2 wx^2 y = a^{k+r+s} b^{k^2}$$

In the second case we have

$$uv^2 wx^2 y = a^k b^{k^2 + r + s}$$

In both of these cases, when at least one of r or s is greater than or equal to 1 (as is required by the pumping lemma), the resulting string fails to be in L. In the third case we have

$$uv^i wx^i y = a^{k+(i-1)r} b^{k^2 + (i-1)s}$$

which fails to be in L for all except finitely many i. Thus L cannot be context-free since the pumping lemma fails to hold.

The pumping lemma has other uses besides showing that certain languages are not context-free. We first consider the following problem: Is $L(G)$ finite for an arbitrary cfg G?

Suppose that $G = (N, \Sigma, S, P)$ is an arbitrary cfg that is in Chomsky normal form. Assume that N contains n elements. Then, from the proof of Lemma 3.6.1, we know that, if any string in $L(G)$ has length greater than 2^{n-1}, then $L(G)$ is infinite. Conversely, since the collection of terminals in G is finite, if $L(G)$ is infinite, then some string in $L(G)$ contains more than 2^{n-1} symbols. Now suppose that $z \in L(G)$ is the shortest string in $L(G)$ with the property that $|z| \geq 2^{n-1}$. We claim that

$$2^{n-1} \leq |z| \leq 2^{n-1} + 2^n$$

To see this, suppose that $|z| > 2^{n-1} + 2^n$. Then, from the proof of Lemma 3.6.1, $z = uvwxy$ and $uwy \in L(G)$, for appropriate substrings $u, v, w, x,$ and y. Now, since $|vwx| \leq 2^n$, we have that $|uwy| \geq |z| - 2^n > 2^{n-1}$.

On the other hand, $|uwy| < |uvwxy| = |z|$. But we assumed that z is the shortest string longer than 2^{n-1}, and so we have a contradiction. Consequently,

$$2^{n-1} \le |z| \le 2^{n-1} + 2^n$$

Thus $L(G)$ is infinite if and only if there is a $z \in L(G)$ for which

$$2^{n-1} \le |z| \le 2^{n-1} + 2^n$$

There are only finitely many such strings in Σ^*, and we may therefore test all such strings if necessary to see if any are in $L(G)$. Hence we have an algorithm for checking a context-free language to see if it is finite or not.

Note that in the elimination of useless symbols we inadvertently supplied an algorithm to answer another question about a language specified by a context-free grammar. $L(G)$ is nonempty if and only if its start symbol actually generates a string of terminals. We have an algorithm for eliminating nonterminals that do not generate terminal strings. Thus $L(G) = \emptyset$ if the start symbol doesn't appear in the collection of nonterminals for the transformed grammar.

Another question about context-free languages that we can answer is that of membership: Given a context-free language L over an alphabet Σ and a string $w \in \Sigma^*$, is $w \in L$ or not?

Lemma 3.6.2. Let $G = (N, \Sigma, S, P)$ be a context-free grammar with no ε productions that is in Chomsky normal form. Let x be a string in Σ^*. It is possible to determine for every $A \in N$ and for every substring w of x whether $A \overset{*}{\Rightarrow} w$.

Proof. Let $n = |x|$. Since there are many possible substrings of x, let us name them by their starting position and length. Let w_{ij} be the substring starting at position i having length j. We then prove that the statement holds for all w_{ij}. We proceed by induction on the length of the substring, that is, on j.

Suppose that $j = 1$. Then $|w_{ij}| = 1$ and so w_{ij} is a terminal symbol. Since the grammar is in Chomsky normal form, for any nonterminal A we have $A \overset{*}{\Rightarrow} w_{ij}$ if and only if there is a production $A \to w_{ij}$ in P. Since P is finite, it is possible to make this determination.

Now suppose that $j > 1$ and that the statement holds for all substrings of length less than j. Note that $A \overset{*}{\Rightarrow} w_{ij}$ if and only if $A \to BC$ for some pair of nonterminals B and C for which $B \overset{*}{\Rightarrow} w_{ik}$ and $C \overset{*}{\Rightarrow} w_{i+k,j-k}$ for some k between 1 and $j-1$. Now both w_{ik} and $w_{i+k,j-k}$ have length less than j, so by the induction hypothesis it is possible to determine if $B \overset{*}{\Rightarrow} w_{ik}$ and if $C \overset{*}{\Rightarrow} w_{i+k,j-k}$. We can therefore determine if $A \overset{*}{\Rightarrow} w_{ij}$ for each i between 1 and n and any j between 1 and $n-i+1$. ∎

In the preceding proof, note that if $j = n$ then we can determine if

$$S \overset{*}{\Rightarrow} w_{1j} = w_{1n} = x$$

That is, we can determine if $x \in L(G)$ for any $x \in \Sigma^*$.

We have that $x \in L(G)$ if and only if $S \overset{*}{\Rightarrow} x$, and from Lemma 3.6.2 we know that it is actually possible to determine if $S \overset{*}{\Rightarrow} x$. Of course, knowing that something is possible and actually doing it are not the same. A number of algorithms for determining if $x \in L(G)$ are known. We present one here due to Cocke, Younger, and Kasami called the CYK algorithm. The CYK algorithm simply constructs sets N_{ij} of nonterminals that generate the substrings w_{ij} of x. When done, if $S \in N_{1n}$, then $x \in L(G)$ (where $|x| = n$). Note that much work can be eliminated by the fact that there is no substring of length greater than $n - i + 1$ that begins at position i.

The CYK algorithm is given as follows:

1. For each $i = 1, 2, \ldots, n$, let

$$N_{i1} = \{A \mid A \to w_{i1}\}$$

That is, N_{i1} is the set of all nonterminals that produce the ith symbol of x.

2. For $j = 2, 3, \ldots, n$, do the following:
   For $i = 1, 2, \ldots, n - j + 1$, do the following:
   a. Set $N_{ij} = \emptyset$.
   b. For $k = 1, 2, \ldots, j - 1$, add to N_{ij} all nonterminals A for which $A \to BC$ with $B \in N_{ik}$ and $C \in N_{i+k, j-k}$.

3. If $S \in N_{1n}$, then $x \in L(G)$.

Note that the CYK algorithm requires a context-free grammar in Chomsky normal form. The algorithm essentially follows the idea of the proof of Lemma 3.6.2 in constructing the nonterminal sets N_{ij}. In step 2b, the step that builds the N_{ij}, we pair up nonterminals from N_{ik} and $N_{i+k, j-k}$, attempting to find right-hand sides of productions. When and if we find such a right-hand side, we add the nonterminal from the left-hand side to N_{ij}.

Example 3.6.1

Consider the context-free grammar

$$
\begin{aligned}
S &\to AB \mid BC \\
A &\to BA \mid a \\
B &\to CC \mid b \\
C &\to AB \mid a
\end{aligned}
$$

For the string $x = bbab$, we have the following table, where each box represents the set N_{ij}:

		$j=1$	$j=2$	$j=3$	$j=4$
b	$j=1$	B	$\emptyset$	A	S, C
b	$j=2$	B	A, S	S, C	
a	$j=3$	A, C	S, C		
b	$j=4$	B			

Since S is in N_{14}, x is generated from the start symbol S. Consequently, x is in the language generated by this grammar.

Suppose that $G_1 = (N_1, \Sigma_1, S_1, P_1)$ and $G_2 = (N_2, \Sigma_2, S_2, P_2)$ are two context-free grammars for which N_1 and N_2 are disjoint. Define the context-free grammar $G = (N, \Sigma, S, P)$, where

$$N = N_1 \cup N_2 \cup \{S\}$$
$$\Sigma = \Sigma_1 \cup \Sigma_2$$
$$P = P_1 \cup P_2 \cup \{(S, S_1), (S, S_2)\}$$

with S a new symbol. That is, P contains all productions from P_1 and P_2 and the two new productions $S \rightarrow S_1 \mid S_2$. It is easy to see that $L(G) = L(G_1) \cup L(G_2)$. First, if $w \in L(G_1)$, then we have $S_1 \overset{*}{\Rightarrow} w$, so $S \Rightarrow S_1 \overset{*}{\Rightarrow} w$, and thus we have $w \in L(G)$. Similarly, if $w \in L(G_2)$, then we have $w \in L(G)$, and so $L(G_1) \cup L(G_2) \subseteq L(G)$. On the other hand, if $w \in L(G)$, then $S \overset{*}{\Rightarrow} w$. But $S \rightarrow S_1 \mid S_2$ are the only productions with S on the left side. Thus either

$$S \Rightarrow S_1 \overset{*}{\Rightarrow} w$$

or

$$S \Rightarrow S_2 \overset{*}{\Rightarrow} w$$

Now, since $N_1 \cap N_2 = \emptyset$, only productions in P_1 can be used in $S_1 \overset{*}{\Rightarrow} w$, so if $S \Rightarrow S_1 \overset{*}{\Rightarrow} w$, we must have $w \in L(G_1)$. Similarly, if $S \Rightarrow S_2 \overset{*}{\Rightarrow} w$, we must have $w \in L(G_2)$. Thus $L(G) \subseteq L(G_1) \cup L(G_2)$. We have proved the following theorem.

Theorem 3.6.3.   If L_1 and L_2 are context-free languages, then $L_1 \cup L_2$ is a context-free language.

That is, the collection of context-free languages is closed with respect to union. This collection is also closed with respect to star closure.

Theorem 3.6.4.   If L is a context-free language, then so is L^*.

Proof.   Let $L = L(G)$ for $G = (N, \Sigma, S, P)$. We construct a context-free grammar $G' = (N', \Sigma, S', P')$ that generates L^* by letting $N' = N \cup \{S', T\}$, where S' and T are new symbols, and adding the productions $S' \rightarrow ST \mid \varepsilon$ and $T \rightarrow ST \mid \varepsilon$. Note that if $w_1, w_2, \ldots, w_n \in L(G)$, we have

$$
\begin{aligned}
S' \Rightarrow ST &\Rightarrow SST \\
&\overset{*}{\Rightarrow} \underset{\text{(n terms)}}{S \cdots ST} \\
&\Rightarrow S \cdots S\varepsilon \\
&\overset{*}{\Rightarrow} w_1 w_2 \cdots w_n
\end{aligned}
$$

Consequently, $L^* \subseteq L(G')$.   ∎

Theorem 3.6.5.   The concatenation of context-free languages is context-free.

Proof.   See Exercise 3.6.5.   ■

We have three *closure properties* of context-free languages in Theorems 3.6.3, 3.6.4, and 3.6.5. Unfortunately, context-free languages are not closed with respect to intersection. The language

$$L = \{a^i b^i c^i \mid i \geq 0\}$$

is not a context-free language as an application of the pumping lemma (Lemma 3.6.1) shows. Note that $L_1 = \{a^i b^j c^j \mid i, j \geq 0\}$ is generated by the context-free grammar

$$S \rightarrow AC$$
$$A \rightarrow aA \mid \varepsilon$$
$$C \rightarrow bCc \mid \varepsilon$$

and the language $L_2 = \{a^i b^i c^j \mid i, j \geq 0\}$ is generated by

$$S \rightarrow AC$$
$$A \rightarrow aAb \mid \varepsilon$$
$$C \rightarrow cC \mid \varepsilon$$

and so are context-free languages. But we have $L = L_1 \cap L_2$, and so the intersection of context-free languages is not necessarily a context-free language.

The context-free languages are not closed under complementation either. If we denote $\Sigma^* - L_i$ by $\overline{L_i}$, then

$$L_1 \cap L_2 = \overline{(\overline{L_1} \cup \overline{L_2})}$$

Since unions of context-free languages result in context-free languages, note that, if complementation of context-free languages always produces context-free languages, the preceding intersection would have to be context-free.

Exercises for Section 3.6

3.6.1. Show that each of the following are not context-free languages.

(a) $\{a^i b^i c^i \mid i \geq 1\}$

(b) $\{a^i b^i c^j \mid j \geq i\}$

(c) $\{a^i b^j c^k \mid i \leq j \leq k\}$

(d) $\{a^i \mid i \text{ is prime}\}$

(e) $\{w \in \{a, b, c\}^* \mid w \text{ has an equal number of } a\text{'s, } b\text{'s, and } c\text{'s}\}$

(f) $\{a^n b^n c^m \mid n \leq m \leq 2n\}$

(g) $\{ww \mid w \in \{a, b\}^*\}$.

3.6.2. Determine if the language generated by

$$S \rightarrow aaA \mid B$$
$$B \rightarrow aA \mid b$$
$$A \rightarrow aS \mid B \mid \varepsilon$$

is finite or infinite.

3.6.3. Determine if *bba*, *bab*, and *babba* are in $L(G)$ for G as in Example 3.6.1 using the CYK algorithm.

3.6.4. Let $G = (N, \Sigma, S, P)$ be a cfg and construct $G' = (N', \Sigma, S, P')$ as in the proof of Theorem 3.6.4. Show that $L(G') \subseteq L^*$.

3.6.5. Prove Theorem 3.6.5.

3.7 PUSHDOWN AUTOMATA

We have seen that context-free grammars extend our language specification ability to include some languages that cannot be recognized by finite automata. In this section we consider automata capable of recognizing all context-free languages.

Intuitively, the problem with finite automata is that they only have finite "memory" ability. Such simple context-free languages as $\{a^n b^n \mid n \geq 0\}$ require keeping track of arbitrarily large amounts of information; we must not only verify that all a's precede b's, but also count the a's. Since the number of a's is arbitrary, we need to avoid placing a limit on the number of a's that we can count.

The context-free language $\{wcw^R \mid w \in \{a, b, c\}^*\}$ suggests an additional consideration. Here we need more than an unrestricted ability to count. We must retain symbols from the string w to compare with the symbols of the string w^R.

In this section we define an automaton having a mechanism allowing unbounded storage and operating like a stack. These automata are called *pushdown automata*. In the following section we explore the connection between pushdown automata and context-free languages.

A pushdown automaton behaves similarly to the finite automata of Chapter 2. It exists in some state at all times and changes state depending on its current state and other information. In the case of the finite automata of Chapter 2, the "other information" consisted simply of the current input symbol. In the case of the pushdown automaton, we include both the current input symbol *and* the symbol currently on the top of the stack. In addition to changing state, the pushdown automaton may also change the top of the stack.

Definition 3.7.1. A *nondeterministic pushdown automaton* (npda) is a 7-tuple, $M = (Q, \Sigma, \Gamma, \Delta, s, F, z)$, where

Q is a finite set of *states*

Σ is an *input alphabet*

Γ is an alphabet called the *stack alphabet*

Δ is a *transition rule*

$s \in Q$ is the *initial* or *start state*

$z \in \Gamma$ is the *stack start symbol*

$F \subseteq Q$ is the set of *final* or *accepting states*.

From our previous description, a transition rule must look at the current state, the current input symbol, and the current top of the stack to indicate a next state and a stack action. Consequently, Δ is defined for triples of the form (q, σ, γ), where q is a state in Q, σ is a symbol in $\Delta \cup \{\varepsilon\}$, and $\gamma \in \Gamma$. The result of Δ applied to such a triple is a collection of pairs (p, w), where $p \in Q$ is the next state and $w \in \Gamma^*$ is a string placed (or pushed) on the stack *in place of* the symbol γ that was there before. Thus we may define the relation Δ as

$$\Delta \subseteq Q \times (\Sigma \cup \{\varepsilon\}) \times \Gamma \times Q \times \Gamma^*$$

Since we are defining a *nondeterministic* pushdown automaton, we would expect that Δ is not required to be a function (although it certainly is not restricted from being one). Thus, if Δ applied to a triple (q_1, a, b) yields the set $\{(q_2, cd), (q_2, dce), (q_3, efc)\}$, one of the three pairs in this set is nondeterministically chosen as the result, and the pushdown automaton is altered to reflect that choice. Note, too, that since the resulting pairs are from $Q \times \Gamma^*$ and since $\varepsilon \in \Gamma^*$ we may have $\Delta(q, a, b)$, yielding, say, (p, ε). Such a result indicates that the next state is p and that the symbol b is removed (or popped) from the top of the stack.

By defining $\Delta \subseteq Q \times (\Sigma \cup \{\varepsilon\}) \times \Gamma \times Q \times \Gamma^*$, we have forced Δ to consider a stack symbol in *all* moves. That is, no move is possible if the stack is empty. For that reason we assume that the stack initially contains some symbol, the stack start symbol z. On the other hand, a move such as

$$\Delta(q, \varepsilon, a) = \{(p, aa)\}$$

indicates that the npda may change to state p and push an a on the stack without consuming any input. Finally, note that if $\Delta(q, \sigma, \gamma) = \emptyset$, no move is possible from state q on the input symbol σ with the stack symbol γ. In this case the npda ceases execution.

Consider the nondeterministic pushdown automaton defined by

$$Q = \{q_1, q_2, q_3, q_4\}$$
$$\Sigma = \{a, b\}$$
$$\Gamma = \{A, B\}$$
$$z = A$$
$$F = \{q_4\}$$
$$s = q_1$$

and Δ given by the following table:

Δ	(a, A)	(b, A)	(ε, A)	(a, b)	(b, B)	(ε, B)
q_1	$\{(q_2, BA), (q_4, A)\}$		$\{(q_4, \varepsilon)\}$			
q_2				$\{(q_2, BB)\}$	$\{(q_3, \varepsilon)\}$	
q_3			$\{(q_4, A)\}$		$\{(q_3, \varepsilon)\}$	

Since Δ depends on current state, current input symbol, and current top of stack, the table has rows corresponding to states and columns corresponding to pairs of input and stack symbols.

Note that transitions are not given for all possible triples of state, input symbol, and stack symbol. Thus, if the npda enters some state where no next state and stack action are specified for the current stack and input symbols, the npda cannot move again. In other words, its activity stops. In particular, there are *no* transitions for any combination of stack and input symbols when this npda is in state q_4, the accepting state.

The actions of the npda are straightforward. The transition $\Delta(q_2, a, B) = \{(q_2, BB)\}$ pushes a B onto the stack and does not change the state. The transition $\Delta(q_2, b, B) = \{(q_3, \varepsilon)\}$ pops the B from the stack and changes state. The transition $\Delta(q_1, a, A) = \{(q_2, BA), (q_4, \varepsilon)\}$ indicates that a nondeterministic choice of action is made. Since, for this transition, the npda begins in state q_1 with A on the top of the stack, this transition indicates that we either push a B on the stack and move to state q_2 or else pop the A from the stack and move to the accepting state q_4. If this is done, then, since no moves are defined for state q_4, the npda halts.

On the other hand, if the npda moves to state q_2, then note that whenever an a is encountered in the input a B is pushed on the stack. Moreover, since the npda stays in state q_2 until the first b is encountered and then moves to state q_3, no b may precede any a. Finally, once in state q_3 only b's may be seen, and whenever a b is encountered, a B is popped from the stack. (Only as many B's can be popped as were pushed as a result of encountering a's in the input.)

The reader should verify that the only input strings that, when they are completely consumed, cause this npda to end in the final state q_4 are strings in the language $\{a^n b^n \mid n \geq 0\} \cup \{a\}$.

The nondeterministic pushdown automaton of the previous example *accepts* the language $\{a^n b^n \mid n \geq 0\} \cup \{a\}$ because the strings whose consumption cause it to move from its initial configuration to its final state are exactly these strings. We proceed to formalize what it means for an npda to accept a language by first introducing some useful notation.

During the processing of a string, each successive configuration of the npda can be described in terms of its current state, the contents of the stack, and the unread input. The triple (q, w, u), where q is the current state, w is the remaining input string, and u is the stack contents (with the symbol on the top of the stack in the leftmost position), is called an *instantaneous description* (ID) of the automaton. It describes the configuration of the pushdown automaton at some instant in its operation. We indicate a move from one configuration to another by placing the symbol $\vdash$ between instantaneous descriptions. Thus

$$(q_1, aw, bx) \vdash (q_2, w, yx)$$

represents a move as a result of $(q_2, y) \in \Delta(q_1, a, b)$. We can denote moves having an arbitrary number of steps by $\overset{*}{\vdash}$ and $\overset{+}{\vdash}$ (where * indicates "zero or more steps" and | indicates "one or more steps").

We now formally define what it means for a nondeterministic pushdown automaton to accept a language.

Definition 3.7.2.   Let $M = (Q, \Sigma, \Gamma, s, z, F, \Delta)$ be a nondeterministic pushdown automaton. The *language accepted by M* is denoted $L(M)$ and is the set

$$L(M) = \{w \in \Sigma^* \mid (s, w, z) \overset{*}{\vdash} (p, \varepsilon, u) \text{ for } p \in F \text{ and } u \in \Gamma^*\}$$

Note that acceptance requires that M move into a final state as the string w is exhausted. M may or may not terminate with an empty stack. (Note, however, that whenever the stack becomes empty the npda *must* stop, because all transitions require a stack symbol.)

Example 3.7.1

Suppose we want to construct a nondeterministic pushdown automaton that accepts the language

$$L = \{w \in \{a, b\}^* \mid w \text{ contains equally may } a\text{'s and } b\text{'s}\}$$

We must count the occurrences of a's and b's. This can be done by pushing symbols on the stack when one input character is seen and removing them when the other is seen. Let M be the npda given by

$$Q = \{q_1, q_2\}$$
$$\Sigma = \{a, b\}$$
$$\Gamma = \{A, B, Z\}$$
$$s = q_1$$
$$z = Z$$
$$F = \{q_2\}$$

and transition rule Δ given by the list

$$\Delta(q_1, \varepsilon, Z) = \{(q_2, Z)\}$$
$$\Delta(q_1, a, Z) = \{(q_1, AZ)\}$$
$$\Delta(q_1, b, Z) = \{(q_1, BZ)\}$$
$$\Delta(q_1, a, A) = \{(q_1, AA)\}$$
$$\Delta(q_1, b, A) = \{(q_1, \varepsilon)\}$$
$$\Delta(q_1, a, B) = \{(q_1, \varepsilon)\}$$
$$\Delta(q_1, b, B) = \{(q_1, BB)\}$$

In processing the string *abba*, M makes the following moves:

$$(q_1, abba, Z) \vdash (q_1, bba, AZ)$$
$$\vdash (q_1, ba, Z)$$
$$\vdash (q_1, a, BZ)$$
$$\vdash (q_1, \varepsilon, Z)$$
$$\vdash (q_2, \varepsilon, Z)$$

at which point the npda halts in the accepting state q_2. Thus *abba* is in $L(M)$.

Example 3.7.2

We can make use of the fact that symbols can be retrieved from a stack in the reverse of their order of insertion. Consider the language $L = \{wcw^R \mid w \in \{a, b\}^*\}$. An npda accepting L might push input characters on the stack until the c is found and then compare input characters and the top of stack, popping the stack if a match is found. Such an npda M may be given by

$$Q = \{q_1, q_2, q_3\}$$
$$\Sigma = \{a, b\}$$
$$\Gamma = \{a, b, z\}$$
$$s = q_1$$
$$z = \text{stack start symbol}$$
$$F = \{q_3\}$$

and Δ given by the following list:

$$\Delta(q_1, a, z) = \{(q_1, az)\} \qquad \Delta(q_1, c, z) = \{(q_2, z)\}$$
$$\Delta(q_1, a, a) = \{(q_1, aa)\} \qquad \Delta(q_1, c, a) = \{(q_2, a)\}$$
$$\Delta(q_1, a, b) = \{(q_1, ab)\} \qquad \Delta(q_1, c, b) = \{(q_2, b)\}$$
$$\Delta(q_1, b, z) = \{(q_1, bz)\} \qquad \Delta(q_2, a, a) = \{q_2, \varepsilon)\}$$
$$\Delta(q_1, b, a) = \{(q_1, ba)\} \qquad \Delta(q_2, b, b) = \{q_2, \varepsilon)\}$$
$$\Delta(q_1, b, b) = \{(q_1, bb)\} \qquad \Delta(q_2, \varepsilon, z) = \{(q_3, z)\}$$

Every nondeterministic finite automaton can be viewed as an npda that never operates on its stack. For example, consider the nfa whose transition diagram is

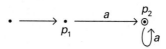

Let the npda M be given by

$$Q = \{q_1, q_2\}$$
$$\Sigma = \{a\}$$
$$\Gamma = \{z\}, \text{ the stack start symbol}$$
$$s = q_1$$
$$F = \{q_2\}$$

and Δ given by

Δ	(a, z)
q_1	$\{(q_2, z)\}$
q_2	$\{(q_2, z)\}$

It is clear that M accepts the same language as the finite automaton.

Exercises for Section 3.7

3.7.1. Find an npda accepting $\{a^n b^n \mid n \geq 0\}$.

3.7.2. Trace the processing of the npda M of Example 3.7.1 on the strings *abaababb* and *abaa*. Are these strings accepted by M?

3.7.3. Trace the execution of the npda M of Example 3.7.2 on the strings *c*, *abcba*, *abcab*, and *babbcbbab*.

3.7.4. The language $L = \{ww^R \mid w \in \{a, b\}^+\}$ is similar to the language of Example 3.7.2 except that there is no character marking the boundary between the w and w^R. Consequently, a nondeterministic pushdown automaton accepting L will have to nondeterministically choose a midpoint and switch from pushing characters on the stack to matching and popping. Use the npda M of Example 3.7.2 as a starting point and construct an npda that accepts L by adding or deleting appropriate transitions.

3.7.5. Find npda's for the following languages:

(a) $\{a^n b^{2n} \mid n \geq 0\}$

(b) $\{a^n b^m c^{n+m} \mid n \geq 0 \text{ and } m \geq 0 \}$

(c) $\{a^n b^m \mid n \leq m \leq 3n\}$

(d) $\{w \in \{a, b\}^* \mid w \text{ contains one more } a \text{ than } b\text{'s}\}$

(e) $\{a^n b^m \mid n \geq 0 \text{ and } m \neq n\}$

(f) $\{w_1 c w_2 \mid w_1, w_2 \in \{a, b\}^* \text{ and } w_1 \neq w_2^R\}$

3.7.6. What language is accepted by M that is given by

$$Q = \{q_1, q_2, q_3\}$$
$$\Sigma = \{a, b\}$$
$$\Gamma = \Sigma \cup \{z\}, \text{ where } z \text{ is the stack start symbol}$$
$$s = q_1$$
$$F = \{q_3\}$$

and Δ is given by the table

Δ	(a, z)	(a, b)	(b, a)	(b, b)
q_1	$\{(q_2, a), (q_3, \varepsilon)\}$			
q_2		$\{(q_3, \varepsilon)\}$	$\{(q_2, b)\}$	$\{(q_2, b)\}$

What language is accepted if we change F to $F = \{q_1, q_2, q_3\}$?

3.7.7. Find an npda that accepts aa^*ba. The presence of a memory device in an automaton can allow for a certain economy of states. A nondeterministic finite automaton for the preceding language necessarily has at least four states, and consequently an npda for this language that ignores its stack must also have at least four states. Find an npda for aa^*ba having only two states.

3.8 PUSHDOWN AUTOMATA AND CONTEXT-FREE LANGUAGES

The main result of this section is that nondeterministic pushdown automata are accepters for context-free languages. This requires that for any context-free language we must be able to find a nondeterministic pushdown automaton accepting it and, conversely, that for any language accepted by a nondeterministic pushdown automaton a context-free grammar can be given. We first show that any context-free language is accepted by some nondeterministic pushdown automaton by giving a construction method for such an npda.

Let $G = (N, \Sigma, S, P)$ be any context-free grammar. We wish to construct a nondeterministic pushdown automaton accepting $L(G)$. The npda we will construct must be able to verify that all strings in $L(G)$ are derivable. The underlying idea is to construct an npda that can carry out a leftmost derivation of any string in the language. It will represent the derivation by keeping the nonterminals in the rightmost part of the derivation on the stack, while the leftmost part (consisting entirely of terminals) is identical with the input that has been read.

We begin by pushing the start symbol (of G) onto the stack. At each subsequent step we do one of the following:

1. If the top of stack symbol is some nonterminal A, we replace it by the right-hand side of some production for A, say $A \to w$, or

2. If the top of stack symbol is a terminal and if it matches the next input symbol, we pop it from the stack.

These actions mimic a leftmost derivation of the input string. If the input string is exhausted and the top of the stack is the stack start symbol, we accept the string, because a derivation of it is possible. Note that nondeterminism is present in step 1 when we select the right-hand side of some production to push on the stack.

To define such a nondeterministic pushdown automaton M, we let

$$Q = \{q_1, q_2, q_3\}$$
$$\Gamma = N \cup \Sigma \cup \{z\}, \text{ where } z \text{ is the stack start symbol}$$
$$\text{(and is different from all symbols in } N \cup \Sigma \text{)}$$
$$F = \{q_3\}$$
$$s = q_1$$

and the transition rule consists of the following four types of transitions:

1. $\Delta(q_1, \varepsilon, z) = \{(q_2, Sz)\}$, which corresponds to initially pushing the start symbol on the stack.

2. $\Delta(q_2, \varepsilon, A) = \{(q_2, w) \mid A \to w \text{ is a production in } P\}$ for each nonterminal A in N.

3. $\Delta(q_2, a, a) = \{(q_2, \varepsilon)\}$ for each terminal symbol a in Σ.

4. $\Delta(q_2, \varepsilon, z) - \{(q_3, z)\}$.

Example 3.8.1

Let G be the context-free grammar whose productions are

$$S \to aSa \mid bSb \mid c$$

Note that $L(G) = \{wcw^R \mid w \in \{a, b\}^*\}$. The corresponding nondeterministic pushdown automaton will have transition rule given by

$$\Delta(q_1, \varepsilon, z) = \{(q_2, Sz)\}$$
$$\Delta(q_2, \varepsilon, S) = \{(q_2, aSa), (q_2, bSb), (q_2, c)\}$$
$$\Delta(q_2, a, a) = \Delta(q_2, b, b) = \Delta(q_2, c, c) = \{(q_2, \varepsilon)\}$$
$$\Delta(q_2, \varepsilon, z) = \{(q_3, \varepsilon)\}$$

The string *abcba* is accepted by the following sequence:

$$
\begin{aligned}
(q_1, abcba, z) &\vdash (q_2, abcba, Sz) \\
&\vdash (q_2, abcba, aSaz) \\
&\vdash (q_2, bcba, Saz) \qquad \text{note that a pop has occurred} \\
&\vdash (q_2, bcba, bSbaz) \\
&\vdash (q_2, cba, Sbaz) \qquad \text{another pop} \\
&\vdash (q_2, cba, cbaz) \\
&\vdash (q_2, ba, baz) \qquad \text{another pop} \\
&\vdash (q_2, a, az) \qquad \text{another pop} \\
&\vdash (q_2, \varepsilon, z) \qquad \text{another pop} \\
&\vdash (q_3, \varepsilon, z) \qquad \text{accept}
\end{aligned}
$$

Suppose that we have constructed an npda from a context-free grammar in the preceding manner. Note that if we have that

$$(q_2, x, A\alpha) \overset{*}{\vdash} (q_2, x, \beta\alpha)$$

then $A \overset{*}{\Rightarrow} \beta$ is possible in the grammar. Thus, if $w = a_1 a_2 \ldots a_n$ is accepted by the npda, we must have that

$$
\begin{aligned}
(q_2, a_1 a_2 \ldots a_n, Sz) &\overset{*}{\vdash} (q_2, a_1 a_2 \ldots a_n, a_1 \beta_1 z) \\
&\vdash (q_2, a_2 \ldots a_n, \beta_1 z) \\
&\overset{*}{\vdash} (q_2, a_n, a_n z) \\
&\vdash (q_2, \varepsilon, z) \\
&\vdash (q_3, \varepsilon, z)
\end{aligned}
$$

and so we have the derivations

$$S \overset{*}{\Rightarrow} a_1 \beta_1 \overset{*}{\Rightarrow} a_1 a_2 \beta_2 \overset{*}{\Rightarrow} \cdots \overset{*}{\Rightarrow} a_1 a_2 \ldots a_n = w$$

Consequently, if w is accepted by the npda, then w is derivable in the grammar.

Conversely, suppose that we have a grammar in Chomsky normal form. If $S \overset{*}{\Rightarrow} a_1 a_2 \ldots a_n$, then we must have a leftmost derivation of $a_1 a_2 \ldots a_n$ of the form

$$S \overset{*}{\Rightarrow} A_1 \alpha_1 \Rightarrow a_1 \alpha_1 \overset{*}{\Rightarrow} a_1 A_2 \alpha_2 \Rightarrow a_1 a_2 \alpha_2 \overset{*}{\Rightarrow} a_1 a_2 \ldots a_n$$

Thus, in any npda derived from this grammar, we would have the sequence

$$
\begin{aligned}
(q_2, a_1 a_2 \ldots a_n, Sz) &\overset{*}{\vdash} (q_2, a_1 a_2 \ldots a_n, a_1 \alpha_1 z) \\
&\vdash (q_2, a_2 \ldots a_n, \alpha_1 z) \\
&\overset{*}{\vdash} (q_2, \varepsilon, z) \\
&\vdash (q_3, \varepsilon, z)
\end{aligned}
$$

That is, the npda would accept the string $w = a_1 a_2 \ldots a_n$. Theorem 3.8.1 then follows.

Theorem 3.8.1.   If L is a context-free language, then there exists an npda M for which $L = L(M)$.

Theorem 3.8.1 represents half of our goal. To show its converse, that any language accepted by an npda is context-free, is our remaining task. For full generality, what we need to do is to take an arbitrary npda and show how to obtain a context-free grammar that generates the language accepted by it. To simplify the discussions, we shall actually deal with an equivalent problem, one in which the npda we start with is, in some sense, well behaved.

Let M be an arbitrary npda. Define the *language accepted by empty stack* by M as

$$N(M) = \{w \mid (q_1, w, z) \overset{*}{\vdash} (p, \varepsilon, \varepsilon)\}$$

Here q_1 is the start state of M and p is *any* state in Q. $N(M)$ is simply the set of all strings that drive M from its initial state to any state in which the stack is empty. Since all transitions are defined in terms of a stack symbol, such a configuration is a halted configuration for M.

Note that for an npda it is not necessarily the case that $N(M) = L(M)$. For example, let M have the three transitions

$$\Delta(q_1, a, z) = \{(q_1, az)\}$$
$$\Delta(q_1, b, z) = \{(q_2, \varepsilon)\}$$
$$\Delta(q_1, a, a) = \{(q_3, a)\}$$

where $Q = \{q_1, q_2, q_3\}$, $F = \{q_3\}$, z is the stack start symbol, and q_1 is the initial state. Note that $N(M) = \{b\}$ while $L(M) = \{a^2\}$.

Let M be any npda. We can transform M into an npda M' so that $L(M) = N(M')$. It will turn out that M' accepts only in a single final state as well.

First note that, if M ever pops z from its stack, it does so by means of a transition of the form $(q', \varepsilon) \in \Lambda(q, \tau, z)$ for some states q and q' and some $\tau \in \Gamma \cup \{\varepsilon\}$. It may or may not be the case that $q' \in F$. Replace all such transitions where q' *is not* in F by new transitions (p_1, z) for a new state p_1. Replace all such transitions where q' *is* in F by (p_2, z) for another new state p_2 and add p_2 to F. After these alterations to M, $N(M) = \emptyset$, but $L(M)$ remains unchanged. We now add transitions and states so that, once M enters a final state, it empties its stack. For all $q \in F$, add transitions

$$\Delta(q, \varepsilon, \gamma) = \{(p_3, \gamma)\}, \qquad \text{for all } \gamma \in \Gamma$$
$$\Delta(p_3, \varepsilon, \gamma) = \{(p_3, \varepsilon)\}, \qquad \text{for all } \gamma \in \Gamma - \{z\}$$
$$\Delta(p_3, \varepsilon, z) = \{(p_4, \varepsilon)\}$$

When this is done, set $F = \{p_4\}$. The resulting npda, M', accepts only in a single final state with an empty stack. Thus $L(M') = N(M') = L(M)$.

In addition to the requirement that the npda's of our discussion accept only in a single state when the stack is empty, we also require that all transitions be of the form

$$\Delta(q, a, A) = \{c_1, c_2, \ldots, c_n\}$$

where each $c_i = (p, \varepsilon)$ or $c_i = (p, BC)$. That is, each transition increases or decreases the contents of the stack by only one symbol.

To construct a context-free grammar for an npda, we reverse the process of the last section so that a derivation simulates the moves of the npda as it accepts a string. To do so, at each step the nonterminal portion of the partially generated string should reflect the contents of the stack, while its terminal prefix is the processed portions of the input string. A configuration of the npda involves a state as well as stack contents. Since we want our derivation to simulate the npda's moves, which in turn depend on the current state, our context-free grammar must also keep track of the state as well. A solution to this problem uses nonterminals of the form $[qAp]$, where we interpret $[qAp] \overset{*}{\Rightarrow} w$ to correspond to the npda's action of removing A from the stack and moving from state q to state p while consuming the input w.

Since we are requiring our npda to meet certain criteria in the way its transitions are formed, the process of listing the corresponding productions is simplified. If $(q_j, \varepsilon) \in \Delta(q_i, a, A)$, then the corresponding production is $[q_i A q_j] \to a$, since the npda moves from q_i to q_j and pops A from the stack on input a.

On the other hand, if $(q_j, BC) \in \Delta(q_i, a, A)$, note that the input of a causes A to be popped from the stack, but then causes B and C to be pushed back on. Since the npda accepts with an empty stack, B and C must eventually be removed. Their removal results in appropriate state changes. Thus, if $(q_j, BC) \in \Delta(q_i, a, A)$, we include all productions of the form $[q_i A q_m] \to a[q_j B q_n][q_n C q_m]$, where q_n and q_m range over all possible states in Q.

Finally, we let the start symbol be $[szq_f]$, where s is the initial state, z is the stack start symbol, and q_f is the (single) accepting state of the npda.

Example 3.8.2

Consider the npda whose transitions are given as

1. $\Delta(q_1, a, z) = \{(q_1, Az)\}$ 4. $\Delta(q_2, b, A) = \{(q_2, \varepsilon)\}$
2. $\Delta(q_1, a, A) = \{(q_1, AA)\}$ 5. $\Delta(q_2, \varepsilon, A) = \{(q_2, \varepsilon)\}$
3. $\Delta(q_1, b, A) = \{(q_2, \varepsilon)\}$ 6. $\Delta(q_2, \varepsilon, z) = \{(q_3, \varepsilon)\}$

where z is the stack start symbol, $F = \{q_3\}$, and q_1 is the initial state. Note that this npda only enters the accepting state when the stack is empty. Moreover, all transitions are of the required forms. In deriving the associated grammar, we have as a start symbol $[q_1 z q_3]$. Transitions 3, 4, 5, and 6 easily translate into the following productions:

$$[q_1 A q_2] \to b$$
$$[q_2 A q_2] \to b \mid \varepsilon$$
$$[q_2 z q_3] \to \varepsilon$$

Transitions 1 and 2 generate the following productions:

From 1: $[q_1 z q_1] \to a[q_1 A q_1][q_1 z q_1] \mid a[q_1 A q_2][q_2 z q_1] \mid a[q_1 A q_3][q_3 z q_1]$
$[q_1 z q_2] \to a[q_1 A q_1][q_1 z q_2] \mid a[q_1 A q_2][q_2 z q_2] \mid a[q_1 A q_3][q_3 z q_2]$
$[q_1 z q_3] \to a[q_1 A q_1][q_1 z q_3] \mid a[q_1 A q_2][q_2 z q_3] \mid a[q_1 A q_3][q_3 z q_3]$

From 2: $[q_1 A q_1] \to a[q_1 A q_1][q_1 A q_1] \mid a[q_1 A q_2][q_2 A q_1] \mid a[q_1 A q_3][q_3 A q_1]$
$[q_1 A q_2] \to a[q_1 A q_1][q_1 A q_2] \mid a[q_1 A q_2][q_2 A q_2] \mid a[q_1 A q_3][q_3 A q_2]$
$[q_1 A q_3] \to a[q_1 A q_1][q_1 A q_3] \mid a[q_1 A q_2][q_2 A q_3] \mid a[q_1 A q_3][q_3 A q_3]$

The string *aabb* is accepted by this npda with the following sequence of configurations:

$$(q_1, aabb, z) \vdash (q_1, abb, Az)$$
$$\vdash (q_2, \varepsilon, z)$$
$$\vdash (q_1, bb, AAz)$$
$$\vdash (q_2, b, Az)$$
$$\vdash (q_3, \varepsilon, \varepsilon)$$

The corresponding derivation in the preceding grammar is

$$[q_1 z q_3] \Rightarrow a[q_1 A q_2][q_2 z q_3]$$
$$\Rightarrow aa[q_1 A q_2][q_2 A q_2][q_2 z q_3]$$
$$\Rightarrow aab[q_2 A q_2][q_2 z q_3]$$
$$\Rightarrow aabb[q_2 z q_3]$$
$$\Rightarrow aabb$$

(Note that the "first q" in each string in the derivation corresponds to the current state in the npda's sequence. Moreover, the sequence of "middle" symbols corresponds to the stack contents as the npda accepts *aabb*.)

This construction often yields a complicated grammar. For example, in the preceding the nonterminal symbols $[q_2 z q_1]$, $[q_3 z q_1]$, $[q_3 z q_2]$, $[q_2 A q_1]$, $[q_3 A q_1]$, $[q_3 A q_2]$, and $[q_3 z q_3]$ never appear as the left-hand side of any production. Consequently, these symbols can never be generated in any derivation of a terminal string. Despite introducing such undesirable complexity, this construction technique may be applied to *any* npda whose transition rules satisfy the given conditions. The simplification techniques of Section 3.5 may be applied to the resulting grammar to remove useless portions of it.

Note that from the way a grammar is constructed from an npda satisfying the given conditions, if we have that

$$(q_i, uv, Ax) \stackrel{*}{\vdash} (q_j, v, x)$$

by means of operation of the pushdown automaton, then in the resulting grammar we have

$$[q_i A q_j] \stackrel{*}{\Rightarrow} u$$

That is, if the npda removes A from the stack by reading the string u and going from state q_i to state q_j, then the nonterminal $[q_i A q_j]$ can derive u.

Conversely, note that if in some derivation we have

$$[q_i A q_k] \stackrel{*}{\Rightarrow} a[q_j B q_r][q_r C q_k]$$

then A can be replaced by BC on the stack while reading a and going from state q_i to q_j.

On the other hand, if $[q_i A q_j] \Rightarrow a$ is a single step derivation, then $\Delta(q_i, a, A)$ contains (q_j, ε) so by consuming a in the input string, A can be popped from the stack. Thus, if $[q_i A q_j] \stackrel{*}{\Rightarrow} u$, the sequence of strings of terminals and nonterminals constituting the derivation corresponds to a sequence of moves in the npda for which $(q_i, uv, Ax) \stackrel{*}{\vdash} (q_j, v, x)$. Consequently, any string of terminals generated in the grammar is accepted by the npda, and vice versa. We have the following theorem:

Theorem 3.8.2.   If L is accepted by some npda, then L is a context-free language.

Nondeterministic pushdown automata give us an alternative characterization of the context-free languages. It is often just as easy to prove that a language is a context-free language by proving an npda accepts it as it is to prove it is context-free by proving a context-free grammar generates it. Occasionally, it is even easier to give the npda description than the grammar description. Additionally, the npda model sometimes eases the business of proving properties about context-free languages.

Theorem 3.8.3.   If L_1 is a context-free language and L_2 is a regular language, then $L_1 \cap L_2$ is a context-free language.

Proof.   Let $M_1 = (Q_1, \Sigma_1, \Gamma, s_1, z, F_1, \Delta_1)$ be an npda that accepts L_1. Let $M_2 = (Q_2, \Sigma_2, s_2, F_2, \delta)$ be a *deterministic* finite automaton accepting the regular language L_2. We construct an npda that accepts $L_1 \cap L_2$ by combining M_1 and M_2. This npda essentially simulates the action of M_1 and M_2 in parallel and accepts a string when and only when both M_1 and M_2 accept. Define the npda $M = (Q, \Sigma, \Gamma, s, z, F, \Delta)$ as follows:

$$Q = Q_1 \times Q_2$$
$$s = (s_1, s_2)$$
$$F = F_1 \times F_2$$
$$\Sigma = \Sigma_1 \cup \Sigma_2$$

and the transition rule Δ is defined so that we have that

$$((q_k, p_l), x) \in \Delta((q_i, q_j), a, b)$$

if and only if both $\delta(p_j, a) = p_l$ and $(q_k, x) \in \Delta_1(q_i, a, b)$. That is,

$$\Delta((q_i, p_j), a, b) = \{((q_k, p_l), x) \mid (q_k, x) \in \Delta_1(q_i, a, b) \quad \text{and} \quad \delta(p_j, a) = \{p_l\}$$

Note that the states of M are labeled by pairs representing the states that M_1 and M_2, respectively, can be in after processing an input. A string is accepted if it causes M to terminate in a state (q, p), where $q \in F_1$ and $p \in F_2$. That is, it is accepted if M_1 accepts the string terminating in state q and M_2 also accepts it terminating in state p. A simple induction on the number of steps in a computation shows that $(s, w, z) \overset{*}{\vdash} ((q, p), \varepsilon, u)$, with $q \in F_1$ and $p \in F_2$, if and only if $(s_1, w, z) \overset{*}{\vdash} (q, \varepsilon, u)$ and $\delta(s_2, w) = p$. ∎

In Section 3.7 we discovered that the intersection of context-free languages is not necessarily a context-free language. That is, the family of context-free languages is not closed under intersection. Theorem 3.8.3 shows that this family is closed under *regular intersection*.

For example, the language $L = \{a^n b^n \mid n \geq 0 \text{ and } n \neq 100\}$ is a context-free language. While such a claim could be proved by constructing a context-free grammar that generates it or an npda that accepts it, a more elegant argument comes from the theorem. Note that $L_1 = \{a^n b^n \mid n \geq 0\}$ is certainly a context-free language. Moreover, we know that both $L_2 = a^* b^*$ and $L_3 = \{a^{100} b^{100}\}$ are regular. Consequently, $L_4 = L_2 - L_3$ is also regular, since the regular languages are closed with respect to language difference. Then note that we have $L = L_1 \cap L_4$, and so L is context-free according to the theorem.

Theorem 3.8.3 can also be used to show that some languages are *not* context-free. For example, we know that $\{a^n b^n c^n \mid n \geq 0\}$ is not context-free. Let

$$L = \{w \in \{a, b, c\}^* \mid w \text{ contain equally as many } a\text{'s, } b\text{'s, and } c\text{'s}\}$$

Then L is not context-free, for if it were, then

$$\{a^n b^n c^n \mid n \geq 0\} = L \cap (a^* b^* c^*)$$

would also be context-free.

Exercises for Section 3.8

3.8.1. For the npda of Example 3.8.1, give the sequence of instantaneous descriptions that accepts the string *babcbab*. At what point does the string *abcab* fail to be accepted?

3.8.2. Find an npda accepting the language generated by the following context-free grammar:

$$S \rightarrow aAA$$
$$A \rightarrow bS \mid aS \mid a$$

3.8.3. Find an npda accepting the language generated by the context-free grammar

$$S \rightarrow aSb \mid aSbb \mid \varepsilon$$

3.8.4. Construct an npda accepting the language generated by the context-free grammar

$$S \rightarrow aABB \mid aAA$$
$$A \rightarrow aBB \mid \varepsilon$$
$$B \rightarrow bBB \mid A$$

3.8.5. Show how to convert an arbitrary npda into one for which all transitions are of the form $\Delta(q, u, A) = \{c_1, c_2, \ldots, c_n\}$, where each $c_i = (p, \varepsilon)$ or $c_i = (p, BC)$.

3.8.6. Find a derivation of $a^3 b^3$ in the grammar of Example 3.8.2.

3.8.7. Apply the preceding construction to the npda given by $M = (Q, \Sigma, \Gamma, s, z, F, \Delta)$, where $Q = \{q_1, q_2, q_3, q_4\}$, $F = \{q_3\}$, $s = q_1$, $\Sigma = \{a, b\}$, $\Gamma = \{A, B, z\}$, and Δ is given as

$$\Delta(q_1, a, z) = \{(q_1, Az)\} \qquad \Delta(q_1, b, A) = \{(q_2, \varepsilon)\}$$
$$\Delta(q_4, \varepsilon, z) = \{(q_1, Az)\} \qquad \Delta(q_2, \varepsilon, z) = \{(q_3, \varepsilon)\}$$
$$\Delta(q_1, a, A) = \{(q_4, \varepsilon)\}$$

3.8.8. Find a context-free grammar generating the same language accepted by the npda $M = (Q, \Sigma, \Gamma, s, z, F, \Delta)$, where $Q = \{q_1, q_2\}$, $\Sigma = \{a, b\}$, $\Gamma = \{a, z\}$, $s = q_1$, $F = \{q_2\}$, and Δ is given by

$$\Delta(q_1, a, z) = \{(q_1, az)\}$$
$$\Delta(q_1, b, a) = \{(q_1, aa)\}$$
$$\Delta(q_1, a, a) = \{(q_2, \varepsilon)\}$$

3.8.9. Find a context-free grammar for the language accepted by the npda $M = (Q, \Sigma, \Gamma, s, z, F, \Delta)$, where $Q = \{q_1, q_2, q_3\}$, $\Sigma = \{a, b\}$, $\Gamma = \{A, z\}$, z is the stack start symbol, $F = \{q_3\}$, and Δ is given by

$$\Delta(q_1, a, z) = \{(q_1, Az)\}$$
$$\Delta(q_1, a, A) = \{(q_1, A)\}$$
$$\Delta(q_1, b, A) = \{(q_2, \varepsilon)\}$$
$$\Delta(q_2, \varepsilon, z) = \{(q_3, \varepsilon)\}$$

Note that this npda does *not* satisfy the two conditions required for the construction of a cfg.

3.8.10. Let $M = (Q, \Sigma, \Gamma, s, z, F, \Delta)$, where $Q = \{q_1, q_2, q_3, q_4\}$, $\Sigma = \{a, b\}$, $\Gamma = \{X, z\}$, $s = q_1$, z is the stack start symbol, $F = \emptyset$ (that is, this npda accepts strictly by the empty stack), and Δ is given by

$$\Delta(q_1, b, z) = \{(q_1, Xz)\}, \qquad \Delta(q_1, \varepsilon, z) = \{(q_1, \varepsilon)\}$$
$$\Delta(q_1, b, X) = \{(q_1, XX)\} \qquad \Delta(q_2, b, X) = \{(q_2, \varepsilon)\}$$
$$\Delta(q_1, a, X) = \{(q_2, X)\} \qquad \Delta(q_2, a, z) = \{(q_1, z)\}$$

After appropriately changing this npda to satisfy the conditions required for the context-free grammar construction, find a context-free grammar for the language accepted by it.

3.8.11. Find a context-free grammar that generates the language accepted by the npda

$$M = (Q, \Sigma, \Gamma, s, z, F, \Delta), \text{ where}$$
$$Q = \{q_1, q_2\}$$
$$\Sigma = \{a, b\}$$
$$\Gamma = \{A, z\}, \text{ and } z \text{ is the stack start symbol}$$
$$s = q_1$$
$$F = \{q_2\}$$

and Δ is given by

$$\Delta(q_1, a, z) = \{(q_1, Az)\}$$
$$\Delta(q_1, b, A) = \{(q_1, AA)\}$$
$$\Delta(q_1, a, A) = \{(q_2, \varepsilon)\}$$

3.8.12. Show that

$$\{a^n b^n \mid n \geq 0 \text{ and } n \text{ is not a multiple of 5}\}$$

is a context-free language.

3.8.13. Let $L = \{a^i b^j c^k \mid i \neq j \text{ or } j \neq k\}$.

(a) Show that L is a context-free language.

(b) Show that if Σ is any alphabet for which $L \subseteq \Sigma^*$ then $\Sigma^* - L$ is not context free. (*Hint:* Consider the regular language $a^*b^*c^*$, again.)

3.8.14. Consider the language consisting of all strings over $\{a, b\}$ that contain equally as many a's and b's, but do not contain the substring aab. Is this language a context-free language?

3.8.15. Show that the set of context-free languages is not closed with respect to complementation. That is, it is not the case in general that both L and $\Sigma^* - L$ are context-free languages.

3.9 GREIBACH NORMAL FORM

Chomsky normal form is one of several useful normal forms for context-free grammars. Another normal form having many important theoretical and practical consequences is *Greibach normal form*. In Greibach normal form, we restrict the position in which terminals and nonterminals can appear. We begin with two useful results.

Theorem 3.9.1.   If $A \to \alpha B \gamma$ is a production in a context-free grammar and if $B \to \beta_1 \mid \beta_2 \mid \ldots \mid \beta_m$ are all productions having B as the left side, then $A \to \alpha B \gamma$ can be replaced by $A \to \alpha \beta_1 \gamma \mid \alpha \beta_2 \gamma \mid \ldots \mid \alpha \beta_m \gamma$ without changing the language generated by the grammar.

Proof.   Let G be the original grammar and let G' be the grammar resulting from the alteration. We have to show that $L(G) = L(G')$. We first show that $L(G') \subseteq L(G)$. Suppose that $w \in L(G')$. If the derivation of w does not involve any of the productions $A \to \alpha \beta_i \gamma$, then $w \in L(G)$, and we are done. On the other hand, if the derivation of w does use a production $A \to \alpha \beta_i \gamma$, then $A \Rightarrow \alpha B \gamma \Rightarrow \alpha \beta_i \gamma$ can be used in G to derive w. Hence $w \in L(G)$. Either way we have $L(G') \subseteq L(G)$.

   To show that $L(G) \subseteq L(G')$, we let $w \in L(G)$. If $A \to \alpha B \gamma$ is not used in the derivation of w, then, since all other productions of G are in G', $w \in L(G')$ and we are done. If $A \to \alpha B \gamma$ is used in the derivation of w, then at some point later B must be replaced by one of the β_i. We may do this immediately, thus combining the two steps into a single step $A \Rightarrow \alpha \beta_i \gamma$. Thus w is derivable in G', and so either way $w \in L(G')$ and we have $L(G) \subseteq L(G')$.   ∎

For example, consider the context-free grammar with productions

$$S \to a \mid aaB \mid Bab \mid abBc$$
$$B \to baabS \mid bba$$

If we make the substitution allowed by Theorem 3.9.1, we get the grammar

$$S \to a \mid aabaabS \mid aabba \mid baabSab \mid bbaab$$
$$\mid abbaabSc \mid abbbac$$
$$B \to baabS \mid bba$$

Note that the B productions $B \to baabS \mid bba$ do not vanish, although they can no longer participate in derivations. In simplifying this resulting grammar, however, one of the simplification techniques of Section 3.5 will remove these useless productions.

   A production of the form $A \to \alpha A$, where $\alpha \in (N \cup \Sigma)^*$, is said to be *right recursive*. Similarly, a *left recursive* production is one of the form $A \to A\alpha$. Right-recursive productions cause parse trees to grow down to the right, while left-recursive productions cause growth down to the left. In many applications of grammars, left recursion is undesirable. The next theorem provides a method for systematically removing left recursion from context-free grammars.

Theorem 3.9.2. Let G be a context-free grammar and A a nonterminal in G. If $A \to A\alpha_1 \mid A\alpha_2 \mid \ldots \mid A\alpha_n$ are all of the left-recursive productions for A, and if $A \to \beta_1 \mid \beta_2 \mid \ldots \mid \beta_m$ are all of the other productions for A, then an equivalent grammar can be constructed by introducing the new nonterminal Z and replacing *all* the preceding productions by

$$A \to \beta_1 \mid \beta_2 \mid \ldots \mid \beta_m \mid \beta_1 Z \mid \beta_2 Z \mid \ldots \mid \beta_m Z$$
$$Z \to \alpha_1 \mid \alpha_2 \mid \ldots \mid \alpha_n \mid \alpha_1 Z \mid \alpha_2 Z \mid \ldots \mid \alpha_n Z$$

Proof. Note that in both cases the strings derivable from A using one or more productions form the regular language

$$\{\beta_1, \beta_2, \ldots, \beta_m\}\{\alpha_1, \alpha_2, \ldots, \alpha_n\}^*. \quad \blacksquare$$

Consider the context-free grammar given by

$$S \to Sa \mid Sb \mid cA$$
$$A \to Aa \mid a \mid \varepsilon$$

Note that there are left-recursive productions with S and A on their left-hand sides. Applying the theorem first to the nonterminal S and introducing the new nonterminal Z_1, we get the transformed context-free grammar

$$S \to cA \mid cAZ_1$$
$$Z_1 \to a \mid b \mid aZ_1 \mid bZ_1$$
$$A \to Aa \mid a \mid \varepsilon$$

Now applying the theorem to the nonterminal A and introducing the new nonterminal Z_2, we get the productions

$$S \to cA \mid cAZ_1$$
$$Z_1 \to a \mid b \mid aZ_1 \mid bZ_1$$
$$A \to a \mid aZ_2 \mid \varepsilon \mid Z_2$$
$$Z_2 \to a \mid aZ_2$$

Note that eliminating left-recursive productions introduces new nonterminals and right-recursive productions.

Definition 3.9.3. *A context-free grammar is in *Greibach normal form* (Gnf) if all productions are of the form $A \to a\alpha$, where a is a terminal symbol and $\alpha \in (\Sigma \cup N)^*$.*

Note that this normal form requires each production to have an alphabet symbol as the first symbol on the right-hand side of its productions. Thus a grammar in Gnf can have no left-recursive productions. Moreover, since each production requires at least one alphabet symbol to be present, only nonempty context-free languages not containing ε can be generated by context-free grammars in Gnf.

It is always possible to construct a context-free grammar in Greibach normal form for any context-free language not containing ε. The algorithm for this consists of several steps.

Suppose that L is a nonempty context-free language that does not contain ε. First we let $G = (\Sigma, N, S, P)$ be a context-free grammar in Chomsky normal form generating L. Assume that $N = \{A_1, A_2, \ldots, A_n\}$, where $A_1 = S$. We then modify the productions so that if $A_r \to A_s \alpha$ is a production then $r < s$. This is accomplished by systematically working through the nonterminals from A_1 to A_n. Assume that we have modified the productions so that, for $1 \leq i \leq k$, if $A_i \to A_j \alpha$, then $i < j$. We then show how to modify the productions for A_{k+1}.

If $A_{k+1} \to A_j \alpha$ is a production with $k+1 > j$, we generate a new set of productions by replacing A_j in the right-hand sides by the right-hand sides of all productions of the form $A_j \to \beta$, as in Theorem 3.9.1. When we make these substitutions, we will get productions of the form $A_{k+1} \to A_r \alpha$. It may be the case that $k+1 \leq r$ or that $r < k+1$. If $k + 1 \leq r$, we have a production of the desired form. If $r < k + 1$, then we repeat the process. Since there are only k indexes less than $k + 1$, after at most $k - 1$ repetitions of this process, we will have eliminated all productions of the form $A_{k+1} \to A_r \alpha$ for which $r < k + 1$. Thus all productions that remain are of the form $A_{k+1} \to A_r \alpha$ with $k + 1 \leq r$. Note that productions for which $k + 1 = r$ are left recursive and can be eliminated by means of Theorem 3.9.2 by introducing the new nonterminal Z_{k+1}.

We repeat this process for each of the original nonterminals A_1 through A_n. This results in productions of only three forms:

1. $A_k \to A_j \alpha$, with $k < j$

2. $A_k \to a \alpha$, for $a \in \Sigma$

3. $Z_k \to \alpha$, for $\alpha \in (N \cup \{Z_1, Z_2, \ldots, Z_n\})^*$

Note that, since A_n is the highest-numbered nonterminal, any productions for A_n must be of type 2. That is, the leftmost symbol on the right-hand side of any production for A_n must be a terminal. Also, any production for A_{n-1} has either a terminal or A_n as its leftmost symbol on the right-hand side. If it is A_n, we can replace A_n by the right-hand side of productions for A_n as in Theorem 3.9.1. These productions begin with a terminal. We then proceed to the productions for A_{n-2}, A_{n-3}, and so on, until the right-hand sides of each production for the original nonterminals begin with a terminal.

Finally, we consider the productions for $Z_1, Z_2, \ldots, Z_n$. Since we began with a context-free grammar in Chomsky normal form and applied only Theorems 3.9.1 and 3.9.2 to it, none of the productions $Z_i \to \alpha$ have another Z_j as a leftmost symbol on their right-hand sides. Thus all the productions for Z_i have right-hand sides that begin with either terminals or A_i's. For the Z_i's having right-hand sides beginning with one of the A_k's, we apply Theorem 3.9.1 one more time, and the resulting productions are of the desired form.

The preceding conversion gives us the following theorem:

Theorem 3.9.4.   Every nonempty context-free language that does not contain ε can be generated by a context-free grammar $G = (N, \Sigma, S, P)$ in which all productions in P are of the form $A \to aw$ for $A \in N$, $a \in \Sigma$, and $w \in N^*$.

Consider the context-free grammar in Chomsky normal form (which has had its nonterminals suitably relabeled)

$$A_1 \to A_2 A_2 \mid a$$
$$A_2 \to A_1 A_2 \mid b$$

Note that the productions $A_1 \to A_2 A_2 \mid a$ are already in suitable form for the first intermediate step. (The productions must satisfy $A_i \to A_j \alpha$ for $i < j$ only when a nonterminal is present on the right-hand side. Thus $A_1 \to a$ is acceptable.) We then consider the productions for A_2. The production $A_2 \to b$ is already acceptable, but $A_2 \to A_1 A_2$ is not. We substitute for A_1, getting the productions $A_2 \to A_2 A_2 A_2 \mid a A_2$. We now remove left recursion, giving the production set

$$A_1 \to A_2 A_2 \mid a$$
$$A_2 \to a A_2 \mid a A_2 Z \mid b \mid bZ$$

Finally, we substitute for A_2 appropriately to begin all right-hand sides with a terminal. This gives

$$A_1 \to a A_2 A_2 \mid a A_2 Z A_2 \mid b A_2 \mid b Z A_2 \mid a$$
$$A_2 \to a A_2 \mid a A_2 Z \mid b \mid bZ$$
$$Z \to a A_2 A_2 \mid a A_2 Z A_2 \mid b A_2 \mid b Z A_2 \mid a A_2 A_2 Z$$
$$\qquad \mid a A_2 Z A_2 Z \mid b A_2 Z \mid b Z A_2 Z$$

Note that all productions of the form given in Theorem 3.9.4 are necessarily of the proper form for *Gnf*. Thus we have the following corollary:

Corollary 3.9.5.   Every nonempty context-free language L that does not contain ε can be generated by a context-free grammar in Greibach normal form.

Actually, an alternate definition of Gnf requires that all productions be of the form $A \to aw$ for $A \in N$, $a \in \Sigma$, and $w \in N^*$. The two definitions of Gnf are equivalent (Exercise 3.9.5).

Exercises for Section 3.9

3.9.1. Eliminate left recursion from

$$S \to Sa \mid aAc \mid c$$
$$A \to Ab \mid ba$$

3.9.2. Eliminate left recursion from $S \to aSb \mid SS \mid \varepsilon$.

3.9.3. In the remarks preceding Theorem 3.9.3, the statement that "none of the productions $Z_i \to \alpha$ have another Z_j as a leftmost symbol on their right-hand sides" depends on the fact that the right-hand sides of every production for A_i begin with either a terminal or $A_j A_k$ for some j and k. Use induction on the number of applications of Theorems 3.9.1 and 3.9.2 to prove this.

3.9.4. Convert to Greibach normal form

    (a) $S \to aSb \mid ab$

    (b) $S \to AA \mid a$
        $A \to SS \mid b$

    (c) $S \to Sa \mid Sb \mid cA$
        $A \to Aa \mid a \mid \varepsilon$

3.9.5. Show that the following definition of Greibach normal form is equivalent to definition 3.9.3: A context-free grammar $G = (N, \Sigma, S, P)$ is in Greibach normal form if all productions in P are of the form $A \to aw$ for $A \in N$, $a \in \Sigma$, and $w \in N^*$.

PROBLEMS

3.1. Consider the language $L = \{a^i b^i c^i \mid i \geq 1\}$ from Exercise 3.6.1(a). This language is not a context-free language since, for a given k, we may choose $z = a^k b^k c^k$ and proceed to show (by means of cases) that no choices for the substrings u, v, w, x, and y satisfy the pumping lemma (3.6.1). This language illustrates a major inconvenience of the pumping lemma: we have no way of telling which portion of the string to focus on as our vwx part. This uncertainty leads to exhausting subcases, which, while an effective technique, can be tedious. In this first exercise we give a stronger pumping lemma that allows us to control our focus on the parts of the string that are pumped.

    Let $G = (N, \Sigma, S, P)$ be a context-free grammar in Chomsky normal form with $\mid N \mid = k$, and let $n = 2^k + 1$. Suppose that $z \in L(G)$ with $\mid z \mid > n$, and let us "mark" at least n positions of z (that is, we are distinguishing the marked positions from the unmarked ones). We desire to find a path in the derivation tree for w analogous to the one in the proof of the pumping lemma. We construct our path by starting with the root and then descending left or right. We descend into the left or right subtree by determining which subtree generates the larger number of marked positions of z (ties can be broken arbitrarily). The resulting path then extends from the root to some marked position.

    Note that any node in the parse tree (and hence in the path we have found) has zero, one, or two children and that each child roots a subtree that may or may not generate any marked positions. If a node in the tree has two children both of which root subtrees that generate marked positions, we will call it a *branch point*.

    1. Prove that any branch point in the path we have constructed has at least half as many marked descendants as the previous branch point.

    2. Show that the path we constructed contains at least $k + 1$ branch points.

    The result that we want here is a weak form of a result due to W. Ogden. We shall refer to it as "Ogden's lemma."

Ogden's Lemma. Let L be a context-free language. Then there is a constant n for which, if $z \in L$ and we mark at least n positions of z, then we can write $z = uvwxy$ in such a manner that

    1. vx has at least one marked position.

    2. vwx has at most n marked positions.

    3. $uv^i wx^i y \in L$ for all $i \geq 0$.

3. Prove Ogden's lemma. *Hint:* By exercise 2, there are at least $k+1$ branch points in a suitably chosen path. Proceed as with the proof of the pumping lemma for the last $k+1$ of them.

3.2. In the following problems we make use of Ogden's lemma.

1. Apply Ogden's lemma to show that the language

$$\{a^i b^i c^i \mid i \geq 1\}$$

is not context-free.

2. Use Ogden's lemma to show that

$$\{a^i b^j c^k d^l \mid i = 0 \text{ or else } j = k = l\}$$

is not a context-free language.

3. Use Ogden's lemma to show that

$$\{a^i b^j c^k \mid i < j < k\}$$

is not context-free.

4. Is the language

$$\{a^i b^j c^k \mid i \neq j, j \neq k, \text{ and } i \neq k\}$$

a context-free language? Why or why not? How about

$$\{a^i b^j c^k \mid i \neq j, \text{ and } j \neq k\}$$

3.3. Let $L = \{ww \mid w \in \{a, b\}^*\}$. In Exercise 3.6.1 (g) the reader was asked to show that L is not context-free. Show that $\overline{L}$, the complement of L in $\{a, b\}^*$, *is* context free. *Hint:* Note that any string of odd length over $\{a, b\}^*$ is automatically in $\overline{L}$. On the other hand, any string of even length in $\overline{L}$ may be written as $u_1 x_1 v_1 u_2 x_2 v_2$, where x_1 and x_2 are in $\{a, b\}$, $x_1 \neq x_2$, and $\mid u_1 \mid = \mid u_2 \mid$, and $\mid v_1 \mid = \mid v_2 \mid$. Consider the union of two context-free languages, one containing only the odd-length strings over $\{a, b\}^*$ and one containing those strings of form $u_1 x_1 v_1 u_2 x_2 v_2$.

3.4. Similar to an npda, a *two-stack pushdown automaton* is a 7-tuple $M = (Q, \Sigma, \Gamma, \Delta, s, F, z)$. Here Q, Σ, Γ, s, and F are the same as in the case of the npda, but the transition relation, Δ, is of the form

$$\Delta \subseteq Q \times (\Sigma \cup \{\varepsilon\}) \times \Gamma \times \Gamma \times Q \times \Gamma^* \times \Gamma^*$$

Note that Δ takes into account a symbol from each of the two stacks when describing a transition. For example, a transition of the form $\Delta(q, \sigma, \tau_1, \tau_2) = \{(p, \alpha, \varepsilon)\}$ would change from state q to state p, replace the symbol τ_1 on the first stack by the symbol (or string) α, and pop the symbol τ_2 from the second stack.

1. Show that any context-free language is accepted by a two-stack pushdown automaton.

2. Show that the language $L = \{a^i b^i c^i \mid i \geq 0\}$ is accepted by a two-stack pda.

3. Describe a technique whereby a two-stack pda can recognize the language

$$L = \{a^i b^i c^i d^i \mid i \geq 0\}$$

3.5. Determinism is present in an automaton when there is no choice in the manner in which it can behave. One condition that must be satisfied for a pushdown automaton to be deterministic is that there cannot be more than one element in any of the sets $\Delta(q, \sigma, \tau)$. This is not sufficient to guarantee determinism, however. Consider the pda that contains the transitions

$$\Delta(q, a, A) = \{(p, w)\}$$
$$\Delta(q, \varepsilon, A) = \{((p', w')\}$$

Note that this pda has a choice in how it behaves once it enters state q. Hence, even if all sets $\Delta(q_i, \sigma, \tau)$ contain single elements, nondeterminism is still present. We define a *deterministic pushdown automaton* (dpda) to be a pda in which there is no configuration in which the pda has a choice of more than one move. In other words a pda is deterministic if (a) each $\Delta(q, a, A)$ has at most one element, and (b) if $\Delta(q, a, A) \neq \emptyset$, then $\Delta(q, \varepsilon, A) = \emptyset$. A context-free language is a *deterministic context-free language* (dcfl) if it is accepted by a dpda.

1. Show that every regular language is a dcfl.

2. Show that not every dcfl is regular.

3. Obviously, any dcfl is a cfl since any dpda is an npda. Use the fact that if L is a dcfl, then L is a cfl to prove that not every cfl is a dcfl. *Hint:* In Problem 3.3 we found a context-free language whose complement is not context-free.

4

Turing Machines

4.1 BASIC DEFINITIONS

Recall that the collection of regular languages forms a proper subset of the context-free languages. Thus, in terms of the ability to accept languages, finite automata are less powerful than pushdown automata. On the other hand, many languages are not context-free, some of which are quite simple, such as

$$\{a^n b^n c^n \mid n \geq 0\}$$

and

$$\{ww \mid w \in \Sigma^*\}$$

In this chapter we investigate a third type of language recognition device, the Turing machine. Turing machines are more general than either finite automata and pushdown automata in that they can recognize regular languages, context-free languages, and many other types of languages as well. Although they are more powerful than the two earlier types of automata, they are quite similar to them in terms of actions and components.

When we moved from finite automata to pushdown automata, we introduced a memory or storage device, the stack, that provided sufficient ability to "remember" information necessary for the recognition of context-free languages. A stack is restrictive in that our access to information is limited to the item on the top. To access data lower in the stack, we must remove data from the top—data that we may not wish to lose.

For example, attempting to recognize $\{a^n b^n c^n \mid n \geq 0\}$ by means of a nondeterministic pushdown automaton might mean counting the number of a's that appear in the input string by pushing some symbol on the stack. Then, to count b's, one might pop stack symbols. When it comes time to count c's, the stack is empty—our count is lost. The underlying problem here is not a lack of memory, but rather the manner in which the memory is organized.

Suppose we allow the stack to be "traversed" without popping. That is, we allow pushing and popping as before, but in addition we allow looking at data on the stack under the top position. We could recognize $\{a^n b^n c^n \mid n \geq 0\}$ by again pushing some symbol on the stack at each a. To recognize b's, we could set a pointer to the top of the stack and at each b move the pointer lower in the stack. This would not destroy our count, so when reading the c portion of the input string, we could still make use of the count. The additional ability to traverse the stack adds substantial recognition capability.

Although we might experiment with various organizations of memory and their operations, the organization we introduce for Turing machines is actually quite simple. It consists of a one-dimensional array of storage cells extending infinitely in either direction—essentially an endless *tape*. Each cell is capable of storing a single symbol. The array has no first or last cell and can thus hold an unlimited amount of information. We allow the contents of cells to be accessed in any order. Associated with the tape is a read/write head that can move about on the tape and read or write a symbol on each move.

We make the following definition:

Definition 4.1.1.   A *Turing machine* is a 7-tuple $M = (Q, \Sigma, \Gamma, s, \flat, F, \delta)$, where

> Q is a finite set of states
> Σ is an input alphabet
> Γ is an alphabet called the *tape alphabet*
> $s \in Q$ is the initial state
> $\flat \in \Gamma$ is the *blank* symbol (and is not in Σ)
> $F \subseteq Q$ is the set of final or accepting states
> $\delta \colon Q \times \Gamma \to Q \times \Gamma \times \{L, R\}$ is a *partial function*
>   called the transition function.

In this definition the tape symbol $\flat$ is assumed to be the initial value of all tape cells. The definition has required that $\flat \notin \Sigma$. Generally, we allow that $\Sigma \subseteq \Gamma - \{\flat\}$. The transition function δ maps pairs (q, σ) of current state and tape symbols to triples (p, t, X), where p is the next state, t is a symbol written to the tape, and X is a read/write head movement, one of L or R, corresponding to left or right movement (the tape is envisioned as extending from left to right).

For example, the transition $\delta(q_1, a) = (q_5, b, R)$ causes the Turing machine to move from a configuration

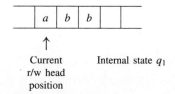

	a	b	b		

↑
Current   Internal state q_1
r/w head
position

to the configuration

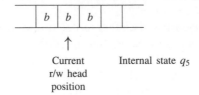

Recall that a partial function is not necessarily defined for every element of the set that it maps *from*. Consequently, δ may not have an image for some pairs in $Q \times \Gamma$.

Note that the transitions depend only on the current state and the contents of the tape cell currently under the read/write head. Thus any input must be presented to a Turing machine on its tape. This is why we require that $\Sigma \subseteq \Gamma - \{b\}$ (and that b not be an input symbol).

Consider the Turing machine defined by

$$Q = \{q_1, q_2\}$$
$$\Sigma = \{a, b\}$$
$$\Gamma = \{a, b, b\}$$
$$F = \{q_2\}$$
$$s = q_1$$

and δ given by

$$\delta(q_1, a) = (q_1, a, R)$$
$$\delta(q_1, b) = (q_1, a, R)$$
$$\delta(q_1, b) = (q_2, b, L)$$

This Turing machine begins operation in state q_1. If the contents of the tape cell under the read/write head are a, the applicable transition is $\delta(q_1, a) = (q_1, a, R)$. The Turing machine will overwrite the a on the tape with another a (that is, causing no change in the tape contents), move right one cell, and stay in state q_1. Any subsequent a's on the tape in this new position or any positions to the right will be unaltered, but b's will be replaced by a's [by means of the transition $\delta(q_1, b) = (q_1 a, R)$]. If the Turing machine encounters a blank (the symbol b), it will move left one cell and enter the final state q_2. There are no transitions from the state q_2, so the Turing machine will halt once in this state.

Following are several stages of the process for this Turing machine begun with a simple initial configuration:

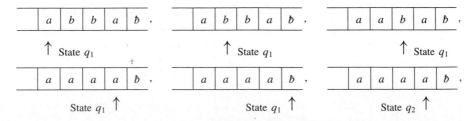

It is cumbersome to represent the configurations of a Turing machine in the preceding manner. Any configuration is determined by current state, tape contents, and the position of the read/write head on the tape. Two notations are commonly employed to capture this information in a convenient manner. The first represents a configuration as a pair $(q_i, w_1 \underline{\sigma} w_2)$, where q_i is the current state, w_1 is the string on the tape preceding the cell under the read/write head, $\underline{\sigma}$ is the tape symbol currently under the read/write head, and w_2 is the string following the read/write head. Thus, in the preceding example the initial configuration of the Turing machine would be given as $(q_1, \underline{b}abba)$, the second as $(q_1, a\underline{b}ba)$, and so on. An alternative notation is to write a string $a_1 a_2 \ldots a_{k-1} q_i a_k \ldots a_n$ to represent the configuration $(q_i, w \underline{a_k} u)$; that is, the read/write head is positioned on the cell containing a_k and the current state is q_i. Note that the string $a_1 a_2 \ldots a_{k-1} q_i a_k \ldots a_n$ indicates that the read/write head is over the tape symbol immediately *following* the state. Thus the first two configurations in the preceding example would be represented as $q_1 abba$ and $aq_1 bba$. We will use these two notations interchangeably. Configurations of a Turing machine are referred to as *instantaneous descriptions* (IDs).

Whichever notation is used to represent a configuration, we will denote a move from one configuration to another by the familiar symbol $\vdash$. Thus, in the preceding example, we have

$$(q_1, \underline{a}bba) \vdash (q_1, a\underline{b}ba) \vdash (q_1, aa\underline{b}a) \vdash (q_1, aaa\underline{a})$$
$$\vdash (q_1, aaaa\underline{b}) \vdash (q_2, aaa\underline{a})$$

or

$$q_1 abba \vdash aq_1 bba \vdash aaq_1 ba \vdash aaaq_1 a \vdash aaaaq_1 \underline{b}$$
$$\vdash aaaq_2 a$$

The notations $\overset{*}{\vdash}$ and $\overset{+}{\vdash}$ have their usual meanings as "zero or more" and "one or more" moves, respectively.

As another example, consider the Turing machine given by

$$Q = \{q_1, q_2, q_3\}$$
$$\Sigma = \{a, b\}$$
$$\Gamma = \{a, b, b\!\!\!/\,\}$$
$$F = \{q_3\}$$
$$s = q_1$$

and the transition function, δ, given by

$$\delta(q_1, a) = (q_1, a, L)$$
$$\delta(q_1, b) = (q_1, b, L)$$
$$\delta(q_1, b\!\!\!/\,) = (q_2, b\!\!\!/\,, R)$$
$$\delta(q_2, a) = (q_3, a, L)$$
$$\delta(q_2, b) = (q_3, b, L)$$
$$\delta(q_2, b\!\!\!/\,) = (q_3, b\!\!\!/\,, L)$$

example

This Turing machine searches left on the tape until it encounters the first blank cell. It then halts, positioning itself on that blank. Thus we might have

$$(q_1, aab\underline{a}bb) \vdash (q_1, aa\underline{b}abb) \vdash (q_1, a\underline{a}babb)$$
$$\vdash (q_1, \underline{a}ababb) \vdash (q_1, \underline{b}aababb)$$
$$\vdash (q_2, \underline{a}ababb) \vdash (q_3, \underline{b}aababb)$$

or, equivalently,

$$aabq_1abb \vdash aaq_1babb \vdash aq_1ababb \vdash q_1aababb$$
$$\vdash q_1\underline{b}aababb \vdash q_2aababb \vdash q_3\underline{b}aababb$$

Note that whenever $\delta(q, a)$ is undefined and the Turing machine is in the configuration $(q, w_1\underline{a}w_2)$, it is impossible for it to move. In this case we say that the Turing machine is *halted*. It may or may not be the case that $q \in F$, the set of final states. In many cases we would like to attach significance to halting in some state in F. In fact, to simplify the discussion, we will assume that no transition is defined for *any* state in F, so the Turing machine will halt whenever it enters a final state. In all cases, however, the sequence of moves leading to a halted configuration is called a *computation*.

Consider the Turing machine given by

$$Q = \{q_1, q_2\}$$
$$\Sigma = \{a, b\}$$
$$\Gamma = \{a, b, \flat\}$$
$$s = q_1$$
$$F = \emptyset$$

and δ defined by

$$\delta(q_1, a) = (q_2, a, R)$$
$$\delta(q_1, b) = (q_2, b, R)$$
$$\delta(q_1, \flat) = (q_2, \flat, R)$$
$$\delta(q_2, a) = (q_1, a, L)$$
$$\delta(q_2, b) = (q_1, b, L)$$
$$\delta(q_2, \flat) = (q_1, \flat, L)$$

If this Turing machine is started with the read/write head on the a of a string of the form abw, we have the following sequence of moves:

$$q_1abw \vdash aq_2bw \vdash q_1abw \vdash aq_2bw \vdash \cdots$$

The Turing machine will run forever with the read/write head moving alternately right and left. This is an instance of a Turing machine that never halts (this particular Turing machine is said to be in an "infinite loop," to borrow from computer programming terminology). This situation, of never halting, is fundamental in the theory of Turing machines, and so we will represent it by $(q, w_1\underline{\sigma}w_2) \overset{*}{\vdash} \infty$ or $w_1q\underline{\sigma}w_2 \overset{*}{\vdash} \infty$. This indicates that the Turing machine begun in the initial configuration $w_1q\sigma w_2$ never halts.

Exercises for Section 4.1

4.1.1. Construct a Turing machine that scans a string over $\{a, b\}^+$ on the tape from left to right, replacing all occurrences of b by c. The Turing machine should start with the read/write head on the first (leftmost) symbol of the string and end with its read/write head on the trailing blank (the blank that follows the rightmost a or c of the transformed string).

4.1.2. Construct a Turing machine that halts whenever presented with a string from

$$L = \{a^n b^m \mid n, m \geq 0 \text{ and not both } n = 0 \text{ and } m = 0\}$$

Begin processing with the read/write head on the first (leftmost) symbol of the string.

4.1.3. Construct a Turing machine that enumerates all binary integers in numerical order in one place on its tape when started as $(q_1, \underline{0}\flat)$ (equivalently, when started as $(\flat q_1 \underline{0} \flat)$). That is, your Turing machine should perform as follows:

$$(q_1, \underline{0}\flat) \overset{*}{\vdash} (q_1, \underline{1}\flat) \overset{*}{\vdash} (q_1, 1\underline{0}\flat) \overset{*}{\vdash} (q_1, 1\underline{1}\flat) \overset{*}{\vdash} \cdots$$

Note that this Turing machine necessarily fails to halt.

4.1.4. Construct a Turing machine that enumerates all binary integers in numerical order separated by $\flat$'s on its tape when started as $(q_1, \underline{0}\flat)$.

4.2 TURING MACHINES AS LANGUAGE ACCEPTERS

A Turing machine can act as a language accepter in much the same manner that a finite automaton or a pushdown automaton does. We place a string w on the tape, position the read/write head on w's leftmost symbol, and start the Turing machine in its initial state. After a sequence of moves, if the Turing machine enters a final state and halts, then w is accepted. Thus w is accepted if $qw \overset{*}{\vdash} w_1 p w_2$ for some final state p and strings w_2 and w_1. (Recall that we are assuming that the Turing machine halts whenever it enters any final state.) We thus have the following definition:

Definition 4.2.1. Let $M = (Q, \Sigma, \Gamma, s = q_1, \flat, F, \delta)$ be a Turing machine. Then the *language accepted by M* is

$$L(M) = \{w \in \Sigma^* \mid q_1 w \overset{*}{\vdash} w_1 p w_2 \text{ for } p \in F \text{ and } w_i \in \Gamma^*\}$$

Example 4.2.1

Consider designing a Turing machine to accept the regular language a^* over $\Sigma = \{a, b\}$. Starting at the left end of a string, we scan right by reading each symbol, checking that it is an a, and, if it is, moving right. If we encounter a blank ($\flat$) without reading any symbol that is not a, we halt and accept. If, on the other hand, we encounter a symbol that is not an a or a $\flat$, we can halt in a nonaccepting state.

Let $Q = \{q_1, q_2\}$, $s = q_1$, and $F = \{q_2\}$, and let δ be defined by

$$\delta(q_1, a) = (q_1, a, R)$$
$$\delta(q_1, \flat) = (q_2, \flat, R)$$

Note that this Turing machine halts in state q_2 only if a string of 0 or more a's is scanned.

To reject a string as unacceptable, we are only required to avoid entering a final state. In the Turing machine of Example 4.2.1, unacceptable strings caused the Turing machine to halt in a nonfinal state. Note that if the Turing machine enters an infinite loop it cannot enter a final state (we are continuing to assume that there are no transitions defined for final states). Thus an alternative way of rejecting a string is to enter an infinite loop. The language of Example 4.2.1 could be accepted by

$$M = (\{q_1, q_2, q_3\}, q_1, \{a, b\}, \{a, b, \flat\}, \flat, \{q_3\}, \delta)$$

where δ is defined by

$$\delta(q_1, a) = (q_1, a, R), \qquad \delta(q_2, a) = (q_2, a, R)$$
$$\delta(q_1, b) = (q_2, b, R), \qquad \delta(q_2, b) = (q_2, b, R)$$
$$\delta(q_1, \flat) = (q_3, \flat, R), \qquad \delta(q_2, \flat) = (q_2, \flat, R)$$

Note that if a b is encountered, this Turing machine enters state q_2. In state q_2 the Turing machine moves right forever.

Example 4.2.2

Consider the language $\{a^n b^n \mid n \geq 1\}$. To recognize this language, we must not only count a's and b's, but also verify that all a's appear left of all b's. One way of approaching this problem might be to check off a's and b's in corresponding positions in the a portion and b portion of the string. That is, starting with the leftmost a, we could convert it to some other symbol and then search right until we encountered the first b. We then convert the b to some other symbol and search for the leftmost a again. We repeat this process until no a's and b's remain.

Let q_1 be the initial state and suppose that we use c's to replace the a's and d's to replace the b's. The transitions

$$\delta(q_1, a) = (q_2, c, R), \qquad \delta(q_2, d) = (q_2, d, R)$$
$$\delta(q_2, a) = (q_2, a, R), \qquad \delta(q_2, b) = (q_3, d, L)$$

will cause the Turing machine to replace the leftmost a by c and then scan right until the first b is encountered. This b is then replaced by d. Note that for $a^n b^n$, where $n > 1$, there may be intervening d's from previous passes.

The transitions

$$\delta(q_3, d) = (q_3, d, L)$$
$$\delta(q_3, a) = (q_3, a, L)$$
$$\delta(q_3, c) = (q_1, c, R)$$

cause the Turing machine to scan back to the left for the leftmost a. Since the Turing machine will only get to state q_3 by means of transitions in the first set, we can be assured that the leftmost a is preceded by a c.

If all a's have been exhausted, the Turing machine will be in state q_1 and positioned on a tape cell containing a d as a result of the last transition in the preceding set. A final check must be made to see if all b's have been converted. The transitions

$$\delta(q_1, d) = (q_4, d, R)$$
$$\delta(q_4, d) = (q_4, d, R)$$
$$\delta(q_4, \flat) = (q_5, \flat, L)$$

perform this check and leave the Turing machine in state q_5 positioned on the last d if the check is successful (that is, if there are no remaining b's). Thus we have the Turing machine that accepts $\{a^n b^n \mid n \geq 1\}$ given by

$$M = (\{q_1, q_2, q_3, q_4, q_5\}, \{a, b\}, \{a, b, c, d\}, q_1, \flat, \{q_5\}, \delta)$$

where δ is given by the preceding 10 transitions.

Exercise 4.2.6 shows that the language $\{a^n b^n c^n \mid n \geq 0\}$ is accepted by a Turing machine. Since this language is known to be a language that is *not* context-free, Turing machines can accept some languages that nondeterministic pushdown automata cannot.

A language that is accepted by a Turing machine is called a *recursively enumerable* language (often abbreviated r.e. language). The term enumerable comes from the fact that it is exactly these languages whose strings can be listed (enumerated) by a Turing machine. This class of languages is quite large, including the context-free languages.

We have remarked that a Turing machine need not halt on all input strings to accept some language. It need only halt in an accepting/final state for those strings that are actually in the language. In fact there are r.e. languages for which no Turing machine that accepts them halts on *all* inputs (of course, any Turing machine for such a language must halt on the strings actually *in* the language). The subclass of the recursively enumerable languages which are accepted by at least one Turing machine that halts on all input strings (whether accepting the string or not) is called the *recursive* languages. We will return to a discussion of recursively enumerable and recursive languages later.

Because Turing machines can both read and write on their tape, they have the ability to transform input into output. We have actually made use of this in recognizing the language $\{a^n b^n \mid n \geq 1\}$; a string of a's and b's is transformed into a string of c's and d's. Transforming input into output is the primary purpose of digital computers and thus a Turing machine provides a simple abstract model of a computer. We assume that the input to the Turing machine is all the nonblank symbols on the tape. The output is whatever symbols are left on the tape at the completion of the computation.

For example, consider the Turing machine $M = (Q, \Sigma, \Gamma, s, \flat, F, \delta)$, where

$$Q = \{q_1, q_2, q_3\}$$
$$\Sigma = \{a, b\}$$
$$\Gamma = \{a, b, \flat\}$$
$$s = q_1$$
$$F = \{q_3\}$$

and δ is given by

$$\delta(q_1, a) = (q_1, b, R), \qquad \delta(q_2, a) = (q_2, a, L)$$
$$\delta(q_1, b) = (q_1, a, R), \qquad \delta(q_2, b) = (q_2, b, L)$$
$$\delta(q_1, b) = (q_2, b, L), \qquad \delta(q_2, b) = (q_3, b, R)$$

This Turing machine *complements* strings over the alphabet Σ. That is, it converts a's into b's, and vice versa. If begun in the configuration $(q_1, \underline{\sigma_1}\sigma_2 \ldots \sigma_n)$, it halts in the configuration $(q_3, \underline{\alpha_1}\alpha_2 \ldots \alpha_n)$, where α_i is a if σ_i is b, and vice versa.

Note that we can view such a Turing machine as an implementation of a string function f that is defined by $f(w) = u$ whenever $q_s w \overset{*}{\vdash} q_f u$, where q_s is the initial state and q_f is a final state. For the sake of convenience and clarity, we will require that the read/write head begin and end on the leftmost symbol of the input and output strings, respectively.

We make the following definition:

Definition 4.2.2. A string function f is said to be *Turing computable* if there is a Turing machine $M = (Q, \Sigma, \Gamma, q_1, b, F, \delta)$ for which $q_1 w \overset{*}{\vdash} q_f u$ for some $q_f \in F$, whenever $f(w) = u$.

Although Turing computability is defined only for string functions, it is easy to extend the idea to integer functions, as the next example shows.

Example 4.2.3

Suppose we let $\Sigma = \{a, b\}$ and represent positive integers by strings of a's. Thus the positive integer n would be represented by a^n. The addition function $f(n, m) = n + m$ could then be implemented by transforming $a^n b a^m$ into $a^{n+m} b$. An appropriate Turing machine for addition might then be given by $M = (Q, \Sigma, \Gamma, s, b, F, \delta)$, where

$$Q = \{q_1, q_2, q_3, q_4, q_5\}$$
$$F = \{q_5\}$$

and δ is given by the following:

$$\delta(q_1, a) = (q_1, a, R), \qquad \delta(q_3, a) = (q_4, b, L)$$
$$\delta(q_1, b) = (q_2, a, R), \qquad \delta(q_4, a) = (q_4, a, L)$$
$$\delta(q_2, a) = (q_2, a, R), \qquad \delta(q_4, b) = (q_5, b, R)$$
$$\delta(q_2, b) = (q_3, b, L)$$

This Turing machine simply moves the b to the right end of a^{n+m}. In doing so, an extra a is created. The Turing machine "remembers" that it created an additional a by shifting to a state q_2 once the separating b is found and then writing the b over an a at the end of the string. Note, too, that the Turing machine parks the read/write head over the leftmost a when it is finished.

Exercises for Section 4.2

4.2.1. Alter the Turing machine of Example 4.2.1 to halt in an accepting state with the read/write head on the first blank trailing an accepted string if an acceptable string is presented to it.

4.2.2. Construct a Turing machine that accepts the language $\{a^{2n} \mid n \geq 0\}$ over $\Sigma = \{a, b\}$.

4.2.3. Trace the execution of the Turing machine of Example 4.2.2 when started in each of the following configurations: $(q_1, \underline{a}abb)$, $(q_1, \underline{a}ab)$, and $(q_1, \underline{a}aabbb)$.

4.2.4. Design a Turing machine that accepts the language $\{a^n b^n \mid n \geq 0\}$. Note that in addition to the considerations in the Turing machine of Example 4.2.2 you must also check for the empty string. Alter your Turing machine so that if an unacceptable string is found it does not halt.

4.2.5. Design a Turing machine that accepts the language $\{a^n b^n \mid n \geq 1\}$ by means of checking off a's and b's from *opposite ends* of the string. That is, using c and d again, the string $aaabbb$ would be transformed first to $caabbd$ then to $ccabdd$ and then, finally, to $cccddd$.

4.2.6. Design a Turing machine to accept $\{a^n b^n c^n \mid n \geq 0\}$.

4.2.7. Construct Turing machines that accept the following languages over $\Sigma = \{a, b\}$:

(a) aba^*b

(b) $\{w \mid$ length of w is even$\}$

(c) $\{a^n b^m \mid n \geq 1$ and $m \neq n\}$

(d) $\{w \mid w$ contains equally many a's as b's$\}$

(e) $\{a^n b^m a^{n+m} \mid n \geq 0$ and $m \geq 1\}$

(f) $\{a^n b^n a^n b^m \mid n \geq 0$ and $m \geq 0\}$

(g) $\{a^n b^{2n} \mid n \geq 1\}$

(h) $\{ww \mid w \in \{a, b\}^+\}$

(i) $\{w \mid w = w^R\}$

(j) $\{a^{n^2} \mid n \geq 1\}$

(k) $\{a^{2^n} \mid n \geq 0\}$

4.2.8. Trace the Turing machine of Example 4.2.3 on input $a^2 ba^3$ and $a^2 b$. How does this Turing machine behave when adding $2 + 0$?

4.2.9. An alternative approach to the method of Example 4.2.3 for adding $n + m$ is to append $a^n b$ to a^m when the input is given as $a^n ba^m$. In this case the original $a^n b$ must be removed from the tape. Construct a Turing machine that implements addition in this manner.

4.2.10. All natural numbers are either even or odd. Construct a Turing machine that computes the *parity function* for natural numbers, that is, that computes

$$f(n) = \begin{cases} 0, & \text{if } n \text{ is even} \\ 1, & \text{if } n \text{ is odd} \end{cases}$$

4.2.11. In Exercise 4.2.10 we mapped strings of symbols to strings consisting of only single symbols. Some languages can be recognized by means of this technique. If L is a language (of an appropriate type as we shall later see), the *indicator function* for L, χ_L, maps a string w over the alphabet into the single symbol strings 0 or 1 depending on whether w is in L or not. That is, χ_L is defined as

$$\chi_L(w) = \begin{cases} 1, & \text{if } w \in L \\ 0, & \text{if } w \notin L \end{cases}$$

Construct a Turing machine that computes $\chi_L(w)$ for the following languages over $\Sigma = \{a, b\}$:

(a) $L = aba^*b$

(b) $L = \{w \mid \text{the length of } w \text{ is even}\}$

(c) $L = \{a^n b^{2n} \mid n \geq 0\}$

Are these languages recursive? Are they recursively enumerable.

4.2.12. Many everyday activities can be viewed as string mappings. For example, parity checking requires that strings of n bits be transformed into strings of $n + 1$ bits in which there are either always an even number of 1 bits (even parity) or always an odd number of 1 bits (odd parity). Construct a Turing machine that transforms strings of eight 0's and 1's into strings of nine 0's and 1's in which the number of 1's is always odd. Start your Turing machine in the cell containing the leftmost bit of the string. Assume that the parity bit is the ninth bit from the left.

4.2.13. Given a k-tuple of natural numbers $(n_1, n_2, \ldots, n_k)$, the *projection* p_i of $(n_1, n_2, \ldots, n_k)$ is just n_i. That is, p_i returns the ith component of the k-tuple. Construct a Turing machine P_i that computes the projection function p_i.

4.3 TURING MACHINE CONSTRUCTION KIT

As the reader may gather from the previous discussion and exercises, Turing machines can perform many activities in addition to language recognition. In fact, Turing machines are generally taken as theoretical models of computers, a topic we will pursue later. For now we will look at the process of simplifying Turing machine construction in a reasonable manner. The basic idea is to construct a collection of simple Turing machines and then combine them in various ways to create more complex devices.

We can combine two Turing machines by allowing them to share the same tape and, when one finishes its execution, we allow the other to begin. The contents of the tape at the beginning of execution of the second Turing machine consists of whatever the first Turing machine left there, and the second is begun with its read/write head on the tape cell that the first terminated on.

Example 4.3.1

Let M_1 be given by

$$
\begin{aligned}
Q_1 &= \{q_1, q_2, q_3, q_4\} \\
\Sigma &= \{a\} \\
\Gamma &= \{a, b\} \\
s_1 &= q_1 \\
F_1 &= \{q_4\}
\end{aligned}
$$

with δ_1 as follows:

$$\delta_1(q_1, a) = (q_2, a, R)$$
$$\delta_1(q_1, b) = (q_2, b, R)$$
$$\delta_1(q_2, a) = (q_2, a, R)$$
$$\delta_1(q_2, b) = (q_3, b, L)$$
$$\delta_1(q_3, b) = (q_4, b, R)$$
$$\delta_1(q_3, a) = (q_4, a, R)$$

Let M_2 be given by

$$Q_2 = \{p_1, p_2\}$$
$$\Sigma \text{ and } \Gamma \text{ the same as with } M_1$$
$$s_2 = p_1$$
$$F_2 = \{p_2\}$$

with δ_2 as follows:

$$\delta_2(p_1, a) = (p_2, a, R)$$
$$\delta_2(p_1, b) = (p_2, a, R)$$

Note that M_1 searches for the first occurrence of b to the right of the position in which it is started, while M_2 writes out an a and stops. (An a is written regardless of the current contents of the cell.) By combining these two Turing machines so that M_1's computation is followed by M_2's, we have a device that searches right on the tape for the first b and then writes an a in that cell. We represent the combination of these two Turing machines in this manner by $M_1 M_2$, indicating that the computation of M_1 is followed by that of M_2.

We formally define this composition or combination of Turing machines as follows:

Definition 4.3.1.   Let M_1 and M_2 be two Turing machines over the same input alphabet Σ and same tape alphabet Γ, where

$$M_1 = (Q_1, \Sigma, \Gamma, s_1, b, F_1, \delta_1)$$

and

$$M_2 = (Q_2, \Sigma, \Gamma, s_2, b, F_2, \delta_2)$$

Assume that $Q_1 \cap Q_2 = \emptyset$. The Turing machine $M = (Q, \Sigma, \Gamma, s, b, F, \delta)$ is the *composition* of M_1 and M_2, denoted $M_1 M_2$, where

$$Q = Q_1 \cup Q_2$$
$$s = s_1$$
$$F = F_2$$

$$\delta(q, \sigma) = \begin{cases} \delta_1(q, \sigma), & \text{if } q \in Q_1 \text{ and } \delta_1(q, \sigma) \neq (p, \tau, X) \\ & \text{for any } p \in F_1 \\ \delta_2(q, \sigma), & \text{if } q \in Q_2 \\ (s_2, \tau, X), & \text{if } q \in Q_1 \text{ and } \delta_1(q, \sigma) = (p, \tau, X) \\ & \text{for some } p \in F_1 \end{cases}$$

Note that the composition $M_1 M_2$ acts like M_1 until M_1 enters a final state. At that time it switches to the initial state of M_2 and behaves like M_2 until termination.

In our previous example, $M_1 M_2$ would have transitions given by

$$\delta(q_1, a) = (q_2, a, R), \qquad \delta(q_3, a) = (p_1, a, R)$$
$$\delta(q_1, b) = (q_2, b, R), \qquad \delta(q_3, b) = (p_1, b, R)$$
$$\delta(q_2, a) = (q_2, a, R), \qquad \delta(p_1, a) = (p_2, a, R)$$
$$\delta(q_2, b) = (q_3, b, L), \qquad \delta(p_1, b) = (p_2, b, R)$$

with $s = q_1$ and $F = \{p_2\}$.

Let us denote the Turing machine M_1 of Example 4.3.1 by R_b. That is, R_b searches for the first b to the right of the current head position. Consider a tape

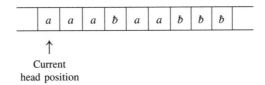

Current
head position

The composite Turing machine $R_b R_b$ would terminate in the position

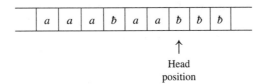

Head
position

while the composite Turing machine $R_b R_b R_b$ would terminate in the position

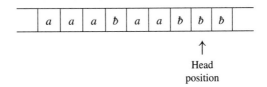

Head
position

An alternative way of specifying transitions is to use a table. The transition table of R_b would be

$\delta(q, \sigma)$	$\sigma \neq b$	$\sigma = b$
q_1	(q_2, σ, R)	(q_2, b, R)
q_2	(q_2, σ, R)	(q_3, b, L)
q_3	(q_4, σ, R)	(q_4, b, R)

Note that one column is specified for a particular symbol on the tape and another specifies all other tape symbols. The transition $\delta(q_2, \sigma) = (q_2, \sigma, R)$ in the column labeled $\sigma \neq \flat$ indicates that, for all tape symbols σ other than $\flat$, the Turing machine writes σ back to the tape, moves right, and stays in state q_2. Although we originally specified $R_\flat$ only for the tape alphabet $\Gamma = \{a, \flat\}$, we now have specified $R_\flat$ for *any* tape alphabet that includes $\flat$ as the blank.

Consider the Turing machine whose transition table is

δ	$\sigma = \flat$	$\sigma \neq \flat$
q_1	$(q_2, \flat, L)$	(q_2, σ, L)
q_2	$(q_2, \flat, L)$	(q_3, σ, R)
q_3	$(q_4, \flat, L)$	(q_4, σ, L)

where $F = \{q_4\}$ and $s = q_1$. This Turing machine searches left for the first nonblank tape symbol and terminates with its read/write head on that cell. This Turing machine will be denoted $L_{\bar{\flat}}$ (the $\bar{\flat}$ is used to denote "any symbol except $\flat$"). Combining $L_{\bar{\flat}}$ and $R_\flat$, we have $R_\flat L_{\bar{\flat}}$, which positions the read/write head on the tape symbol preceding the first $\flat$ right of the current position. Thus, if started on

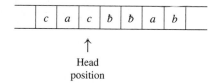

Head position

the combined Turing machine would terminate in

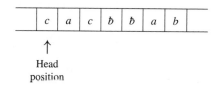

Head position

In Example 4.3.1 we also gave a Turing machine (M_2) that wrote out a single symbol. It would be convenient to specify a Turing machine that writes out a single symbol, a, and then remains on that cell. Let us specify this Turing machine where $s = q_1$ and $F = \{q_3\}$ by the following table:

$\delta(q, \sigma)$	$\sigma \in \Gamma$
q_1	(q_2, a, R)
q_2	(q_3, σ, L)

If we denote this Turing machine by the symbol that it writes out, a, we can then compose it with others. For example, $R_b a R$ would search for the first b right of the current head position, write an a in that cell, and then move right to the next cell.

We may wish to combine our simple Turing machines so that a specific simple Turing machine follows another on specific conditions. For example, suppose that $L_b R$ is to be followed by either writing an a if the cell is blank or writing a b if the cell contains an a. We effectively need to fork the execution path. Consider the Turing machine whose transition table is

$\delta(q, \sigma)$	$\sigma = b$	$\sigma = a$
q_1	(q_2, b, L)	(q_4, a, L)
q_2	(q_3, b, R)	(q_3, a, R)
q_4	(q_5, b, R)	(q_5, a, R)

where $F = \{q_3, q_5\}$ and $s = q_1$ (note that there are no transitions for q_3 or q_5). Suppose we combine this Turing machine with the Turing machines for writing a and b so that, if it terminates in q_3, execution of the a-writing Turing machine is initiated, and if it terminates in q_5, execution of the b-writing Turing machine is begun. We have caused a branch in the execution. This could be denoted by the diagram

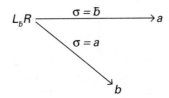

Here we are denoting the Turing machine that causes the branch simply by the arrows.

For example, a Turing machine that scans a string converting all a's to b's and all b's to a's could be constructed thus

Note that we identify the simple Turing machine that begins this execution sequence with an arrow, much like the initial state of a finite automaton. Moreover, since there is no next state from R with the current tape symbol is b, the composite must halt in that case.

Multiple arrows can be eliminated in various ways. For example, if $\Gamma = \{a, b, c, b\}$, the composite Turing machine denoted by

$$R \xrightarrow{\quad a, b, \not b \quad} R$$

accomplishes the same thing as does the composite

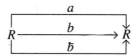

That is, it moves right one cell and then, if the tape symbol there contains an a, b, or $\not b$, it moves right again.

In the same manner, the Turing machine denoted by

$$R \xrightarrow{\quad a, b, c, \not b \quad} R$$

or

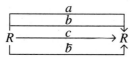

or

$$R \xrightarrow{\hspace{3cm}} R$$

or even by RR or R^2 simply moves the read/write head right two cells (note that since Γ consists only of the symbols $a, b, c, \not b$; all tape symbols cause the second R to occur).

A common problem is to branch one way on a specific tape symbol and another way on all others. This can be denoted in various ways. For example, if $\Gamma = \{a, b, c, \not b\}$, then

$$Q \overset{\sigma = a}{\underset{R \xrightarrow{\quad \sigma \neq a \quad} b}{\Big\downarrow}}$$

searches right for the first cell containing something other than a and then writes a b there. The diagram

$$Q \overset{a}{\underset{R \xrightarrow{\quad \bar{a} \quad} b}{\Big\downarrow}}$$

denotes the same thing.

Consider the problem of shifting a string one cell to the right on the tape. Suppose that we require the string that is to be shifted to be preceded and followed by $\not b$'s. Thus we wish to transform $\underline{b}wb$ into $bb\underline{w}$ (here the symbol where the read/write head is located is indicated as the underlined symbol). If we assume that the tape alphabet, Γ, is $\{a, b, \flat\}$, such a Turing machine could be constructed as follows:

$$R_\flat R \longrightarrow L^2 \xleftarrow{\ \sigma = a\ } \flat Ra$$

with paths $\sigma = \flat \rightarrow R$, $\sigma = b \rightarrow \flat R_\flat$

This Turing machine moves the string over one symbol at a time from the right until it finds the $\flat$ originally preceding the string. It then moves right and halts. We can abbreviate two of the paths as

$$R_\flat R \longrightarrow L^2 \xrightarrow{\ \sigma \neq \flat\ } \flat R\sigma$$

with path $\sigma = \flat \rightarrow R$

Here the σ in $\flat R\sigma$ means that this composite "remembers" the symbol that it just overwrote with the $\flat$. (This was accomplished originally by having two separate paths.) This right shifter is relatively simple and useful. Let us denote it by S_R.

Consider the process of recognizing $\{ww^R \mid w \in \Sigma\}$. One approach would be to compare the leftmost and rightmost symbols. If a match is made, we then erase them and repeat. The string is accepted when all symbols have been erased. On the other hand, if two symbols fail to match, we terminate immediately in a nonaccepting state. We begin with $\underline{b}u\flat$ and hope to discover that $u = ww^R$. Consider the composite Turing machine

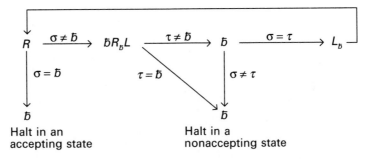

Note that here we are abbreviating possible paths by remembering two tape symbols σ and τ. The states in which this Turing machine terminates are either accepting states or not and are denoted by the three paths on various conditions.

Recall that language acceptance only requires that the Turing machine halt in an accepting state if the string presented to it is in the language. Thus an alternative to the preceding composite might be

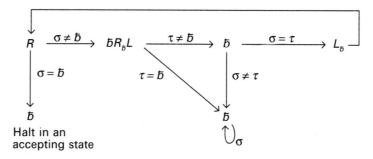

This Turing machine halts in an accepting state for strings of the form ww^R and fails to halt at all for strings not of that form, instead infinitely writing a $ƀ$.

Exercises for Section 4.3

4.3.1. What would the combined Turing machine M_2M_1 of Example 4.3.1 accomplish?

4.3.2. Formally construct the composite Turing machine M_2M_1 of Example 4.3.1 (give Q, F, s, and δ).

4.3.3. Construct the following Turing machines:

$L_ƀ$ Positions the read/write head on the first $ƀ$ left of the current head position.

$R_ƀ$ Positions the read/write head on the first non-$ƀ$ right of the current head position.

R Moves the read/write head right one cell from its current position.

L Moves the read/write head left one cell from its current position.

4.3.4. What effect does S_R have on $ƀaabbbƀ$? What effect does S_R^2 have on $ƀaabbbbccƀ$?

4.3.5. Construct a left shifter S_L as a composite of simple Turing machines. S_L should change $ƀabƀ$ into $abƀƀ$, for example.

4.3.6. Construct a copy machine C. C should transform $ƀwƀ$ into $ƀwƀwƀ$.

4.3.7. Make use of C in Exercise 4.3.6 (as well as other elementary Turing machines) to construct a Turing machine that computes $f(n, m) = nm$ (that is, integer multiplication).

4.3.8. Subtraction of natural numbers is not defined for all pairs since the difference may be negative. Define the operation *monus* as

$$n \overset{.}{-} m = \begin{cases} n - m, & \text{if } n \geq m \\ 0, & \text{if } n < m \end{cases}$$

Construct a Turing machine that computes $n \overset{.}{-} m$ (your Turing machine should take $ƀa^nƀa^mƀ$ and return $ƀa^{n-m}ƀ$).

4.3.9. Construct a Turing machine that accepts $\{wcw \mid w \in \{a, b\}^*\}$.

4.3.10. Let $L(n, m) = \{a^n b^{n - m} \mid n, m \geq 0\}$ (the monus operator, $\dot{-}$, is defined in Exercise 4.3.8). For a given n and m, construct a Turing machine accepting $L(n, m)$.

4.3.11. Construct a Turing machine accepting $\{w \mid w = w^R\}$.

4.3.12. (a) Construct a Turing machine that computes the integer function $f(n) = \lfloor n/2 \rfloor$, where $\lfloor x \rfloor$ is the floor function at x (that is, the greatest integer less than or equal to x).

    (b) Construct a Turing machine that, when given a string w and an integer $n \leq \mid w \mid$, positions the read/write head on the nth symbol of w (from the left).

    (c) Construct a variant S_R' of S_R that doesn't require the string to be preceded by a b symbol. For example, S_R' should transform $\underline{a}bbab b$ into $\underline{b}abbab b$.

    (d) Construct a Turing machine that accepts $\{ww \mid w \in \Sigma^*\}$ by making use of the Turing machines in parts a through c.

4.4 MODIFICATIONS TO TURING MACHINES

A number of other definitions of Turing machines are equivalent to our definition. Some of these alternative models are much more complicated than ours, yet all have the same computational power. Such variations on our definition occasionally allow greater flexibility in designing a Turing machine to solve a particular problem. We begin with some minor variations on our original definition.

Recall that the simple Turing machine L_b positions the read/write head on the first b left of the current position. To do so, it actually searches *beyond* that tape cell and then backs up. This is because our definition requires each transition to move the tape head. Our definition of the transition function

$$\delta : Q \times \Gamma \to Q \times \Gamma \times \{R, L\}$$

can be modified to

$$\delta : Q \times \Gamma \to Q \times \Gamma \times \{R, L, S\}$$

where the directive S means "stay," that is, do *not* move the read/write head. Thus $\delta(q, \sigma) = (p, \sigma', S)$ means to change state to p, write σ' to the current cell, and leave the read/write head in the current cell on the tape. Note that our original definition is contained in this definition, so this is an extension of the Turing machine we've defined.

On the other hand, any Turing machine for which $\delta(q, \sigma) = (p, \sigma', S)$ is defined can be simulated by one of our original definition by simply adding states and moves of the form $\delta(q, \sigma) = (p', \sigma', R)$ and $\delta(p', \tau) = (p, \tau, L)$ and/or of the form $\delta(q, \sigma) = (p', \sigma', L)$ and $\delta(p', \tau) = (p, \tau, R)$ for all $\tau \in \Gamma$.

For example, let M_1 have transitions defined by the table

$\delta(q, \sigma)$	$\sigma \neq b$	$\sigma = b$
q_1	(q_2, σ, L)	(q_2, σ, L)
q_2	(q_2, σ, L)	(q_3, b, S)

where $s = q_1$ and $F = \{q_3\}$. Note that this is an implementation of L_b as a Turing machine having the no-move ability. A Turing machine of our original definition that is derived from M_1 by means of this transformation is M_2, whose transitions are given by the table

$\delta(q, \sigma)$	$\sigma \neq b$	$\sigma = b$
q_1	(q_2, σ, L)	(q_2, σ, L)
q_2	(q_2, σ, L)	(q_4, b, L)
q_4	(q_3, σ, R)	(q_3, b, R)

where $s = q_1$ and $F = \{q_3\}$.

Another simple variation of our basic Turing machine is one in which each tape cell is subdivided into subcells. Each subcell is capable of containing a tape symbol. The tape

b	b	b
a	a	b
a	a	b

$\cdots$ (left) $\cdots$ (right)

has each cell divided into three subcells. Such a tape is said to have *multiple tracks*. Since each tape cell on such a Turing machine contains multiple characters, we represent the tape cell contents by ordered tuples. In the preceding example, the tape cells contain (b, a, a), (b, a, a), and (b, b, b). In making moves, such a Turing machine depends on its current state and the tuple that makes up the contents of the current tape cell.

Suppose that Γ is a tape alphabet. A Turing machine having a k-track tape each of whose cells contains symbols from Γ could be viewed as one having as its tape alphabet all k-tuples over Γ. For example, if $\Gamma = \{a, b, b\}$ and M is a two-track Turing machine whose cells contain pairs of symbols from Γ, M could be viewed as having as its tape alphabet $\Gamma \times \Gamma$. Viewed in this manner, it is clear that multitrack Turing machines are no more powerful than our original Turing machine. However, they do allow for easier construction of Turing machines for certain problems.

Example 4.4.1

Suppose we wish to construct a Turing machine that adds two binary numbers. Let us construct a three-track Turing machine to do this. Input is assumed to be two binary numbers occupying the top two tracks of the tape. Let us assume that their rightmost digits are aligned and that their binary representations are of the same length (which can be accomplished by padding with 0's as necessary) and that the read/write head is positioned on the leftmost cell of the strings. Thus, if we were to add 101 and 10, the tape would contain

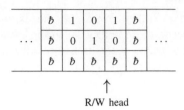

b	1	0	1	b
b	0	1	0	b
b	b	b	b	b

$\uparrow$

R/W head

The Turing machine will form the sum in the third track. Consequently, the tape alphabet must consist of the following triples:

$$
\begin{array}{llll}
(b, b, b) & (1, 1, b) & (1, 1, 0) & (1, 1, 1) \\
(0, 0, b) & (0, 0, 0) & (0, 0, 1) & (b, b, 1) \\
(0, 1, b) & (0, 1, 0) & (0, 1, 1) & \\
(1, 0, b) & (1, 0, 0) & (1, 0, 1) &
\end{array}
$$

This Turing machine will first search right for the right end of the numbers to be added. It will then add pairs of digits, working from right to left, keeping track of any carries that are generated, and adding them in as it goes. Thus we have (assuming that q_1 is the initial state)

$$
\delta(q_1, \sigma) = \begin{cases} (q_1, \sigma, R), & \text{if } \sigma \neq (b, b, b) \\ (q_2, \sigma, L), & \text{if } \sigma = (b, b, b) \end{cases}
$$

$$
\begin{array}{ll}
\delta(q_2, (0, 0, b)) = ((q_2, (0, 0, 0), L) & \delta(q_3, (0, 0, b)) = (q_2, (0, 0, 1), L) \\
\delta(q_2, (0, 1, b)) = ((q_2, (0, 1, 1), L) & \delta(q_3, (0, 1, b)) = (q_3, (0, 1, 0), L) \\
\delta(q_2, (1, 0, b)) = (q_2, (1, 0, 1), L) & \delta(q_3, (1, 0, b)) = (q_3, (1, 0, 0), L) \\
\delta(q_2, (1, 1, b)) = (q_3, (1, 1, 0), L) & \delta(q_3, (1, 1, b)) = (q_3, (1, 1, 1), L) \\
\delta(q_2, (b, b, b)) = (q_4, (b, b, b), S) & \delta(q_3, (b, b, b)) = (q_4, (b, b, b), S)
\end{array}
$$

Note that we are allowing the no-move ability in this Turing machine. This Turing machine will transform

b	1	0	1	b
b	0	1	0	b
b	b	b	b	b

into

b	b	1	0	1	b
b	b	0	1	0	b
b	0	1	1	1	b

Another simple (and quite common) variation on our original Turing machine definition is to use a tape that extends infinitely in only *one* direction. Generally, we view such a tape as having a leftmost cell and extending infinitely to the right. No left move is permitted from the leftmost cell. Certainly, any such Turing machine can easily be simulated by one of our original definition. We simply distinguish some cell on our two-way infinite tape and treat it as the leftmost cell in any computation.

A Turing machine with a one-way infinite tape can also simulate one with a two-way infinite tape by making use of two tracks. Let M be a Turing machine with a two-way infinite tape. A one-way infinite-tape Turing machine, M', which simulates M has two tracks on its tape. The upper track contains information from M's tape to the right of some reference point. The lower track contains the left portion of M's tape (in reverse order). Thus, if M's tape contained

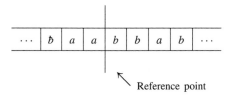

Reference point

the tape for M' might look like

*	b	b	a	b	...
*	a	a	b	b	

A special symbol, $*$, is used to mark the left boundary of the tape. When M would cross the reference point on its tape, M' would encounter the cells marked with $*$. If M is operating on cells to the right of the reference point, M' is operating on the upper track. When M operates on cells left of the reference point, M' operates on the lower track. When M moves across the reference point, M' encounters the $*$'s, changes direction, and also changes which track it is working on.

A more complicated variation of our original definition is the *multitape* Turing machine. This Turing machine has several tapes, each of which has its own read/write head. The individual read/write heads are independently controlled (that is, they do not all have to move in the same direction at once, the same amount, or even at all). On a single move such a Turing machine

1. Changes state depending on its current state and the contents of *all* tape cells currently scanned by the read/write heads.
2. Writes a new symbol in each of the tape cells under its read/write heads.
3. Moves each read/write head either left or right (independently of the other read/write heads).

Thus the transition function for such a Turing machine with n tapes is of the form

$$\delta : Q \times \Gamma^n \to Q \times \Gamma^n \times \{L, R\}^n$$

where a transition of the form

$$\delta(q, (\sigma_1, \sigma_2, \ldots, \sigma_n)) = (p, (\tau_1, \tau_2, \ldots, \tau_n), (X_1, X_2, \ldots, X_n))$$

means change state from q to p, replace σ_i by τ_i on tape i, and move the read/write head in the direction X_i on tape i.

Example 4.4.2

Multitape Turing machines greatly simplify some of the things we would like to do with Turing machines. Consider the process of recognizing $\{a^n b^n | n \geq 1\}$. This is quite laborious with a single-tape Turing machine. It is much easier with a two-tape Turing machine. Suppose that we initially place the string to be checked on tape 1 and that q_1 is the initial state. If the read/write head of tape 1 is initially placed on the leftmost character of the string, the following four transitions are the important transitions for recognition (all other transitions would be for an incorrectly formed string and may be assumed to lead to a nonaccepting state):

$$\delta(q_1, (a, \flat)) = (q_1, (a, a), (R, R))$$
$$\delta(q_1, (b, \flat)) = (q_2, (b, \flat), (S, L))$$
$$\delta(q_2, (b, a)) = (q_2, (b, a), (R, L))$$
$$\delta(q_2, (\flat, \flat)) = (q_3, (\flat, \flat), (R, L))$$

Although a multitape Turing machine appears somewhat different from, and possibly more powerful than, our originally defined Turing machine, the two are actually equivalent in the sense that each can simulate the other.

Let M_1 be a k-tape Turing machine. M_1 may be simulated with a Turing machine, M_2, having a single tape split into $2k + 1$ tracks. Each of M_1's tapes corresponds to two tracks for M_2. One track keeps track of the contents of the corresponding tape of M_1, while the other is used to record a marker that corresponds to the position of M_1's read/write head for that tape. The $(2k + 1)^{st}$ track is used to record end markers. The end markers mark the positions of the leftmost and rightmost head markers. Each move of M_1 is simulated by M_2 by making a sweep of its read/write head from left to right and then from right to left. M_2's head begins in the cell marked as the left end (by the left end marker). To simulate a move of the k-tape M_1, M_2 sweeps right, recording (by means of states) the symbols marked as being scanned by each of M_1's heads. When M_2's read/write head encounters the right end marker, the Turing machine has seen all symbols that M_1's read/write heads scan and so has enough information to determine a move. Now M_2's read/write head sweeps left, updating the tape contents and adjusting the head markers as it goes, until it encounters the left end marker. Note that in making this sweep M_2 needs to be able to move the head markers either to the left or right of their current positions. This suggests that the pattern of movement that the read/write head makes during the sweep consists of two left moves followed by two right moves and then followed by a single left move. Finally, M_2 adjusts its state to correspond to M_1's next state.

Another modification that we can make to our original Turing machine is to allow the tape to extend in multiple dimensions. For example, a two-dimensional tape extends up and down, as well as left and right. Depending on the Turing machine's current state and the symbol scanned, it changes state, writes a symbol in the current tape cell, and moves left, right, up, or down. Thus the transition function for such a Turing machine is of the form

$$\delta : Q \times \Gamma \rightarrow Q \times \Gamma \times \{L, R, U, D\}$$

It is easy for a multidimensional Turing machine to simulate a standard Turing machine. It simply does all its computation in one dimension. A standard Turing machine can also simulate a multidimensional Turing machine and, consequently, the additional complexity and freedom of multiple dimensions adds no real ability. To simulate a two-dimensional Turing machine on a standard Turing machine, we first associate an address with all tape cells. One way of doing this is to arbitrarily fix a location on the tape and give cells coordinate addresses as in the coordinate plane.

For example,

$-1, 1$		$1, 1$		
$-1, 0$	$0, 0$	$1, 0$	$2, 0$	
	$0, -1$			

We then use a two-track tape in the simulating Turing machine. One track keeps track of the contents of cells, and the other keeps track of the coordinates. In this scheme, if cell $(1, 2)$ contains an a and cell $(-3, 12)$ contains a b, the simulating Turing machine's tape would look like

a				b					
1	*	2	*	$-$	3	*	1	2	

Note that a new tape symbol, *, must be introduced to mark the boundaries between coordinate values. To simulate a move of the two-dimensional Turing machine, this Turing machine first computes the address of the cell to which the two-dimensional machine would move. It then locates the cell with this address on the lower track and changes the contents of the cell on the upper track accordingly.

An important final modification of our original definition is to relax the requirement that the transition rule be a function. In such a Turing machine, called a *nondeterministic Turing machine*, for a combination of current state and current tape symbol there may be finitely many choices of moves. Thus the transition rule, Δ, of such a machine satisfies

$$\Delta(q, \sigma) \subseteq Q \times \Gamma \times \{L, R\}$$

For example, if such a Turing machine has a transition

$$\Delta(q_1, a) = \{(q_1, b, R), (q_2, a, L)\}$$

then the moves

$$(q_1, ab\underline{a}b) \vdash (q_1, abb\underline{b}b) \quad \text{and} \quad (q_1, ab\underline{a}b) \vdash (q_2, a\underline{b}ab)$$

are both possible.

Since any deterministic Turing machine is also nondeterministic, it is certainly the case that a deterministic Turing machine can be simulated by a nondeterministic Turing machine. It is also the case that a deterministic Turing machine can simulate a nondeterministic one. Consequently, no additional power is gained by the nondeterminism.

To see how such a simulation can occur, let M_1 be a nondeterministic Turing machine accepting some language. We describe a (deterministic) three-tape Turing machine M_2 that simulates M_1. Note that for any current state and tape symbol of M_1 there are finitely many choices of next move. We can number these moves $1, 2, \ldots, k$. Since both Q_1 and Γ_1 of M_1 are finite sets, there are only finitely many pairs of current state and tape symbol. Thus we can find which pair has the maximum number of possible next moves. Let this number be n. Now any computation by M_1 can be represented by a finite sequence of numbers chosen between 1 and n, each number representing the choice of next move at that step in the computation. Note that not all finite sequences of numbers between 1 and n represent valid computations since there might be less than n choices for some state-tape symbol pairs.

In the three-tape Turing machine M_2, the first tape will hold the input, and the second will generate finite sequences of numbers between 1 and n in some systematic manner. For each sequence, M_2 will copy the input string onto the third tape and then simulate M_1 on that tape using the sequence on the second tape to guide the computation. If a sequence of choices leads M_1 to accept the string, then that sequence will eventually be generated by M_2, and the string will be accepted. If no sequence of choices leads to acceptance by M_1, then M_2 will also not accept.

Note that this argument is phrased in terms of accepting a language. Nondeterministic Turing machines are usually viewed as language accepters. Note, too, that this argument readily generalizes to simulating a nondeterministic multitape Turing machine.

In this section we have described various modifications to our original Turing machine, all of which are neither more nor less powerful than the original. It is reasonable to ask why we even bother with these variations if there is no gain in computational ability or, for that matter, why we do not restrict our attention to one of the simpler variations. One reason is that we now have a number of different ways of solving Turing machine problems. If one of the variants lends itself more readily to a solution to a problem than the originally defined Turing machine, there is no loss of generality in using the variant.

Another, deeper reason for studying these variations and their equivalence to the original is that in doing so we gain a sense of the ultimacy of the Turing machine. Any computation that can be performed by one of the new arrangements still falls into the category of "computable by a Turing machine" and, hence, is mechanically computable.

This has hardly been an exhaustive look at Turing machine variations. Indeed, we shall look at several more variations of our original definition later.

Exercises for Section 4.4

4.4.1. Remove the restriction that the shorter of the two binary numbers be padded with 0's in Example 4.4.1.

4.4.2. Construct a three-track Turing machine that will subtract the binary number on its second track from the one on its first track and leave the result on the third track.

As a variation, suppose that the Turing machine has only two tracks and the result is to be left on track 2.

As another variation, suppose the result is to be left on track 1.

4.4.3. Construct a three-track Turing machine that determines if the binary number on its first track is smaller than the binary number on its second track. If it is smaller, write the character S on the third track; if it isn't, write the characters GE on the third track. How could you add a check for equality?

4.4.4. A Turing machine can check if a binary number greater than 2 is prime. The number to be checked is written on track 1. The Turing machine then writes the number 2, in binary, on the second track and copies the first track onto the third. It then subtracts the second track from the third as many times as possible (leaving the result on track 3 each time). This effectively divides the number on track 1 by the number on track 2, leaving the remainder on track 3. If the remainder is 0, then the number is not prime. If the remainder is not 0, then increment the number on track 2. If the numbers on tracks 1 and 2 are now equal, the number is prime (why?). If the number on track 2 is less than the number on track 1, repeat the whole process for the new number on track 2. Construct a Turing machine that performs this prime check.

4.4.5. Multiple tracks are also useful for nondestructively recognizing strings in a language. The string in question is placed on one track and an additional track is used to check off the symbols that have been considered (as opposed to erasing them or overwriting them by other symbols). This is accomplished by placing markers on the second track under or over the symbols that have been considered on the first track. Construct such a Turing machine to recognize the language $\{wcw \mid w \in \{a, b\}^*\}$.

4.4.6. Let M be a two-way infinite-tape Turing machine having transitions given by

$\delta(q, \sigma)$	$\sigma = a$	$\sigma = b$	$\sigma = \flat$
q_1	(q_1, c, R)	(q_1, b, R)	$(q_2, \flat, L)$
q_2	(q_2, a, L)	(q_2, d, L)	$(q_3, \flat, S)$

Suppose that q_1 is the start state of M. Construct a Turing machine with a one-way infinite tape that simulates M's actions for an input string placed in any position on M's tape.

4.4.7. Design a one-way infinite-tape Turing machine that, when started in the configuration $(q_1, w\flat)$, will accept

$$L = \{w \subset \{a, b\}^* \mid w \text{ contains at least 1 } a\}$$

(*Note:* Keep in mind that our requirement for acceptance is that the Turing machine halt in an accepting state.)

4.4.8. Trace the execution of the two-tape Turing machine of Example 4.4.2 on input a^2b^2.

4.4.9. Construct a two-tape Turing machine that recognizes $L = \{ww^R \mid w \in \{a, b\}^+\}$. Assume that strings to be checked are placed initially on tape 1.

4.4.10. Suppose that M is a two-tape Turing machine with tape alphabet $\Gamma = \{a, b\}$. Define the appropriate parts of a five-track Turing machine M' in order to simulate the move $\delta(q_1, (a, b)) = (q_2, (b, a), (R, L))$ of M.

4.4.11. Suppose we define a *multihead* Turing machine as one that has a single (two-way) tape, but has several read/write heads on that tape. Each move depends on the current state as well as all the symbols scanned by the heads. At each move, some convention arbitrates if more than one head is positioned over the same cell.

   (a) Construct a two-head "copy machine" that transforms bwb into $bwbwb$ on the tape.

   (b) Give a simulation similar to that of a k-tape Turing machine by a 1-tape Turing machine for a multihead Turing machine to be simulated by a Turing machine with a single two-way tape.

4.4.12. How can a multitape Turing machine simulate a Turing machine of our original definition? How can a multihead Turing machine simulate one of our original definitions?

4.4.13. Construct a Turing machine with a two-dimensional tape that will "draw" a 2×3 rectangle on the tape, with lower-left corner the tape cell that the Turing machine began in.

4.4.14. Construct a Turing machine of our original description that generates all finite sequences of the numbers 1, 2, and 3 on its tape so that the shorter sequences appear first and so that sequences of the same length appear in lexicographical order. How would you generalize to sequences of the numbers $1, 2, \ldots, n$?

4.4.15. Construct a nondeterministic Turing machine accepting $L = \{ww \mid w \in \{a, b\}^+\}$.

4.4.16. Construct a nondeterministic Turing machine accepting

$$L = \{xww^R y \mid x, y, w \in \{a, b\}^+ \text{ and } |x| \geq |y|\}$$

How would you solve this problem deterministically?

4.4.17. Carefully explain *why* the statement "If no sequence of choices leads to acceptance by M_1, then M_2 will not accept either" is a true statement in the description of the simulation of a nondeterministic Turing machine by a (deterministic) Turing machine.

4.5 UNIVERSAL TURING MACHINES

A *universal* Turing machine is a Turing machine that, when supplied with an appropriate description of a Turing machine M and an input string w, will simulate M's behavior on w. In this section we describe such a Turing machine. We shall need this development later in our studies of the language hierarchy and of decidability, but it also serves to fortify our intuitive connection between Turing machines and modern digital computers.

We first must find a way of describing an arbitrary Turing machine $M = (Q, \Sigma, \Gamma, s, b, F, \delta)$ so that its description can be supplied as input to a universal Turing machine. This requires that such a description be encoded over a finite alphabet. By adopting some simple conventions, such an encoding is actually quite simple.

To begin with, we require that M have a single accepting state. It is a simple process to transform an arbitrary Turing machine into one that accepts in a single state.

We simply add appropriate transitions and states so that from each old accepting state q the Turing machine can move to the new accepting state p and leave the read/write head in the position it was in upon reaching q.

Now let us assume that $Q = \{q_1, q_2, \ldots, q_n\}$, where q_1 is the initial state and q_2 is the single final state of M. Moreover, let us assume that $\Gamma = \{\sigma_1, \sigma_2, \ldots, \sigma_m\}$, where σ_1 is the blank. With these assumptions, M is completely described by means of its transition function δ. Thus, to encode M, we must only encode δ. To do this, we represent q_1 by 1, q_2 by 11, and so on. Similarly, we represent σ_i by a string of i 1's. Finally, represent the read/write head directives by 1 for L and 11 for R. If we use 0's as separators, we may encode a transition such as

$$\delta(q_3, \sigma_1) = (q_4, \sigma_3, L)$$

by the string 011101011110111010. It follows that M has an encoding as a finite string of 0's and 1's. Moreover, given an encoding, we can decode it correctly.

A universal Turing machine M_u can be implemented as a three-tape Turing machine whose input alphabet includes 0 and 1. The first tape contains the encoding of M with its read/write head positioned on the initial 0 of the string of 0's and 1's. The second tape contains the encoded contents of M's tape with its read/write head positioned on the leading 1 of the current encoded tape symbol. The third tape is used to keep track of M's current state. This tape initially contains the encoded version of M's initial state (state q_1, hence a single 1) surrounded by b's. Its read/write head is positioned on the first 1 of the encoded string.

M_u scans and compares the contents of the second and third tapes with the first tape until it either finds a transition for the encoded configuration or exhausts all possibilities. If a transition for the given configuration is found, the two tapes are adjusted to reflect the result of the transition. If no transition for the given configuration is found, M_u halts, as M must. In either case, M_u behaves as M would (modulo the encoding).

If M halts when presented with the string w, then M_u will halt when presented with the encoded M and the encoded w on its tapes. Moreover, the final string on M_u's tape will be the encoding of the string that M would leave on its tape. When M halts, M_u can tell if it is in the single accepting state and so move to an accepting state of its own (or not).

Exercises for Section 4.5

4.5.1. Let M be given by

$$
\begin{aligned}
Q &= \{q_1, q_2, q_3, q_4, q_5, q_6, q_7, q_8\} \\
\Sigma &= \{a, b\}, \\
\Gamma &= \{a, b, b\}, \\
s &= q_1 \\
F &= \{q_6, q_7\}
\end{aligned}
$$

and with δ given by the following:

$$\delta(q_1, \flat) = (q_1, \flat, R) \qquad \delta(q_3, b) = (q_4, \flat, L)$$
$$\delta(q_1, a) = (q_2, \flat, R) \qquad \delta(q_3, a) = \delta(q_2, \flat) = (q_8, \flat, L)$$
$$\delta(q_1, b) = (q_6, \flat, R) \qquad \delta(q_4, a) = (q_4, a, L)$$
$$\delta(q_2, a) = (q_2, a, R) \qquad \delta(q_4, b) = (q_4, b, L)$$
$$\delta(q_2, b) = (q_2, b, R) \qquad \delta(q_4, \flat) = (q_5, \flat, R)$$
$$\delta(q_2, \flat) = (q_3, \flat, L) \qquad \delta(q_5, a) = (q_1, a, L)$$
$$\delta(q_5, \flat) = (q_7, \flat, R) \qquad \delta(q_5, b) = (q_6, b, R)$$
$$\delta(q_8, a) = \delta(q_8, b) = \delta(q_8, \flat) = (q_8, \flat, L)$$

Convert M into a Turing machine with a single final state.

4.5.2. Give a complete encoding of the Turing machine given by

$$\delta(q_1, \sigma_1) = (q_1, \sigma_1, R)$$
$$\delta(q_1, \sigma_2) = (q_3, \sigma_1, L)$$
$$\delta(q_3, \sigma_1) = (q_2, \sigma_2, L)$$

4.5.3. Give an algorithm that will determine if a string $w \in \{0, 1\}^+$ is an encoded Turing machine.

4.5.4. Sketch a procedure that will enumerate encodings of all Turing machines. *Hint:* From Exercise 4.1.4 you can enumerate all binary integers in order. Combine this with Exercise 4.5.3.

Exercise 4.5.4 has an important consequence given in the following:

4.5.5. Show that the collection of all Turing machines is countable.

PROBLEMS

In this chapter we saw that it is not possible to extend the computational power of the standard Turing machine by complicating its tape structure. It turns out that it *is* possible to limit its power by restricting the manner in which the tape can be used. One possible such restriction that yields an interesting device occurs when we limit the number of tape cells that the Turing machine can use to some number based on the length of the input string. Thus more space could be available for computations on long input strings than for short ones.

We define a *linear-bounded automaton* (*lba*) to be a nondeterministic Turing machine $M = (Q, \Sigma, \Gamma, s, \flat, F, \Delta)$ in which the tape alphabet contains two additional special symbols, $<$ and $>$. M begins in the configuration $(q_1, < w >)$ (where q_1 is the initial state of M). M is not permitted to replace the symbols $<$ or $>$ or to move its read/write head left of $<$ or right of $>$. Note that a linear-bounded automaton is restricted to performing its computation in only the tape cells originally occupied by the input string.

For example, consider the lba defined by

$$Q = \{q_1, q_2\}$$
$$\Sigma = \{a, b\}$$
$$\Gamma = \{a, b, <, >\}$$
$$s = q_1$$
$$F = \{q_2\}$$

Δ is given by

$$\Delta(q_1, <) = (q_1, <, R)$$
$$\Delta(q_1, a) = (q_1, b, R)$$
$$\Delta(q_1, b) = (q_1, a, R)$$
$$\Delta(q_1, >) = (q_2, >, S)$$

This lba complements its input strings by converting a's to b's and vice versa. Note that, while it can recognize and act on the special symbols $<$ and $>$, it cannot replace them or move beyond them.

Assume that an lba is always started with its read/write head positioned on the $<$ symbol.

4.1. Find a linear-bounded automaton that accepts the language $\{a^n b^n c^n \mid n \geq 1\}$.

4.2. Find an lba that determines if its input string has odd length. Assume that the input strings are from $\{a, b\}^*$.

4.3. Find an lba that determines if its input string, taken from $\{a, b\}^*$, is a palindrome.

Linear-bounded automata may have multiple-track tapes. In the case of multiple tracks, the cells available for computation are still restricted to the ones that originally contained input. For example, if $w = abaa$ is the input string for a two-track lba, the tape would look like

	$<$	a	b	a	a	$>$		
	$<$					$>$		

(where blank cells are assumed to contain b's).

4.4. Construct a two-track lba that accepts the language

$$\{a^{n!} \mid n \geq 0\}$$

where $n!$ is the factorial function. (*Hint:* Repeatedly divide the input string by $2, 3, 4, \ldots$ by placing a divisor on the second track. When and how do you determine if there are $n!$ a's on the first track?)

4.5. Let $k > 0$ be a fixed integer. Construct an lba that, when presented with two integers n and m (as a^n and a^m), determines if $n - m$ is divisible by k.

5

Turing Machines and Languages

5.1 LANGUAGES ACCEPTED BY TURING MACHINES

In Chapter 4 we introduced the Turing machine and investigated some of its properties. In particular, the development of a universal Turing machine suggests that a Turing machine may be thought of in a manner analogous to a computer program and, thus, that Turing machines might reasonably model mechanical computation. We pursue this connection further in Chapter 6, where we investigate the limits of mechanical computation by studying decidability. In the present chapter we investigate the kinds of languages accepted by Turing machines. In doing so, we encounter a problem for Turing machines in general. This problem is called the *halting problem*. The halting problem will become our key in the discussion of decidability. We close with a theorem (the hierarchy theorem) that relates all the types of languages we've studied.

Recall that a string w over some alphabet is accepted by a Turing machine M when a computation begun with w on M's tape and with M in its initial state results in M entering a final/accepting state. On the other hand, w can be rejected in two different manners, either by causing M to halt in some nonaccepting state or else by causing M to never halt. Although we are currently unable to show the distinction at this point, the two methods of rejecting strings are *not* equivalent. Consequently, we have defined *recursively enumerable* languages to be those languages accepted by a Turing machine (in any manner) and *recursive* languages to be those accepted by some Turing machine that always halts on any input. Formally, we have the following definition:

Definition 5.1.1. A language L over an alphabet Σ is said to be *recursively enumerable* if it is accepted by some Turing machine. That is, L is recursively enumerable if for some

Turing machine M we have

$$L = \{w \in \Sigma^* \mid qw \overset{*}{\vdash} upv \text{ for } p \in F \text{ and } u, v \in \Sigma^*\}$$

(where q is the initial state of M and F is the set of final states of M).

A language L is *recursive* if L is recursively enumerable and there is some Turing machine that halts on *all* inputs that accept L.

It is immediate from the definition that any language that is recursive is also recursively enumerable. We shall see in Section 5.4 that there are recursively enumerable languages that are not recursive.

Exercises for Section 5.1

5.1.1. Show that L is recursive if and only if the indicator function for L, χ_L, is a Turing computable function (see Exercise 4.2.11). (For this reason, if L is a recursive language and T is a Turing machine that accepts L and halts on all inputs, then T is sometimes said to *decide* L, since for any string wI decides whether or not w is in L.)

5.1.2. Suppose that M is a Turing machine that halts on all inputs and accepts the language L. Convert M into M', where $L = L(M')$ and M' rejects strings by not halting.

5.2 REGULAR, CONTEXT-FREE, RECURSIVE, AND RECURSIVELY ENUMERABLE LANGUAGES

Let $M = (Q, \Sigma, s, F, \delta)$ be a deterministic finite automaton. We may construct a Turing machine $M' = (Q', \Sigma', \Gamma, s', b, F', \delta')$ for which $L(M) = L(M')$ by means of the following:

$$Q' = Q \cup \{q'\}, \qquad \text{where } q' \text{ is a new state not in} Q$$
$$\Sigma' = \Sigma$$
$$\Gamma = \Sigma \cup \{b\}$$
$$F' = \{q'\}$$
$$\delta'(q, \sigma) = (\delta(q, \sigma), \sigma, R), \qquad \text{for } q \in Q \text{ and } \sigma \in \Sigma'$$
$$\delta'(q, b) = (q', b, S), \qquad \text{for all } q \in F, \text{ where } S \text{ is the stay tape directive}$$

The resulting Turing machine scans its input string from left to right. At each input symbol it changes its state to reflect the corresponding state change in the finite automaton. When it encounters the b at the right end of the input string, It moves to its accepting state only if the finite automaton would accept the string.

Note that, since pairs of the form (q, b) never occur in M, defining δ' to mimic δ where possible and $\delta'(q, b) = (q', b, S)$ for states $q \in F$ results in a transition function that is well defined.

Since any regular language may be accepted by some deterministic finite automaton, we have the following theorem:

Theorem 5.2.1.   If L is a regular language, then L is also a recursive language.

We know from Example 4.2.2 that there is a Turing machine that halts on all inputs and accepts $\{a^n b^n \mid n \geq 1\}$. From Example 2.9.1 we know that this language is not regular. Consequently, there are recursive languages that are not regular.

Let M be a nondeterministic pushdown automaton. We may construct a Turing machine that emulates M's behavior in accepting or rejecting strings. Such an emulation must account for M's state changes and the changes in M's stack while consuming its input string. For simplicity we will use a two-tape Turing machine. Tape 1 will hold the input string and tape 2 will hold the contents of M's stack. A push will correspond to a move right followed by writing on tape 2. Thus the read/write head of tape 2 will always scan the current top of the stack. The state changes of the Turing machine will reflect M's state changes. Consider the npda M given by

$$Q = \{q_1, q_2, q_3\}, \qquad s = q_1$$
$$\Sigma = \{a, b\}, \qquad F = \{q_3\}$$
$$\Gamma = \{a, b, z\},$$
$$\Delta(q_1, \varepsilon, z) = \{(q_3, \varepsilon)\}, \qquad \Delta(q_1, a, z) = \{(q_1, az)\}$$
$$\Delta(q_1, a, a) = \{(q_1, aa)\}, \qquad \Delta(q_1, b, a) = \{(q_2, \varepsilon)\}$$
$$\Delta(q_2, b, a) = \{(q_2, \varepsilon)\}, \qquad \Delta(q_2, \varepsilon, z) = \{(q_3, \varepsilon)\}$$

This npda accepts the context-free language $\{a^n b^n \mid n \geq 0\}$.

The Turing machine that we construct will have start state q'. We begin with the read/write head of tape 1 on the leftmost symbol of the input string and tape 2 empty (that is, all blanks). We first mark the "bottom" of the stack on tape 2. Thus we have the transitions

$$\delta(q', (a, \flat)) = (q_1, (a, z), (S, S))$$
$$\delta(q', (\flat, \flat)) = (q_1, (\flat, z), (S, S))$$

(Here the S tape directive again indicates that the corresponding tape's read/write head is not moved.) The two instances in which this npda performs a push are handled by first moving the read/write head of the stack tape (tape 2) right and then writing the new character. At this point the input character is then "consumed" by moving the read/write head of tape 1 right. Thus we have the transitions

$$\delta(q_1, (a, z)) = (p_1, (a, z), (S, R))$$
$$\delta(q_1, (a, a)) = (p_1, (a, a), (S, R))$$
$$\delta(p_1, (a, \flat)) = (q_1, (a, a), (R, S))$$

which push a's on the stack. Here p_1 is a new state. A pop by the npda simply corresponds to moving tape 2's read/write head toward the bottom of the stack, that is, to the left. Thus we have the transitions

$$\delta(q_1, (b, a)) = (q_2, (b, a), (R, L))$$
$$\delta(q_2, (b, a)) = (q_2, (b, a), (R, L))$$

Finally, acceptance occurs when the input string has been exhausted and the stack emptied. The transition of the npda $\Delta(q_2, \varepsilon, z) = \{(q_3, \varepsilon)\}$ corresponds to the move

$$\delta(q_2, (\flat, z)) = (q_3, (\flat, z), (S, L))$$

of the Turing machine.

Since context-free languages are exactly those languages accepted by the nondeterministic pushdown automata, we have the following theorem:

Theorem 5.2.2.   If L is a context-free language, then L is a recursive language.

If we intersect two recursive languages, a recursive language results. To see this, suppose that M_1 and M_2 are Turing machines that halt on all inputs. Then, if $w \in L(M_i)$, we know that M_i will halt in an accepting state, and if $w \notin L(M_i)$, then M_i will halt in a nonaccepting state for each $i = 1, 2$. Let M be a Turing machine that has two tapes. The input string w is presented on tape 1 and a copy of it is made on tape 2. M then emulates M_1 on tape 1 until M_1 would halt. If M_1 would halt in a nonaccepting state, then M also halts in a nonaccepting state. On the other hand, if M_1 would accept w, then M emulates M_2 on tape 2 (with the copy of w). If M_2 would halt in a nonaccepting state, then M also halts in a nonaccepting state. On the other hand, if M_2 would accept w, then M accepts w. Thus $w \in L(M)$ if and only if $w \in L(M_1)$ and $w \in L(M_2)$, so we have $L(M) = L(M_1) \cap L(M_2)$. Finally, note that M halts on all inputs since both M_1 and M_2 do. Thus $L(M)$ is a recursive language. We have the following theorem:

Theorem 5.2.3.   If L_1 and L_2 are recursive languages, then so is $L_1 \cap L_2$.

We know from Chapter 3 that $L = \{a^i b^i c^i \mid i \geq 0\}$ is the intersection of two context-free languages, but is not itself a context-free language. Combining Theorems 5.2.2 and 5.2.3, we have that L is a recursive language. Thus the converse of Theorem 5.2.2 does not hold. That is, there are recursive languages that are not context-free.

Exercises for Section 5.2

5.2.1. If L is regular, is L recursively enumerable? Why or why not?

5.2.2. This deterministic finite automaton M accepts strings of even length over $\Sigma = \{a, b\}$. Construct a Turing machine from this dfa that accepts $L(M)$.

$$M = (Q, \Sigma, s, F, \delta)$$

where

$$Q = \{q_1, q_2\}$$
$$\Sigma = \{a, b\}$$
$$s = q_1$$
$$F = \{q_1\}$$
$$\delta(q_1, a) = \delta(q_1, b) = q_2$$
$$\delta(q_2, a) = \delta(q_2, b) = q_1$$

5.2.3. Use the technique given in this section to construct a Turing machine that accepts the language accepted by the following deterministic finite automaton:

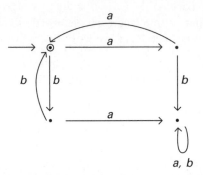

5.2.4. Use the construction technique of this section to construct a Turing machine that accepts the same strings as the npda given by

$$Q = \{q_1, q_2\} \qquad s = q_1$$
$$\Sigma = \{a, b\} \qquad F = \{q_2\}$$
$$\Gamma = \{a, b, z\}$$

Δ is given by

$$\Delta(q_1, \varepsilon, z) = \{(q_2, z)\} \qquad \Delta(q_1, a, a) = \{(q_1, aa)\}$$
$$\Delta(q_1, a, z) = \{(q_1, az)\} \qquad \Delta(q_1, b, a) = \{(q_1, \varepsilon)\}$$
$$\Delta(q_1, b, z) = \{(q_1, bz)\} \qquad \Delta(q_1, a, b) = \{(q_1, \varepsilon)\}$$
$$\Delta(q_1, b, b) = \{(q_1, bb)\}$$

5.2.5. (a) How would a transition of the form

$$\Delta(q, a, b) = \{(p, baaba)\}$$

be handled in the construction of a Turing machine that corresponds to an npda?

(b) How would a transition of the form

$$\Delta(q, a, b) = \{(q_1, b), (q_2, a)\}$$

be handled in the construction of a Turing machine to correspond to an npda? Note that since npda's are likely to be nondeterministic this problem is certainly likely to occur. (*Hint:* What do we know about nondeterministic Turing machines?)

(c) Combine your answers to parts (a) and (b) with the technique for constructing Turing machines for npda to build a Turing machine that accepts the language that the following npda accepts:

$$Q = \{q_1, q_2, q_3, q_4, q_5, q_6\} \qquad s = q_1$$
$$\Sigma = \{a, b\} \qquad F = \{q_6\}$$
$$\Gamma = \{a, b, z\}$$

and Δ is given by the following:

$$\Delta(q_1, \varepsilon, z) = \{(q_6, \varepsilon)\}$$
$$\Delta(q_1, a, z) = \{(q_2, babz)\}$$

$$\Delta(q_2, a, b) = \{(q_2, babb), (q_3, babb)\}$$
$$\Delta(q_3, b, b) = \{(q_4, \varepsilon)\}$$
$$\Delta(q_4, a, a) = \{(q_5, \varepsilon)\}$$
$$\Delta(q_5, b, b) = \{(q_3, \varepsilon)\}$$
$$\Delta(q_5, \varepsilon, z) = \{(q_6, \varepsilon)\}$$

[Note that the language accepted by this npda is $\{a^n(bab)^n \mid n \geq 0\}$.]

5.2.6. Formally define the construction technique of Exercise 5.2.5, which constructs a Turing machine M' that accepts the same language as an npda $M = (Q, \Sigma, \Gamma, s, F, z, \Delta)$.

5.2.7. In the construction of a Turing machine from an npda, what ensures that the Turing machine constructed will halt on all inputs, thus making it possible to assert that context-free languages are recursive (instead of only that they are recursively enumerable)?

5.2.8. Show that the union of recursive languages is also a recursive language. Is the union of two arbitrary *recursively enumerable* languages a recursively enumerable language?

5.2.9. Show that the intersection of recursively enumerable languages results in a recursively enumerable language.

5.2.10. Show that the following language L over the alphabet $\Sigma = \{a, b\}$ is a recursive language. (*Hint:* Find appropriate context-free languages to intersect.)

$$L = \{w \mid w \text{ contains equally many } a\text{'s and } b\text{'s and no substring } aab\}$$

5.3   RECURSIVE AND RECURSIVELY ENUMERABLE LANGUAGES

Suppose that L is a recursive language over the alphabet Σ. Then there is some Turing machine $M = (Q, \Sigma, \Gamma, s, \flat, F, \delta)$ that halts on all inputs and accepts L. Consider the Turing machine $M' = (Q, \Sigma, \Gamma, s, \flat, Q - F, \delta)$. Note that any string in L causes M' to halt in some state in F, and so M' rejects all strings in L. On the other hand, if $w \notin L$, then M halts in some state that is not in F when begun with w on its tape. That is, M halts in some state in $Q - F$. But then so does M', and so if $w \notin L$, then $w \in L(M')$. Thus $L(M') = \Sigma^* - L$. Moreover, since M halts on all inputs, we have that M' does, too. Thus we have the following lemma:

Lemma 5.3.1.   If L is a recursive language, then $\Sigma^* - L$ is also a recursive language.

This is a property of recursive languages that does not hold for recursively enumerable languages in general. To see this, suppose that Σ is an alphabet. Since Σ^* is countable, we may enumerate Σ^* as $\Sigma^* = \{w_1, w_2, w_3, \ldots\}$. In our discussion of universal Turing machines we noted that we can enumerate all Turing machines over Σ (by means of generating strings of symbols representing encoded Turing machines). Thus we may list all Turing machines over Σ by, say, $M_1, M_2, \ldots$. Let

$$L = \{w_i \mid w_i \text{ is accepted by } M_i\}$$

This language is recursively enumerable, but its complement is *not*.

First, to see that L is recursively enumerable, we give a Turing machine M that accepts L. M is actually a combination of several Turing machines. Given a string w over Σ, note that $w = w_i$ for some i. M first generates $w_1, w_2, \ldots$ until it finds i for which $w = w_i$. M then generates the (encoded) ith Turing machine M_i, encodes w_i, and passes the encoded M_i and w_i to a universal Turing machine U that emulates M_i on w_i. If M_i halts and accepts w_i, then U halts in an accepting state, and so M halts and accepts w_i.

On the other hand, M_i may either halt without accepting w_i or else not halt. In either case, M does not halt and therefore does not accept w_i. Thus $w_i \in L(M)$ if and only if we have $w_i \in L(M_i)$.

Second, we observe that $\Sigma^* - L$ is *not* recursively enumerable. To see this, suppose that $\Sigma^* - L$ actually *is* recursively enumerable. Then it must be accepted by some Turing machine, say, M_j. Consider w_j. If $w_j \in L(M_j)$, we must have that $w_j \in L = \Sigma^* - L(M_j)$, and so $w_j \notin L(M_j)$. Conversely, if $w_j \notin L(M_j)$, then $w_j \notin L$, and so we must have that $w_j \in \Sigma^* - L = L(M_j)$. In either case we arrive at a contradiction, and so it must be the case that $\Sigma^* - L$ is not accepted by any Turing machine. We have the following theorem:

Theorem 5.3.2.   There is a recursively enumerable language L for which $\Sigma^* - L$ is not recursively enumerable.

Note that the language L described here cannot be recursive since, if it were, its complement would also be recursive and so L would be recursively enumerable. Thus we have a recursively enumerable language that is not recursive. Consequently, the converse of the statement that any recursive language is also recursively enumerable is not true.

As mentioned earlier, Turing machines can be thought of as models of mechanical computation. A Turing machine that accomplishes a task—whether recognizing a language or drawing a pattern on a multidimensional tape—models a process. Processes that always terminate have come to be called algorithms and so Turing machines that halt on all inputs are models of algorithms. This means that for recursive languages there is an algorithm that determines if a string w is in a language L. This algorithm is modeled by some Turing machine that halts on all inputs and accepts L.

On the other hand, if L is recursively enumerable but not recursive, there is *no* Turing machine that halts on all inputs and accepts L. It follows that there is no model of an algorithm that determines if $w \in L$ for an arbitrary string w. The membership problem (is w in L?) for arbitrary recursively enumerable languages that are not recursive is an example of an *undecidable problem*, one for which no algorithm is sufficient to answer yes or no. We will return to questions of decidability in Chapter 6.

Theorem 5.2.3 together with Exercises 5.2.8 and 5.2.9 indicate that the collection of recursive languages is closed with respect to intersection and union. It is also the case that the recursively enumerable languages are closed with respect to intersection and union. The proof that the intersection of recursive enumerable languages results in another recursively enumerable language is similar to the proof of that statement for recursive languages and was Exercise 5.2.8. The proof that the union of recursively enumerable languages is also recursively enumerable provides a useful and interesting proof technique.

Theorem 5.3.3.   If L_1 and L_2 are recursively enumerable languages, then $L_1 \cup L_2$ is also recursively enumerable.

Proof.   If both L_1 and L_2 are recursive, then we know that their union is also recursive and hence recursively enumerable. In this case there is nothing to prove.

Suppose that at least one of L_1 and L_2 is recursively enumerable but not recursive. Let $L_i = L(M_i)$, where $M_i = (Q_i, \Sigma, \Gamma_i, s_i, b, F_i, \delta_i)$ are Turing machines for $i = 1$ and $i = 2$. We sketch the construction of a Turing machine $M = (Q, \Sigma, \Gamma, s, b, F, \delta)$ that accepts $L_1 \cup L_2$. In other words, M accepts w if and only if w is accepted by at least one of M_1 or M_2. M will be a two-tape Turing machine that essentially simultaneously simulates M_1 on tape 1 and M_2 on tape 2. If either M_1 or M_2 halts in an accepting state, M will also halt and accept. If one of M_1 or M_2 halts in a nonaccepting state before the other Turing machine halts, M will shift its attention to the Turing machine that hasn't halted. If neither Turing machine halts on input w (and so if $w \notin L_1 \cup L_2$), M also never halts and so never accepts w.

This simulation is accomplished by including in Q the pairs in $Q_1 \times Q_2$ and allowing every possible move of the form

$$\delta((q_1, q_2), (\sigma_1, \sigma_2)) = ((p_1, p_2), (\tau_1, \tau_2), (X_1, X_2))$$

where for each $i = 1, 2$,

$$\delta_i(q_i, \sigma_i) = (p_i, \tau_i, X_i)$$

is a transition in M_i.

Additionally, to accommodate situations in which one Turing machine halts in a nonaccepting state before the other halts, we need to include transitions that allow M to continue simulating the other Turing machine. For example, if M_1 would halt in the nonaccepting state q_3 (M_1 would have no transitions from q_3 on any tape symbol in this case), we might include in M all transitions of the form

$$\delta((q_3, q), (\sigma_1, \sigma_2)) = ((q_3, p), (\sigma_1, \tau_2), (S, X_2))$$

where $\delta_2(q, \sigma_2) = (p, \tau_2, X_2)$ is a transition in M_2. If we do this for all such states in which M_1 or M_2 halts without accepting, then M will fail to halt at all when both M_1 and M_2 would halt without accepting a string (why is this behavior acceptable?).

Finally, for any pair (q_1, q_2) in which one of q_1 or q_2 is an accepting state of its corresponding Turing machine, we include transitions of the form

$$\delta((q_1, q_2), (\sigma_1, \sigma_2)) = (q, (\sigma_1, \sigma_2), (S, S))$$

where $q \in Q$ is a new state that is the single accepting state of M.   ∎

The proof of Theorem 5.3.3 suggests a technique that we may use to show that any recursively enumerable languages whose complement is recursively enumerable must be a recursive language. To prove this, suppose that L and $\Sigma^* - L$ are both recursively enumerable. We use the construction in the proof of Theorem 5.3.3 to construct a Turing machine that accepts $L \cup (\Sigma^* - L)$. Of course, this union is all of Σ^*, but since $L \cap (\Sigma^* - L) = \emptyset$, any string $w \in \Sigma^*$ lies in only one of L or $\Sigma^* - L$. Thus, if we have

Turing machines M_1 and M_2 accepting L and $\Sigma^* - L$, respectively, then for any $w \in \Sigma^*$ only one of M_1 or M_2 will halt and accept w. We modify the Turing machine M in the preceding proof so that, if M_1 would halt and accept w, then M accepts it, whereas if M_2 accepts w, then M halts and rejects it. We then have a Turing machine that halts on all inputs and accepts L. Thus we have the following theorem:

Theorem 5.3.4.   If L is a recursively enumerable language for which $\Sigma^* - L$ is also recursively enumerable, then L is a recursive language.

A language is *enumerated* by a Turing machine M if M generates the strings of the language on its tape separating them by some marker symbol. Note that if the language is finite the Turing machine may halt. On the other hand, if the language is infinite, then the Turing machine necessarily continues forever.

If L is enumerated by the Turing machine M, then we can construct a Turing machine M' that accepts L. M' has one more tape than M, which is used as its input tape. To check the string w, we place it on this extra tape. M' then simulates M on the other tape(s), except that, each time M generates a string, M' pauses and compares the newly generated string with w. If a match occurs, M' halts in an accepting state; otherwise, M' continues. It follows that any language enumerated by a Turing machine is a recursively enumerable language.

On the other hand, if L is recursively enumerable, then we may construct a Turing machine that enumerates it. To see this, suppose M is a Turing machine that accepts L. We may construct M' that enumerates L as a three-tape Turing machine. The basic idea is essentially the following: The strings of L will be enumerated on tape 1. On tape 2, M' generates the strings of Σ^* in an orderly manner. On tape 3, M' simulates M's actions on the strings generated. If a string would be accepted by M, then M' writes it to tape 1, thus enumerating L. Note that, since we have only required L to be recursively enumerable and *not* necessarily recursive, simulating M's action on a string might lead to problems if M never halts on that string.

We avoid this problem by having M' simulate longer and longer (finite) sequences of moves of M, rather than attempt to completely process the strings. M' generates the strings of Σ^* in lexicographical (alphabetic) order. Suppose that $\Sigma = \{\sigma_1, \sigma_2, \ldots, \sigma_n\}$. M' first generates ε, the empty string. Then M' generates all strings of length 1 in order $\sigma_1, \sigma_2, \ldots, \sigma_n$. Then M' generates all strings of length 2; $\sigma_1\sigma_1, \sigma_1\sigma_2, \ldots, \sigma_1\sigma_n, \sigma_2\sigma_1, \sigma_2\sigma_2, \ldots, \sigma_2\sigma_n, \ldots, \sigma_n\sigma_n$, and so on. (Note that the original order in which Σ is listed determines the lexicographical order of the strings.)

To organize the simulations of sequences of moves of M on these strings, M' first generates ε and simulates one move on it. On the second pass, M' simulates two moves in ε (if possible), generates σ_1, and simulates one move on it. On the third pass, M' will simulate three moves on ε, two on σ_1, and then generate σ_2 and simulate one move on it. Tape 2 is used for keeping track of the strings generated so far and numbers of moves to be performed on them. Thus after i passes tape 2 will contain i strings from Σ^* as well as counts of the numbers of moves performed on them. As M' makes its next pass, it processes each of these i strings by incrementing the move counter for each string, copying it to tape 3 and simulating M on it for the specified number of moves. If M accepts the string, M' copies it to tape 1.

Note that the problem of M never halting on a specific string is eliminated. Any string in L is eventually generated on tape 2 and is eventually accepted during the simulation of M. Consequently, any string in L eventually appears on tape 1. We have the following theorem:

Theorem 5.3.5.   A language L is recursively enumerable if and only if L is enumerated by some Turing machine.

Thus the ability to be enumerated by a Turing machine completely characterizes the recursively enumerable languages.

Exercises for Section 5.3

5.3.1. In the construction in the proof of Theorem 5.3.3, if both M_1 and M_2 would reject a string by halting in nonaccepting states, the Turing machine M would reject the string by failing to halt. Sketch a way in which M could be constructed so as to also halt in a nonaccepting state in this instance.

5.3.2. Use the same sort of construction as in the proof of Theorem 5.3.3 to show that $L_1 \cap L_2$ is recursively enumerable if both L_1 and L_2 are recursively enumerable.

5.3.3. Sketch the Turing machine that is described in the remarks preceding Theorem 5.3.4. Specifically, how does it determine which of M_1 or M_2 accepts the input string?

5.3.4. Suppose that $L_1, L_2, \ldots, L_n$ are languages that form a partition of Σ^*. If all the L_i are recursively enumerable, show that each language must also be recursive.

5.3.5. The technique described in this section to enumerate a recursively enumerable language with a Turing machine is certainly not very efficient. Strings in the language actually appear on tape 1 repeatedly, since once their move count is greater than or equal to the number of moves M needs to accept them they will be written to tape 1 on every pass. Suggest a technique for eliminating this redundancy (keep in mind that the strings may need to remain on tape 2 in order that the process of generating Σ^* in lexicographical order may continue).

5.3.6. Suppose that L is recursively enumerable but not recursive. Show that for any Turing machine M that accepts L there are infinitely many strings that cause M to fail to halt.

5.4   UNRESTRICTED GRAMMARS AND RECURSIVELY ENUMERABLE LANGUAGES

Throughout our investigation of languages we have discussed two general techniques for specifying languages. We can specify a language by describing a procedure to recognize its strings. Such procedures have taken the form of automata of various sorts. Alternatively, we can specify a language by providing a technique that generates its strings. Grammars have provided this method.

In both regular and context-free grammars, the way in which productions could be formed was restricted. To what extent may we relax these restrictions and still make sense of the languages that result? Moreover, how do such languages relate to the languages that are accepted by Turing machines?

In terms of Cartesian products of sets the productions of regular grammars are pairs in $N \times \Sigma^*(N \cup \varepsilon)$ (for right-regular grammars), reflecting that the left-hand side must consist of a single nonterminal, while the right side can consist of any string of terminals possibly followed by a nonterminal. In moving to context-free grammars we relaxed the restriction on the structure of the right side, allowing productions to be pairs in the product $N \times (N \cup \Sigma)^*$. In this case the right side may include any number of nonterminals, while the left side is still restricted to a single nonterminal.

Although in context-free grammars the structure of the right side of the productions seems to be as general as we can get, at least two possibilities suggest themselves for the left sides. We may allow nonempty strings of nonterminals or even strings of nonterminals and terminals to form the left sides. Of the two, a nonempty string consisting of terminals, nonterminals, or both is the most general form. In such a situation, our productions would be pairs in the product $(N \cup \Sigma)^+ \times (N \cup \Sigma)^*$. In this case we have removed all possible restrictions on the formation of the productions. (Note that if we allow the empty string as a left side then we have the possibility of more than one starting point for derivations, which is undesirable. Thus we will *not* allow ε as a left side in productions.)

We define the following:

Definition 5.4.1. An *unrestricted grammar* (also known as a *phrase-structured grammar*) is a 4-tuple $G = (N, \Sigma, S, P)$, where

N is an alphabet of nonterminal symbols

Σ is an alphabet of terminal symbols with $N \cap \Sigma = \emptyset$

$S \in N$ is the start symbol

P is a finite set of productions of the form $\alpha \to \beta$, where $\alpha \in (N \cup \Sigma)^+$

and $\beta \in (N \cup \Sigma)^*$ (that is, $P \subset (N \cup \Sigma)^+ \times (N \cup \Sigma)^*$ and is a finite set)

Note that any regular or context-free grammar is also an unrestricted grammar. As would be expected, by relaxing the restrictions on production formation, we gain additional generative power over what we had in regular and context-free grammars.

For example, consider the unrestricted grammar given by

$$S \to aSBC \mid aBC$$
$$CB \to BC$$
$$aB \to ab$$
$$bB \to bb$$
$$bC \to bc$$
$$cC \to cc$$

(Here we are continuing with the conventions adopted in the discussion of regular and context-free grammars. That is, unless otherwise specified, S is always the start symbol, lowercase symbols are terminals, and uppercase are nonterminals.)

There are always equally many a's, B's, and C's in the string that exists when the start symbol vanishes. Moreover, all the a's precede the B's and C's. The production $CB \to BC$ allows us to interchange the nonterminals C and B, resulting in a string of the form $a^n B^n C^n$. The productions $aB \to ab$ and $bB \to bb$ allow us to convert all B's to b's, giving $a^n b^n C^n$. Finally, the productions $bC \to bc$ and $cC \to cc$ transform this string into $a^n b^n c^n$.

On the other hand, if $n = 1$, then abc is derivable in this grammar by means of $S \Rightarrow aBC \Rightarrow abC \Rightarrow abc$. If $n \geq 1$, then the string $a^n b^n c^n$ is derivable by means of

$$S \overset{n-1}{\Rightarrow} a^{n-1} S(BC)^{n-1} \Rightarrow a^n (BC)^n \overset{n}{\Rightarrow} a^n B^n C^n \overset{n}{\Rightarrow} a^n b^n C^n \overset{n}{\Rightarrow} a^n b^n c^n$$

Thus any string of the form $a^n b^n c^n$ for $n \geq 1$ is derivable in G.

It follows that $L(G) = \{a^n b^n c^n \mid n \geq 1\}$. Thus we may derive languages that are not context-free with these new grammars.

As another example of the generative power of unrestricted grammars, consider the grammar

$$
\begin{array}{ll}
S \to ACaB, & Ca \to aaC \\
CB \to DB \mid E, & aD \to Da \\
AD \to AC, & aE \to Ea \\
AE \to \varepsilon &
\end{array}
$$

This grammar generates $L = \{a^{2^k} \mid k > 0\}$. To get an idea of how it generates strings in L, consider the derivation of $a^{2^2} = a^4$. We have

$$
\begin{aligned}
S &\Rightarrow ACaB \Rightarrow AaaCB \Rightarrow AaaDB \Rightarrow AaDaB \Rightarrow ADaaB \Rightarrow ACaaB \\
&\Rightarrow AaaCaB \Rightarrow AaaaaCB \Rightarrow AaaaaE \Rightarrow AaaaEa \Rightarrow AaaEaa \\
&\Rightarrow AaEaaa \Rightarrow AEaaaa \Rightarrow aaaa
\end{aligned}
$$

Here A and B act as end markers of the string of a's being generated. C migrates right, doubling the a's until it is next to B, at which point it turns into a D. D migrates left until it finds A, at which point it turns back into C. When CB is replaced by E, the generation of additional a's is over. The E migrates left until it encounters the A, at which point the AE vanishes.

Suppose G is an unrestricted grammar. We can list all w for which $S \Rightarrow w$, that is, all strings that are derived in one step. Since the collection of productions is finite, there will be a finite number of such strings. We can also list all strings derivable in two steps, three steps, and so on. Each of these collections is similarly finite. It follows that $L(G)$ can be listed in this manner. This, in turn, suggests that we should be able to find a Turing machine that enumerates $L(G)$. This is not surprising since grammars generate strings in a well-defined, orderly manner.

Applying Theorem 5.3.5 to the preceding remarks, we have the following theorem:

Theorem 5.4.2.   If G is an unrestricted grammar, then $L(G)$ is a recursively enumerable language.

It is also the case that any recursively enumerable language is generated by some unrestricted grammar. To see this, suppose that L is a recursively enumerable language accepted by the Turing machine $M = (Q, \Sigma, \Gamma, s = q_1, \flat, F, \delta)$. We construct an unrestricted grammar G based on M. If $w \in L(M)$, then $q_1 w \overset{*}{\vdash} x q_f y$, where $q_f \in F$ is an accepting state of M and x and y are some strings in $(\Gamma - \{\flat\})^*$. The grammar G produces the string w by working backward from $x q_f y$ to $q_1 w$ and then removing q_1. G is defined as $G = (N, \Sigma, S, P)$, where $N = (\Gamma - \Sigma) \cup Q \cup \{A_1, A_2, S\}$, where $A_1, A_2,$ and S are new symbols.

The productions in P are of four types. We want G to first derive a final configuration of the form $x q_f y$. This can be accomplished by including all productions of the form

$$S \rightarrow \flat S \mid S\flat \mid A_1 A_2$$
$$A_2 \rightarrow aA_2 \mid A_2 a \mid q$$

for all $a \in \Gamma - \{\flat\}$ and all $q \in F$. [Note that $\flat \in \Gamma \subseteq N$ so that the forms $\flat S$ and $S\flat$ are in $(N \cup \Sigma)^*$.] A_1 is introduced as a marker, which we will remove only at the end of a derivation. These rules allow derivations of the form

$$S \overset{*}{\Rightarrow} \flat \cdots \flat A_1 x q_f y \flat \cdots \flat$$

for all x and y in $(\Gamma - \{\flat\})^*$ and final states q_f in F. Now since we are working backward through M's acceptance of a string, we must ultimately move from the configuration $x q_f y$ back to $q_1 w$. In terms of generating strings, this means we need to replace $A_1 x q_f y$ with $A_1 q_1 w$ eventually. To accomplish this, we add to P productions of the form $b q_j \rightarrow q_i a$, where $\delta(q_i, a) = (q_j, b, R)$ is a transition in M, and productions of the form $q_j cb \rightarrow cq_i a$ for every symbol c in Γ, where $\delta(q_i, a) = (q_j, b, L)$ is a transition of M. The first types of productions (corresponding to right moves) "undo" what the corresponding transition in M does by replacing b with a and moving the nonterminal corresponding to the state left of the a. In the productions resulting from left moves, we replace strings of the form $q_j cb$ by strings of the form $cq_i a$, where c is whatever symbol was originally to the left of M's read/write head. Consequently, for a left transition $\delta(q_i, a) = (q_j, b, L)$, we include all productions of the form $q_j cb \rightarrow cq_i a$ where $c \in \Gamma$.

Finally, since $\flat$'s may remain and certainly the symbols A_1 and q_1 are still present, we clean up the string with the following productions:

$$A_1 q_1 \rightarrow \varepsilon$$
$$\flat \rightarrow \varepsilon$$

As a very simple example of the construction of such a grammar, consider the Turing machine $M = (Q, \Sigma, \Gamma, s = q_1, \flat, F, \delta)$, where we have

$$Q = \{q_1, q_2, q_3\}$$
$$\Sigma = \{a\}$$
$$\Gamma = \{a, \flat\}$$
$$F = \{q_3\}$$
$$\delta(q_1, a) = (q_1, a, R)$$
$$\delta(q_1, \flat) = (q_2, \flat, R)$$
$$\delta(q_2, \flat) = (q_3, \flat, L)$$

This Turing machine accepts a^*. Applying the preceding construction, we get the following groups of productions:

$$\left.\begin{array}{l} S \rightarrow \bar{b}S \mid S\bar{b} \mid A_1A_2 \\ A_2 \rightarrow aA_2 \mid A_2a \mid q_3 \end{array}\right\} \text{from the first step}$$

$$\left.\begin{array}{l} aq_1 \rightarrow q_1a \\ \bar{b}q_1 \rightarrow q_1\bar{b} \end{array}\right\} \begin{array}{l} \text{from the transition moving} \\ M\text{'s read/write head right} \end{array}$$

$$\left.\begin{array}{l} q_3a\bar{b} \rightarrow aq_2\bar{b} \\ q_3\bar{b}\bar{b} \rightarrow \bar{b}q_2\bar{b} \end{array}\right\} \begin{array}{l} \text{from the transition moving} \\ M\text{'s read/write head left} \end{array}$$

$$\left.\begin{array}{l} A_1q_1 \rightarrow \varepsilon \\ \bar{b} \rightarrow \varepsilon \end{array}\right\} \text{from the last step}$$

To understand the connection between the way in which M accepts a string and the way in which G generates the same string, consider $w = a^2$. M accepts w by means of the following transitions:

$$q_1a^2 \vdash aq_1a \vdash a^2q_1\bar{b} \vdash a^2\bar{b}q_2\bar{b} \vdash a^2q_3\bar{b}\bar{b}$$

Correspondingly, G first generates $A_1a^2q_3\bar{b}\bar{b}$ and then works back through the preceding configurations of M to $A_1q_1a^2$, at which point it erases the substring A_1q_1. We have the derivation

$$S \Rightarrow S\bar{b} \Rightarrow S\bar{b}\bar{b} \Rightarrow A_1A_2\bar{b}\bar{b} \Rightarrow A_1aA_2\bar{b}\bar{b} \Rightarrow A_1a^2A_2\bar{b}\bar{b}$$
$$\Rightarrow A_1a^2q_3\bar{b}\bar{b} \Rightarrow A_1a^2\bar{b}q_2\bar{b} \Rightarrow A_1a^2q_1\bar{b}\bar{b} \Rightarrow A_1aq_1a\bar{b}\bar{b}$$
$$\Rightarrow A_1q_1a^2\bar{b}\bar{b} \stackrel{*}{\Rightarrow} A_1q_1a^2 \Rightarrow a^2$$

Theorem 5.4.3.   If $L = L(M)$ is a recursively enumerable language and G is constructed in the manner described previously, then $L = L(G)$.

Proof.   We must show that if $w \in L(M)$, then $w \in L(G)$, and vice versa.

First, suppose $w \in L(M)$. Then we must have that $q_1w \stackrel{*}{\vdash} xq_fy$ for some strings x and y in $(\Gamma - \{\bar{b}\})^*$. From the preceding construction of G, we then have that

$$S \stackrel{*}{\Rightarrow} \bar{b} \cdots \bar{b}A_1xq_fy\bar{b} \cdots \bar{b}$$

This is always possible, since we constructed the first collection of productions so that they would derive *any* string of this form.

Now suppose that, during its computation accepting w, M applies the transition $\delta(q_i, b_1) = (q_j, c, L)$, giving, say,

$$a_1 \ldots a_nq_ib_1 \ldots b_m \vdash a_1 \ldots a_{n-1}q_jcb_2 \ldots b_m$$

as consecutive configurations. Since the transition $\delta(q_i, b_1) = (q_j, c, L)$ yields the production $q_ja_nc \rightarrow a_nq_ib_1$ in G, we have that

$$a_1 \ldots a_nq_ib_1 \ldots b_m \Rightarrow a_1 \ldots a_{n-1}q_jcb_2 \ldots b_m$$

is a legal step in a derivation in G. A similar argument applies to right moves by M. It follows, by an inductive argument, that

$$\not{b} \cdots \not{b} A_1 x q_f y \not{b} \cdots \not{b} \overset{*}{\Rightarrow} \not{b} \cdots \not{b} A_1 q_1 w \not{b} \cdots \not{b}$$

Finally, applying the "clean-up" productions to remove $A_1 q_1$ and any blanks, we have that $S \overset{*}{\Rightarrow} w$. That is, $w \in L(G)$.

Conversely, if $w \in L(G)$, then $S \overset{*}{\Rightarrow} w$, and so we have

$$S \overset{*}{\Rightarrow} \not{b} \cdots \not{b} A_1 x q_f y \not{b} \cdots \not{b}$$
$$\overset{*}{\Rightarrow} \not{b} \cdots \not{b} q_1 w \not{b} \cdots \not{b}$$
$$\overset{*}{\Rightarrow} w$$

so that we have $x q_f y \overset{*}{\Rightarrow} q_1 w$. Since $q_1 w$ corresponds to the initial configuration of M when it begins processing w, a simple induction argument shows that $q_1 w \overset{*}{\vdash} x q_f y$, and so $w \in L(M)$. ∎

Combining Theorems 5.4.2 and 5.4.3, we have the following result:

Theorem 5.4.4.   A language L is recursively enumerable if and only if $L = L(G)$ for some unrestricted grammar G.

Thus the languages arising from unrestricted grammars are exactly those that are accepted by Turing machines.

Exercises for Section 5.4

5.4.1. What language is generated by this grammar?

$$S \rightarrow Ba \mid a, \qquad Sa \rightarrow Bb$$
$$Sb \rightarrow \varepsilon, \qquad B \rightarrow bS \mid BB \mid b$$

Is this language context-free? Is it regular?

5.4.2. Find an unrestricted grammar for each of these languages.

   (a) $\{a^n b^n a^n b^n \mid n \geq 0\}$
   (b) $\{a^i b^j c^k \mid i < j < k\}$
   (c) $\{ww \mid w \in \{a, b\}^*\}$
   (d) $\{www \mid w \in \{a, b\}^*\}$

5.4.3. Some texts define an unrestricted grammar to be one in which all productions are of the form $\alpha \rightarrow \beta$, where $\alpha \in (N \cup \Sigma)^* N (N \cup \Sigma)^*$ and β is as in our definition. That is, α contains at least one nonterminal. This was the definition we gave informally in Section 4.3. Show why grammars of this type have neither more nor less generative power than those of our definition. (*Hint:* How could you transform a grammar of each type into one of the other? Does this transformation affect anything?)

5.4.4. Sketch the design of a Turing machine that enumerates $L(G)$ for an unrestricted grammar G. (*Hint:* Consider a Turing machine with at least three tapes. Tape 1 is the output tape on which $L(G)$ is enumerated, tape 2 contains the list of productions of G, and tape 3 is the work tape. Find some manner in which this Turing machine can first generate those strings that are derivable in one step in G in an orderly manner on tape 3. As each is generated, copy it to tape 1. Then generate strings derivable in two steps in G, and so on.)

5.4.5. In the remarks before Theorem 5.4.3 and its proof there are two implicit requirements of the Turing machine that is being converted into the unrestricted grammar. First, the Turing machine must be *non-erasing*. That is, it may not have any transitions of the form $\delta(q, \sigma) = (p, \flat, X)$ for any $\sigma \neq \flat$. Second, the Turing machine is assumed to halt (on acceptance) with its read/write head on the first blank following the nonblank string, which is left on its tape.

(a) Show that if L is accepted by an arbitrary Turing machine M, then L is also accepted by a non-erasing Turing machine M'.

(b) Construct a non-erasing Turing machine that accepts $\{a^n b^m \mid n, m \geq 0\}$ which halts on the first blank following the nonblank string it leaves on its tape.

(c) Use the technique of this section to find the associated unvestricted grammar for this language.

(d) Give both a derivation (using the grammar from part c) and the sequence of ID's of the Turing machine in part b that leads to acceptance for the string $a^2 ba$.

5.4.6. Show that, if L_1 and L_2 are recursively enumerable languages, then $L_1 L_2$ and L_1^* are recursively enumerable languages.

5.5 CONTEXT-SENSITIVE LANGUAGES AND THE CHOMSKY HIERARCHY

Between the unrestricted grammars and the somewhat restricted form of context-free grammars, various grammars with differing levels of restriction can be defined. Not all such grammars yield interesting classes of languages, but one that does is the collection of context-sensitive grammars. Context-sensitive grammars produce a class of languages lying strictly between the context-free languages and the recursive languages.

Definition 5.5.1.   A grammar $G = (N, \Sigma, S, P)$ is a *context-sensitive grammar* if all productions are of the form $\alpha \rightarrow \beta$, where $\alpha, \beta \in (N \cup \Sigma)^+$ and $|\alpha| \leq |\beta|$.

For example, the grammar given by

$$S \rightarrow abc \mid aAbc$$
$$Ab \rightarrow bA$$
$$Ac \rightarrow Bbcc$$
$$bB \rightarrow Bb$$
$$aB \rightarrow aa \mid aaA$$

is a context-sensitive grammar. This grammar generates the language $\{a^n b^n c^n \mid n \geq 1\}$

so that we have an example of a context-sensitive language that is *not* a context-free language.

Recall that any context-free grammar can be put into Chomsky normal form in which all productions are of the form $A \to \alpha$ or else $A \Rightarrow BC$. Since productions of this form satisfy the definition of context-sensitive grammars, it follows that any context-free grammar is also a context-sensitive grammar. Thus we immediately have the following:

Lemma 5.5.2.   The collection of context-sensitive languages properly contains the collection of context-free languages.

The restriction that the right-hand side of productions in a context-sensitive grammar be at least as long as the left-hand side is said to make the grammar *noncontracting*. Since the empty string, ε, has length 0, it follows from the definition that $\varepsilon \notin L(G)$ for any context-sensitive grammar G. It is sometimes convenient to allow the empty string into a language that is otherwise generated by a context-sensitive grammar. We shall extend our definition to allow productions of the form $S \to \varepsilon$ (for S the start symbol), provided that S does not appear on the right-hand side of any production.

Lemma 5.5.3.   Let $G = (N, \Sigma, S, P)$ be any context-sensitive grammar. Then there exists a context-sensitive grammar $G_1 = (N_1, \Sigma, S_1, P_1)$ for which $L(G) = L(G_1)$ and S_1 never appears on the right-hand side of any productions in P_1.

Proof.   Let $N_1 = \{S_1\} \cup N$, where S_1 is a new symbol. Let $P_1 = P \cup \{S_1 \to \alpha \mid S \to \alpha$ is a production in $G\}$. Note that P_1 satisfies the condition that S_1 never appears on the right-hand side in any production. Moreover, if $S \overset{*}{\Rightarrow} w$ is a derivation in G, then some production $S \to \alpha$ is the initial step (that is, we have $S \Rightarrow \alpha \overset{*}{\Rightarrow} w$). But then $S_1 \to \alpha$ is a production in P_1, and so we have $S_1 \Rightarrow \alpha \Rightarrow w$ in G_1. Thus $w \in L(G)$ if and only if $w \in L(G_1)$. ∎

Suppose that $G = (N, \Sigma, S, P)$ is a context-sensitive grammar and that $w \in L(G)$. If $w = \varepsilon$, then we must have $S \to \varepsilon$. If $w \neq \varepsilon$, then there is some derivation $S \Rightarrow \alpha_1 \Rightarrow \cdots \Rightarrow \alpha_m = w$. Since a context-sensitive grammar is noncontracting, we must have that

$$\mid \alpha_1 \mid \le \mid \alpha_2 \mid \le \cdots \le \mid \alpha_m \mid = \mid w \mid$$

If $m > \mid w \mid$ (that is, the derivation involves more steps than w has symbols), then for some i, j, and p we must have

$$\mid \alpha_i \mid = \mid \alpha_{i+1} \mid = \cdots = \mid \alpha_{i+j} \mid = p$$

That is, during these $j + 1$ steps in the derivation, the string being generated does not increase in length. Now, since N and Σ are finite sets, we have that $\mid N \cup \Sigma \mid = k$ for some k, and thus there are k^p possible strings of length p. If the number of steps in the derivation where the partially derived string stays of length p is greater than the number of possible strings of that length (that is, if $j + 1 > k^p$), then at least two of

$\alpha_i, \alpha_{i+1}, \ldots, \alpha_{i+j}$ must be the same. In this case we can eliminate at least one step in the derivation. That is, if $\alpha_r = \alpha_s$, then

$$S \Rightarrow \alpha_1 \Rightarrow \cdots \Rightarrow \alpha_r \Rightarrow \alpha_{s+1} \Rightarrow \cdots \Rightarrow \alpha_m = w$$

eliminating $\alpha_{r+1} \Rightarrow \cdots \Rightarrow \alpha_s$, and gives a shorter derivation.

The idea in the preceding is that if w is derivable in G then there is some derivation of w that is "not too long." This, in turn, suggests that there is an algorithm for determining if $w \in L(G)$. That is, we can find a Turing machine which halts on all inputs and accepts $L(G)$.

Lemma 5.5.4.   Let $G = (N, \Sigma, S, P)$ be a context-sensitive grammar. Then there exists a Turing machine, T, that halts on all inputs and accepts $L(G)$.

Proof.   We describe a three-tape nondeterministic Turing machine M that accepts $L(G)$. Tape 1 is the input tape. Tape 3 records the entire derivation of the input string w, if such a derivation exists. Tape 2 holds the production rules of G, where the rule $u \rightarrow v$ is represented by $u \flat v$.

A computation of M with input string w consists of the following three steps:

1. The string $S \flat$ is written to tape 3.

2. M generates the productions of G on tape 2.

3. The following steps are repeated until M halts:

    3a. A production $u \flat v$ is chosen from tape 2.

    3b. If $\flat x \flat$ is the rightmost string on tape 2 (the most recently derived string), an instance of the substring u in x is chosen if one exists. If u does not appear as a substring of x, then M halts.

    3c. Replace the instance of u in $\flat x \flat$ by v and write the new string that results, x', on tape 3 immediately following $\flat x \flat$. (Thus, if, say, $\flat x \flat$ is the string $\flat x_1 u x_2 \flat$, we would write $x' = x_1 v x_2$ on tape 3 immediately following $\flat x \flat$.)

    3d. If $x' = w$, then M halts in an accepting state.

    3e. If x' occurs at another position on tape 3, then M halts, rejecting w.

    3f. If $|x'| > |w|$, then M halts in a rejecting state.

Since there are only finitely many strings in $(N \cup \Sigma)^*$ of length less than or equal to $|w|$, every derivation halts, enters a cycle, or derives a string of length greater than $|w|$. Each of these possibilities is covered in (3b), (3d), (3e), or (3f). Thus M halts on all inputs. As was noted in the remarks preceding this theorem, every string in $L(G)$ can be derived by a noncyclic derivation. If w can be derived by such a derivation, M simulates the derivation and halts. ■

Theorem 5.5.5 follows immediately from Lemma 5.5.4.

Theorem 5.5.5.   If L is a context-sensitive language, then L is recursive.

Consider the collection of all context-sensitive grammars with $\Sigma = \{a, b\}$. Since each set of nonterminals is finite, suppose that we rename them all so that, if $G = (N, \Sigma, S, P)$ is any one of these context-sensitive grammars, then we have $N \subseteq \{A_1, A_2, \ldots\}$. Let us assume that the start symbol is always A_1. We are going to encode all context-sensitive grammars over $\{a, b\}$ as strings of 0's and 1's.

First we encode the symbols a and b as 00 and 001. Next we encode each nonterminal A_i as 01^i. We represent the production arrow ($\rightarrow$) by 0011 and the comma (,) as 00111. Any context-sensitive grammar over $\{a, b\}$ can be described by a string of productions separated by commas (using the arrow, $\rightarrow$, to separate the left- and right-hand sides of the productions) and so can be encoded as a string of 0's and 1's in the preceding fashion.

Note that any context-sensitive grammar so encoded can easily be decoded. Also note that not all strings of 0's and 1's represent encoded context-sensitive grammars, but, given a string, we can easily tell if it does represent an encoded context-sensitive grammar over $\{a, b\}$.

If we generate strings of 0's and 1's in lexicographical (alphabetic) order, we may then check each one to determine if it is an encoded context-sensitive grammar. Thus we may find the ith encoded context-sensitive grammar G_i by generating strings in this order until the ith string that is an encoded context-sensitive grammar gets generated. Hence we can index the context-sensitive grammars over $\{a, b\}$ in a meaningful manner, $G_1, G_2, \ldots$.

Now suppose we enumerate $\{a, b\}^*$ in lexicographical order $w_1, w_2, \ldots$. Define $L = \{w_i \mid w_i \notin L(G_i)\}$. It is easy to see that L is recursive. Given $w \in \{a, b\}^*$, determine i for which $w = w_i$. Then generate G_i and determine if $w = w_i \in L(G_i)$ by the preceding algorithm (Lemma 5.5.4). By composing appropriate Turing machines, we get a Turing machine M that halts on all inputs with $L = L(M)$.

A simple diagonalization shows that L is not generated by any context-sensitive grammar. Suppose that $L = L(G)$ for some context-sensitive grammar G over $\{a, b\}$. Then $G = G_i$ for some i. If $w_i \in L = L(G_i)$, then by the definition of L we must have that $w_i \notin L(G_i)$, a contradiction. Conversely, if $w_i \notin L = L(G_i)$, then $w_i \in L$, again from the definition of L. This, again, gives a contradiction. Thus we conclude that L is not generated by any context-sensitive grammar over $\{a, b\}$. It follows that L is a recursive language that is not a context-sensitive language.

Thus we have the following lemma:

Lemma 5.5.6.   There are recursive languages that are not context-sensitive languages.

Combining Lemma 5.5.2, Theorem 5.5.5, and Lemma 5.5.6, we have the following theorem:

Theorem 5.5.7.   The context-free languages are properly contained in the context-sensitive languages, which, in turn, are properly contained in the recursive languages.

In 1959, Noam Chomsky classified four families of grammar types. Unrestricted, context-sensitive, context-free, and regular grammars are referred to as type 0, type 1, type 2, and type 3, respectively. The languages arising from these types of grammars are identified as types 0, 1, 2, and 3 as well. As we have noted, every context-free language that contains the empty string is generated by a context-free grammar in which $S \to \varepsilon$ is the only ε rule. Similarly, we've shown that any context-sensitive language containing ε is derived from a suitably "cleaned up" grammar in which $S \to \varepsilon$ is the only ε rule. Ignoring the complications presented by the empty string, we have seen that every type i language is also type $i - 1$, with inclusion being proper.

This hierarchy of languages is referred to as the *Chomsky hierarchy*. Figure 5.1 illustrates the relationships clearly.

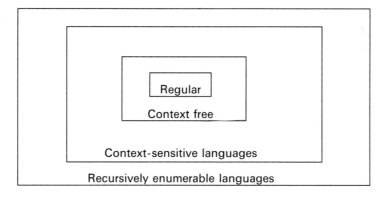

Figure 5.1

In addition to the language/grammar categories originally studied by Chomsky, we have studied recursive languages/grammars that fit between the recursively enumerable languages and the context-sensitive ones. Other language families can be defined and their places in this hierarchy studied. Often they do not have the neatly nested relationships with other languages as in this hierarchy.

We close this section and chapter with the *hierarchy theorem*, which summarizes the language/grammar relationships just described.

Theorem 5.5.8.   Over a given alphabet the collection of recursively enumerable languages properly contains the collection of recursive languages that properly contains the collection of context-sensitive languages that properly contains the collection of context-free languages that, in turn, properly contains the regular languages. Summarizing, let $\mathcal{L}_x$ represent the collection of x languages. We have

$$\mathcal{L}_{\text{regular}} \subset \mathcal{L}_{\text{cf}} \subset \mathcal{L}_{\text{cs}} \subset \mathcal{L}_{\text{recursive}} \subset \mathcal{L}_{\text{r.e.}}$$

Exercises for Section 5.5

5.5.1. If we allow the production $S \rightarrow \varepsilon$ in an otherwise context-sensitive grammar, why do we require that S never appear on the right-hand side in any production?

5.5.2. In the Turing machine described in the proof of Lemma 5.5.4, where does nondeterminism occur?

5.5.3. In the Turing machine M described in the proof of Lemma 5.5.4, why must M generate the production rules of G on tape 2?

5.5.4. While the Turing machine in Lemma 5.5.4 provides a model of a membership algorithm for context-sensitive languages, it is hardly efficient. This exercise explores a more efficient algorithm.

Let $G = (N, \Sigma, S, P)$ be a context-sensitive grammar. To determine if $w \in L(G)$, we can easily determine by inspection if $\varepsilon \in L(G)$. Suppose that $w \in \Sigma^*$ and that $|w| = n > 0$. Let $T_0 = \{S\}$ and, in general, let

$$T_m = \{\alpha \in (N \cup \Sigma)^+ \mid S \overset{k}{\Rightarrow} \alpha \text{ for } k \leq m \text{ and } |\alpha| \leq n\}$$

(a) Show that $T_m = T_{m-1} \cup \{\alpha \mid \beta \overset{*}{\Rightarrow} \alpha \text{ for } \beta \in T_{m-1} \text{ and } |\alpha| \leq n\}$.

(b) Show that $T_m = A \cap B$ for the sets

$$A = \{\alpha \in (N \cup \Sigma)^* \mid |\alpha| \leq n\}$$

$$B = \{\alpha \in (N \cup \Sigma)^* \mid S \overset{*}{\Rightarrow} \alpha \text{ in no more than } m \text{ steps}\}$$

Note the following:

  i. If $S \overset{*}{\Rightarrow} \alpha$ and $|\alpha| \leq n$, then for some m we must have that $\alpha \in T_m$.

  ii. If S does not derive α or if $|\alpha| > n$, then $\alpha \notin T_m$ for all m.

  iii. $T_{m-1} \subseteq T_m$.

  iv. If $T_{m-1} = T_m$, then $T_m = T_{m+1} = \cdots$.

(c) Show that (iv) occurs.

Thus, to determine if $w \in L(G)$, we calculate T_0, T_1, and so on, until we find that $T_{m-1} = T_m = \cdots$. At this point all strings of length less than or equal to n have been generated, and we can simply check T_{m-1} for w. If $w \in T_{m-1}$, then $w \in L(G)$; otherwise, $w \notin L(G)$.

(d) Let G be given by the productions

$$
\begin{aligned}
S &\rightarrow aSBC \mid aBC, & bB &\rightarrow bb \\
CB &\rightarrow BC, & bC &\rightarrow bc \\
aB &\rightarrow ab, & cC &\rightarrow cc
\end{aligned}
$$

  1. Use the algorithm to show that $abac \notin L(G)$.

  2. Use the algorithm to determine if $abaa$ and $aabbcc$ are strings in $L(G)$.

5.5.5. Given a string of 0's and 1's, suggest a technique for determining if it represents a context-sensitive grammar over $\{a, b\}$ encoded in the manner described preceding Lemma 5.5.6.

5.5.6. Encode

$$A_1 \rightarrow aA_2A_1 \mid b$$
$$A_2a \rightarrow aA_2 \mid ab$$
$$bA_2 \rightarrow bb$$

by the method described preceding Lemma 5.5.6.

5.5.7. Let $G = (N, \Sigma, S, P)$ be an unrestricted grammar. Let c be some terminal symbol not in Σ. Construct a context-sensitive grammar $G' = (N, \Sigma \cup \{c\}, S, P')$ based on G for which $w \in L(G)$ if and only if $wc^k \in L(G')$ for some $k \geq 0$.

5.5.8. Let $\mathcal{C}$ be a class of devices of some sort. Suppose that $\mathcal{C}$ can be enumerated as $M_1, M_2, \ldots$ and that there is an algorithm that, when given a device M in $\mathcal{C}$ and an input w, will determine if M accepts w. Show that not every recursive language over some alphabet Σ is accepted by some device in $\mathcal{C}$.

5.5.9. Is the collection of all context-sensitive languages closed with respect to union, concatenation, or star closure? Why or why not?

PROBLEMS

5.1. Is it the case that, if $L_1, L_2, \ldots$ are recursively enumerable languages over Σ, then $\bigcup_{i=1}^{\infty} L_i$ is recursively enumerable? Why or why not?

5.2. Show that the complement of a context-free language must be recursive.

5.3. If L_1 is recursive and L_2 is recursively enumerable, show that $L_1 - L_2$ is recursively enumerable. Is $L_2 - L_1$ recursive? Is it recursively enumerable?

5.4. If L_1 and L_2 are recursively enumerable languages over Σ, sketch the construction of Turing machines that accept L_1L_2 and L_1^*. (*Hint:* Consider nondeterministic Turing machines.)

5.5. Our argument that the languages generated by unrestricted grammars are recursively enumerable (Theorem 5.4.2) was based on the ability to find a Turing machine that enumerates the strings of the language in some orderly manner. An alternative argument can be given by constructing a nondeterministic Turing machine that accepts strings in the language.

　　　Let G be an unrestricted grammar. The Turing machine M that we construct nondeterministically chooses a derivation in G and simulates it on its tape. It then compares the derived string to the input string and accepts if they match. If a match is not found, M simulates another derivation, and so on. If the input string is in $L(G)$, then eventually M will simulate a derivation of it; otherwise, M will never halt.

　　　The simulation is accomplished by first writing the start symbol S on the tape. M then enters a loop, which it may terminate after any number of passes. Each pass corresponds to nondeterministically selecting both a production in G to try to apply and a position in the string on the tape at which to try to apply it. Once a position is selected, M checks to see if that position begins a sequence of symbols corresponding to the left-hand side of the selected production, and if it does, the sequence is replaced by the right-hand side of that production. This loop is repeated until M nondeterministically chooses to exit it. At this point the string that has been generated is compared with the input string to determine if a match is found.

1. Note that nondeterminism is present in three places in the simulation that M performs: choosing a production to use, choosing a starting position, and deciding when to exit the loop. Why is nondeterminism necessary when deciding to exit the loop?

2. Describe the Turing machine M.

   a. How will M represent G's productions in a manner that it can nondeterministically select among them?

   b. What will the tape and input alphabet need to include?

   c. Describe the major components of M.

3. Carefully describe *all* steps necessary in performing one pass through the loop.

   a. What is involved in nondeterministically choosing a production? a starting position? exiting the loop?

   b. How is a production applied when it has been chosen and a match for its left-hand side found?

5.6. In problem 4.1, the language $L = \{a^n b^n c^n | n \geq 1\}$ is seen to be accepted by a linear bounded automaton. This suggests a possible connection between context-sensitive languages and linear bounded automata.

1. Show that if G is a context-sensitive grammar then there is some linear bounded automaton M that accepts $L(G)$. To keep things simple, suppose that $L(G)$ does not contain the empty string. (*Hints:* Consider a two-track linear bounded automaton in which the production rules of G are encoded in states and transitions. Also, review the proof of Lemma 5.5.4.)

   The converse of the preceding is also true. That is, if M is a linear bounded automaton, then $L(M)$ is a context-sensitive language and so there is a context-sensitive grammar generating it. The remarks preceding Theorem 5.4.3 suggest a technique for constructing a grammar based on an arbitrary Turing machine. Note that all productions that result are noncontracting except for $A_1 q_1 \to \varepsilon$ and $\flat \to \varepsilon$. In the case that the Turing machine is a linear bounded automaton, the production $\flat \to \varepsilon$ is unnecessary because a linear bounded automaton never moves outside its end markers. If we omit the production $A_1 q_1 \to \varepsilon$, then the language generated is $\{A_1 q_1 w | w \in L(M)\}$. Note that if M is a linear bounded automaton then this language differs from $L(M)$ only in that every word has an undesirable prefix. Since in a context-sensitive grammar we cannot erase symbols, we do not have the ability to eliminate that undesirable prefix.

   Let $M = (Q, \Sigma, \Gamma, q_1, \flat, F, \Delta)$ be a linear bounded automaton and assume that $\varepsilon \notin L(M)$. We define a context-sensitive grammar $G = (N, \Sigma, S, P)$ for which $L(G) = L(M)$. The context-sensitive grammar we construct generates two copies of a string and then simulates M's actions on one of the copies. If M accepts the string, G eliminates the string resulting from M's activity, leaving only the acceptable string. To make G context-sensitive, we avoid the need for productions that eliminate symbols by building nonterminals that contain a great deal of information. If a and b are in Σ and $q \in Q$, N would include (as individual nonterminals) pairs of the form

$$(*) \begin{cases} (a, a), \quad (a, < b), \quad (a, b >), \quad (a, < b >), \quad (a, qb), \quad (a, q < b) \\ (a, < qb), \quad (a, qb >), \quad (a, bq >), \quad (a, q < b >), \quad (a, < qb >), \quad (a, < bq >) \end{cases}$$

N includes all such pairs for all $a, b \in \Sigma$ and all $q \in Q$. [Note that if a nonterminal $(a, bq >)$ is replaced by the terminal a we have not violated the context-sensitive condition by contracting.] In each case the first element represents the terminal symbol originally in that position and will not be altered during the simulation of M. The second element is used in the simulation of M, as will be described shortly.

N also contains the symbols S and A. S is the start symbol of G, and A is used to generate strings of pairs representing an input string to M. The productions for S and A are

$$S \rightarrow (a, q_1 < a)A \mid (a, q_1 < u >), \quad \text{for every } a \in \Sigma \text{ (here } q_1 \text{ is } M\text{'s initial state)}$$

$$A \rightarrow (a, a)A \mid (a, a >), \qquad\qquad \text{for every } a \in \Sigma$$

These productions can generate strings of the form

$$(a_{i_1}, q_1 < a_{i_1})(a_{i_2}, a_{i_2}) \cdots (a_{i_k}, a_{i_k} >)$$

Note that the string consisting of the second elements is

$$q_1 < a_{i_1} a_{i_2} \cdots a_{i_k} >$$

which represents an initial configuration of M on the input string formed by the first elements. We wish to simulate M's activity on this string of second elements while leaving the string of first elements alone.

2. Suggest or outline a general approach to constructing the productions that simulate M's computation on the string of second components of a string of ordered pairs. *Hints:* These productions should consist of nonterminals in the preceding set (*). Also, as a simple example consider the action of an lba M (with initial state q_1 and accepting state q_n) that accepts the language of all strings of a's and b's in which there is at least one each of a and b. M accepts aba in the following manner:

$$q_1 < aba > \vdash < q_1 aba > \vdash < a q_2 ba > \vdash < ab q_3 a > \vdash < aba q_3 > \vdash < aba q_4 >$$

If the string originally generated by G corresponds to a string in $L(M)$, the simulation of M on the string of second elements will eventually enter an accepting state and terminate. At that point we wish to convert to a string of terminal symbols— the string of first elements. This is accomplished by productions of the form

(1)
$$\begin{array}{llll}
(a, q < b) \rightarrow a, & (a, bq >) \rightarrow a, & \\
(a, < qb) \rightarrow a, & (a, q < b) \rightarrow a, & \text{for all } q \in F \\
(a, qb) \rightarrow a, & (a, < qb) \rightarrow a, & \text{and all } b \in \Sigma \\
(a, qb >) \rightarrow a, & (a, < bq) \rightarrow a &
\end{array}$$

and of the form

(2)
$$\begin{array}{ll}
(a, r)b \rightarrow ab, & \\
b(a, x) \rightarrow ba, & \text{for all } b \in \Sigma \text{ and } (a, x) \in N
\end{array}$$

3. Why is it necessary that the productions in (1) depend on q while those in (2) do not?

4. a. Give an lba accepting the language of palindromes over $\{a, b\}$.

   b. Use the preceding technique to convert this lba into a context-sensitive grammar.

5.7. Let $\alpha \rightarrow \beta$ be a noncontracting production (that is, $|\alpha| \leq |\beta|$).

1. Construct a sequence of noncontracting productions, each of whose right side has length 2 or less, that produces β from α (that is, $\alpha \overset{*}{\Rightarrow} \beta$ by means of these productions).

2. Construct a sequence of productions of the form $uAv \to uwv$ (that is, $\alpha \to \beta$ where

$$\alpha \in (N \cup \Sigma)^* N (N \cup \Sigma)^* \quad \text{and} \quad \beta \in (N \cup \Sigma)^* \Sigma^+ (N \cup \Sigma)^*)$$

which produces the same result as $AB \to CD$.

3. Show that any context-sensitive language is generated by a context-sensitive grammar in which each production is of the form $uAv \to uwv$ for $w \in \Sigma^+$ and $u, v \in (N \cup \Sigma)^*$.

6

Decidability

6.1 HALTING PROBLEM

In Definition 4.2.2 we defined a function f to be *Turing computable*, or just *computable*, if there is a Turing machine that computes $f(w)$ for all w in the domain of f. As a practical example of computable functions, the indicator function for a recursive language is computable. [Recall that the indicator function, χ_L, is the function that evaluates to 1 (yes) or 0 (no) depending on whether its argument is in or not in the language.] From Chapter 5 we intuitively know that the indicator function for a recursively enumerable language that is not also recursive is *not* computable, since in such a language some strings cause any Turing machine accepting the language to fail to halt. Thus we have examples of both computable and uncomputable functions.

In this chapter we will further investigate questions of computability by means of situations in which the result of a computation is yes or no (equivalently, 1 or 0). Problems of this sort are called *decision problems* and this kind of computability is referred to as *decidability*.

For example, the problem "given a context-free grammar G, is $L(G)$ empty?" is such a problem. Note that there are infinitely many *instances* of this problem—one instance for each context-free grammar. Furthermore, for each instance an answer of either yes or no can be determined (see Section 2.6).

As another example, consider the question "given a context-sensitive grammar G and a string w, is $w \in L(G)$?" Again, note that there are infinitely many instances of this problem. In this case each instance is determined by a context-sensitive grammar and a string. Moreover, again, each instance has a yes or no answer (see Section 5.5).

Decision problems are said to be *decidable* if an algorithm exists that is capable of answering yes or no for any instance. If no algorithm exists, the problem is said to be *undecidable*. Both of the problems in the preceding examples are decidable since such algorithms exist for them.

Perhaps the most well known undecidable problem is the *halting problem* for Turing machines. The halting problem is simply stated as follows:

> Let M be an arbitrary Turing machine with input alphabet Σ. Let $w \in \Sigma^*$. Will M halt when begun on the input string w?

An individual *instance* of the halting problem consists of a Turing machine–input string pair. A solution to the halting problem would be an algorithm that correctly answers yes or no for any instance, that is, an algorithm general enough to answer the halting problem correctly for every possible combination of Turing machine and input string.

Throughout our discussion of Turing machines we have emphasized the close connection between them and algorithms. In Chapter 5 we made this connection specific: our model of an algorithm is a Turing machine that halts on all inputs. Consequently, we may seek a solution to the halting problem by seeking a Turing machine that halts on all inputs and provides a yes or no answer when presented with information about any Turing machine and input string.

In Section 4.5 we discussed universal Turing machines and, in particular, a technique for encoding Turing machines over some input alphabet Σ as strings of 0's and 1's. There are countably many strings of 0's and 1's, and certainly not every such string of 0's and 1's is an encoding of a Turing machine. Thus there are at most countably many Turing machines with input alphabet Σ. We may enumerate the Turing machines over Σ as, say, $M_1, M_2, \ldots$. Furthermore, since Σ^* is also countable, we may enumerate it as $\Sigma^* = \{w_1, w_2, \ldots\}$.

Consider the language

$$L = \{w_i \mid w_i \text{ is not accepted by } M_i\}$$

We claim that L is not a recursively enumerable language. To see this, suppose that L actually *is* a recursively enumerable language. Then L must be accepted by some Turing machine, say M_k. Consider w_k. Note that if $w_k \in L$ then w_k must not be accepted by M_k, so we have $w_k \notin L(M_k) = L$, a contradiction. On the other hand, if $w_k \notin L$, then since $L = L(M_k)$ we have that $w_k \notin L(M_k)$, and so w_k must be in L, another contradiction. It follows that L is not accepted by any Turing machine and so cannot be recursively enumerable.

Now suppose that the halting problem has a solution. That is, there is a Turing machine that halts on all inputs and, when presented with a description of any Turing machine M and any input string w (both encoded in some manner), determines if M halts on input w. We may then construct a Turing machine M_L that accepts the preceding language L. Let w be a string. M_L first enumerates $w_1, w_2, \ldots$ until it determines k for which $w = w_k$. M then generates M_k and passes the appropriate encodings of w_k and M_k to the alleged Turing machine, which determines if M_k halts on input w_k. If it is determined that M_k does not halt on input w_k, then M_L halts and accepts $w_k = w$

(why?). On the other hand, if it is determined that M_k halts on input w_k, then appropriate encodings of M_k and w_k are passed to a universal Turing machine that simulates M_k on w_k. In this case the universal Turing machine will eventually halt, determining if M_k accepts w_k. If M_k does accept w_k, then M_L halts and rejects w_k. If M_k does not accept w_k, then M_L halts and accepts w_k.

It follows that $w \in L(M_L)$ if and only if $w \in L$, and so we have that $L = L(M_L)$. This, in turn, contradicts the fact that L is not recursively enumerable. Consequently, there can be no general algorithm that answers the halting problem for an arbitrary Turing machine–input string combination. Thus we have the following theorem:

Theorem 6.1.1.   The halting problem for Turing machines is undecidable.

We may use the undecidability of the halting problem to show that other problems are undecidable. One way of doing this is to show that if a certain other problem is decidable, then the halting problem would also be decidable.

For example, the *blank tape problem* is the problem of deciding if an arbitrary Turing machine will halt when started with a blank tape. To show that the blank tape problem must be undecidable, we will show that if it *were* decidable then the halting problem would be decidable. Thus suppose that the blank tape problem is decidable. Let M be any Turing machine and let w be any string. Let M' be the Turing machine that starts with a blank tape, writes w on the tape, and then acts like M begun in the configuration $q_1 w$ (where q_1 is the initial state of M). Note that M' is a Turing machine that we have begun with a blank tape. If we have an algorithm that determines if an arbitrary Turing machine begun with a blank tape will halt, we may determine if M' halts. But M' halts if and only if the original Turing machine M halts with the input string w. Thus we would have a solution to the halting problem if such a general algorithm existed for the blank tape problem. This contradicts Theorem 6.1.1 and so the blank tape problem is also undecidable.

The technique of connecting the halting problem to the blank tape problem in a manner that allows us to use the undecidability of the halting problem to conclude the undecidability of the blank tape problem is called *reduction*. We say that the halting problem is *reduced* to the blank tape problem, because decidability of the blank tape problem would allow us to conclude decidability of the halting problem. (A problem X is reduced to a problem Y if by solving Y we can solve X.)

Exercises for Section 6.1

6.1.1. Show that if the halting problem is decidable then every recursively enumerable language is recursive.

6.1.2. Let M be a Turing machine with input alphabet Σ. Let w_m be an encoding of M over $\{0, 1\}$. Let

$$L = \{w_m w \mid M \text{ halts on the input string encoded as } w\}$$

Show that L is recursively enumerable. Show that L is *not* recursive.

6.1.3. The *state entry problem* for Turing machines can be stated as follows: For an arbitrary Turing machine $M = (Q, \Sigma, \Gamma, s, b, F, \delta)$, state q, and string $w \in \Sigma^*$, does M ever enter state q when begun on the string w? Show that the state entry problem is undecidable by an appropriate reduction of the halting problem.

6.1.4. The *emptiness problem*, "does $L(M) = \emptyset$" for an arbitrary Turing machine, is also an undecidable problem. Show that this problem is undecidable by reducing the blank tape problem to it.

6.1.5. By appropriate reductions, show that each of the following problems is undecidable:

(a) For an arbitrary Turing machine M with input alphabet Σ, does $L(M) = \Sigma^*$?

(b) For arbitrary Turing machines M_1 and M_2, does $L(M_1) = L(M_2)$?

(c) For an arbitrary Turing machine M with tape alphabet Γ and $a \in \Gamma$, if M is started on an empty tape, does it ever write the symbol a to the tape?

6.2 POST'S CORRESPONDENCE PROBLEM

The undecidable problems that we've considered so far have been concerned with properties of Turing machines. The fact that the halting problem is undecidable has many consequences of interest in other areas as well. In many cases it is awkward to use the halting problem itself to derive these consequences. In this section we establish the unsolvability of an intermediate result, the Post correspondence problem (herein after referred to as PCP).

An instance of the PCP is called a *Post correspondence system* and consists of three things: an alphabet Σ and two sets, A and B, of strings from Σ^+, where both A and B contain the same number of strings. Suppose that $A = \{u_1, u_2, \ldots, u_k\}$ and $B = \{v_1, v_2, \ldots, v_k\}$. A *solution* for this instance of the PCP (that is, a solution for this Post correspondence system) is a sequence of indexes, $i_1, i_2, \ldots, i_n$, such that $u_{i_1} u_{i_2} \ldots u_{i_n} = v_{i_1} v_{i_2} \ldots v_{i_n}$.

For example, if $\Sigma = \{a, b\}$, $A = \{a, abaaa, ab\}$ and $B = \{aaa, ab, b\}$, this Post correspondence system has a solution given by $i_1 = 2, i_2 = i_3 = 1$, and $i_4 = 3$ since $u_2 u_1 u_1 u_3 = abaaaaaab = v_2 v_1 v_1 v_3$.

It is convenient to view a Post correspondence system as a collection of blocks of the form

Thus the preceding Post correspondence system is viewed as

a		$abaaa$		ab
aaa	,	ab	,	b
$i=1$		$i=2$		$i=3$

A solution corresponds to some way of laying blocks next to each other so that the string in the top cells corresponds to the string in the bottom cells. Thus the preceding solution corresponds to

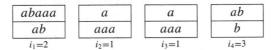

Consider the Post correspondence system given by

$$
\begin{array}{|c|}\hline ab \\\hline aba \\\hline\end{array}\quad
\begin{array}{|c|}\hline baa \\\hline aa \\\hline\end{array}\quad
\begin{array}{|c|}\hline aba \\\hline baa \\\hline\end{array}
$$

$$
i=1 \qquad\qquad i=2 \qquad\qquad i=3
$$

Note that any solution must begin with $i_1 = 1$ since this is the only block where both strings begin with the same letter. The next block in such a solution must begin with an a in the top cell; hence either $i_2 = 1$ or $i_2 = 3$. But $i_2 = 1$ will not work since we would have

$$
\begin{array}{|c|c|}\hline ab & ab \\\hline aba & aba \\\hline\end{array}
$$

$$
i_1=1 \qquad i_2=1
$$

and the upper and lower strings cannot be equal. Thus i_2 must be 3, giving

$$
\begin{array}{|c|c|}\hline ab & aba \\\hline aba & baa \\\hline\end{array}
$$

$$
i_1=1 \qquad i_2=3
$$

A similar argument shows that i_3 must be 3, giving

$$
\begin{array}{|c|c|c|}\hline ab & aba & aba \\\hline aba & baa & baa \\\hline\end{array}
$$

$$
i_1=1 \qquad i_2=3 \qquad i_3=3
$$

But this argument must go on forever, since there is never a choice of next index that allows the string in the top cells to catch up to the string in the bottom cells in length. Consequently this Post correspondence system does not have a solution.

The problem of determining if an arbitrary Post correspondence system has a solution is the *Post correspondence problem* (PCP).

In the preceding examples we were able to give an argument (or a specific construction) that solutions to individual instances of the PCP exist. In general, though, there is no algorithm for deciding if an arbitrary Post correspondence system has a solution. We will prove this statement by showing that if PCP were decidable then we could solve the halting problem for Turing machines, that is, by reducing the halting problem for Turing machines to the PCP. We begin by introducing a modification to the PCP and showing that if PCP were solvable then this *modified PCP* would also be solvable.

In the *modified PCP* (MPCP) we seek a solution for a Post correspondence system in which the sequence of indexes must begin with 1 (that is, we must have $i_1 = 1$). So, we seek a sequence of indexes $1, i_2, \ldots, i_n$ so that $u_1 u_{i_2} \ldots u_{i_n} = v_1 v_{i_2} \ldots v_{i_n}$. We first show the necessary connection between MPCP and PCP.

Lemma 6.2.1.   If the PCP is decidable, then the MPCP is also decidable.

Proof.   Let $A = \{u_1, u_2, \ldots, u_k\}$ and $B = \{v_1, v_2, \ldots, v_k\}$ be an instance of the MPCP with the alphabet Σ. Suppose that each $u_i = a_{i_1} a_{i_2} \ldots a_{i_{m_i}}$ and that each $v_i = b_{i_1} b_{i_2} \ldots b_{i_{n_i}}$, where the a's and b's are alphabet symbols in Σ. For each i, let

$$y_i = a_{i_1} \$ a_{i_2} \$ \ldots \$ a_{i_{m_i}} \$ \quad \text{and} \quad z_i = \$ b_{i_1} \$ b_{i_2} \ldots \$ b_{i_{n_i}}$$

where $\$$ is some new symbol not in Σ. Note that y_i is just u_i with a $\$$ appended to each of its symbols, and z_i is v_i with the $\$$ prefixed to each of its symbols. Let $\%$ be another symbol not in Σ and let

$$\begin{aligned} y_0 &= \$ y_1, & z_0 &= z_1 \\ y_{k+1} &= \%, & z_{k+1} &= \$\% \end{aligned}$$

Consider the instance of the PCP given by the following set of blocks:

y_0		y_1		y_k		y_{k+1}
z_0	$\ldots$	z_1		z_k		z_{k+1}

We claim that this instance of the PCP has a solution if and only if the original instance of MPCP given by A and B has a solution. To see this, note that if $i_1, i_2, \ldots, i_r$ provides a solution to this instance of PCP then, since all z_i begin with $\$$ and only y_0 begins with $\$$, we must have that $i_1 = 0$. Moreover, i_r must be $k + 1$ since only y_{k+1} and z_{k+1} match in their last symbol. Thus, if there is a solution to this instance of the PCP, it must have form $0, i_2, i_3, \ldots, k + 1$. That is, we must have a

y_0				y_{k+1}
z_0	$\ldots$			z_{k+1}

or, equivalently,

$$\$ a_{1_1} \$ a_{1_2} \$ \ldots \$ a_{1_{m_1}} \$ \ldots \$ \% = \$ b_{1_1} \$ b_{1_2} \$ \ldots \$ b_{1_n} \$ \ldots \$ \%$$

Ignoring the $\$$ signs, we get

$$u_1 u_{i_2} \ldots u_{i_r} = v_1 v_{i_2} \ldots v_{i_r}$$

which is a solution to the preceding instance of MPCP. Thus, if PCP is decidable, then MPCP is decidable.   ∎

Lemma 6.2.1 gives us the ability to show that PCP is undecidable by means of showing that MPCP is undecidable. This simplifies our problem because the MPCP is somewhat more structured. We show that if MPCP were decidable then the halting problem for Turing machines would also be decidable, and so MPCP cannot be decidable.

Suppose that the MPCP is decidable; that is, there is some general algorithm that can be used to determine if any instance of the MPCP has a solution. Our object is to show that there then is an algorithm that can determine if an arbitrary Turing machine M will halt when begun with an arbitrary string w on its tape.

To accomplish this, we first note that any Turing machine can be converted into one that only halts in an accepting state. This is easy to do since, if the Turing machine halts in a nonaccepting state, we may add transitions that cause it to loop forever. Note that the language accepted by the converted Turing machine is exactly the same language that the original accepted. For our discussion, then, we may assume that any Turing machine is of this form.

Now suppose that $M = (Q, \Sigma, \Gamma, s, \flat, F, \delta)$ is any Turing machine and w is any string over Σ. We show how to construct an instance of the MPCP for which the ability to determine if a solution exists gives the ability to determine if M halts on input w [and, consequently, to determine if $w \in L(M)$].

Let \$ be some symbol not in Γ. We construct the lists $A = \{u_1, u_2, \ldots, u_n\}$ and $B = \{v_1, v_2, \ldots, v_n\}$ of the MPCP in five groups. For simplicity let us represent the lists as blocks.

The first group consists of the single block

$$\frac{u_1}{v_1} = \frac{\$}{\$q_1 w \$}$$

where q_1 is the initial state of M.

The second group of blocks consists of the block

$$\frac{\$}{\$}$$

and all blocks of the form

$$\frac{\sigma}{\sigma}$$

where σ is any nonblank symbol in Γ.

The third group is derived from M's transitions. If $\delta(q, \sigma) = (p, \tau, R)$ we include a block

$$\frac{q\sigma}{\tau p}$$

If $\delta(q, \sigma) = (p, \tau, L)$, we include all blocks of the form

$$\frac{\gamma q \sigma}{p \gamma \tau}$$

for $\gamma \in \Gamma - \{\flat\}$. If $\delta(q, \flat) = (p, \tau, R)$, we include the block

$$\frac{q\$}{\tau p \$}$$

and if $\delta(q, \flat) = (p, \tau, L)$, we include all blocks of the form

$$\frac{\gamma q \$}{p \gamma \tau \$}$$

for all $\gamma \in \Gamma - \{b\}$.

The fourth group is derived from the collection of accepting states of M. For each $q \in F$ and all σ and τ in $\Gamma - \{b\}$, we include blocks

$$\frac{\sigma q \tau}{q} \quad , \quad \frac{\sigma q \$}{q\$} \quad , \quad \frac{\$ q \tau}{\$ q} \quad , \quad \text{and} \quad \frac{q\$\$}{\$}$$

Example 6.2.1

Suppose that M has initial state q_1 and accepting state q_3 with transitions given by the table

$\delta(q_i, \sigma)$	$\sigma = a$	$\sigma = b$	$\sigma = b$
q_1	(q_2, b, R)	(q_2, a, L)	(q_2, b, L)
q_2	(q_3, a, L)	(q_1, a, R)	(q_2, a, R)

Let $w = ab$. The instance of the MPCP given by this Turing machine and this string would be represented by the following blocks:

Group 1:
$$\frac{\$}{\$q_1ab\$}$$
$i=1$

Group 2:
$$\frac{a}{a} \quad \frac{b}{b} \quad \frac{\$}{\$}$$
$i=2 \qquad i=3 \qquad i=4$

Group 3:
$$\frac{q_1a}{bq_2} \qquad \text{from } \delta(q_1, a) = (q_2, b, R)$$
$i=5$

$$\frac{aq_1b}{q_2aa} \quad \frac{bq_1b}{q_2ba} \qquad \text{from } \delta(q_1, b) = (q_2, a, L)$$
$i=6 \qquad i=7$

$$\frac{aq_1\$}{q_2ab\$} \quad \frac{bq_1\$}{q_2bb\$} \qquad \text{from } \delta(q_1, b) = (q_2, b, L)$$
$i=8 \qquad i=9$

$$\frac{aq_2a}{q_3aa} \quad \frac{bq_2a}{q_3ba} \qquad \text{from } \delta(q_2, a) = (q_3, a, L)$$
$i=10 \qquad i=11$

$$\frac{q_2b}{aq_1} \qquad \text{from } \delta(q_2, b) = (q_1, a, R)$$
$i=12$

$$\frac{q_2\$}{aq_2\$} \qquad \text{from } \delta(q_2, b) = (q_2, a, R)$$
$i=13$

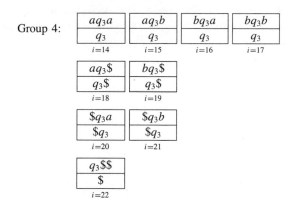

Group 4:

aq_3a	aq_3b	bq_3a	bq_3b
q_3	q_3	q_3	q_3
$i=14$	$i=15$	$i=16$	$i=17$

$aq_3\$$	$bq_3\$$
$q_3\$$	$q_3\$$
$i=18$	$i=19$

$\$q_3a$	$\$q_3b$
$\$q_3$	$\$q_3$
$i=20$	$i=21$

$q_3\$\$$
$\$$
$i=22$

Suppose that we try to find a solution to this instance of the MPCP. We must begin with

u_1
v_1

This leaves a "remainder" of $q_1ab\$$ in the v_i's that we must accommodate with u_i's. By choosing $u_5u_3u_4$, we offset this remainder and introduce a new remainder of $bq_2b\$$. This remainder can be covered by $u_3u_{12}u_4$, which introduces yet a new remainder of $baq_1\$$. Continuing in this manner of offsetting and generating remainders (possibly backtracking if a poor choice is made when several options are available), we get the solution:

$\$$	q_1a	b	$\$$	b	q_2b	$\$$	b	$aq_1\$$	bq_2a	b	$\$q_3b$	a	b	$\$q_3q$	b	$\$q_3b$	$\$$	$q_3\$\$$
$\$q_1ab\$$	bq_2	b	$\$$	b	aq_1	$\$$	b	$q_2ab\$$	q_3ba	b	$\$q_3$	a	b	$\$q_3$	b	$\$q_3$	$\$$	$\$$
Index 1	5	3	4	3	12	4	3	8	11	3	21	2	3	20	3	21	4	22

The string composed in this solution is

$$\$q_1ab\$bq_2b\$baq_1\$bq_2ab\$q_3bab\$q_3ab\$q_3b\$q_3\$\$$$

Note that $ab \in L(M)$, for it is accepted by means of the computation

$$q_1ab \vdash bq_2b \vdash baq_1 \vdash bq_2ab \vdash q_3bab$$

The individual configurations of this computation appear separated by $ signs and in order in the string composed in the solution of the MPCP.

Let us look back at the way in which the u_i's and v_i's were defined in constructing the instance of the MPCP from the Turing machine M. We are forced to choose the block

$$\frac{u_1}{v_1} = \frac{\$}{\$q_1w\$}$$

to begin a solution (if one actually exists). The portion q_1w that appears between the $\$$ signs in v_1 represents M's initial configuration as it begins computation on w. Now, if w begins with σ and if $\delta(q_1, \sigma) = (q_k, \tau, R)$, we construct a (u_i, v_i) pair as

$$\begin{array}{|c|}\hline q_1\sigma \\ \hline \tau q_k \\ \hline \end{array}$$

so that, in order to make up the remainder that the string in the top square lacks, we must begin constructing the next configuration of M in the bottom square. The existing remainder is then filled out by adding the remaining symbols of w in both the top and bottom strings. Thus we include all the pairs

$$\begin{array}{|c|}\hline \sigma_i \\ \hline \sigma_i \\ \hline \end{array} \quad \text{and} \quad \begin{array}{|c|}\hline \$ \\ \hline \$ \\ \hline \end{array}$$

When the string in the top boxes has caught up to the string that appears in the bottom of the first box, the bottom string has grown to represent the next configuration of M. We extend this string in the same way. At each step the lower string stays one step ahead of the top string, so every time the top string completes a configuration of M, the bottom string has built the next configuration. All that remains is to include appropriate (u_i, v_i) pairs so that the top string can actually catch up to the bottom string once an accepting configuration of M has been achieved.

First note that, if the string of u_i's is of the form $\alpha\$$ and the string of v_i's is of the form $\alpha\$x\$$, then we may extend the u_i's to $\alpha\$x\$$ and the v_i's to $\alpha\$x\$y\$$, where y represents the configuration of M one move later. In addition, this string of v_i's is the only one that can result corresponding to the new string of u_i's.

To see this, assume that the string of u_i's is $\alpha\$$ while the string of v_i's is $\alpha\$\sigma_1\sigma_2\ldots\sigma_kq\sigma_{k+1}\ldots\sigma_{k+m}\$$ for some $m > 0$. Suppose that $\delta(q, \sigma_{k+1}) = (q', \tau, R)$. The other possibilities are similar. The blocks that allow us to extend the string of u_i's are

$$\begin{array}{|c|}\hline \sigma_i \\ \hline \sigma_i \\ \hline \end{array}, \quad \text{for } i = 1, 2, \ldots, k$$

the block

$$\begin{array}{|c|}\hline q\sigma_{k+1} \\ \hline \tau p \\ \hline \end{array}$$

blocks of the form

$$\begin{array}{|c|}\hline \sigma_i \\ \hline \sigma_i \\ \hline \end{array}, \quad \text{for any } i = k + 2, \ldots, k + m$$

and finally the block

$$\begin{array}{|c|}\hline \$ \\ \hline \$ \\ \hline \end{array}$$

The string resulting in the v_i's is

$$\alpha\$\sigma_1 \ldots \sigma_kq\sigma_{k+1} \ldots \sigma_{k+m}\$\sigma_1 \ldots \sigma_k\tau p\sigma_{k+2} \ldots \sigma_{k+m}\$$$

Note that $y = \sigma_1 \ldots \sigma_k \tau p \sigma_{k+2} \ldots \sigma_{k+m}$ is exactly the configuration of M resulting from this transition. Moreover, since there is no choice in this process as to which (u, v) pair to use, there is no other possible resulting string of v_i's.

Recall that we are assuming that a Turing machine M halts only when accepting.

Lemma 6.2.2. M halts on input w if and only if there is a solution to the derived instance of the MPCP.

Proof.   Suppose that M halts on input w. Thus there is some sequence of configurations of M beginning with $q_1 w$ and ending in an accepting state. Suppose that this sequence is represented by the strings $x_1, x_2, \ldots, x_k$ for some k. From the preceding remarks, in the derived instance of MPCP we may construct a sequence of u_i's of the form $\$x_1\$x_2 \ldots \$x_{k-1}\$$ and a sequence of v_i's of the form $\$x_1\$x_2 \ldots \$x_{k-1}\$x_k\$$. Since M halts in the configuration x_k, we must have $x_k = yqz$ for some state $q \in F$ and strings y and z in Γ^*. If at least one of y and z is not the empty string, we may extend the u_i string and the v_i string by means of one of the (u, v) pairs from the fourth group and possibly several of the type

σ_i
σ_i

or

$\$$
$\$$

making the string of u_i's look like $\$x_1\$x_2\$ \ldots \$x_{k-1}\$x_k\$$ and the string of v_i's look like $\$x_1\$x_2\$ \ldots \$x_{k-1}\$x_k\$x_{k'}$ where $x_{k'}$ has at least one less symbol than x_k. We repeat this, shortening the resulting string between the last pair of $\$$ signs of the v_i string until we have strings of the following form:

$$u_i\text{'s}: \quad \$x_1\$x_2\$ \ldots \$x_k\$ \ldots \$$$
$$v_i\text{'s}: \quad \$x_1\$x_2\$ \ldots \$x_k\$x_{k'}\$ \ldots \$q\$$$

The last group of (u, v) pairs contains a block of the form

$q\$\$$
$\$$

which may now be appended to make equal strings. Thus, if M halts on input w, we may find a solution to the derived instance of MPCP.

Conversely, suppose that M does not halt input w. By the preceding remarks, the strings of u_i's and v_i's in the derived instance of MPCP represent consecutive configurations of M. Since M never enters a halting state (all of which are accepting states), none of the (u_i, v_i) pairs from the fourth group is ever appended. A simple induction shows that the growing strings of u_i's and v_i's always have different numbers of $\$$ signs, and so this instance of MPCP has no solution.   ∎

We thus conclude the following theorem:

Theorem 6.2.3.   The PCP is not solvable.

Proof. Let M be an arbitrary Turing machine and w an arbitrary string (we assume that M halts only on acceptance). If PCP is decidable, then by Lemma 6.2.1 we may determine if the instance of MPCP derived from M has a solution. Thus, by Lemma 6.2.2 we may determine if M halts on input w. Since M was an arbitrary Turing machine and w an arbitrary string, we have an algorithm for deciding an arbitrary instance of the halting problem, a contradiction of Theorem 6.1.1. Thus PCP is not solvable. ∎

Exercises for Section 6.2

6.2.1. The Post correspondence system given by

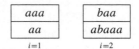

has a solution. Find it.

6.2.2. Does this Post correspondence system have a solution?

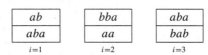

6.2.3. For each of the following Post correspondence systems, either find a solution or show that none exists.

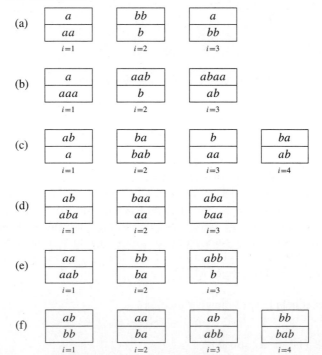

6.2.4. Although the PCP is undecidable, it is easy to alter the problem so that it becomes decidable. Show that there is a decision algorithm for the PCP for Post correspondence systems with a single-symbol alphabet.

6.2.5. Show that in the proof of Lemma 6.2.1 if there is a solution to the instance of MPCP given by A and B then the derived instance of the PCP also has a solution.

6.2.6. In the remarks after Lemma 6.2.1 it is claimed that the conversion of a Turing machine M into one that only halts when it accepts is an easy conversion. In fact, the conversion involves two steps.

(a) Give a technique to identify any nonaccepting states in which $M = (Q, \Sigma, \Gamma, s, b, F, \delta)$ would halt if it entered them.

(b) Suppose that q is a nonaccepting state from which there are no transitions. Show how to construct transitions that would cause M to never halt in case it ever entered q.

6.2.7. For the Turing machine M of Example 6.2.1 and the string $w = abb$, does the derived instance of MPCP have a solution? How about if $w = a$?

6.2.8. An interesting alternative approach to showing that the MPCP is undecidable comes from unrestricted grammars rather than Turing machines.

(a) Show that the *membership problem* for recursively enumerable languages is undecidable. (The membership problem for recursively enumerable languages may be stated as follows: "Is there an algorithm for deciding if $w \in L$ for L an arbitrary recursively enumerable language and w an arbitrary string?")

(b) Let $G = (N, \Sigma, S, P)$ be an unrestricted grammar and $w \in \Sigma^+$. Construct an instance of MPCP in the following manner: Let $u_1 = F$ and $v_1 = FS \Rightarrow$, where F is some symbol not in $N \cup \Sigma$. Thus we have the block

F
$FS \Rightarrow$

$$i = 1$$

For every $x \in N \cup \Sigma$, include a block

x
x

Let E be some symbol not in $N \cup \Sigma$ and include the block

$\Rightarrow wE$
E

For every production $\alpha \rightarrow \beta$ in P, include a block

α
β

Finally, include the block

$\Rightarrow$
$\Rightarrow$

    i. For the following unrestricted grammar and the string a^3b^3 construct such an instance of the MPCP:

$$S \rightarrow aASB|aBb$$
$$aA \rightarrow aa$$
$$aB \rightarrow ab$$
$$bB \rightarrow bb$$

    ii. Find a derivation of a^3b^3 with this grammar.

    iii. Find a solution to the instance of the MPCP that you've constructed.

(c) Sketch a proof of the following statement: If G is any unrestricted grammar and $w \in \Sigma^+$ is any string, the instance of MPCP constructed as in part (b) has a solution if and only if $w \in L(G)$.

(d) Prove that if MPCP is decidable then the membership problem for recursively enumerable languages is also decidable (thereby proving that the MPCP is undecidable).

6.2.9. Show that the PCP remains unsolvable even if restricted to Post correspondence systems over two-symbol alphabets.

6.2.10. Use the PCP to prove that the emptiness problem for context-sensitive grammars is undecidable. [The emptiness problem for CSG's is, "For an arbitrary CSG G is $L(G) = \emptyset$?"] *Hint:* It is a consequence of Problem 5.6 that for any linearly bounded automaton M we can construct a context-sensitive grammar generating $L(M)$. We wish to show that PCP is decidable if the emptiness problem for context-sensitive grammars is decidable, so consider an LBA that accepts only strings y for which $u_{i_1} \ldots u_{i_k} = v_{i_1} \ldots v_{i_k} = y$.

6.3 UNDECIDABILITY AND CONTEXT-FREE LANGUAGES

In Chapter 3 we established algorithms for certain decision problems for context-free grammars and languages. In particular, we found solutions to the membership problem for context-free languages, the problem of whether a context-free grammar generates any terminal strings (the emptiness problem), and the problem of whether or not a context-free grammar generates an infinite language. It turns out that many of the kinds of questions that we were able to answer for regular languages become undecidable when asked for context-free languages. The undecidability of the PCP provides a useful tool in establishing the undecidability of some of these problems.

    Our first approach to showing that a question about context-free grammars or languages is undecidable is to show that, if it were decidable, then the PCP would be decidable. For each such question we show how to construct a context-free grammar from an arbitrary Post correspondence system in a manner that, if the question about the grammars were decidable, then an arbitrary instance of the PCP would also be decidable.

    Suppose that Σ, A, and B is an arbitrary instance of the PCP, where A is $u_1, u_2, \ldots, u_k$ and B is $v_1, v_2, \ldots, v_k$, both lists of strings over Σ. Suppose that $C = \{a_1, a_2, \ldots, a_k\}$ are symbols not in Σ. We construct two context-free grammars G_A and G_B derived from A, B, and C.

Let $G_A = (\{S_A\}, \Sigma \cup C, S_A, P_A)$ and $G_B = (\{S_B\}, \Sigma \cup C, S_B, P_B)$, where S_A and S_B are new symbols. The production set P_A consists of all productions of the form $S_A \rightarrow u_i S_A a_i | u_i a_i$ for $i = 1, 2, \ldots, k$. Similarly, P_B contains all productions of the form $S_B \rightarrow v_i S_B a_i | v_i a_i$ for $i = 1, 2, \ldots, k$.

Note that the language generated by G_A consists of all nonempty strings of the form

$$u_{i_1} u_{i_2} \ldots u_{i_{n-1}} u_{i_n} a_{i_n} a_{i_{n-1}} \ldots a_{i_2} a_{i_1}$$

Similarly, G_B generates all nonempty strings of the form

$$v_{i_1} v_{i_2} \ldots v_{i_{n-1}} v_{i_n} a_{i_n} a_{i_{n-1}} \ldots a_{i_2} a_{i_1}$$

If the preceding instance of the PCP has a solution, say, where

$$u_{i_1} u_{i_2} \ldots u_{i_{n-1}} u_{i_n} = v_{i_1} v_{i_2} \ldots v_{i_{n-1}} v_{i_n}$$

then we have that the string

$$u_{i_1} u_{i_2} \ldots u_{i_{n-1}} u_{i_n} a_{i_n} a_{i_{n-1}} \ldots a_{i_2} a_{i_1} \in L(G_A) \cap L(G_B)$$

Conversely, if for some string w we have that $w \in L(G_A) \cap L(G_B)$, then w must be of the form

$$w = w' a_{i_n} a_{i_{n-1}} \ldots a_{i_2} a_{i_1}$$

for some $w' \in \Sigma^+$ and suffix $a_{i_n} a_{i_{n-1}} \ldots a_{i_2} a_{i_1}$. But the only way this suffix can be generated is by generating the prefix $u_{i_1} u_{i_2} \ldots u_{i_{n-1}} u_{i_n}$ in G_A and the prefix $v_{i_1} v_{i_2} \ldots v_{i_{n-1}} v_{i_n}$ in G_B; thus

$$\begin{aligned} w &= u_{i_1} u_{i_2} \ldots u_{i_{n-1}} u_{i_n} a_{i_n} a_{i_{n-1}} \ldots a_{i_2} a_{i_1} \\ &= v_{i_1} v_{i_2} \ldots v_{i_{n-1}} v_{i_n} a_{i_n} a_{i_{n-1}} \ldots a_{i_2} a_{i_1} \end{aligned}$$

and so the string $u_{i_1} u_{i_2} \ldots u_{i_{n-1}} u_{i_n}$ is a solution to this instance of the PCP. It follows that this instance of the PCP has a solution if and only if $L(G_A) \cap L(G_B) \neq \emptyset$.

Theorem 6.3.1.   The empty intersection problem for context free grammars is undecidable.

Proof.   Suppose that this problem *is* decidable. Then there is an algorithm to decide if $L(G_1) \cap L(G_2) = \emptyset$. Let A, B, and Σ be any instance of the PCP. By the preceding construction, derive the two context-free grammars G_A and G_B. Use the algorithm to decide if $L(G_A) \cap L(G_B) = \emptyset$. This instance of the PCP has a solution if and only if $L(G_A) \cap L(G_B) \neq \emptyset$. Thus we are able to determine if an arbitrary instance of the PCP is solvable, a contradiction of Theorem 6.2.3.   ■

Recall that a context-free grammar is ambiguous if there are two distinct leftmost derivations of the same string. The context-free grammar

$$S \rightarrow aSB | SS | \varepsilon$$
$$B \rightarrow b$$

is ambiguous since there are two leftmost derivations of a^2b^2.

Unfortunately, it is not possible to determine, in general, if a context-free grammar is ambiguous. That is, the *ambiguity question for context-free grammars*, "Is G an ambiguous context-free grammar?" is undecidable. To see this, we suppose that the question *is* decidable; that is, there is an algorithm that decides it for arbitrary context-free grammars. We show that the PCP would then be decidable.

Again, let Σ, A, and B be an arbitrary instance of the PCP and construct the grammars G_A and G_B as before. We define a new grammar G based on G_A and G_B. Let $G = (\{S, S_A, S_B\}, \Sigma, S, P)$, where the production set P is given as $P_A \cup P_B \cup \{S \to S_A, S \to S_B\}$. Note that G generates $L(G_A) \cup L(G_B)$. Moreover, because of the structure of the productions in G_A and G_B, all derivations in G are leftmost derivations.

It is not hard to see that the grammars G_A and G_B are unambiguous. For example, in $L(G_A)$ any string ending in a_i must have been derived beginning with a production $S_A \to u_i S_A a_i$. Also, at any later stage in the derivation we can tell which production had to be applied. It follows, then, that if G is an ambiguous context-free grammar then it is because there is a string w for which

$$S \Rightarrow S_A \overset{*}{\Rightarrow} w = u_{i_1} u_{i_2} \dots u_{i_n} a_{i_n} \dots a_{i_2} a_{i_1}$$

and also

$$S \Rightarrow S_B \overset{*}{\Rightarrow} w = v_{i_1} v_{i_2} \dots v_{i_n} a_{i_n} \dots a_{i_2} a_{i_1}$$

That is, $w \in L(G_A) \cap L(G_B)$. But $L(G_A) \cap L(G_B) \neq \emptyset$ is equivalent to having a solution for this instance of the PCP.

Thus, if there is an algorithm for determining if an arbitrary context-free grammar is ambiguous, then we may determine if a solution exists for an arbitrary instance of the PCP. This, of course, is a contradiction, and so we may state the following theorem:

Theorem 6.3.2.   The ambiguity problem for context-free grammars is undecidable.

While the PCP is useful in showing the undecidability of many problems about context-free grammars and languages, another method is also available. This method involves the emptiness problem for Turing machines (see Section 6.2). Suppose that $M = (Q, \Sigma, \Gamma, s = q_1, \flat, F, \delta)$ is a Turing machine. Suppose that $q_1 w \vdash x_1 \vdash \dots \vdash x_n$ is a computation by M [with $w \in L(M)$]. Then the string $q_1 w \$ x_1^R \$ x_2 \$ x_3^R \$ \dots$ will be called a *valid computation* (here $\$$ is assumed to be some symbol not in Γ). Note that each configuration x_i is a string in $\Gamma^* Q \Gamma^*$ and does not begin or end with $\flat$. Also, x_n is necessarily a string in $\Gamma^* F \Gamma^*$.

Note that each valid computation of M may be viewed as a string over $\Gamma \cup Q \cup \{\$\}$. We define the set of *invalid computations* of M to be the complement of the set of valid computations with respect to $\Gamma \cup Q \cup \{\$\}$.

It is reasonable to ask what a string that comprises an invalid computation looks like. If the string w is an invalid computation, then w satisfies one of the following conditions:

1. w is not of the form $y_0\$y_1\$y_2\$\ldots\$y_k\$$, where y_i is a configuration of M if i is even or else y_i^R is a configuration of M if i is odd.

2. y_0 is not of the form $q_1 x$ for some $x \in \Sigma^*$.

3. y_k is not an accepting configuration of M; that is, $y_k \notin \Gamma^* F \Gamma^*$.

4. It is not the case that $y_i \vdash y_{i+1}^R$ for some even i.

5. It is not the case that $y_i^R \vdash y_{i+1}$ for some odd i.

It is easily seen that the set of strings satisfying condition 1 forms a regular language, as do the sets satisfying conditions 2 and 3. Thus the strings satisfying conditions 1 or 2 or 3 constitute a regular language (Theorem 2.8.1). Consequently, a finite automaton for this language can be constructed and so a regular (hence context-free) grammar can be given.

The sets of strings satisfying conditions 4 and 5 are both context-free languages. To see this for the language in condition 4, we sketch a nondeterministic pushdown automaton M' that accepts this language. M' nondeterministically selects some i for which y_i is preceded by an even number of $\$$ signs. It then consumes y_i and, as it does so, it pushes x on the stack, where $y_i \vdash x$ in M. Once M' encounters the $\$$ at the right end of y_i, it compares y_{i+1} with the contents of the stack, popping symbols as they match. Note that a successful match occurs only if $y_{i+1} = x^R$. If at any point a match fails to occur, M' scans its remaining input and accepts. (Note that it would be an easy exercise to also empty the stack at acceptance as well.) The construction for the language in condition 5 is similar.

Thus the set of invalid computations is the union of two context-free languages and a regular language and, therefore, is a context-free language (Theorem 3.6.3). Moreover, we may construct a context-free grammar for this set from the two npda's and the regular grammar.

We have shown the following:

Lemma 6.3.3.   The set of invalid computations of the Turing machine M is a context-free language.

We may then prove Theorem 6.3.4.

Theorem 6.3.4.   For an arbitrary context-free grammar G, the question "Does $L(G) = \Sigma^*$?" is undecidable.

Proof.   Suppose that this problem *is* decidable. We show that then the emptiness problem for Turing machines is decidable, contradicting Exercise 6.1.4.

Let $M = (Q, \Sigma, \Gamma, q_1, \flat, F, \delta)$ be an arbitrary Turing machine. By Lemma 3.3 we may construct a context-free grammar G generating all invalid computations of M. Note that $L(M) = \emptyset$ if and only if $L(G) = \Sigma^*$. Thus, if this question were decidable, then the emptiness question would also be decidable.   ∎

A number of results follow immediately from Theorem 6.3.4. For example, if G_1 is any context-free grammar and G_2 is a grammar generating Σ^* (where Σ is the terminal alphabet of G_1), then the statement "Does $L(G_1) = L(G_2)$?" is equivalent to the statement of the theorem. Thus it is undecidable if $L(G_1) = L(G_2)$ for two arbitrary context-free grammars G_1 and G_2.

If R is an arbitrary regular language and G_1 an arbitrary context-free grammar, the statement "Is $L(G_1) = R$?" is undecidable. To see this, we take $R = \Sigma^*$, where Σ is the terminal alphabet of G_1. Again note that the statement "Is $L(G_1) = R$?" is equivalent to the statement in Theorem 6.3.4.

Exercises for Section 6.3

6.3.1. Is the following problem decidable? Let G_1 be an arbitrary regular grammar and G_2 be an arbitrary context-free grammar. Does $L(G_1) \cap L(G_2) = \emptyset$?

6.3.2. The languages $L(G_A)$ and $L(G_B)$ have an interesting property. If $L(G_A) \cap L(G_B)$ is regular, then it is empty. Prove this property; then use it to show that, for an arbitrary context-free grammar G, the problem "Is $L(G)$ regular?" is undecidable.

6.3.3. Suppose that there are no valid computations for M. What does this say about $L(M)$?

6.3.4. Construct regular expressions for each of the languages in conditions 1, 2, and 3, in the discussion preceding Lemma 6.3.3.

6.3.5. Show that it is undecidable if $L(G_1) \subseteq L(G_2)$ for arbitrary context-free grammars G_1 and G_2.

6.3.6. Show that it is undecidable if $R \subseteq L(G)$ for an arbitrary regular language R and an arbitrary context-free grammar G.

6.3.7. For G an arbitrary context-free grammar and R an arbitrary regular language, is the question "Is $L(G) \subseteq R$?" a decidable question? [*Hint:* $L(G) \subseteq R$ if and only if $L(G) \cap \overline{R} = \emptyset$. What do we know about the language $L(G) \cap \overline{R}$? What do we, therefore, know about the decidability of the emptiness problem for $L(G) \cap \overline{R}$?]

PROBLEMS

6.1. In this problem we use a different technique to arrive at the conclusion of Theorem 6.3.1; that is, the empty intersection problem for context-free grammars is undecidable.

Let $M = (Q, \Sigma, \Gamma, s = q_1, \flat, F, \delta)$ be a Turing machine for which the symbol $\$ \notin F$. Recall that one way in which we represent configurations of a Turing machine is as strings of the form $\sigma_1 \sigma_2 \dots \sigma_k q \sigma_{k+1} \dots \sigma_n$, where the $\sigma_i \in \Gamma$ and $q \in Q$. That is, a configuration is a string over $\Gamma^* Q \Gamma^*$. Let

$$A = \{y\$z^R \mid y, z \in \Gamma^* Q \Gamma^* \text{ and } y \vdash z \text{ in } M\}$$
$$B = \{y^R\$z \mid y, z \in \Gamma^* Q \Gamma^* \text{ and } y \vdash z \text{ in } M\}$$

1. Show that A and B are context-free languages. [*Hint:* Sketch a npda accepting A (or B) and then apply Theorem 3.8.2.]

2. Show that the languages L_1 and L_2 are context-free languages, where

$$L_1 = (A\$)^*(\varepsilon \cup \Gamma^* F \Gamma^* \$)$$
$$L_2 = q_1 \Sigma^* \$(B\$)^*(\varepsilon \cup \Gamma^* F \Gamma^* \$)$$

3. Show that $L_1 \cap L_2$ is exactly the set of valid computations of M.

4. Suppose that the empty intersection problem for context-free grammars *were* decidable. Construct an algorithm to answer the problem "Is $L(M)$ empty?" for an arbitrary Turing machine M. Conclude that the empty intersection problem for context-free languages is not decidable.

6.2. 1. Let M be a Turing machine that makes at least three moves for every input string. (Note that any Turing machine can be converted into one of this type.) Show that the set of valid computations of M is a context-free language if and only if $L(M)$ is finite. [*Hint:* If $L(M)$ is finite, then the set of valid computations is also finite and we are done. On the other hand, if $L(M)$ is infinite and the valid computations form a context-free language, then there is a valid computation of the form $w_1\$w_2\$w_3\$\ldots$ with $|w_2|$ of a size that Ogden's lemma (see Problems 3.1 and 3.2) can be applied.]

2. Show that for an arbitrary context-free grammar G it is undecidable whether $\overline{L(G)}$ is a context-free language.

3. Show that for arbitrary context-free grammars G_1 and G_2 it is undecidable whether $L(G_1) \cap L(G_2)$ is a context-free language.

7

Introduction to
Computational Complexity

In Section 4.4 we showed that alternative definitions of the Turing machine did not increase the computational power of the basic model. We did this by showing how a Turing machine of one type could simulate a Turing machine of another type.

When simulating the actions of a Turing machine of a more complex type with one of our basic definitions, much more time and space are often consumed. Issues of computational power or the ability to decide a problem are unaffected by the Turing machine model used. However, the time and space requirements of the computation are clearly affected by the model chosen. The complexity of a computation measures the space or time requirements of that computation. In this chapter we briefly introduce *computational complexity theory* as it relates to automata and languages.

7.1 SPACE COMPLEXITY

The complexity of a computation is measured in its consumption of time and space resources. Efficient computations have small resource requirements ("small" being relative). The resource requirements of computations that accept strings in some language may well depend on the size (length) of the input string. We begin by considering the space resource.

Definition 7.1.1. Let M be a k-tape Turing machine. Suppose that, on any input of length n, M's read/write heads visit at most $S(n)$ tape cells on any tape, where $S: \mathbb{N} \to \mathbb{N}$ is a function. Then M is said to have *space complexity* $S(n)$ or to be an $S(n)$ *space-bounded* Turing machine. $L(M)$ is said to be a language of space complexity $S(n)$ also.

Example 7.1.1

Consider the language

$$L = \{xyzy^R | x, y \in \Sigma^*, z \in \Sigma^+\}$$

A two-tape nondeterministic Turing machine accepting L takes input w on tape 1. As it scans w, it (nondeterministically) guesses where y begins and copies it to tape 2. It continues scanning after y is copied by ignoring z, and then it (nondeterministically) guesses where y^R begins. While scanning y^R, it compares the symbols on tape 1 with those on tape 2. Assuming that the Turing machine is begun with the read/write head of tape 1 on the first symbol of the input, note that all of w is scanned, as well as the $\flat$ that follows w. Moreover, on tape 2 y as well as the $\flat$'s before and after it are scanned. Thus a space bound for this Turing machine is

$$S(n) = \max\{n + 1, n + 2\} = n + 2$$

Note, too, that any $S': \mathbb{N} \to \mathbb{N}$ for which $S(n) \leq S'(n)$ is also a space bound.

Since any Turing machine necessarily scans at least one cell for each tape that it has, every space bound is at least 1. In discussing space complexity, it is often convenient to assume a Turing machine that has a read-only input tape and one or more *work tapes*. We modify the definition of space complexity to mean that the read/write heads of the work tapes visit at most $S(n)$ cells. The effect of this is that we do not count the cells scanned by simply scanning the input string. Thus in some circumstances we may have space complexity that is less than linear.

Recall that in Section 4.4 we gave a simulation of a k-tape Turing machine by a one-tape Turing machine having $2k + 1$ tracks. It is easy to see that the same simulation allows us to simulate a Turing machine having k work tapes and one input tape by a Turing machine having one work tape and one input tape. Moreover, if $S(n)$ is a space bound for the k-tape Turing machine, the simulation uses no more than $S(n)$ cells of its $2k + 1$ track work tape so that $S(n)$ is also a space bound for the simulation. Thus we have the following theorem:

Theorem 7.1.2.   If L is accepted by a k-work tape Turing machine having space bound $S(n)$, then it is also accepted by a one-work-tape Turing machine having space bound $S(n)$.

Theorem 7.1.2 says that the number of work tapes used in accepting a language L does not affect L's space complexity. We can, in fact, compress by a constant factor the amount of tape space used to accept a language by encoding several tape symbols into one. For example, if the tape alphabet consists of a, b, and $\flat$, we could consider encoding pairs of symbols. This would increase the size of the tape alphabet, but it would also reduce the tape space by half.

Theorem 7.1.3.   Let L be accepted by a k-work-tape Turing machine M having space bound $S(n)$. For any $c > 0$, there is a $cS(n)$ space-bounded Turing machine that accepts L.

Proof. (*sketch*) Let r be an integer satisfying $rc \geq 1$. Recode the tape alphabet of M as blocks of r symbols. Use the transitions of M to define new transitions based on the blocks of r symbols. ∎

As a result of Theorem 7.1.3, we may compare asymptotic behavior of space bounds when comparing the space requirements of Turing machines. Thus, Turing machine M_1 with space bound $S_1(n) = n^2 + 2n + 1$ and Turing machine M_2 with space bound $S_2(n) = 3n^2 - 1$ are both of space complexity $S(n) = n^2$. On the other hand, a space complexity of n^3 is smaller than space complexities of n^4 or 2^n.

Recall that an ID of a Turing machine takes into account the current state as well as the current tape contents. A space bound for a Turing machine thus provides a bound on the size of an ID. Combining the information present in a space bound with the knowledge about the sizes of the sets of states and tape symbols, we arrive at a bound on the number of moves in an accepting sequence of moves. For example, a k-work-tape Turing machine with state set Q, tape alphabet Γ, and space bound $S(n)$ has $n + 2$ positions for its input head, $S(n)$ positions for the read/write heads on each of the k work tapes, $|\Gamma|^{S(n)}$ possible tape contents on each of the k work tapes, and $|Q|$ choices of current state. Thus there are at most $|Q|(n + 2)|\Gamma|^{kS(n)}(S(n))^k$ IDs possible. If M accepts its input in more than $|Q|(n + 2)|\Gamma|^{kS(n)}(S(n))^k$ moves, then some ID is repeated. Thus this accepting computation involves a loop that can be omitted. It follows that, if M accepts an input of length n, it does so in at most $|Q|(n + 2)|\Gamma|^{kS(n)}(S(n))^k$ moves. Note that if $S(n) \geq \log n$ then we can find a constant c for which $|Q|(n + 2)|\Gamma|^{kS(n)}(S(n))^k \leq c^{S(n)}$ (see Exercise 7.1.2). We have the following lemma:

Lemma 7.1.4.   Let M be a k-tape Turing machine with space complexity $S(n)$, where $S(n) \geq \log n$. Then there exists a constant c for which, if w is any input with length $|w| = n$, then:

1. M has at most $c^{S(n)}$ IDs.
2. If M accepts w, then it does so in at most $c^{S(n)}$ moves.

By removing loops (that is, sequences of repeated IDs) in an accepting computation of M, we have the following corollary:

Corollary 7.1.5.   Let M be a k-tape Turing machine with space complexity $S(n)$, where $S(n) \geq \log n$. Then there exists a constant c for which if M accepts input w then there exists a computation $\alpha_1 \vdash \alpha_2 \vdash \cdots \vdash \alpha_m$, where the α_i are distinct and $m \leq c^{S(n)}$.

In Section 4.4 we showed that nondeterministic and deterministic Turing machines are equivalent in terms of accepting power. The simulation of a nondeterministic Turing machine by a deterministic one amounted to exhaustively searching all finite sequences of moves until an accepting computation is found (if one exists). In fact, we will see that under certain circumstances, it is possible to construct a deterministic Turing machine that accepts the same language as a nondeterministic one and has space complexity that is the square of that of the nondeterministic one.

First note that if M is a k-tape nondeterministic Turing machine we may construct a deterministic Turing machine M_1 that, when given two IDs of M, I_1 and I_2, checks if $I_1 \vdash I_2$. M_1 systematically attempts to find a transition of M that yields I_2 from I_1. If one is found, it accepts or returns "true." If none are found, it rejects or returns "false."

Suppose that I_1 and I_2 are IDs of M and $m \geq 0$. Define the predicate YIELDS(I_1, I_2, m) to return the answer to the question "Does $I_1 \overset{(t)}{\vdash} I_2$ for any $t \leq m$?"

Note that YIELDS(I_1, I_2, m) behaves as follows:

1. If $m = 0$ and $I_1 = I_2$, it returns "true."
2. If $m = 1$ and $I_1 \vdash I_2$, it returns "true."
3. If $m > 1$ and YIELDS$(I_1, I', \lceil \frac{m}{2} \rceil)$ and YIELDS$(I', I_2, \lfloor \frac{m}{2} \rfloor)$ both return "true," then it returns "true."
4. Otherwise, it returns "false."

By adding a work tape that acts like a stack to the deterministic Turing machine M_1, we can compute the predicate YIELDS(I_1, I_2, m). At each recursive call, M_1 pushes I_1, I_2, and I' on the stack. All have length at most $S(n)$. In this case, to determine if M accepts input w, we must evaluate YIELDS(I_1, I_f, m), where I_1 is M's initial ID, I_f is some accepting ID, and $m = c^{S(n)}$. [Note that m can be encoded in binary using at most $S(n) \log c$ bits or cells. Thus each push would push $(3 + \log c) S(n)$ symbols on the stack.] Since the parameter m is halved at each recursive call, at most $1 + \lceil \log c^{S(n)} \rceil = 1 + \lceil S(n) \log c \rceil$ calls are made. Thus the stack requires $(1 + \lceil S(n) \log c \rceil)(3 + S(n) \log c)$ space. That is, M_1 has space bound $c_1 (S(n))^2$, where $S(n)$ is the space bound of M and c_1 is a constant. Since M_1 is deterministic, this suggests that we may be able to use a deterministic Turing machine of space complexity $c_1 (S(n))^2$ to accept the same language that the nondeterministic Turing machine M uses space $S(n)$ to accept.

Note that the preceding sketch relies heavily on knowing the value of $S(n)$. For input w of length $|w| = n$, if we know the value of $S(n)$, we may compute $m = c^{S(n)}$ and can determine the IDs I_1, I_2, and I' of proper length, so determining if M accepts w can be done deterministically in $c_1 (S(n))^2$ space. If we don't know the value of $S(n)$, we cannot determine the maximum length of any ID or the maximum length of an accepting computation.

Definition 7.1.6.   A function $S(n)$ is said to be *fully space constructible* if there is a Turing machine M_S that has space bound $S(n)$ and, on all inputs of length n, M_S uses exactly $S(n)$ tape cells on its work tape.

Note that if $S(n)$ is fully space constructible then, given input w of length $|w| = n$, we may use M_S to mark off exactly $S(n)$ tape cells on a work tape. The preceding deterministic Turing machine M_1 may then use these $S(n)$ cells to generate IDs and compute $m = c^{S(n)}$. Note that M_S is necessarily a deterministic Turing machine, and so the composite M' constructed from M_1 and M_S is also deterministic. Finally, note that, by Theorem 7.1.2, M' has space bound $(S(n))^2$. We have proved the following theorem:

Theorem 7.1.7. **(Savitch's theorem)** If $S(n)$ is fully space constructible and M is a nondeterministic Turing machine of space complexity $S(n)$, then there is a deterministic Turing machine M' of space complexity $(S(n))^2$ for which $L(M) = L(M')$.

Space-bounded languages form a hierarchy in terms of the space required to accept them.

Definition 7.1.8. The family of languages accepted by deterministic Turing machines of space complexity $S(n)$ is $DSPACE(S(n))$. The family of languages accepted by nondeterministic Turing machines of space complexity $S(n)$ is $NSPACE(S(n))$. These language classes are called *space complexity classes*.

We summarize the relationships that we have already discovered between these complexity classes in Theorem 7.1.9.

Theorem 7.1.9. Let S, S_1, and S_2 be functions from $\mathbb{N}$ into $\mathbb{N}$. Assume that $S_1(n) \leq S_2(n)$ for all n and that $c > 0$. Then

1. $DSPACE(S_1(n)) \subseteq DSPACE(S_2(n))$.

2. $NSPACE(S_1(n)) \subseteq NSPACE(S_2(n))$.

3. $DSPACE(S(n)) \subseteq NSPACE(S(n))$.

4. $DSPACE(S(n)) = DSPACE(cS(n))$.

5. $NSPACE(S(n)) \subseteq DSPACE((S(n)^2)$.

The containment in part (1) of Theorem 7.1.9 is proper under certain circumstances. We offer, without proof, the following theorem:

Theorem 7.1.10. If $S_2(n)$ is fully space constructible and

$$\lim_{n \to \infty} \frac{S_1(n)}{S_2(n)} = 0$$

and if $S_1(n) \geq \log n$ and $S_2(n) \geq \log n$, then there exists a language

$$L \in DSPACE(S_2(n)) - DSPACE(S_1(n))$$

Note that Theorem 7.1.10 does not require that $S_1(n) \leq S_2(n)$ for all n. If, in addition to the requirements of Theorem 7.1.10, we also have that $S_1(n) \leq S_2(n)$ holds for all n, then $DSPACE(S_1(n)) \subset DSPACE(S_2(n))$, that is, proper containment holds.

Definition 7.1.11. If L is accepted by a deterministic Turing machine with space complexity $S(n) = a_k n^k + a_{k-1} n^{k-1} + \cdots a_0$, then L is said to be in the language class *PSPACE*. If

L is accepted by a nondeterministic Turing machine with polynomial space bound, then L is in the language class *NSPACE*.

Note that since

$$a_k n^k + a_{k-1} n^{k-1} + \cdots a_0 \leq (|a_k| + |a_{k-1}| + \cdots + |a_0|) n^k$$

by Theorem 7.1.3 we have that

$$\text{DSPACE}(a_k n^k + a_{k-1} n^{k-1} + \cdots a_o) \subseteq \text{DSPACE}(n^k)$$

Thus we may characterize $\text{PSPACE} = \bigcup_{k=1}^{\infty} \text{DSPACE}(n^k)$. Similarly $\text{NPSPACE} = \bigcup_{k=1}^{\infty} \text{NSPACE}(n^k)$. Note that Savitch's theorem (Theorem 7.1.7) says that $\text{NPSPACE} = \text{PSPACE}$ since $\text{NSPACE}(n^k) \subseteq \text{DSPACE}(n^k)$.

Exercises for Section 7.1

7.1.1. Let M be the one-tape Turing machine defined by the transitions given below, where q_3 is the single accepting state and q_1 is the initial state. Assume that the tape alphabet is $\{a, b, \flat\}$. Note that $L(M) = \{a^{2k+1}b | k \geq 0\}$. Construct a Turing machine M' for which $L(M') = L(M)$, but M' has as its tape symbols encodings of pairs of tape symbols of M (see Theorem 7.1.3).

$$\Delta(q_1, a) = \{(q_2, a, R)\}, \qquad \Delta(q_2, a) = \{(q_1, a, R)\}$$
$$\Delta(q_2, b) = \{(q_3, b, R)\}$$

7.1.2. In this problem we derive the constant c of Lemma 7.1.4. Refer to the remarks that precede Lemma 7.1.4.

(a) For $\log n \leq S(n)$, show that $\log_{|\Gamma|}(n+2) \leq (k+1)S(n)$ so that $(n+2) \leq |\Gamma|^{(k+1)S(n)}$.

(b) Use part (a) to show that $(n+2)(S(n))^k \leq |\Gamma|^{(2k+1)S(n)}$.

(c) Give a constant c for which $|Q|(n+2)|\Gamma|^{kS(n)}(S(n))^k \leq c^{S(n)}$.

7.1.3. Which space complexity class or classes do each of the following types of languages belong to? Regular languages, context-free languages, context-sensitive languages.

7.1.4. Show that if L is accepted by a Turing machine with space bound $S(n) \geq \log n$ then L is accepted by an $S(n)$ space-bounded Turing machine that halts on all inputs. (Thus space-bounded languages are recursive languages.)

7.2 TIME COMPLEXITY

Although space is an important resource in any Turing machine, computation time is also important. In this section we consider the time complexity of Turing machine computations as it depends on the size of the input string. Time is measured in the number of moves that are made by the Turing machine.

Definition 7.2.1.   Let M be a k-tape Turing machine. Suppose that, on every input of length n, M makes at most $T(n)$ moves for some function $T : \mathbb{N} \to \mathbb{N}$. Then M is said to have *time complexity* $T(n)$ or to be a $T(n)$ *time-bounded* Turing machine. $L(M)$ is said to be a $T(n)$ time-bounded language or to have time complexity $T(n)$.

Note that in order to read its input a Turing machine must make at least $n + 1$ moves. Thus $T(n) \geq n + 1$ for any time bound $T(n)$.

Example 7.2.1

Consider the language $L = \{xcx^R | x \in \Sigma^*\}$. In recognizing L with a one-tape Turing machine, we may scan back and forth over the input matching symbols at the beginning with symbols at the end until the middle c is encountered. Each complete scan across the input requires $2t$ moves, where t is the current length of the "unchecked" input string. At each complete scan, t is reduced by 1. This continues until $t = 1$ (the c in the middle). Thus we have

$$T(n) = n^2 + n - 2$$

We could also recognize L with a two-tape Turing machine. The Turing machine copies input symbols to its second tape until the middle c is found. It then moves the tape head on the second tape left at each step, comparing the symbol on the second tape with that on the first tape. This Turing machine requires $n + 1$ moves to recognize an input of length n. Thus, for it, $T(n) = n + 1$.

Example 7.2.1 suggests that the time complexity of a Turing machine is related to the number of tapes available for the computation.

Theorem 7.1.3 said that by cleverly treating multiple tape symbols as a single symbol we could linearly compress the space required for a computation. The same applies in the case of time; under certain restrictions we can linearly speed up a computation.

Suppose that M is any one-tape Turing machine. Consider M', which is derived from M by combining a block of m tape symbols of M into a single tape symbol. (The tape alphabet of M' would just be $\Gamma' = \Gamma^m$, where Γ is the tape alphabet of M.) Now, when M's read/write head enters a block of m tape cells, it enters on either the right or left side. Initially, M's read/write head is on the leftmost cell of the first block of m cells on its tape. M' can use states to record where M's read/write head is located in a block of m tape cells that corresponds to a single cell of the tape of M'. Once M's read/write head enters a block of m tape cells, it performs a sequence of moves before it leaves. Those moves may change the contents of that block of m cells. That is, when the read/write head of M' moves from a tape cell, we must write in that cell the block of m symbols that corresponds to the contents of M's tape when *its* read/write head moves from the corresponding block of m cells. But we can determine what this block of m symbols is by simply looking at M's behavior on a tape containing the block of symbols. Thus, given an m-symbol block, we may determine what m-symbol block replaces it. That is, we can determine what M' should write on its tape when it moves its read/write head off the current symbol.

Consider the Turing machine M that computes the string function $f((ab^n) = (ab)^{n+1}$ given by the following transitions:

$$\Delta(q_1, a) = (q_2, a, R) \qquad \Delta(q_1, b) = (q_5, b, S)$$
$$\Delta(q_2, b) = (q_1, b, R) \qquad \Delta(q_2, a) = (q_5, a, S)$$
$$\Delta(q_1, \flat) = (q_3, a, R) \qquad \Delta(q_3, a) = (q_5, a, S)$$
$$\Delta(q_3, \flat) = (q_4, b, R) \qquad \Delta(q_3, b) = (q_5, b, S)$$

(Here the initial state is q_1, and q_4 is the single final state.) To build Turing machine M', which combines two tape cells of M into one cell, we need an alphabet

$$\Gamma' = \{`aa', `ab', `ba', `bb', `b\flat', `a\flat', `\flat a', `b\flat', `\flat b'\}$$

Note that this is essentially $\Gamma \times \Gamma$. The transitions of M' take into account M's actions on each block of two tape symbols. Thus M' has the following transitions:

$$\Delta'(p_1, `ab') = (p_1, `ab', R) \qquad \Delta'(p_1, `\flat\flat') = (p_2, `ab', R)$$
$$\Delta'(p_1, `a\flat') = (p_3, `a\flat', R) \qquad \Delta'(p_1, `aa') = (p_3, `aa', R)$$
$$\Delta'(p_1, `\flat a') = (p_3, `\flat a', R) \qquad \Delta'(p_1, `b\flat') = (p_3, `b\flat', R)$$
$$\Delta'(p_1, `\flat b') = (p_3, `\flat b', R) \qquad \Delta'(p_1, `bb') = (p_3, `bb', R)$$

Note that a computation of M on input $(ab)^n$ takes $T(n) = 2n+2$, while the corresponding computation of M' on $(ab)^n$ takes $T'(n) = n + 1$.

We may actually do better than this, however. If we know the contents of the m-symbol blocks occupying the tape cells left and right of the current block of m cells of M, we can determine their contents after M moves its head to the left or right of the current block of m cells. Thus we may determine the contents of the two-tape cells left and right of the current tape cell of M'. Since M requires at least m moves to move from the corresponding region of $3m$ cells, we may simulate at least m moves of M by adjusting the three-tape cells of M' and moving its head.

Suppose that M' moves its head left one cell, right two cells, then left one cell, recording (by means of states) the contents of the cells left and right of the current one. At this point it has enough information to determine what the contents of those three cells should be when M's read/write head moves out of the corresponding $3m$ cells in its tape. In four more moves, M' can adjust the contents of the left, right, and current cell accordingly and move its read/write head to the appropriate cell corresponding to the position of M's read/write head at the end of those moves. Thus in eight moves M' can simulate at least m moves of M. If M makes $T(n)$ moves, M' makes at most $8\lceil \frac{T(n)}{m} \rceil$ moves.

Although we've restricted our attention to a one-tape Turing machine, no problems arise by extending our discussion to a k tape Turing machine. The above *does* assume that the input is presented to M' in encoded form, however. If M is a k-tape Turing machine with $k > 1$, we may construct M' as before with the added ability to take the same input as M and encode it. M' simply scans the tape that the input is on, encoding and combining m symbols into one and writing the result on a second tape. This second tape becomes the input tape, while the first becomes a work tape (we could blank the cells as we go about the encoding). Note that it takes n moves to scan the input and $\lceil \frac{n}{m} \rceil$ moves to position the read/write head of the new work tape to begin computation on the encoded input string. Thus, in $n + \lceil \frac{n}{m} \rceil + 8\lceil \frac{T(n)}{m} \rceil$ moves, M' can perform the same computation that M does in $T(n)$ moves.

We consider the quantity $n + \lceil \frac{n}{m} \rceil + 8 \lceil \frac{T(n)}{m} \rceil$. First note that, for any number x, $\lceil x \rceil < x + 1$. Second, note that, when $n \geq 6$, $T(n) \geq 7$. Finally, assume that $\inf_{n \to \infty} \frac{T(n)}{n} = \infty$, so for any constant d there is an N such that, for $n \geq N$, we have $\frac{T(n)}{n} \geq d$. Assuming that $n \geq N \geq 6$, we have the following:

$$
n + \lceil \frac{n}{m} \rceil + 8 \lceil \frac{T(n)}{m} \rceil \leq n + \frac{n}{m} + 1 + 8 \left(\frac{T(n)}{m} + 1 \right)
$$

$$
= (n + 2) + \frac{n}{m} + 8 \frac{T(n)}{m} + 7
$$

$$
\leq 2n + \frac{n}{m} + 8 \frac{T(n)}{m} + T(n)
$$

$$
\leq \frac{2T(n)}{d} + \frac{T(n)}{dm} + T(n) \left(\frac{8}{m} + 1 \right)
$$

$$
= T(n) \left(\frac{2}{d} + \frac{1}{dm} + \frac{8 + m}{m} \right)
$$

Thus, given any $c > 0$, we can adjust m and d so that the number of moves of M' is at most $cT(n)$. This is the linear speedup that we want.

Theorem 7.2.2.   Let $k > 1$. Suppose that $\inf_{n \to \infty} \frac{T(n)}{n} = \infty$. If L is accepted by a k-tape Turing machine with time complexity $T(n)$ then, for $c > 0$, L is accepted by a k-tape Turing machine with time complexity $cT(n)$.

Note that if L is accepted by a one-tape Turing machine with time bound $T(n)$ then it is also accepted by a k-tape Turing machine with time complexity $T(n)$ for any $k > 1$. Thus we have the following corollary:

Corollary 7.2.3.   Let $\inf_{n \to \infty} \frac{T(n)}{n} = \infty$. If L is accepted by a Turing machine having time complexity $T(n)$, then, for all $c > 0$, L is accepted by a Turing machine having time complexity $cT(n)$.

If $T_1(n) \leq T_2(n)$ for all n and L is a language of time complexity $T_1(n)$, then L is also of time complexity $T_2(n)$. In particular, if L is of time complexity

$$
T_1(n) = a_k n^k + a_{k-1} n^{k-1} + \cdots + a_0
$$

note that $T_1(n) \leq (|a_k| + |a_{k-1}| + \cdots + |a_0|) n^k$ for all n. Applying the preceding with

$$
c = \frac{1}{|a_k| + |a_{k-1}| + \cdots + |a_0|}
$$

we have that L has time complexity n^k.

In Example 7.2.1 we looked at the time complexity of $L = \{xcx^R | x \in \Sigma^*\}$. When using a Turing machine with one tape, we observed a time complexity of n^2. With two tapes though, L has time complexity n. This suggests the following theorem:

Theorem 7.2.4.   If L is accepted by a k-tape Turing machine having time complexity $T(n)$ and if $\inf_{n\to\infty} \frac{T(n)}{n} = \infty$, then L is accepted by a one-tape Turing machine having time complexity $(T(n))^2$.

Proof.   If L is accepted by a one-tape Turing machine having time complexity $T(n)$, then, since $T(n) \leq (T(n))^2$ for all n, L is also accepted by a one-tape Turing machine of time complexity $(T(n))^2$. Suppose that L is accepted by a Turing machine having $k > 1$ tapes and time bound $T(n)$. Consider a simulation of a k-tape Turing machine by a one-tape Turing machine as in Section 4.4. After t moves, the head markers may be $2t$ cells apart. Each move of the k-tape Turing machine corresponds to a sweep across all cells marked as being scanned by the k read/write heads, followed by a sweep back adjusting the head markers and cell contents. The sweep back as described takes five moves per cell. Thus move t of the k-tape Turing machine may correspond to $12t$ moves in the simulation. Hence $T(n)$ moves may require

$$\sum_{t=1}^{T(n)} 12t = 6(T(n))^2 + 6T(n)$$

moves in the simulation. We may speed up the simulation via Theorem 7.2.2 to $(T(n))^2$.   ■

Analogous with the space complexity classes DSPACE and NSPACE, we define the following:

Definition 7.2.5.   The family of languages accepted by deterministic Turing machines having time complexity $T(n)$ is *DTIME* $(T(n))$. The family of languages accepted by nondeterministic Turing machines having time complexity $T(n)$ is *NTIME* $(T(n))$. These classes are called *time complexity classes* of languages.

Some observations are immediate.

Theorem 7.2.6.

1. If $T_1(n) \leq T_2(n)$, then DTIME $(T_1(n)) \subseteq$ DTIME $(T_2(n))$.

2. If $T_1(n) \leq T_2(n)$, then NTIME $(T_1(n)) \subseteq$ NTIME $(T_2(n))$.

3. DTIME $(T(n)) \subseteq$ NTIME $(T(n))$.

4. If $\inf_{n\to\infty} \frac{T(n)}{n} = \infty$, then DTIME $(T(n))$ = DTIME $(cT(n))$ for all $c \geq 0$.

Parts 1 and 2 of Theorem 7.2.6 say that any language with time complexity $T_1(n)$ also has time complexity $T_2(n)$ for any $T_2(n)$ that is "larger" than $T_1(n)$. It is reasonable to ask just how much larger $T_2(n)$ must be so that there are languages of time complexity $T_2(n)$ that are *not* of time complexity $T_1(n)$. Part 4 of Theorem 7.2.6 says that if $T_1(n)$ satisfies $\inf_{n\to\infty} \frac{T(n)}{n} = \infty$, then $T_2(n)$ must be larger than a constant multiplied by $T_1(n)$. Theorem 7.2.8, which we offer without proof, gives sufficient conditions for the existence of languages in DTIME $(T_2(n))$ that are not in DTIME $(T_1(n))$. Theorem 7.2.8 depends on the following definition, which is analogous to Definition 7.1.6.

Definition 7.2.7.   A function $T(n)$ is *fully time constructible* if there is a $T(n)$ time-bounded Turing machine that uses exactly $T(n)$ time on all inputs of length n.

Theorem 7.2.8.   If $T_2(n)$ is fully time constructible and

$$\inf_{n \to \infty} \frac{T_1(n) \log(T_1(n))}{T_2(n)} = 0$$

then there is a language $L \in$ DTIME $(T_2(n))-$ DTIME $(T_1(n))$.

An important relationship between time and space is given in Theorem 7.2.9.

Theorem 7.2.9.   If $L \in$ DTIME $(f(n))$, then $L \in$ DSPACE $(f(n))$.

Proof.   Suppose that L is accepted by a Turing machine M that makes at most $f(n)$ moves on input of length n. Then M can visit at most $1 + f(n)$ tape cells, and so $L \in$ DSPACE $(f(n) + 1)$. But $f(n) + 1 \le 2f(n)$, since time bounds are at least $n + 1$, so by Theorem 7.1.3 $L \in$ DSPACE $(f(n))$.   ■

Deterministic time and nondeterministic time are related in an important way. Suppose that M is a nondeterministic Turing machine with time bound $T(n)$. Let us count (and bound) the number of possible IDs of M. If M has k tapes, then M can visit at most $T(n) + 1$ cells of any tape in time $T(n)$. Thus in $T(n)$ moves any tape contains a string of length at most $T(n) + 1$. If Γ is the tape alphabet of M, there are $|\Gamma|^{T(n)+1}$ possible strings of length $T(n) + 1$. This is the number of possible strings that M can leave on any one tape. Since there are k tapes, there are $|\Gamma|^{k(T(n)+1)}$ possible strings that describe M's tape contents after $T(n)$ moves. Moreover, each read/write head may be in any one of $T(n) + 1$ possible tape cells on each of the k tapes. If Q is the state set of M, then the number of possible IDs of M on input of length n is

$$|Q|(T(n) + 1)^k |\Gamma|^{k(T(n)+1)} \le c^{T(n)}$$

for appropriate choice of constant c. To systematically search for an accepting ID that is accessible from M's initial ID in $T(n)$ moves using a deterministic Turing machine, we generate and check IDs. We first look among all IDs accessible in 1 move, then in 2 moves, and so on, up to $T(n)$ moves. Let r be the length of an ID. Assuming that we generate IDs one after the other on the tape, it takes at most $3r$ moves to generate and check each ID. At any step there are at most $c^{T(n)}$ next IDs. Thus each step requires at most $3rc^{T(n)}$ moves. There are at most $T(n)$ steps in this search, so such a search requires $3rT(n)c^{T(n)}$ moves. The length of an ID is at most $r = 1 + k(T(n) + 2)$; so for an appropriately chosen constant d, the search requires at most $d^{T(n)}$ moves. We have the following theorem:

Theorem 7.2.10.   If L is accepted by a nondeterministic Turing machine with time complexity $T(n)$, then L is accepted by a deterministic Turing machine with time complexity $d^{T(n)}$ for some constant d. That is, if $L \in$ NTIME $(T(n))$, then there is a constant d for which $L \in$ DTIME $(d^{T(n)})$.

In Lemma 7.1.4 we observed that if M has space complexity $S(n) \geq \log n$, then we can bound the number of distinct IDs that M has by $c^{S(n)}$ for some constant c. If M is a deterministic Turing machine, then the same ID appearing twice indicates that M has entered a loop and so will never halt or accept. It follows that a deterministic Turing machine M' can be constructed that simulates M and maintains a count of moves on an additional tape. If the count exceeds $c^{S(n)}$, the simulation has repeated an ID of M, and so M' can halt and reject the input. Clearly, M' has time bound $2c^{S(n)}$. Applying Theorem 7.2.2 we have the following theorem:

Theorem 7.2.11.   If $L \in$ DSPACE $(S(n))$ and $S(n) \geq \log n$, then $L \in$ DTIME $(c^{S(n)})$ for some constant c.

In Definition 7.1.11, we grouped all languages that are accepted by deterministic Turing machines with polynomial space bound into one class and all those accepted by nondeterministic Turing machines with polynomial space bound into another. Savitch's theorem shows that those two classes of languages are the same because changing from nondeterministic space to deterministic space only squares the space bound. Theorem 7.2.10 suggests that we may not be able to get such a nice result for the analogous time complexity classes because the change from nondeterministic to deterministic may exponentiate the time bound.

Definition 7.2.12.   The class $\mathcal{P}$ consists of all languages accepted by deterministic Turing machines having polynomial-time bound. The class $\mathcal{NP}$ consists of all languages accepted by nondeterministic Turing machines having polynomial-time bound.

Note that for any n

$$a_k n^k + a_{k-1} n^{k-1} + \cdots + a_0 \leq (|a_k| + |a_{k-1}| + \cdots + |a_0|) n^k$$

so that applying Corollary 7.2.3 gives

$$\text{DTIME}(a_k n^k + a_{k-1} n^{k-1} + \ldots + a_0) \subseteq \text{DTIME}(n^k)$$

It follows that we may characterize

$$\mathcal{P} = \bigcup_{n \geq 1} \text{DTIME}(n^k)$$

Similarly,

$$\mathcal{NP} = \bigcup_{n \geq 1} \text{NTIME}(n^k)$$

Finally, since DTIME $(n^k) \subseteq$ NTIME (n^k) for all k, we have $\mathcal{P} \subseteq \mathcal{NP}$. Unfortunately, this is as far as current knowledge takes us. One of the most important unsolved problems in computer science is the question of equality for $\mathcal{P}$ and $\mathcal{NP}$. Answering affirmatively involves showing that any language in $\mathcal{NP}$ is also in $\mathcal{P}$. This would require finding some way in which to convert a nondeterministic Turing machine with a polynomial-time bound into a deterministic Turing machine with a polynomial-time bound (the polynomials need not be of the same degree). Theorem 7.2.10 says that we can make the transformation from nondeterministic to deterministic Turing machine and increase the time bound to exponential. This does *not* say that transformation to a polynomially time bounded Turing machine is impossible, only that so far we don't know how to do it.

On the other hand, to show that $\mathcal{P} \neq \mathcal{NP}$ requires that we find a language in $\mathcal{NP}$ that is not in $\mathcal{P}$. If L is such a language, we must show that *no* deterministic polynomially time bounded Turing machine accepts L. While there are languages in $\mathcal{NP}$ that are not known to be in $\mathcal{P}$, they are also not known to *not* be in $\mathcal{P}$.

Exercises for Section 7.2

7.2.1. Show that, if L is accepted by a k-tape Turing machine with time bound $T(n) = cn$ for $k > 1$ and some constant c then, for every $\varepsilon > 0$, L is accepted by a k-tape Turing machine with time bound $(1 + \varepsilon)n$.

7.2.2. Is it the case that DTIME $(2^{2^n}) \subseteq$ DTIME (2^{2^n+n})? Why or why not?

7.3 INTRODUCTION TO COMPLEXITY THEORY

In Definition 4.2.2, we defined a string function f to be Turing computable if there is a Turing machine M that, when given input string w, computes u whenever $f(w) = u$. A string function that is Turing computable is said to be *polynomial-time computable* if there is a Turing machine that computes it and has a polynomial time bound.

Definition 7.3.1.   A language L_1 is said to be *polynomial-time reducible* to a language L_2 if there is a polynomial-time computable string function for which $f(u) \in L_2$ if and only if $u \in L_1$.

Polynomial-time reductions are important tools in determining which class ($\mathcal{P}$ or $\mathcal{NP}$) a language belongs, to as the following theorem indicates.

Theorem 7.3.2.   If L_1 is polynomial-time reducible to L_2, then

a. If $L_2 \in \mathcal{P}$ then $L_1 \in \mathcal{P}$.

b. If $L_2 \in \mathcal{NP}$ then $L_1 \in \mathcal{NP}$.

Proof.   (b) Suppose $L_2 \in \mathcal{NP}$ and that f is the function that polynomial-time reduces L_1 to L_2. To check if a string w is in L_1, we can compute $f(w)$ in polynomial-time and then use a nondeterministic Turing machine with polynomial-time bound for L_2 to check if $f(w) \in L_2$. Since the composition of polynomials with polynomials is again polynomial, we are done.

The proof of (a) is similar.   ■

The notation $L_1 <_p L_2$ is used to indicate that L_1 is polynomial-time reducible to L_2. Note that if $L_1 <_p L_2$ then determining if $w \in L_1$ is no harder than determining if $f(w) \in L_2$, where f is the function that polynomial-time reduces L_1 to L_2.

Definition 7.3.3.   For any class $\mathcal{C}$ of languages, a language L is said to be $\mathcal{C}$-*hard* (or hard for the class $\mathcal{C}$) if, for any $L' \in \mathcal{C}$, $L' <_p L$. That is, all languages in $\mathcal{C}$ polynomial-time reduce to L.

In particular L is $\mathcal{NP}$-*hard* if for any language $L' \in \mathcal{NP}$, $L' <_p L$.

Note that the definition of $\mathcal{C}$-hard language L says nothing about *where* L, itself, is. That is, L may or may not be in $\mathcal{C}$.

Definition 7.3.4.   If L is $\mathcal{C}$-hard and $L \in \mathcal{C}$, then L is said to be $\mathcal{C}$-*complete*.

In particular, if L is $\mathcal{NP}$-hard and L is also a language *in* $\mathcal{NP}$, then L is $\mathcal{NP}$-complete.

Theorem 7.3.5.   If L is an $\mathcal{NP}$-complete language and $L \in \mathcal{P}$, then $\mathcal{P} = \mathcal{NP}$.

Proof.   Let $L_1 \in \mathcal{NP}$ be any language. Then, since L is $\mathcal{NP}$-hard, we have that $L_1 <_p L$. Since $L \in \mathcal{P}$, Theorem 7.3.2 applies and thus $L_1 \in \mathcal{P}$.   ■

Theorem 7.3.5 provides the important tool for trying to establish equality between $\mathcal{P}$ and $\mathcal{NP}$. That is, we can show $\mathcal{P} = \mathcal{NP}$ by showing that some $\mathcal{NP}$-complete language is in $\mathcal{P}$. Of course, this requires that we actually *have* an $\mathcal{NP}$-complete language. We now develop an $\mathcal{NP}$-complete language and show that it, in fact, is $\mathcal{NP}$-complete. Theorem 7.3.8 and its corollary show a relatively easy way to get more $\mathcal{NP}$-complete languages.

The first $\mathcal{NP}$-complete language found is a language called L_{sat}. It consists of all encoded Boolean expressions that have a truth assignment that makes them evaluate to true.

A *Boolean variable* is a variable that takes on the values true or false. We represent true by 1 and false by 0. A variable or its negation is called a *literal*. We recall the logical connectives $\land$ (AND/conjunction), $\lor$ (OR/disjunction), and negation from Chapter 0. These connectives are used to form *Boolean expressions*. A *clause* is a kind of Boolean expression consisting of a disjunction of literals. Thus $y \lor \bar{z} \lor \bar{x}$ is a clause. A *truth assignment* for a set of Boolean variables is just an assignment of the values 0 and 1 to the Boolean variables in the set. A clause X is *satisfiable* if there is a truth assignment to its variables that makes X true. A collection of clauses is satisfiable if there is a truth assignment to the variables of the clauses that satisfies each clause simultaneously.

For example, let

$$C = \{x_1 \vee \bar{x}_2, \bar{x}_1 \vee \bar{x}_2 \vee \bar{x}_3, \bar{x}_1 \vee x_2 \vee x_3\}$$

A satisfying truth assignment for C is $x_1 = 1$, $x_2 = 0$, and $x_3 = 1$. Not every collection of clauses is satisfiable. For example, the set

$$D = \{\bar{x}_1, x_1 \vee x_2, x_1 \vee \bar{x}_2\}$$

is clearly not satisfiable. The *satisfiability problem (SAT)* is the problem of deciding if an arbitrary collection of clauses is satisfiable.

Note that we have described a decision problem: "Given a set of clauses, is that set of clauses satisfiable?" We can convert SAT into a language L_{sat} by encoding instances of SAT. Suppose that an instance of SAT contains the variables $x_1, x_2, \ldots, x_n$. We may encode x_i as the symbol '&' followed by i written as a binary string (of 0's and 1's). To represent an instance of SAT then requires the alphabet $\Sigma = \{ ',', '\vee', '-', '\&', '0', '1' \}$, where ' $-$ ' is used to indicate negation. We let

$$L_{\text{sat}} = \{w \in \Sigma^* \mid w \text{ represents a satisfiable set of clauses}\}$$

Given an encoded clause and a truth assignment for the variables, it is easy to see that we can evaluate the clause in polynomial time. Thus, given a truth assignment, we can determine if an encoded set of clauses is satisfied in polynomial time. Thus L_{sat} is in $\mathcal{NP}$ since a nondeterministic Turing machine can determine if $w \in L_{\text{sat}}$ by first guessing a truth assignment for the variables and then evaluating the clauses in polynomial time. We have the following lemma:

Lemma 7.3.6. $L_{\text{sat}} \in \mathcal{NP}$.

Thus, if we can show that L_{sat} is $\mathcal{NP}$-hard, we will then have an $\mathcal{NP}$-complete language. To show that L_{sat} is $\mathcal{NP}$-hard, we must take an arbitrary language $L \in \mathcal{NP}$ and polynomial time reduce it to L_{sat}. Since L is arbitrary, we cannot depend on any characteristics of L except that it is in $\mathcal{NP}$. That is, we only know that L is accepted by some nondeterministic Turing machine having polynomial time bound. It turns out that this is enough information to construct a polynomial-time reduction!

Suppose that $L \in \mathcal{NP}$ is accepted by the nondeterministic Turing machine M having polynomial time bound $T(n)$. Given an input $w = \sigma_1 \sigma_2 \ldots \sigma_n$ to M, we transform it into an instance of SAT, E_w, in such a manner that E_w is satisfiable if and only if $w \in L$. Note that E_w is necessarily a collection of clauses; thus the transformation must involve Boolean variables and disjunction.

If an input of length n is accepted by M, then there is an accepting computation that requires at most $T(n)$ steps. By Theorem 7.2.4, we may assume that M has a single tape. Suppose that we number the cells of M's tape so that an input occupies cells $1, 2, \ldots, n$ and the tape cells left of the first symbol are numbered $0, -1, \ldots$. Note that in $T(n)$ moves M can only visit tape cells with numbers $-T(n), -T(n) + 1, \ldots, T(n) + 1$. Thus we can specify M's read/write head positions during computation by Boolean variables

H_{ij} for $0 \leq i \leq T(n)$, $-T(n) \leq j \leq T(n) + 1$, where $H_{ij} = 1$ means that M's read/write head scans tape cell j after move i.

Suppose that M has states $q_0, q_1, \ldots, q_p$, where q_0 is M's initial state and q_p is the single accepting state. In a computation we can define Boolean variables Q_{ij} to be true if, after move i, M is in state q_j, where $0 \leq i \leq T(n)$ and $0 \leq j \leq p$.

Finally, suppose that M's tape alphabet is $\Gamma = \{\tau_0, \tau_1, \ldots, \tau_m\}$, where τ_0 is the blank (that is, $\tau_0 = b$). We define Boolean variables S_{ijk} for $0 \leq i \leq T(n)$, $-T(n) \leq j \leq T(n) + 1$, and $0 \leq k \leq m$ to be true if and only if after move i tape cell j contains τ_k. If M doesn't require $T(n)$ moves on a computation, let us agree to "pad out" the remaining moves by requiring that the configuration remain unchanged in all subsequent moves up to $T(n)$ once it accepts. In this manner every computation of M corresponds to a truth assignment to the variables H_{ij}, Q_{ij}, and S_{ijk}.

Note that, while a computation by M naturally induces a truth assignment of the variables, the converse is not true. That is, an arbitrary truth assignment to the variables does not necessarily need to correspond to a computation of M. The transformation of the problem of determining if M accepts w is one in which the set E_w of clauses over H_{ij}, Q_{ij}, and S_{ijk} is satisfiable if and only if M accepts w in $T(n)$ moves. The clauses in E_w restrict how a truth assignment may assign values to the variables in a number of different ways.

There are four situations necessary for a truth assignment to correspond to an accepting computation of M. The truth assignment must reflect the following:

1. The read/write head can scan only one cell, each cell can contain only one symbol, and M can be in only one state.

2. At time 0, M must be in an initial configuration: w must occupy tape cells $1, 2, \ldots, n$ and the rest of the cells must be b's. M's read/write head must scan cell 1, and M's state must be q_0.

3. After move $T(n)$, M must be in an accepting configuration. That is, the current state must be q_p.

4. After move i, the configuration of M that the truth assignment indicates must follow from its configuration before move i by an application of a transition rule of M.

At each time i, $0 \leq i \leq T(n)$, if at least one of $H_{i,-T(n)}$, $H_{i,-T(n)+1}$, ..., $H_{i,T(n)+1}$ is true, then M's read/write head scans at least 1 tape cell. If, in addition, all clauses of the form $\overline{H_{ij}} \vee \overline{H_{ij'}}$ are true for $j < j'$, then M's read/write head scans only one cell. Thus, to satisfy the requirement that, after move i, M's read/write head scans exactly one tape cell, we include in E_w all (singleton) clauses of form H_{ii} for $-T(n) \leq j \leq T(n) + 1$ and all clauses of the form $\overline{H_{ij}} \vee \overline{H_{ij'}}$ for $-T(n) \leq j < j' \leq T(n) + 1$. We include similar clauses for the requirements that, after move i, M must be in exactly one state and that each tape cell must contain exactly one symbol. We do this for all i.

The requirement that, at time 0, M be in an initial configuration is expressed by the following clauses:

Q_{00}	that is, M is in state q_0
H_{01}	M's read/write head scans cell 1
S_{0tk_t}	for each $1 \leq t \leq n$, where $w = \tau_{k_1} \ldots \tau_{k_n}$
S_{0t0}	for $-T(n) \leq t \leq 0$ and $n + 1 \leq t \leq T(n) + 1$ (recall that τ_0 is b)

We add these clauses to E_w.

The requirement that, after move $T(n)$, M be in an accepting state is expressed by $Q_{T(n)p}$ (recall that q_p is the single accepting state of M). We include this clause in E_w.

Finally, the requirement that M's configuration after move i be consistent with a transition of M based on its configuration before the move will be expressed by three clauses. Suppose that at time $i - 1$ (that is, just before the ith move) M's read/write head scans cell j, containing τ_t, and M is in state q_s. If the transition $(q_{s'}, \tau_{t'}, X)$ of $\Delta(q_s, \tau_t)$ is applied (where X is R or L), then we must have the following Boolean expression satisfied:

$$H_{ij} \wedge Q_{is} \wedge S_{ijt} \wedge H_{i+1,j+d} \wedge Q_{i+1,s'} \wedge S_{i+1,j,t'}$$

(Here $d = -1$ if $X = L$ and $d = 1$ if $X = R$). The clauses

$$\overline{H_{ij}} \vee \overline{Q_{is}} \vee \overline{S_{ijt}} \vee H_{i+1,j+d}$$
$$\overline{H_{ij}} \vee \overline{Q_{is}} \vee \overline{S_{ijt}} \vee Q_{i+1,s'}$$
$$\overline{H_{ij}} \vee \overline{Q_{is}} \vee \overline{S_{ijt}} \vee S_{i+1,j,t'}$$

are satisfied exactly when the preceding Boolean expression is true. The special case where we repeat an accepting ID is expressed as

$$H_{ij} \wedge Q_{ip} \wedge S_{ijt} \wedge H_{i+1,j} \wedge Q_{i+1,p} \wedge S_{i+1,j,t}$$

(Here q_p is M's accepting state.) The following clauses are true exactly when this expression is true:

$$\overline{H_{ij}} \vee \overline{Q_{ip}} \vee \overline{S_{ijt}} \vee H_{i+1,j}$$
$$\overline{H_{ij}} \vee \overline{Q_{ip}} \vee \overline{S_{ijt}} \vee Q_{i+1,p}$$
$$\overline{H_{ij}} \vee \overline{Q_{ip}} \vee \overline{S_{ijt}} \vee S_{i+1,j,t}$$

We add all such clauses to E_w. Note that the number of clauses in E_w depends on $T(n)$ and the number of states and tape symbols of M. Since the number of states and tape symbols does not depend on the length of the input string, the number of clauses is polynomial in $T(n)$, say $T(n)^r$. It is not hard to see that the restrictions arising from the clauses in E_w force truth assignments to the Boolean variables to correspond to accepting computations of M. Thus $w \in L$ if and only if E_w is satisfiable.

Note that we have

$$(T(n) + 1)(p + 1) + 2(T(n) + 1)^2 + 2(m + 1)(T(n) + 1)^2$$

variables. Since clauses may contain a variable or its negation, there are thus at most $c(T(n) + 1)^2$ distinct variables and their negations for an appropriate choice of the constant c. Thus the maximum number of literals in a clause is $c(T(n) + 1)^2$. It follows that the size of E_w is at most $T(n)^r c(T(n) + 1)^2$, which is bounded by some polynomial in $T(n)$, say $T(n)^{r'}$. The encoding of each variable that we suggested requires space that is bounded by the log of the number of variables, since we encode the variables' indexes in binary. This requires that the variables have a single index, however, and so we must reindex the $2(T(n) + 1)$ variables before encoding them. This may be accomplished in time polynomial in the length of E_w, which itself is polynomial in

$T(n)$. Thus the reduction of L to L_{sat} requires polynomial time, and so L_{sat} is $\mathcal{NP}$-hard.

We have shown Cook's theorem.

Theorem 7.3.7.   **(Cook)** L_{sat} is $\mathcal{NP}$-complete.

Once a known $\mathcal{NP}$-complete language has been found, language reduction provides a technique for showing that other languages are $\mathcal{NP}$-complete.

Lemma 7.3.8.   If L_1 is $\mathcal{NP}$-complete and $L_1 <_p L_2$, then L_2 is $\mathcal{NP}$-hard.

Proof.   Suppose that $L \in \mathcal{NP}$. Then, since L_1 is $\mathcal{NP}$-complete, there is a polynomial-time computable function $f_1 : L \to L_1$ with the property that $w \in L$ if and only if $f_1(w) \in L_1$. Since $L_1 <_p L_2$, there is also a polynomial-time computable function $f_2 : L_1 \to L_2$, so that $u \in L_1$ if and only if $f_2(u) \in L_2$. Note that we then have $w \in L$ if and only if $f_1(w) \in L_1$ if and only if $f_2(f_1(w)) \in L_2$. Moreover, since both f_1 and f_2 are computable in time that is polynomial in the length of their arguments, $f_2(f_1(w))$ is computable in time polynomial in the length of $f_1(w)$, which by Theorem 7.2.9 is polynomial in the length of w. Thus the composite function $f_2(f_1(w))$ is computable in polynomial-time. It follows that $L <_p L_2$, so L_2 is $\mathcal{NP}$-hard.   ∎

Corollary 7.3.9.   If L_1 is $\mathcal{NP}$-complete and $L_2 \in \mathcal{NP}$ with $L_1 <_p L_2$, then L_2 is $\mathcal{NP}$-complete.

Corollary 7.3.9 provides a technique for finding other $\mathcal{NP}$-complete languages. Given a language L in $\mathcal{NP}$, if we can polynomial-time reduce a known $\mathcal{NP}$-complete language to it, then L is also $\mathcal{NP}$-complete. When confronted with a language L that is suspected to be $\mathcal{NP}$-complete, we often may be able to apply Corollary 7.3.9 easily and prove that L is $\mathcal{NP}$-complete. In other cases, L may be similar to another language L' that has been shown to be $\mathcal{NP}$-complete. Sometimes the similarity is close enough that the proof of $\mathcal{NP}$-completeness of L' can be adapted to proving the same for L.

Exercises for Section 7.3

7.3.1. We discussed encoding clauses as strings over the alphabet $\Sigma = \{\text{'}, \text{'}, \text{'}\vee\text{'}, \text{'}-\text{'}, \text{'\&'}, \text{'0'}, \text{'1'}\}$ Given a truth assignment how might we encode it so that it could be presented to a Turing machine that could evaluate an encoded clause?

7.3.2. Describe how a set of clauses can be evaluated in polynomial time by a Turing machine.

7.3.3. Describe a technique whereby the literals of E_w can be reindexed in time that is polynomial in the size of E_w.

7.3.4. Show that if $T(n)$ is a polynomial in n then the following expression is also a polynomial in n:

$$a_k T(n)^k + a_{k-1} T(n)^{k-1} + \cdots + a_1 T(n) + a_0$$

PROBLEMS

7.1. Numerous languages have been shown to be $\mathcal{NP}$-complete. In this problem we investigate a language derived from a problem called 3SAT. 3SAT is a satisfiability problem like SAT, except the clauses involved consist of exactly three literals (in SAT the number of literals in the clauses was unrestricted).

Obviously, any Turing machine that can accept L_{sat} can be adapted to accept L_{3sat}. All the alteration that is needed is a "submachine" to check that the encoded instance consists of clauses containing exactly three literals each. The remainder of the L_{sat} machine, which guesses a truth assignment and checks it, can remain unchanged. Thus $L_{3sat} \in \mathcal{NP}$.

To polynomial-time reduce L_{sat} to L_{3sat} requires that we take potential strings in L_{sat} and make them look like potential strings in L_{3sat}. Instead of dealing with this problem at the language level, however, we will work at the level of the clauses themselves. That is, we will take an instance of SAT and transform it into an instance of 3SAT.

Suppose that we have a set C of clauses; that is, we have an instance of SAT. If all clauses consist of three literals, we are done. If not all clauses consist of three literals, we must somehow alter C to C', where all clauses in C' consist of three literals, so that C' is satisfiable if and only if C is and so that any truth assignment that satisfies C' will also satisfy C. Suppose that c is a clause in C that does not contain three literals. There are three cases to consider. The clause c may contain one, two, or more than three literals. Suppose that c contains two literals, say, $c = x_1 \vee x_2$. We can construct two three-literal clauses c_1 and c_2 from c with the property that any satisfying truth assignment for the set $\{c_1, c_2\}$ induces a truth assignment for the variables in c, and vice versa. Let α be a new Boolean variable (which occurs in none of the clauses of C). Note that $c_1 = x_1 \vee x_2 \vee \alpha$ and $c_2 = x_1 \vee x_2 \vee \bar{\alpha}$ are the required two clauses.

1. Suppose that c is a clause consisting of a single literal x. Show how to construct a set D of clauses having the property that any satisfying truth assignment for D induces a truth assignment for the variable in x, and vice versa. *Hint:* This can be accomplished with four clauses.

In the case that c is a clause consisting of more than three literals, we may construct a clause set D with the desired property in the following manner. Suppose that c is the clause $x_1 \vee x_2 \vee \ldots \vee x_k$. Let $\alpha_1, \alpha_2, \ldots, \alpha_{k-3}$ be new Boolean variables. Let D consist of the clauses $x_1 \vee x_2 \vee \alpha_1, x_2 \vee \bar{\alpha}_1 \vee \alpha_2, x_3 \vee \bar{\alpha}_2 \vee \alpha_3, \ldots, x_{k-1} \vee x_k \vee \bar{\alpha}_{k-3}$. Note that D has the desired property. That is, a truth assignment to the variables $x_1, x_2, \ldots, x_k$ making c true then induces a truth assignment that satisfies D, and vice versa.

Thus any collection of clauses can be transformed into a collection of clauses consisting of exactly three literals with the property that any truth assignment satisfying the original set induces a truth assignment for the transformed set, and vice versa.

2. Show that the preceding transformation can be accomplished in polynomial time.

3. Show that L_{3sat} is $\mathcal{NP}$-complete.

References
and Bibliography

The material in this book is derived from many sources, as is the manner in which it is presented. In the following short annotation, we mention certain topics whose sources are particularly important. The bibliography that follows lists many of the sources that the author used in preparation of this text. Neither the annotation nor the bibliography is intended to be particularly exhaustive or complete, however.

Problem 1.8 comes from Salomaa [11]. Lemma 2.8.2 is a modification of a theorem of Arden [1]. This lemma is used in the development of Lemma 2.8.3, which is based on work by Brzozowski [2]. This paper also gives an elegant technique for deriving a finite automaton from a regular expression. Problem 2.4 is from Harrison [4]. Section 4.3 owes its origin to Lewis and Papadimitriou [7]. Their book does substantially more with this "Turing machine construction kit" than we do.

The books mentioned so far, as well as the remaining books listed, have been sources for portions of this development and presentation. The excellent books of Lewis and Papadimitriou [7], Harrison [4], and Hopcroft and Ullman [6] are classics in the area. All three are appropriate sources of study to pursue after this book, as is Wood [13]. The earlier book by Hopcroft and Ullman [5] is a compendium of the known (at that time) material on formal languages, automata theory, and computational complexity, which appears to have grown into [6]. The books by Linz [8], Carroll and Long [3], Rayward-Smith [10], Martin [9], and Sudkamp [12] are introductions to the area and are similar to this book. All five are excellent references during the reading of the present text.

REFERENCES

[1] ARDEN, D. N. "Delayed Logic and Finite State Machines," in *Theory of Computing Machine Design*. Ann Arbor, MI: University of Michigan Press, 1960.

[2] BRZOZOWSKI, J. A. "Derivatives of Regular Expressions," *Journal of the Association for Computing Machinery*, 11, no. 4 (October 1964), pp. 481–494.

[3] CARROLL, JOHN, and DARRELL LONG. *Theory of Finite Automata with an Introduction to Formal Languages*, Englewood Cliffs, NJ: Prentice Hall, 1989.

[4] HARRISON, MICHAEL. *Introduction to Formal Language Theory*, Addison-Wesley Series in Computer Science. Reading, MA: Addison-Wesley, Inc., 1978.

[5] HOPCROFT, JOHN E., and JEFFREY D. ULLMAN. *Formal Languages and Their Relation to Automata*, Addison-Wesley Series in Computer Science. Reading, MA: Addison-Wesley, Inc., 1969.

[6] HOPCROFT, JOHN E., and JEFFREY D. ULLMAN. *Introduction to Automata Theory and Computation*, Addison-Wesley Series in Computer Science. Reading, MA: Addison-Wesley, Inc., 1979.

[7] LEWIS, H. R., and C. H. PAPADIMITRIOU. *Elements of the Theory of Computation*, Englewood Cliffs, NJ: Prentice Hall, 1981.

[8] LINZ, PETER. *An Introduction to Formal Languages and Automata*, Lexington, MA: D. C. Heath and Company, 1990.

[9] MARTIN, JOHN C. *Introduction to Languages and the Theory of Computation*, New York: McGraw-Hill, Inc., 1991.

[10] RAYWARD-SMITH, V. J., *A First Course in Formal Language Theory*, Computer Science Texts Series. Oxford, UK: Blackwell Scientific Publications, 1983.

[11] SALOMAA, ARTO. "Morphisms on Free Monoids and Language Theory," in *Formal Language Theory: Perspectives and Open Problems*, ed. Ronald V. Book. New York: Academic Press, Inc.

[12] SUDKAMP, THOMAS A. *Languages and Machines, An Introduction to the Theory of Computer Science*, Addison-Wesley Series in Computer Science. Reading, MA: Addison-Wesley, Inc., 1988.

[13] WOOD, DERICK. *Theory of Computation*, New York: John Wiley & Sons, Inc., 1987.

Index

W

Wood, Derick, 229, 230
Word, 23
Work tapes, 211

Y

Yield of derivation tree, 95